THE BUFFALO SOLDIERS

THE BUFFALO SOLDIERS

A Narrative of the Black Cavalry in the West

REVISED EDITION

WILLIAM H. LECKIE
WITH SHIRLEY A. LECKIE

UNIVERSITY OF OKLAHOMA PRESS   NORMAN

ALSO BY WILLIAM H. LECKIE

The Military Conquest of the Southern Plains (Norman, 1963)

The Buffalo Soldiers: A Narrative of the Negro Cavalry in the West (Norman, 1967)

(with Shirley A. Leckie) *Unlikely Warriors:*
General Benjamin Grierson and His Family (Norman, 1984)

(ed.) *Indian Wars of the Red River Valley* (Sacramento, 1986)

ALSO BY SHIRLEY A. LECKIE

(with William H. Leckie) *Unlikely Warriors:*
General Benjamin Grierson and His Family (Norman, 1984)

(ed.) *The Colonel's Lady on the Western Frontier:*
The Correspondence of Alice Kirk Grierson (Lincoln, 1989)

Elizabeth Bacon Custer and the Making of a Myth (Norman, 1993)

Angie Debo: Pioneering Historian (Norman, 2000)

LIBRARY OF CONGRESS CATALOGING-IN-PUBLICATION DATA
Leckie, William H.
The buffalo soldiers : a narrative of the Black cavalry in the West /
William H. Leckie, with Shirley A. Leckie.—Rev. ed
p. cm.
Includes bibliographical references and index.
ISBN-13: 978-0-8061-3840-4 (paper)
1. United States. Army. Cavalry, 10th.
2. United States. Army. Cavalry, 9th.
3. United States. Army—African American troops.
4. West (U.S.)—History, Military—19th century.
I. Leckie, Shirley A., 1937–   II. Title.
UA31 10th .L4197 2003
978'.00496073—dc21
2002032478

The paper in this book meets the guidelines for permanence and durability of the Committee on Production Guidelines for Book Longevity of the Council on Library Resources, Inc. ∞

2 3 4 5 6 7 8 9 10

To Betty and Hazel and
their children and grandchildren

Contents

Illustrations

following page 216
Entrance to Hembrillo Canyon
Captain Thomas C. Lebo
Tenth Cavalry at Battle of Rattlesnake Springs
Colonel Edward Hatch
Captain Henry Carroll

following page 259
Company K, Ninth Cavalry
Company E, Tenth Cavalry
Brigade Drill of Tenth Cavalry
Ninth Cavalry, Fort Davis
Aerial view of Fort Davis
Lieutenant Powhatan Clarke
Boomer leaders, 1884
Boomers, circa 1883

following page 287
Ninth Cavalry honor guard
Buffalo soldier statue
"The Sentinel"

DRAWINGS

MAPS

Preface to the Revised Edition

The University of Oklahoma Press published *The Buffalo Soldiers: A Narrative of the Negro Cavalry in the West* in May 1967. Sales were encouraging enough for the press to issue a second hardback in 1971, and additional paperbacks have followed to this day. Reviewers generally praised the book but had criticisms that fell into four areas. They noted that the work paid too little attention to the Twenty-fourth and Twenty-fifth Infantry Regiments, units of black soldiers that also served in the West. Other critics felt that *The Buffalo Soldiers* devoted too little space to social and family relations among the enlisted men and that it failed to include enough detail on enlisted Medal of Honor winners. They also observed the need for more photographs of the soldiers themselves.

Arlen Fowler rectified the lack of attention to the Twenty-fourth and Twenty-fifth Infantry when he published *The Black Infantry in the West, 1861 to 1868* in 1971. The University of Oklahoma Press reissued that work in 1996. Over time other historians have addressed many of the questions raised by the initial critiques of the first edition of *The Buffalo Soldiers*. In doing so, they have added to scholarly understanding of all these issues. In addition, historians have identified new historical concerns and have questioned some longstanding beliefs. Archival and private collections have yielded new photographs. These new insights and findings have made it possible to revise and enlarge a work that is now well into its fourth decade of existence.

At heart, this study remains what it was in the beginning—an account of the battles, campaigns, and peacekeeping activities that the black soldiers of the Ninth and Tenth Cavalry were involved in during the period of the Indian wars of the post–Civil War era. Wherever possible, we have introduced new information regarding the poignant situation that American Indians found themselves in as they faced ecological disasters and severe challenges from newcomers who wished to take from them both their homeland and their way of life.

In writing about the buffalo soldiers, we have tried to correct those statements or interpretations that appeared in the earlier work and are no longer valid on the basis of the most recent research and evidence. Without obstructing the flow of the narrative, we have also tried to work into this revision more information on relations between the enlisted men and their officers and insights into the educational opportunities that the army made available to them and what those opportunities meant. We have also woven into the last chapter some discussion of family life, recreational opportunities, and the emergence of a new generation of buffalo soldiers who had been born after slavery ended.

Finally, we have added to this work a brief epilogue that traces developments after the end of the Indian wars. We have also tried to tie these developments into the larger context of race relations in the United States and the ways in which the U.S. Army as an institution reflected those changes, often to the detriment of black soldiers. Later, in the twentieth century, the army changed course and became an institution that led the way toward integration and a larger measure of justice for individuals of all races in American life.

We wish to thank the staffs of the Illinois State Historical Library; the Western History Collections at the University of Oklahoma, especially John Lovett; and Mary Williams, historian at the Fort Davis National Historic Site. The staff at the University of Central Florida Library, especially those in Interlibrary Loan, was unfailingly helpful.

Many individuals also gave us the benefit of their interest and knowledge of the buffalo soldier story. These include Durwood Ball, historian at the University of New Mexico; Eddie Dixon, sculptor, Lubbock, Texas; Mark and Patricia Erickson, photographers, Silver City, New Mexico; Frank Schubert, historian, Joint History Office, Office of the Chairman, Joint Chiefs of Staff; Bob Snead, artist, El Paso, Texas; and Fred Jones, Don Lee, John Russell, and other members of the Ninth and Tenth Horse Cavalry Association. Finally, Chris Blacklock, computer technician, kept our IBM clone and email system operating. Jean Hurtado, acquisitions editor at the University of Oklahoma Press, encouraged us as we began the task of revision.

The mistakes are entirely our own.

William H. Leckie
Shirley A. Leckie
June 15, 2002

Preface to the First Edition

My interest in the American Negro soldier goes back two decades to the close of World War II. At that time I was placed in charge of two hundred Negro airmen en route to separation centers in the United States after long service in the South Pacific. A duty, which I at first regarded as onerous, became one of the most rewarding experiences of my life. Despite more than two years of arduous service and a low priority for discharge from the Army Air Corps, the men were obedient, cheerful, proud of their uniform, and altogether a credit to themselves and to their country. On the long voyage home, I made many friends among them, and when our destination was reached, to a man they came by to shake my hand and express appreciation for "fair" treatment.

In the years that followed, casual reading revealed that the Negro had played a far greater role in American military history than I had ever imagined. Serious interest was aroused with my discovery that for a generation following the Civil War, two regiments of Negro cavalry, the Ninth and Tenth, had served continuously on the western frontier. An intensive search in the existing literature proved frustrating. In thousands of pages the Third, Fourth, Fifth, Sixth, and Seventh Cavalry, great regiments all, rode and fought their way to glory, but the Negro troopers were usually dismissed with a bare mention, ignored completely, or their efforts mocked. Only a handful of books and articles proved helpful, and virtually nothing was found in way of letters, diaries, or journals—not surprising in view of the fact that most of the troopers were illiterate.

It was not until I turned to the wealth of material in the military records of the National Archives that the true character and contributions of the Ninth and Tenth stood clearly revealed. For twenty-four years these regiments campaigned on the Great Plains, along the Rio Grande, and in New Mexico, Arizona, Colorado, and finally the Dakotas. Their antagonists were the enemies of peace, order, and settlement: warring Indians, bandits, cattle thieves, murderous gunmen, bootleggers, trespassers, and Mexican revolutionaries. All these they met many times, and with success, regardless of extremes of climate and terrain that ranged from the broken, rugged, and torrid Big Bend of Texas to the rolling plains, badlands, and subfreezing temperatures of South Dakota.

Their work was not limited to fighting. Many a frontier post arose as a result of their labors, and the foundations thus were laid for future cities. Fort Sill, Oklahoma, and the thriving city of Lawton are prime examples. Scouting detachments stripped the mystery from little-known areas; located water, wood, and grass; and paved the way for eager settlers. Many a frontier official owed his life and his job to the support given him by these black men in blue, and many more farmers and ranchers slept soundly in their beds because a thin line of Negro troopers guarded them from harm.

The only obstacles the Ninth and Tenth could not overcome were those of prejudice and discrimination. These twin foes were constant enemies, ever harassing, hampering, and embarrassing their efforts, and denying recognition for tasks well done. Three quarters of a century have passed since the work of these regiments on the frontier came to a close, and their contributions still go largely unknown and unheralded. This book is an effort to tell the story of the Ninth and Tenth Cavalry, in the conviction that they deserve recognition for what they were—first-rate regiments by any standards one wishes to apply and major spearheads in the settlement of the West. It is a story of significant achievement under many handicaps, and a record in which every American can take justifiable pride.

In the research and writing of this book, I am indebted to many people. The assistance of Sara Jackson of the National Archives is gratefully acknowledged, and Anne Henry of Washington, D.C., was a tireless research assistant. Savoie Lottinville, director of the University of Oklahoma Press, has been a constant source of guidance and inspiration. Don Rickey, Jr., of the National Park Service provided information I would have otherwise overlooked. President William S. Carlson and Dean Jerome Kloucek of the University of Toledo gave every encouragement along with released time necessary to complete the manuscript. Particular thanks are due John Morgan of the University of Toledo Library for his many courtesies and untiring efforts to secure desired material. Josephine Soukup of Norman, Oklahoma, typed the manuscript with great skill and even greater patience.

My wife, Glorieta Leckie, assisted in the research and made possible the long periods necessary for undisturbed writing. The errors and shortcomings of this book, however, are entirely my own.

William H. Leckie
Toledo, Ohio
November 29, 1966

Abbreviations Used in Notes

AG	Adjutant General
AGO	Adjutant General's Office
AAG	Assistant Adjutant General
AAAG	Acting Assistant Adjutant General
GP-ISHS	Papers of Benjamin H. Grierson, Illinois State Historical Society, Springfield
GP-TTU	Benjamin H. Grierson Papers, Southwest Collection, Texas Technological University, Lubbock
LR	Letters Received
LS	Letters Sent
NA	National Archives
PA	Post Adjutant
RG	Record Group
SDLR	Selected Documents from Letters Received
SLR	Selected Letters Received

THE BUFFALO SOLDIERS

The Early Years

African American troops marched in the ranks of Washington's armies in the cause of independence and served with Andrew Jackson at New Orleans in 1815 to repel the British invader, but their first large-scale employment awaited the coming of the Civil War. When Confederate batteries fired on Fort Sumter early on the morning of April 12, 1861, inaugurating four years of internecine warfare, many black men were eager to wear the Union blue. They found their services were neither wanted then nor contemplated in the future.[1]

As the bitter conflict dragged on, however, casualty lists grew apace, and as thousands of black refugees sought sanctuary behind Union lines, sentiment began to change. On the first anniversary of Fort Sumter, General David Hunter, commanding the Department of the South, organized a black regiment. His effort was abortive, for it brought no joy to the hearts of President Abraham Lincoln and his advisers. The regiment was, according to T. W. Higginson of Massachusetts, "turned off without a shilling, by order of the War Department." Seven months later, Higginson himself was invited to become colonel of the First Regiment of South Carolina Volunteers, the "first slave regiment mustered into the service of the United States."[2]

1 Reddick, "Negro Policy of the United States Army," 14–15; Quarles, *The Negro in the Civil War,* 31.
2 Higginson, *Army Life in a Black Regiment,* 15, 1.

Colonel Higginson accepted, although had "an invitation reached me to take command of a regiment of Kalmuck Tartars, it could hardly have been more unexpected." This experiment, as well as others, proved successful, and with the Emancipation Proclamation of January 1, 1863, enlistment of African Americans began in earnest.[3]

The decision to use black troops was not universally popular and was not motivated by idealism but rather by the dictates of a grueling war. One historian has summarized the impetus as arising "largely out of the dawning realization that, since the Confederates were going to kill a great many more Union soldiers before the war was over, a good many white men would escape death if a considerable percentage of those soldiers were colored."[4]

Such "dawning realization" came slowly to many officers and men in the Union army, for stout opposition developed. In response, General Ulysses S. Grant enjoined his subordinates "that all commanders will especially exert themselves in carrying out the policy of the administration, not only in organizing colored regiments and rendering them effective, but also in removing prejudice against them."[5]

Grant's instruction tempered resistance somewhat, but many officers vowed never to serve with African American troops, and resentment and anger seethed among rank and file. Feeling ran so high in one Ohio division that the men threatened to stack their arms and return home. Adjutant General Lorenzo Thomas, in turn, warned them that any such action would be regarded as treason and the men involved would be shot.[6]

Resistance to the use of African Americans diminished when officers discovered that a commission in a black regiment often meant quick promotion. A number of candidates then came forward to meet the needs of the new organization. Further, as the black man proved his worth as a soldier, general though reluctant acceptance became the rule. Nonetheless, discrimination persisted until the end of the war. Most notably, until June 1864, the Union army paid the black soldier ten dollars per month for his services, while his white counterpart received thirteen dollars. Blacks also received less in bonuses.[7]

3 Ibid., 2; Quarles, *The Negro in the Civil War*, 182.
4 Catton, *This Hallowed Ground*, 222.
5 Williams, *Negro Troops in the War of the Rebellion*, 108.
6 Ibid., 110.
7 Randall, *Civil War and Reconstruction*, 506–7.

Despite such biased treatment, black soldiers demonstrated their courage and patriotism. African Americans fought at Fort Wagner, South Carolina, and Milliken's Bend, Louisiana; at Baxter Springs, Kansas, and Point Lookout, Virginia; and in the slaughterhouse that was Cold Harbor. Hundreds were massacred at Fort Pillow, Tennessee, and they bled and died on scores of other battlefields. If any lingering question of their merit, spirit, and courage persisted, their charge into the "Crater" before Petersburg on July 30, 1864, should have dispelled it.[8]

Union sappers tunneled under a Confederate strongpoint in the Petersburg defenses and mined up. The mine was exploded at dawn, blasting a huge crater in the Confederate line. When General Ambrose Burnside, a master fumbler, failed to attack at once, the Confederates took advantage of the respite to build a new line to the rear of the crater. The Union attack, when finally launched, failed, but even after realizing this, Burnside ordered General Edward Ferrero's Fourth Division comprised entirely of black infantry to assault the Confederate defense. They charged with great spirit and gallantry but met a galling fire in which "hundreds of heroes carved in ebony fell." Although forced to retire, some stood their ground until most were killed.[9]

By the end of the war, nearly 180,000 African Americans had served in the Union army and taps had sounded over the bodies of 33,380 of those who had given their lives for freedom and the Union. Despite that record, many still doubted that black men could be first-rate combat soldiers, and their future in the U.S. Army remained clouded in uncertainty.[10]

On May 23–24, 1865, the Union army staged its last great spectacle. Nearly a quarter of a million men in blue passed in grand review along Pennsylvania Avenue in the nation's capital. Soon after, the United States reverted to its traditional policy of a small peacetime army. Within little more than a year, the military establishment had been all but dismantled. The authorized strength of the army stood at only 54,641 officers and men; the actual

8 Frederick Phisterer, *Statistical Record of the Armies of the United States* (New York: Charles Scribner's Sons, 1883), 68. At Fort Pillow, Tennessee, on April 12, 1864, three hundred black soldiers of the Sixth U.S. Colored Heavy Artillery and the Second Colored Light Artillery were murdered as they sought to surrender to Confederates under General Nathan Bedford Forrest. See Cornish, *Sable Arm*, 173–74.

9 *Battles and Leaders of the Civil War*, 4:564. For an incisive overview of this tragic event, see McPherson, *Battle Cry of Freedom*, 758–60.

10 Cornish, *Sable Arm*, 288; Reddick, "Negro Policy of the United States Army," 17–18.

strength was considerably less.[11] This was the situation as Americans faced a renewed Indian war in the West and conditions approaching anarchy along the Mexican border.

Congress, meanwhile, had cleared up some of the uncertainty surrounding the future of the black man in the armed forces. In doing so, it altered military tradition. Largely because of support from some Radical Republicans desirous of aiding their African American allies and certain, as Senators Benjamin F. Wade and Henry M. Wilson maintained, that blacks were "less likely" to leave their posts for the mining fields, the act passed on July 28, 1866, contained provisions for them to serve in the regular peacetime army. Six regiments of black troops were authorized, two of cavalry, four of infantry. By this legislation Congress began a new chapter in American military history and afforded the erstwhile slave an opportunity to play a major role in the opening up of the West to non-Indian settlement and development.[12]

Since the use of black troops in the peacetime army was regarded as something of an experiment, the authorizing act contained some unusual provisions. Chaplains were normally assigned to a particular post or station, but in the case of African American units, the chaplain was assigned directly to a regiment with both spiritual and educational duties. Since most blacks were former slaves and most southern states had outlawed their education during slavery, few black recruits would be literate. This meant that their officers would have to perform most of the paperwork normally assigned to noncommissioned officers. For that reason and to enhance their skills as soldiers in the regular army, the chaplain was to instruct black regulars in the rudiments of reading, writing, and arithmetic.

It was assumed that all officers of the new regiments would be white. In addition, they would take and pass a special examination before a board of experienced officers appointed by the secretary of war. Finally, their record had to include two years of active field service in the Civil War. Two-thirds of those holding the rank of captain or above, moreover, were to be drawn

11 Actual strength of the army was only 38,540. *Annual Report of the Secretary of War for the Year 1866*, 3–4; Ganoe, *History of the United States Army*, 307.

12 Major John Bigelow, Jr., "Historical Sketch, Tenth United States Cavalry, 1866–1892," U.S. Army Commands, RG 98, NA; Dobak and Phillips, *Black Regulars*, xiii. See also Fletcher, *Black Soldier and Officer*, 20; and Tate, *Frontier Army in the Settlement of the West*, ix–xvi.

from the volunteer regiments and one-third from the regular army. Officers of lower rank were to come exclusively from the volunteer services.[13]

Early in August 1866, General Grant telegraphed General Philip Sheridan, commanding the Division of the Gulf, and General William T. Sherman, commanding the Military Division of the Missouri, to organize a regiment of black cavalry in their respective divisions. The new regiments were designated as the Ninth and Tenth U.S. Cavalry, and Grant recommended two officers with brilliant Civil War records to command them—Colonel Edward Hatch of Iowa and Colonel Benjamin H. Grierson of Illinois.[14]

Edward Hatch, a blond, blue-eyed native of Maine, had gone early to sea before entering the lumber business in Pennsylvania. In 1855 he moved to Iowa, where he resided when the war came. He received appointment as a captain in the Second Iowa Cavalry in August 1861. Less than a year later, he was its colonel. After taking part in Grierson's famous raid through Mississippi in 1863, he received a bullet through his right lung and a broken shoulder at Moscow, Tennessee, in December that same year. Later, he received citations for gallantry and meritorious service at the battles of Nashville and Franklin, also in Tennessee. One of the most underrated cavalrymen of the Union army, he closed out the war as brevet major general of volunteers. Able, decisive, ambitious, and personable, he received Grant's unqualified endorsement to lead the Ninth Cavalry.[15]

Tall, swarthy, scar-faced Benjamin Grierson was a most unlikely candidate for a distinguished career as a cavalryman. Since the age of eight, when a pony kicked him in the face and left a cheek permanently scarred, he had been skittish of horses. A small-town music teacher and an ardent admirer of Abraham Lincoln, he volunteered immediately when the war came and sought a commission in the infantry. When his appointment came through, however, he found himself a major in the Sixth Illinois Cavalry. Despite an almost complete lack of military experience and his dislike of horses, Grierson was soon promoted to colonel. In April 1863 General Grant selected him to lead three regiments of cavalry in a diversionary raid through Mississippi.

---

13 Bigelow, "Historical Sketch"; Hutcheson, "Ninth Regiment of Cavalry," 280.

14 Grant to Sheridan and Sherman, August 4, 1866, SLR Relating to the Ninth and Tenth Regiments, U.S. Cavalry, AGO, RG 94, NA.

15 Heitman, *Historical Register,* 1:510; Brown, *Grierson's Raid,* 61–62; Schubert, *Black Valor,* 11; Kenner, *Buffalo Soldiers and Officers of the Ninth Cavalry,* 30–41.

Grierson's six-hundred-mile, sixteen-day sweep through the Confederate heartland contributed materially to Grant's successful operations around Vicksburg. When the latter described the raid as the most brilliant expedition of the war, the easygoing and tolerant Grierson emerged as a national figure. By the time of Appomattox, he was a brevet major general of volunteers and had the confidence of both Grant and Sherman. Mustered out of service in April 1866, he gave brief thought to a business career and then accepted appointment as commander of the Tenth Cavalry.[16]

He was a good choice. Although he had expressed prejudice against blacks early in the war, his combat experiences convinced him that African Americans were valiant soldiers worthy of respect. In 1863, following an assault on Port Hudson, Louisiana, Grierson wrote his wife, Alice, that a day earlier, any questions about the "good fighting qualities of negroes" had been "settled beyond a doubt." For him they were never reopened.[17]

Hatch and Grierson wasted no time in proceeding with the organization of their regiments. The former established headquarters at Greenville, Louisiana, and the latter at Fort Leavenworth, Kansas. From the first, however, difficulty was encountered in procuring experienced officers; many of them refused to serve with black troops. More than a few agreed with Brevet Major General Eugene A. Carr that black men would not make good soldiers and took a lower rank in order to serve with a white regiment. The dashing "boy general," George A. Custer, refused a lieutenant colonelcy with the Ninth. Instead, he wangled the same rank in the newly formed Seventh Cavalry— a decision that was probably fortunate for the Ninth. Certainly, it launched Custer on the road to the Little Bighorn and a controversial niche in history.[18]

Despite possibilities for greater rank and more rapid promotion in the black regiments, many officers of lower rank shared the feelings expressed in an *Army and Navy Journal* advertisement in which a "First Lieutenant of Infantry (white) stationed at a very desirable post in the Department of the South" expressed a willingness to trade assignment with another officer of the same rank "on equal terms" if the regiment was white. However, "if in a colored regiment," then "a reasonable bonus would be expected."[19]

16 See Dinges, "Making of a Cavalryman"; Leckie and Leckie, *Unlikely Warriors*, 3–140.
17 Leckie and Leckie, *Unlikely Warriors*, 101.
18 Bigelow, "Historical Sketch"; E. D. Townsend, AAG to Sheridan, August 3, 1866, SLR Relating to the Ninth and Tenth Regiments, U.S. Cavalry; King, *War Eagle*, 77; Dobak and Phillips, *Black Regulars*, 27–28.
19 *Army and Navy Journal*, June 10, 1871, 684.

Under such circumstances, officer procurement proceeded at a snail's pace. In November Hatch complained to the adjutant general that he had several hundred recruits on hand at Greenville, was receiving arms and horses, but still did not have a single officer present for duty. Grierson had an additional complaint. He believed that regular-army officers were being assigned to white regiments and only volunteers were staffing the black units. If this was the policy of the government, he wrote his wife, "I will not remain in the army."[20]

Once officer procurement accelerated, the Ninth obtained some excellent men. They included Captain James S. Brisbin, a former abolitionist who had served as commander of the Sixth U.S. Colored Cavalry in the Civil War; Lieutenant Colonel Wesley Merritt; and in March 1867 Major Albert P. Morrow.[21] Still, the flow was much too slow in Hatch's case, for recruits were pouring into the camp at Greenville.

Army recruiters concentrated their efforts in nearby New Orleans and Baton Rouge because of the large number of black Civil War veterans in those towns. White southerners often targeted black veterans for intimidation and violence in this period, and the high unemployment rates in many southern cities where blacks had flocked following natural disasters that had destroyed much of the cotton crop rendered military life more attractive.[22] Thus, recruiters had little difficulty in attracting soldiers. A black man named George Washington was the first to enlist on August 1866 and was immediately placed in Company A. Others followed, seeing in the army social and economic opportunities unavailable to them elsewhere. Thirteen dollars a month was meager pay, but it was the same that white soldiers received and more than most could expect to earn as civilians. When food, clothing, and shelter were added, a better life seemed assured.

20 Hatch to the AG, November 4, 1866, SLR Relating to the Ninth and Tenth Regiments, U.S. Cavalry; Benjamin H. Grierson to Alice Grierson, October 6, 1866, GP-ISHS.
  21 James Brisbin of Pennsylvania was mustered out of service as brevet brigadier general of volunteers in 1865. He became major of the Second Cavalry in 1868 and then returned to the Ninth as lieutenant colonel in 1885. In 1881 he published the best seller *The Beef Bonanza; or, How to Get Rich on the Plains* with Lippincott. Wesley Merritt was a graduate of West Point with a brilliant record during the Civil War. He received seven brevets for gallant meritorious service and held the rank of major general of volunteers when the war ended. He accepted the lieutenant colonelcy of the Ninth Cavalry in July 1866 and remained with the regiment until July 1876, when he was appointed colonel of the Fifth Cavalry. Albert P. Morrow rose through the ranks to become a brevet colonel of the Sixth Pennsylvania Cavalry. He joined the Ninth as a major in March 1867 and served with the regiment for fifteen years. See Heitman, *Historical Register*, 1:246, 706, 729
  22 Dobak and Phillips, *Black Regulars*, 20–21.

Equally important for many young black men undoubtedly was the chance to prove their manhood in a nation that, by and large, but particularly in the South, denigrated their worth as human beings. Although blacks had attained freedom, they were still denied full citizenship rights and subject to discrimination and prejudice. In New Orleans the previous July, some two hundred blacks—many veterans of the Civil War—had marched to support civil rights. White citizens had reacted violently. When the ensuing race riot was over, thirty-four of the thirty-eight who perished were African Americans.[23]

The earliest days of the Ninth were difficult and dangerous for both officers and men. In the midst of a cholera epidemic that raged throughout New Orleans during fall 1866, the recruits were packed into a filthy and poorly ventilated site that had once served as a cotton-bale packing plant. There, without stoves and ventilation, they cooked their meals over open fires and tried to sleep. Not surprisingly, nine soldiers died in October, another fifteen in November, and five more in December. Others simply left, and by the end of the year, thirty had deserted and another sixteen followed suit in 1867. It was an inauspicious beginning for the new regiment.[24]

Nonetheless, despite the continuing tension from the recent riot, the deaths from cholera, the desertions, the lack of facilities, and the scarcity of officers, 818 men were accepted as enlistees in the Ninth Cavalry during its first year. Many came from states outside of Louisiana. Kentucky contributed, among others, farmer George Gray, doomed to die of tetanus in the post hospital at Fort Clark, Texas, and laborer William Sharpe, an Indian arrow awaiting him along the rocky banks of the Pecos River.

Emmanuel Stance, nineteen and scarcely five feet tall, was from northern Louisiana. One of the first to enroll, he was literate, which meant that he would soon be promoted to sergeant. He would also earn a Medal of Honor. From Virginia came Washington Wyatt, who would die at the hands of persons unknown in Austin, Texas, before he reached his twenty-first birthday. And so they came, farmers, teamsters, dyers, cooks, bakers, painters, waiters, and cigar makers, to enlist for five years in the Ninth Regiment of Cavalry, U.S.A.[25]

23 Schubert, *Black Valor*, 11–12; Foner, *Reconstruction*, 262–63.
24 Schubert, *Black Valor*, 11–12.
25 Organizational Returns, Ninth Cavalry, August–September, 1867, AGO, RG 94, NA; Registers of Enlistments in the U.S. Army, 1798–1914, microcopy 233, U.S. Army Commands, RG 98, NA. These registers are arranged alphabetically and by year, giving the name, place of enlistment, place of birth, age, civilian occupation, and condition of service termination. As such they are a mine of information on enlisted men for the period given.

Years later, Lieutenant Grote Hutcheson's regimental history character-ized its early recruits as "ignorant, entirely helpless" men with minds that "were filled with superstition."[26] That defamation and the early troubles that beset the unit during its first year led many to conclude that the recruiters, in their haste to fill the ranks, had enlisted men who were, over-all, inferior to those who enrolled in the Tenth Cavalry.

Historian Charles L. Kenner challenges that interpretation. Hutcheson, he notes, had never campaigned with the buffalo soldiers and provided no evidence for his statements. Moreover, Tenth Cavalry recruiters actually enlisted 1,147 men, which was substantially more than the 818 enrolled in the Ninth Cavalry.[27] Clearly, the Ninth's early difficulties arose not from indis-criminate recruiting but rather from its early problems and the hardships the men endured. In addition, not only was there a lack of officers but some of those who did serve also were brutal and contemptuous of their men.

By February 1867, Hatch had organized all twelve companies of the Ninth, though only eleven officers had reported for duty. A month later, he received orders transferring the regiment to Texas. Two companies, L and M, were assigned to Brownsville along the Rio Grande, while the remaining ten companies would encamp near San Antonio and undergo further training.

When the regiment disembarked from steamers at Indianola, Texas, on March 29, it was poorly prepared for its new assignment. As the ten compa-nies bound for San Antonio began the 150-mile march to that city, they heard inflammatory rumors along the way about the dangers they would soon confront. Subsequently, a disturbance in Company K, commanded by Lieutenant Fred Smith, was suppressed only with great difficulty.

More serious were the events in Lieutenant Edward Heyl's Company E. Heyl, who had risen from the ranks to captain in a Pennsylvanian cavalry regiment during the Civil War, was twenty-three, a heavy drinker, and prone to violence. As Frank N. Schubert notes, "His fitness for command of any kind would be open to question today, but officers who brutalized their men were not uncommon in white or black regiments. In any case, no officer who would name his horse 'Nigger,' as Heyl later did, should have been in the Ninth Cavalry."[28]

26 Kenner, *Buffalo Soldiers and Officers of the Ninth Cavalry*, 10.
27 Ibid., 11.
28 Schubert, *Black Valor*, 13. See also Byron Price, "Mutiny at San Pedro Springs," *By Valor and Arms* 1 (spring 1975): 31–34.

After arrival at San Pedro Springs outside San Antonio, conditions did not improve. On April 9 Heyl attempted to run down one soldier for tardiness and ordered three men hung by their wrists from a tree because they had been slow, he thought, in removing their horses' nosebags. After retreating to a nearby saloon, Heyl returned and began beating a hanging soldier with his saber.

In response, Orderly Sergeant Harrison Bradford began marching Company E to Lieutenant Colonel Wesley Merritt's tent to complain of maltreatment, but Heyl fired at him twice and wounded him with his second shot. Bradford's attempt to defend himself with the help of another soldier left Lieutenants Seth E. Griffin, Fred Smith, and Heyl wounded. Despite his wound, Smith still managed to kill Bradford, and at that point all hell erupted. In fury the soldiers of E Company turned on Smith, and the melee ended only when Merritt appeared and restored order.[29]

Merritt concluded in his report that Heyl's behavior and the regiment's lack of officers had brought about the mutinous turn of events. Colonel Hatch blamed this tragic affair on the shortage of officers. Captain W. S. Abert, Sixth Cavalry, assigned to investigate the mutiny, sustained that assessment. Lieutenant Griffin died of his wounds, and in the trial that followed, Corporal Charles Woods and Private Irving Charles were convicted and sentenced to death, and other soldiers were charged and imprisoned. Later, however, Woods and Charles were pardoned and returned to duty, and the imprisoned soldiers were reinstated. The recruits had never heard about the Articles of War, and they had no way of knowing how to obtain redress when confronted with brutal officers such as Lieutenant Heyl, who would remain with the regiment for another four years. Despite his actions, he was serving as a colonel in the Inspector General's Department of the army when he died in 1895.[30]

In the aftermath of these disturbances, the War Department honored Hatch's request, and the Ninth soon gained new officers. Within a month Hatch reported that both morale and discipline were much improved. It was none too soon, for conditions in the vast expanse of West Texas and along the Rio Grande were fast becoming intolerable, and troops were needed

29 Schubert, *Black Valor,* 13–14.
30 Ibid., 14–15; Hatch to the AAG, District of Texas, May 14, 1867, SDLR, AGO, RG 94, NA; *San Antonio Daily Express,* May 8, 1867.

badly. In May Hatch received orders to march west and occupy Forts Stockton and Davis. Before midsummer all ten companies had reached these posts. An untried regiment with the stain of mutiny on its standard faced the formidable task of guarding hundreds of miles of raw frontier populated by former Confederates who harbored antipathy toward black soldiers.[31]

Meanwhile, at Fort Leavenworth, Grierson struggled with problems that were, if anything, more exasperating than those of Hatch. Organization of the Tenth Cavalry proceeded very slowly because of the lack of officers coupled with Grierson's insistence on accepting only men who met a very high standard. For example, he instructed Captain Louis H. Carpenter, on recruiting service in Philadelphia, to enlist "men sufficiently educated to fill the positions of Non-Commissioned Officers, Clerks and Mechanics in the regiment." In the same vein, Grierson wrote Colonel S. Hendrickson, who was recruiting in Boston, "quality is more important than numbers." Such fastidiousness meant that by the end of September 1866, only one man, Private William Beauman, had arrived at Leavenworth, and he was ill with malaria.[32]

The pace of organization was so slow that Grierson found ample time to write frequently to Alice concerning the social scene at Leavenworth and to relate with considerable relish some details of a grasshopper invasion:

> they [the grasshoppers] were impolite and unceremonious enough to hop up, get up or in some way make their merry way up under the hoops and skirts of the ladies who are bold enough to promenade among them. From the motions I have myself seen made by ladies walking the streets, I am of the opinion that they were being tickled almost to death by grasshoppers—in some instances wiggling was most excruciating—even enough to drive a man with a heart of stone promptly to the rescue . . . should the grasshoppers remain here very long, I have no doubt

31 Organizational Returns, Ninth Cavalry, May–June 1867; Hutcheson, "Ninth Regiment of Cavalry," 280–82. The Ninth was not the only new regiment to face the problem of mutiny. In July 1867 a serous outbreak occurred in the Seventh Cavalry, and three troopers were shot. See Davis, "Summer on the Plains," 306. See also Millbrook, "The West Breaks in General Custer," 113–48.

32 Grierson to Carpenter, March 5, 1867, LS, Tenth U.S. Cavalry, U.S. Army Commands, RG 98, NA; Grierson to Hendrickson, June 3, 1867, ibid.; Organizational Returns, Tenth Cavalry, September 1866, AGO, RG 94, NA.

but what some Yankee will invent some new pattern for the relief
of the ladies in the way of *solid drawers.*[33]

The tempo of enlistment increased slightly in the late fall and winter as
additional officers reported for duty and were detailed immediately on
recruiting service. Early efforts had been concentrated in the states of the
Upper South, but Grierson was dissatisfied with the results. Thus, he shifted
most of the recruiters to northern cities such as Philadelphia, Boston, New
York, and Pittsburgh.

Grierson also kept a watchful eye on the new recruits as they arrived at
Leavenworth to ensure that his standards were being observed. He quickly
took a careless officer to task and wrote a tart letter to Captain H. T. Davis
at Memphis, Tennessee, warning him, "You will have to foot the bill for your
rejects in the future." As if by magic, the quality of Davis's enlistees improved.
The net result, however, was that the slow pace continued. As 1867 opened,
Grierson could report that only seven officers and eighty enlisted men had
joined the regiment.[34]

Spring brought a sharp upswing in enlistments but also increasing friction between Grierson and General William Hoffman, Third Infantry, who
was commanding at Leavenworth. The latter, contemptuous of black troops
and apparently of officers who served with them, made their stay at his post
as uncomfortable as possible. He quartered them on low ground that
became a swamp during rainfall; not surprisingly, many troopers were soon
hospitalized with pneumonia. He also ignored Grierson's pleas for a change
of quarters and refused to provide walkways so the men could at least keep
their feet dry.[35]

Prejudiced and a master of the petty, Hoffman bombarded Grierson with
complaints about his men's untidy quarters, their alleged tardiness at meal-
time, and their commanders' supposedly inadequate training methods and
improper routing of correspondence. One group of Grierson's recruits,
encamped along the road between Leavenworth and the city, was ordered to
"get out of sight." During inspection, Grierson's company commanders were

33   B. H. Grierson to Alice Grierson, October 3, 1866, GP-ISHS.
34   Grierson to Davis, March 6, 1867, LS, Tenth U.S. Cavalry; Organizational Returns,
Tenth Cavalry, January 1867.
35   Grierson to the PA, Fort Leavenworth, February 2, 1867, LS, Tenth U.S. Cavalry;
Annual Report of the Secretary of War for the Year 1867, 39; Organizational Returns, Tenth
Cavalry, February–March 1867.

instructed to keep their men at least ten to fifteen yards from white troops. Moreover, the blacks were not allowed to march in review but, instead, were ordered to remain at parade rest.[36]

Such rank discrimination led Grierson to protest loudly on the parade ground, but Hoffman refused to yield. Grierson fought back as best he could. Tolerant and genuinely fond of his men, he ordered his company commanders not to use the word "colored" in their reports. "The regiment is simply the Tenth Regiment of Cavalry, United States Army." He also complained directly to department headquarters of "invidious distinctions between white and Negro troops" and insisted on impartial treatment for his men.[37]

When Grierson received no satisfactory answers to his complaints, he feared that the future of his regiment was endangered. Determined to organize his companies and get them on the march "double quick," he wrote Alice that "Old Fogies" in the army wished to disband the black regiment. Thankfully, there were few recruits at Leavenworth "for the powers that be to wreak their spite and wrath upon." Despite his problems, he was certain, "Colored troops will hold their place in the Army of the United States as long as the government lasts."[38]

Another difficulty arose at Leavenworth that proved intensely frustrating. The regiment lacked good horses. Grierson journeyed to St. Louis to inspect a herd of fifty animals and found not a single one that was suitable for service. Many, he wrote Alice, were wind-blown cripples of the Civil War and others were more than a dozen years old. What he was encountering was a common problem. All cavalry commanders were often frustrated with the quality of mounts available to their regiments.[39]

The lack of suitable mounts did not delay Grierson's resolve to move at "double quick" to organize his regiment. Company A was outfitted and sent west in February. Although Company B required two more months,

36 Captain George T. Robinson to Grierson, June 30, 1867, GP-ISHS; Hoffman to Grierson, June 27, 1867, ibid; Grierson to the PA, June 21, 1867, LS, Tenth U.S. Cavalry; Lieutenant Henry E. Alvord to the PA, April 17, 1867, ibid.; Hoffman to Grierson, June 27, 1867.

37 Lieutenant Henry Alvord, Acting Adjutant, Tenth Cavalry, to Lieutenant N. D. Badger, June 18, 1867, LS, Tenth U.S. Cavalry; Grierson to the AAG, Department of the Missouri, June 19, 1867, ibid.

38 B. H. Grierson to Alice Grierson, May 24, 1867, GP-ISHS.

39 B. H. Grierson to Alice Grierson, April 26, 1867, ibid.; Dobak and Phillips, *Black Regulars*, xvi; Fletcher, *Black Soldier and Officer*, 22–23; Billington, *New Mexico's Buffalo Soldiers*, 187–90; Kenner, *Buffalo Soldiers and Officers of the Ninth Cavalry*, 28–29.

Company C was "armed, organized, uniformed, equipped, mounted and marched west under Captain [Edward] Byrne at this post [Leavenworth] last week in forty-eight hours after arrival of recruits from St. Louis." When General Hoffman took a parting shot at C Company by denying permission for the laundresses to accompany it, Byrne outmaneuvered him by instructing the women to walk out of the post. Once out of sight, they climbed on the wagons.[40]

Grierson became so impatient that he did not wait for the normal complement of ninety-nine men to fill D Company. He wrote Captain J. W. Walsh, on recruiting duty at Little Rock, Arkansas, to organize the company at Fort Gibson, Indian Territory, with the men on hand. At the same time, he cautioned Walsh to draw one hundred Spencer repeating carbines, sixteen to eighteen revolvers for the noncommissioned officers, and all other supplies necessary for a full company. The remaining personnel could be assigned later.[41]

Organization was thus hastened, and even greater speed could have been achieved but for the illiteracy of the men. A company was fortunate to have one man who could read and write, and invariably that man became quartermaster sergeant. Grierson soon found, however, that literacy was not an absolute prerequisite for noncommissioned rank. Most of the initial companies had illiterate first sergeants, and generally they performed well. But for many months officers had to complete all clerical work themselves, which led inevitably to delays in the organization and training of the regiment. The necessity for officers and men to work closely together, however, meant that over time they developed more intimate relationships than those that characterized most regiments.[42]

---

40 Alvord to Captain J. W. Walsh, May 23, 1867, LS, Tenth U.S. Cavalry; Organizational Returns, Tenth Cavalry, February–May 1867; Alice Grierson to Benjamin Grierson, May 21, 1867, GP-ISHS.

41 Grierson to Walsh, May 4, 1867, LS, Tenth U.S. Cavalry; Alvord to Walsh, May 23, 1867, ibid. Revolvers issued to the cavalry at this time were usually the Colt Army .44, a single-action, six-shot weapon using percussion cartridges. The Spencer carbine, standard for the cavalry until 1873, was of .56-50 caliber with a seven-shot magazine that was inserted into the stock through a hole in the butt plate. The cartridges in the magazine were nose to tail, however, and the gun had a discouraging tendency to discharge accidentally. "Death by accidental gunshot wound" is a common entry in the Organizational Returns of both the Ninth and Tenth Cavalry until the Spencer was replaced by the Model 1873 Springfield in that year. See Whitman, *The Troopers*, 178–88; Koller, *Fireside Book of Guns*, 77–80.

42 Bigelow, "Historical Sketch"; Grierson to Lieutenant Robert Gray, May 9, 1867, LS, Tenth U.S. Cavalry.

Despite the difficulties, including an outbreak of cholera in June and July that took many lives, eight companies of the Tenth were in the field by early August 1867. Companies D, E, and L were assigned to Indian Territory, while the others were stationed at posts and camps along the Kansas Pacific Railroad then under construction in central Kansas. Early in August, Grierson received orders to transfer his headquarters to Fort Riley, Kansas. In a matter of hours he left Fort Leavenworth, General Hoffman, and fears for the future of his regiment behind him.[43]

At Fort Riley, Grierson welcomed the arrival of an old friend and aide of Civil War days, Lieutenant Samuel Woodward. "Sandy" Woodward replaced Captain Henry Alvord as regimental adjutant, while the latter took command of Company M. For the next twenty years, without promotion, Woodward would serve the Tenth Cavalry and its colonel with singular efficiency and unfailing devotion.[44]

Organization of the remaining four companies of the regiment was completed at Riley, although it was October before Company M, the last, was ready for the field. But M had the honor of departing first for the West to the tunes of the regimental band. As a music lover, Grierson managed to find a few musicians and to teach others, but no funds were available for instruments. He solved this dilemma by establishing a band fund to which the enlisted men were asked to contribute fifty cents apiece, while each group of company officers donated fifty dollars.[45]

One year of history was behind the Tenth Cavalry, but the fighting qualities of officers and men were still an unknown quantity. This would not remain so very long.

The movement westward of the Ninth and Tenth Cavalry in the spring and summer of 1867 marked the beginning of more than two decades of

43 Organizational Returns, Tenth Cavalry, June–July 1867. Sixteen men died of cholera in July alone. Grierson to the AG, Washington, D.C., August 7, 1867, SDLR. Fort Riley, the first real home of the Tenth Cavalry, was situated on the north bank of the Kansas River at the junction of the Republican and Smoky Hill Rivers. It was named for Colonel Bennett Riley, First U.S. Infantry, and become a permanent cavalry post in 1855. See Frazer, *Forts of the West,* 57.

44 Alvord to Grierson, September 21, 1867, GP-ISHS; Woodward to Grierson, October 3, 1867, ibid. Woodward, a New Yorker, rose through the ranks in the Sixth Illinois Cavalry and was discharged as a major when the Civil War ended. Commissioned as a lieutenant in the Tenth Cavalry, he was not promoted to captain until 1887. See Heitman, *Historical Register,* 1:1059.

45 Organizational Returns, Tenth Cavalry, July–October 1867; circular, Grierson to All Company Commanders, September 14, 1867, LS, Tenth U.S. Cavalry.

continuous service on the Great Plains and in the mountains and deserts of New Mexico and Arizona. The challenge was a formidable one. Ten years of almost constant campaigning were required before the nomads of the southern plains—the Comanches, Kiowas, Kiowa-Apaches, Southern Cheyennes, and Arapahos—were defeated and confined to their reservations. Half again as long was required before peace prevailed along the tortured Rio Grande frontier, where Kickapoos and Lipans, Mexican bandits and revolutionaries, roamed, raided, stole, and murdered under conditions approaching anarchy. And for as many years, the Ninth and Tenth fought the Apaches of New Mexico and Arizona in their mountain homes and on waterless, desolate desert wastes.

The duties of the regiments would not be limited to fighting Indians. Law and order were little more than a hope in the post–Civil War Southwest, and civil authorities were compelled constantly to call upon the army to assist in rounding up border scum. The region swarmed with cattle thieves as well as men who killed with little or no provocation. Petty, scheming, and sometimes murderous politicians, combined with greedy land and cattle barons, crooked government contractors, heartless Indian agents, and land-hungry homesteaders, were the sources of civil broils of a scope far beyond the control of local or state authority. The result was inevitable involvement in civil affairs for the Ninth and Tenth, with often little hope or expectation of gratitude regardless of outcome or contribution. But in the summer of 1867, Hatch, Grierson, and their troopers rode west with no foreknowledge of the awesome tasks that awaited them. Perhaps it was just as well.

Meanwhile, the four infantry regiments, the Thirty-eighth, Thirty-ninth, Fortieth, and Forty-first, had been easily manned from the available pool of infantrymen still in the service. The Thirty-eighth had been assigned to the Department of the Missouri, while the other regiments had been ordered south for Reconstruction duty. In 1869 these infantry units would be consolidated into two—the Twenty-fourth and Twenty-fifth—and these would be sent to the Texas frontier. They would remain in the West along with their cavalry comrades for the next generation.

The Tenth Moves to the Plains

Colonel Benjamin Grierson and his fledgling regiment marched westward and straight into an Indian war of almost unprecedented scope and violence. In Texas, the coming of the Civil War and the withdrawal of U.S. garrisons had enabled the Kiowas and the Comanches to reclaim lands lost to aggressive whites. Determined to protect their way of life based on the buffalo hunt, these nomadic tribes had staved off and even rolled back non-Indian settlement in the remote areas of Texas for many miles.

The Plains Indians had been under intense and growing stress since the beginning of the overland trails in the 1840s. The livestock that migrating families had driven before them had diminished the forage available to the buffalo herds on which they had based their way of life. These livestock had also introduced diseases and parasites that had taken an additional toll on the buffalo, and the migrants had eliminated much of the game, such as elk, that might have provided Indians an alternative supply of meat. The onset of a severe drought on the plains in 1863 and continuing white intrusion onto American Indian lands along with the accompanying appropriation of pastureland and streams, had left the nomadic tribes of the central plains facing ecological disaster.[1]

1 West, *The Way West,* 52–83; West, *Contested Plains,* 261–62.

With tensions between Plains Indians and newcomers mounting, the Colorado militia under Colonel John M. Chivington had responded in 1864 by massacring a band of Cheyennes camped along Sand Creek (in present-day Colorado) under the leadership of the peace chief Black Kettle. That, in turn, had ignited a war that had left vast areas of the central plains ravaged.

In the uneasy peace achieved with the Cheyennes and their southern plains allies by the Treaty of the Little Arkansas in October 1865, the Dog Soldiers, an important group of largely younger braves among the Cheyennes, remained unappeased. To make matters worse, the lands assigned the plains tribes under terms of the treaty lay partly in Texas and Kansas. Both states refused to countenance reservations within their borders. The result was that for more than two years, the Cheyennes had no official home.[2]

This state of affairs brought a renewal of the conflict, and the Kiowas and Comanches struck once more at their foes in Texas. The Cheyennes, angered by the new threat to the buffalo herds posed by the construction crews of the transcontinental railroad and its proliferating lines, grew increasingly threatening. To forestall a major outbreak, Major General Winfield Scott Hancock, commanding the Department of the Missouri, took to the field in April 1867 to "overawe" or defeat any hostile Indians he might encounter. Hancock's campaign brought disastrous results. He failed to "overawe" a single Indian, and he provoked a full-scale war that rapidly spun out of his control. By the summer of 1867, the Plains Indians, to the consternation of many non-Indian settlers, roamed freely over much of the central and southern plains.[3]

Cheyenne war parties, aided by hostile Arapahos and Sioux, took a heavy toll along the Smoky Hill River, the line of the Kansas Pacific Railroad, and brought work virtually to a halt. In mid-June General Hancock reported that every station along the road for nearly one hundred miles on either side of Fort Wallace had been attacked, some as many as four times. Nor was Fort Wallace itself immune. Four men were killed and scalped near the post early in the month, and on June 21 two teamsters hauling stone from a quarry were killed within sight of the post. Five days later a force of Cheyennes estimated at two to three hundred attacked Pond Creek Station just west of Wallace.

---

2 Utley, *Indian Frontier*, 87–98; Kappler, *Indian Affairs*, 2:887–95; Berthrong, *Southern Cheyennes*, 238–44; *Annual Report of the Commissioner of Indian Affairs for the Year 1868*, 35.

3 *New York Tribune*, September 2, 1857; Berthrong, *Southern Cheyennes*, 277–87; Leckie, *Military Conquest*, 1–62.

Three hours of desperate fighting on the part of Captain Albert Barnitz and Company G, Seventh Cavalry, were required to save the station.[4]

Other hostile warriors congregated in the vicinity of Forts Hays and Harker, killing unwary trappers and travelers and running off stock. Near the latter post a gentleman from Boston, refusing to believe the Indian danger was either real or near, continued to search for geological specimens along Fossil Creek. While walking along the creek bed he met an incoming settler who remarked, "You'll find my partner's body a layin' down there; the Injins was in half an hour ago and tuk his scalp, and I haint had time to get him in since."[5] Interest in gathering fossils ceased then and there.

The Texas frontier and the Five Civilized Tribes of Indian Territory—the Cherokees, Choctaws, Chickasaws, Creeks, and Seminoles—suffered heavily from Kiowa and Comanche raiders. Governor J. W. Throckmorton of Texas telegraphed Secretary of War Edwin M. Stanton that, in the month of July alone, Kiowas and Comanches had killed 18 persons. Furthermore, since the end of the Civil War 162 citizens had lost their lives, 43 had suffered capture, and 24 had been wounded. Cattle numbering 30,838 head had been stolen, along with nearly 4,000 horses. Captain E. L. Smith, Nineteenth Infantry, reported from Fort Arbuckle that a thousand men would be required to protect the lives and property of the Five Tribes.[6]

An ugly and dangerous situation existed, therefore, from the Platte River in the north to the Rio Grande in the south. But Lieutenant General William T. Sherman, commanding the vast Military Division of the Missouri, which encompassed the Great Plains, had far fewer troops at his disposal than needed to provide a solid defense for such a long frontier. Since an economy-minded Congress refused to provide funds to strengthen the military, Sherman had to make do with those he had.[7]

As a partial remedy, therefore, three companies of the Tenth Cavalry, D, E, and L, were assigned to Indian Territory, with the remaining nine compa-

---

4 *Annual Report of the Secretary of War for the Year 1867*, 33; Post Returns, Fort Wallace, June 1867, AGO, RG 94, NA; *Harper's Weekly Magazine* 11 (July 27, 1867): 467–68.

5 *Army and Navy Journal* 4 (July 20, 1867): 770; Post Returns, Fort Hays, June 1867.

6 J. W. Throckmorton to E. M. Stanton, August 5, 1867, in Day and Winfrey, *Texas Indian Papers*, 4:235–36; Capt. E. L. Smith to the AAG, Department of the Arkansas, February 16, 1867, LR by the Office of Indian Affairs, Kiowa Agency, Records of the Office of Indian Affairs, NA.

7 Sherman's resources were slender indeed. In the Department of the Missouri, comprising all of Kansas, Missouri, Indian Territory, and New Mexico Territory, there were only three regiments of cavalry, the Third, Seventh, and Tenth, and four regiments of infantry. See *Annual Report of the Secretary of War for the Year 1866*, 19.

nies taking station at camps and posts along the line of the Smoky Hill and Santa Fe routes. This marked the beginning of more than two decades of continuous frontier defense for Benjamin Grierson's troopers.[8]

From Forts Harker, Hays, and Larned, detachments fanned out to protect railroad-working crews, escort stages and trains, and scout along the Saline, Solomon, and Arkansas Rivers. Initially, disease proved a greater enemy than marauding Indians. Epidemic cholera broke out at Harker and Hays. In ten days it claimed the lives of seven men in Captain George Armes's Company F, which was stationed at the latter post. Losses were also heavy at Fort Harker. Some lives might have been saved with proper food and nursing care, but post commanders were often reluctant to release men for such duties or to provide details to maintain proper hygiene around the military posts.[9]

These were not the only hazards of tenure in a remote post. At Fort Larned a large, rabid, gray wolf invaded the post hospital, bit a finger off a startled Corporal McGillicoddy, Third Infantry, and lacerated badly the right foot of Private Willie Mason, Company C, Tenth Cavalry, who was trying to climb the wall. Having created utter bedlam in the hospital and having undoubtedly promoted some remarkably rapid recoveries, the wolf departed between the legs of a doughty sentinel, who fired and understandably missed. Loping along officers' row and leaving complete demoralization in his wake, the animal paused long enough to sink his fangs into a Lieutenant Thompson before adjourning to the post haystack, where a guard's bullet put an end to the raid.[10]

New dangers threatened. On August 1, word reached Fort Hays that a strong party of Cheyennes had attacked Campbell's Camp, thirteen miles down the railroad, killing seven men. Captain Armes, an able but contentious officer, with thirty-four troopers marched to Campbell's, found the trail, and followed it northeast to the banks of the Saline. On the morning of August 2, he turned upstream and had scouted perhaps a dozen miles when suddenly seventy-five to eighty warriors attacked him.

The command dismounted to fight on foot and soon found itself surrounded as more warriors continually arrived as the battle progressed.

8 Organizational Returns, Tenth Cavalry, June–July, 1867, AGO, RG 94, NA.
9 Medical History, Fort Larned, vol. 164, Medical History of Posts, AGO, RG 94, NA; Medical History, Fort Hays, vol. 412; Armes, *Ups and Downs*, 230–31.
10 Medical History, Fort Larned, vol. 164.

For six hours under a blazing sun, F Company fought off its attackers, and then with ammunition running low, the troopers mounted and shot their way through the encircling Indians. Fifteen miles of skirmishing were necessary, however, before the Cheyennes broke off the action. Armes had suffered a hip wound. Sergeant William Christy, an ex-farmer from Pennsylvania, had been killed by a shot through the head. With the regiment less than two months, his was the first combat death in the Tenth Cavalry. Armes placed Indian casualties at six killed and an undetermined number wounded.[11]

Critically short of cavalry in the face of wide-scale Indian attacks, Sherman authorized Governor Samuel Crawford of Kansas to raise a force of volunteer cavalry. Designated the Eighteenth Kansas Cavalry, the volunteers rendezvoused at Fort Harker under the command of Major Horace L. Moore. Cholera took a heavy toll before Moore received orders to transfer his four companies to Fort Hays. Nonetheless, they were ready for field duty by mid-August.[12]

Captain Armes recovered sufficiently from his wound to return to active duty. Believing that a large concentration of hostile Cheyennes was somewhere along the Solomon River, he proposed to take his F Company and two companies of the Eighteenth Kansas to scout in that area. Moore with the remaining volunteers would scout the same stream. If either found Indians they would unite, thereby concentrating their strength so that together they could defeat any number of warring nomads they might encounter.

On August 20 Armes with forty men of F and ninety Kansans under Captain George Jenness left Fort Hays and set out for the Solomon. They reached it the evening of the following day. That night, when they saw a light some distance to the east, Jenness volunteered to take a small party and investigate. He found the remains of a campfire but saw no Indians in the

---

11 Armes, *Ups and Downs*, 237; Post Returns, Fort Hays, August 1867; Major John Bigelow, Jr., "Historical Sketch, Tenth United States Cavalry, 1866–1892," U.S. Army Commands, RG 98, NA; Registers of Enlistments in the U.S. Army, 1867, microcopy 233, U.S. Army Commands, RG 98, NA. Christy had enlisted in the Tenth on June 4, 1867. Captain Armes was a controversial officer whose long military career was dotted with arrests and quarrels with his superiors. He was dismissed from the service in June 1870, but the dismissal was later amended to provide an honorable discharge. He returned to the Tenth Cavalry in May 1878 and was retired in 1883. His own account of his troubles is found in his book, *Ups and Downs of an Army Officer.*

12 Garfield, "Defense of the Kansas Frontier," 338–39; *Annual Report of the Secretary of War for the Year 1867,* 35–36.

Emblem of the Tenth Regiment, United States Cavalry
Courtesy National Archives

vicinity. Unable to find his way back in the dark, Jenness encamped. At daybreak he returned to the Solomon and located the wagon train, guarded by Lieutenant Price and about thirty men of the Eighteenth Kansas. Armes, meanwhile, had moved on toward Beaver Creek with the rest of the command. There was no sign of Major Moore or of units of the Seventh Cavalry, which were thought to be in the area also.

Jenness and Price moved out to join Armes, but they had gone only a short distance when hundreds of screaming warriors streamed toward them. Jenness formed his men into a hollow square and opened fire with Spencer repeaters. Indian warriors completely surrounded the embattled Kansans, circling and firing with rifles, shotguns, and bows and arrows. One brave, mounted on a superb white horse, led a charge that was broken by the rapid-fire Spencers. The gallant warrior, after riding down one solider who tried to stop him, moved on through the square, escaping without a scratch, although at least fifty shots were fired at him.

Fearful that he would be overrun, Jenness began a slow movement in the direction Armes had taken, with his wounded draped over the few remaining sound animals in his command. The Indian fire proved too hot, and Jenness was forced to halt and take refuge in a ravine. The Kansans had no monopoly on the fighting, however, for Armes was having his own troubles as well. As he entered the valley of the Beaver, an overwhelming number of fast-riding Cheyennes attacked and forced him to take cover in a deep ravine. The fighting raged until dark and was renewed at daybreak the next morning. Not until midafternoon did the warriors draw off sufficiently to permit Armes and Jenness to unite their battered forces.

The Indians still commanded the nearby ridges, however, and shouted insults in good English. A number of them taunted, "Come out of that hole you sons of bitches and give us a fair fight." Armes obliged by charging and driving his tormentors for some distance. Skirmishing, however, continued until dusk, when the Indians left the field and allowed Armes to march his weary command back to Fort Hays. F Company suffered one man killed and thirteen wounded, while Jenness counted two dead and sixteen wounded. Armes placed Indian losses at fifty killed and three times that number wounded. He and Jenness believed that they had been attacked by a force of eight hundred to one thousand warriors.[13]

13 Bigelow, "Historical Sketch"; Jenness, "Battle on Beaver Creek," 447–52; Armes, *Ups and Downs,* 242–46; Organizational Returns, Tenth Cavalry, August 1867.

Company F had done well for raw recruits. True, the troopers had fired too rapidly for accuracy, but they had shown no panic in the face of great odds and had charged with spirit when called upon. Not all their lessons were learned on the battlefield. In scouting, guarding, and escort duty, in the routine of garrison life, and through the iron discipline of the frontier army, pride of self and of regiment grew. They learned, most of them, to accept danger and death as constant companions, whether from enemy bullet, arrow, or lance, or from cholera, pneumonia, "acute gastritis," or other scourges of the day. Armes no longer led a bunch of recruits after August 21, 1867, but a company of fighting men.

Capable noncommissioned officers were quick to emerge. On September 15 Sergeant Ed Davis and nine men of Company G were on guard at a railroad camp forty-five miles west of Fort Hays. Private John Randall, who had been with the regiment less than two months, and two civilians left camp for a hunt. They were barely out of sight before seventy Cheyennes attacked them. Both civilians were killed almost at once, and Randall was severely wounded before he found dubious sanctuary in a hole under a railroad cut. Gleeful warriors probed the hole with lances, inflicting eleven wounds, and then tried to cave the hole in on him. Fortunately for the cornered Randall, they eventually tired of the sport and turned to attack the camp.

Sergeant Davis did not wait to receive the attack but dismounted his men and advanced to fight the enemy on foot. The Cheyennes, apparently surprised at such audacity, turned off to attack two men who came up with an ox team. But Davis, moving swiftly and shooting accurately, forced the Indians to veer off, thereby allowing the men to reach camp in safety. Davis then mounted his little command and rode in search of Randall and his companions.

The warriors, still seeking a fight, returned to the attack but once again were repulsed with a loss of thirteen killed or wounded. When the Indians withdrew, Randall was located by his cries for aid and extricated from his crumbling shelter, seriously but not fatally wounded. That fall, he received a citation for heroism, which added to the honors the Tenth Cavalry was winning.[14]

It was about this time that the Plains Indians gave the black troopers a

14 George W. Ford, formerly First Sergeant, Troop L, Tenth Cavalry, to the editor, *Winners of the West* 3 (November 1925); Organizational Returns, Tenth Cavalry, September 1867; Schubert, *On the Trail of the Buffalo Soldier*, 346.

sobriquet. Called all manner of names—"Moacs," "Brunettes," "niggers," "Africans"—by all manner of people, they were dubbed "buffalo soldiers" by their Indian antagonists. The reasons are not entirely known, but Frances Roe, the wife of Lieutenant Fayette Washington Roe of the Third Infantry, gave this explanation in correspondence to relatives back east. In June 1873 she wrote from Camp Supply that the Indians called the black soldiers buffalo soldiers because "their wooly heads are so much like the matted cushion that is between the horns of the buffalo."[15]

Meanwhile, events were occurring that gave the buffalo soldiers a brief but welcome respite. The federal government was making another effort at a peaceful solution to the Indian problem. In July 1867 Congress created the Indian Peace Commission for the purpose of conferring with the warring tribes and to remove, if possible, the causes of recurring wars. The commission met at St. Louis in August; elected N. G. Taylor, commissioner of Indian affairs, as president; and quickly agreed that the Indians must be placed on permanent reservations away from the roads and railroads.

Considerable difficulties were encountered in making contact with the tribes, but arrangements were finally made to hold a council with the Southern Cheyennes and Arapahos, Kiowas, Comanches, and Kiowa-Apaches near mid-October along Medicine Lodge Creek in Kansas. Pending the outcome of the talks, Sherman notified subordinate commanders that all offensive military operations should cease.

More than a week of talks at Medicine Lodge brought treaties with all the assembled tribes. The Comanches, Kiowas, and Kiowa-Apaches accepted a reservation of some three million acres between the Washita and Red Rivers in Indian Territory, while immediately to the north the Cheyennes and Arapahos received in excess of four million acres. The Indians were promised annuities in the form of ample food, clothing, and other supplies. They also retained the right to hunt buffalo anywhere south of the Arkansas River. Finally, resident agents would assist them in adjusting to the "white man's road." In return the Indians agreed to keep the peace, not to molest the whites, and to stay clear of the great roads.[16]

15 Roe, *Army Letters from an Officer's Wife*, 62–65.
16 *United States Statues at Large*, 15:17; Kappler, *Indian Affairs*, 2:980–89; Alfred A. Taylor, "Medicine Lodge Peace Council," *Chronicles of Oklahoma* 2 (June 1924): 100–101; House, H. Exec. Doc. 97, 40th Cong., 2d sess., 2–3. In addition to Commissioner Taylor, other members of the commission were John B. Henderson, John B. Sanborn, S. F. Tappan, General Sherman, and Brigadier Generals William S. Harney and Alfred H. Terry.

The treaties of Medicine Lodge brought a cessation of warfare on the central plains and strong hopes for a permanent peace. Disturbing factors, however, still remained. Many influential chiefs and headmen among the Cheyennes, along with their followers, were opposed to giving up their hunting grounds since they knew that the buffalo and game were less plentiful south of the Arkansas River.[17] Thus, their future behavior was in grave doubt.

To the south there was no doubt; bands of Kiowas and Comanches continued to antagonize citizens along the Texas frontier, and the Five Civilized Tribes of Indian Territory also suffered from their incursions. Worse yet, the Senate and House fell to haggling over financial provisions of the treaties, and ratification was long delayed. It was expecting too much of a nomad Indian to understand and appreciate what his more "enlightened" white brethren often failed to comprehend—the vagaries of American politics.

During the winter of 1867–68, Grierson found conditions favorable enough on the Kansas frontier to concentrate most of his regiment at Fort Riley. As a precautionary measure, however, detachments were left at railroad camps along the Kansas Pacific to protect the workers. Meanwhile, the troopers of D, E, and L Companies in Indian Territory had seen no fighting, but they had enough work to keep them busy. In November Grierson moved Company M under Captain Henry Alvord to Fort Gibson.[18]

Kiowa and Comanche raids on the herds of the Chickasaws and Choctaws had brought these tribes to the point of open warfare. Bootleggers plied their dangerous and illicit traffic in the territory, and bands of white men stole Indian cattle and horses with impunity. Mail carriers between Forts Gibson and Arbuckle were murdered so often that no white man could be found to accept such employment, and Indian scouts were eventually induced to ride in teams to get the mail through. And as winter deepened, bands of Kiowas and Comanches made their camps along the Washita. With them were a number of white captives taken on raids into Texas.[19]

In such a wild and sparsely settled country, there was little that four untrained troops of cavalry and a few companies of infantry could do.

17 Utley, *Indian Frontier,* 112.
18 Organization Returns, Tenth Cavalry, October–December 1867; Grierson to the AG, September 30, 1867, LS, Tenth U.S. Cavalry, U.S. Army Commands, RG 98, NA; Alvord to Grierson, November 21, 1868, GP-ISHS.
19 House, H. Misc. Doc. 139, 41st Cong., 2d sess., 3; Pratt, *Battlefield and Classroom,* 22–24.

Distances were great and news traveled slowly. Reports of raids or the entry of elusive whisky peddlers reached the lonely little posts long after the intruders had departed. Some success was achieved in recovering white captives, though ransom proved necessary.

More progress was made in rebuilding Fort Arbuckle, a duty the buffalo soldiers would repeat many times over at different locations during their long service on the plains. Captain J. W. Walsh and Captain George T. Robinson of Companies D and E at Arbuckle spent much of their time in training their willing and obedient troopers, who soon became proficient in mounted and dismounted drill. But garrison life was often monotonous, and an occasional trooper kicked over the traces. Private William Alexander of D sold his overcoat to a teamster, bought a jug of whisky from an ever-present peddler, and went on a spree. He no doubt remembered the occasion for a long time, for he was sentenced to stand on the head of a barrel from 9:00 A.M. to 4:00 P.M. each day for ten days and to forfeit fourteen dollars of his pay.

Some of the new troopers developed a quick aversion for army life and took off without bothering to say farewell. Others deserted after a minor infraction brought instant and severe punishment, such as confinement in a barrel from reveille to retreat without relief. But one trooper at Arbuckle, charged with desertion, came to typify the growing spirit and pride that marked the men of the Tenth.

In the dead of winter, Private Filmore Roberts was detailed to carry the mail to Fort Gibson. He never reported there and was listed as a deserter. Many months later his remains were found lodged in some willows along the Canadian River several miles below the fort. Still strapped to his back was the mail pouch for which he had given his life in an attempt to cross a swollen stream and deliver it to Fort Gibson.[20]

The tempo of activity accelerated considerably at Gibson and Arbuckle early in 1868. In February Colonel Jesse Leavenworth, appointed as agent to the Kiowas and Comanches, arrived in the Indian Territory and established a temporary agency at Eureka Valley. He found affairs in a critical state. The failure of Congress to implement the Medicine Lodge treaties left him with little to offer his insolent and restless charges, and they continued to harry the North Texas frontier.

20 Ford to the editor, *Winners of the West* (November 1925); Pratt, *Battlefield and Classroom*, 15–17; Nye, *Carbine and Lance*, 40–41.

In less than a month, Leavenworth became fearful for his own safety and dashed off a note to Captain Walsh at Arbuckle asking for military assistance. Walsh made a forced march to Eureka Valley with D Company, but before they arrived the more belligerent Indians had left. Raids and depredations continued. In May a Comanche war party swept down on the Wichita agency, some one hundred miles northwest of Arbuckle, and burned the buildings after looting them. It was enough for Leavenworth. He departed the country never to return.[21]

The troopers at Gibson and Arbuckle, while improving daily in efficiency and effectiveness, were still much too far to the east to counter the raids quickly. Major General Philip Sheridan, Hancock's successor as commanding general of the Department of the Missouri, ordered Grierson to move his headquarters from Fort Riley to Gibson and then to reconnoiter the country to the west with a view to building a post in the heart of the recently established Kiowa and Comanche reservation. Cavalry could then observe the activities of the Indians and, when necessary, operate against them more effectively.

Grierson left Fort Riley on May 1 with his adjutant, Samuel Woodward, the regimental chaplain, W. M. Grimes, and nineteen troopers. He stayed at Gibson only long enough to mount E and M Companies and then pushed on to Arbuckle. Late in the month he left for the west with D, E, L, M, and a train guarded by a company of the Sixth Infantry. Torrential rains caught the column shortly after it left the post and turned the trail into a quagmire. Long stretches had to be corduroyed to get the train through, and enormous balls of mud formed on the horses' hooves. The men were soaked, bedraggled, and miserable.

Eventually the rains stopped and the column reached a delightful valley in the shadow of the Wichita Mountains. After scouting along Cache and Medicine Bluff Creeks, Grierson was convinced that he had found the most desirable site in the region. There was an abundance of water, timber, grass,

---

21 Leavenworth to the Commanding Officer, Fort Arbuckle, March 26, 1868, LR by the Office of Indian Affairs, Kiowa Agency; Nye, *Carbine and Lance,* 47–48; *Annual Report of the Secretary of War for the Year 1868,* 16. Fort Arbuckle was first situated along the Arkansas River in June 1834 and named for Colonel Matthew Arbuckle, Seventh Infantry. It was abandoned in 1834. A second Fort Arbuckle was built along Wild Horse Creek about five miles from the Washita River in April 1851. It was evacuated by U.S. troops in May 1861 and was not reoccupied by them until November 1866. See Frazer, *Forts of the West,* 116–17.

and limestone, and Grierson hastened to stake out a site for the future post. A buffalo hunt produced plenty of fresh meat, and the command marched on westward to Otter Creek, where they encountered a band of Comanches. Grierson arranged for a council and recovered six captives after a lengthy talk. Feeling his mission accomplished, Grierson returned to Fort Arbuckle and disbanded the expedition.[22]

Need for just such a post became readily more apparent in ensuing months. In September Captain Alvord, writing from Fort Gibson, told Grierson that the Comanches were "getting pretty wild" in Eureka Valley. In response, Lieutenant Robert Gray of D Company had taken every buffalo soldier at Arbuckle and gone there to quiet them.[23]

But if conditions were bad along the Texas frontier and in Indian Territory, they were worse in Kansas. With the approach of summer, large numbers of Kiowas, Comanches, Southern Cheyennes, and Arapahos gathered in the vicinity of Fort Larned to receive their promised annuities. But Congress still dallied, and Agent E. W. Wynkoop had little to offer them. There were other supplies, unfortunately, that lurking bootleggers readily furnished. Angry warriors, seeing their families hungry, lacking in supplies, and able to obtain whiskey, could only spell trouble. Depredations were committed near Forts Zarah and Wallace in May. Later that month a large war party of Cheyennes attacked a band of Kaws at Council Grove, burned several buildings, and stole some cattle.[24]

With an ominous situation developing, Sheridan concentrated seven companies of the Seventh Cavalry under Brevet Brigadier General Alfred Sully at Fort Larned. The eight companies of the Tenth still in Kansas were equally divided between Forts Hays and Wallace. Meanwhile, Congress had finally made funds available to implement the Medicine Lodge treaties, and annuities were issued to the Indians at Fort Larned during the first week of August. Much to Sheridan's disgust, the distribution included guns and ammunition for hunting.[25]

22 Organizational Returns, Tenth Cavalry, May–June 1868; "Reminiscences of John Thomas, Late of Troop 'L,' Tenth Cavalry," *Winners of the West* (May 30, 1934); Bigelow, "Historical Sketch"; Nye, *Carbine and Lance*, 49–50.

23 Alvord to Grierson, September 13, 1868, GP-ISHS.

24 *Annual Report of the Commissioner of Indian Affairs for the Year 1868*, 64–66; Post Returns, Fort Wallace, May, 1868; Doran, "Kansas Sixty Years Ago," 491.

25 *Annual Report of the Commissioner of Indian Affairs for the Year 1868*, 68–70; Post Returns, Fort Larned, Fort Hays, and Fort Wallace, May–June, 1868; Sheridan, *Personal Memoirs*, 2:289.

Agent Wynkoop, relieved that the annuities had been issued at last, wrote the commissioner of Indian affairs that the Indians were pleased and contented. There would be no trouble on the plains, at least for a time. Wynkoop could hardly have been more wrong, for even as he wrote a large Cheyenne war party struck the settlements along the Saline and Solomon Rivers with the fury of a tornado.

Although peace chiefs such as Black Kettle tried to maintain order among their followers, they could not control many of their young braves, particularly the Dog Soldiers, any more than many government authorities could control their youthful hotheads, especially in unsettled regions. Some Cheyenne braves also joined Arapaho raiders and struck a party of wood-choppers along Twin Butte Creek. After killing three of them, they stole twenty-five head of stock, then murdered two men on Pond Creek near Fort Wallace and a herder near Fort Dodge. They then chased the stage to Cheyenne Wells for four miles and attacked a wood train of thirty-five wagons at Cimarron Crossing, killing two men and running off seventy-five head of cattle. Those actions led Governor Frank Hall of Colorado to report that two hundred warriors were devastating the southern part of his territory.[26]

On August 21 an angry General Sherman telegraphed the War Department that he had ordered General Sheridan to force the Indians south of the Kansas line and to kill them if necessary. If President Johnson did not agree, Sherman wished to be notified at once. Consultations between the War and Interior Departments resulted in approval of Sherman's proposal, provided those Indians innocent of any outrages were separated from the guilty. The peaceful ones would be escorted to a rendezvous at Fort Cobb in Indian Territory, where agents could minister to their needs. Arrangements were made, therefore, to remove the Kiowas, Kiowa-Apaches, and Comanches while the army undertook to punish the offending Cheyennes and Arapahos.[27]

Punishing the hostiles was not easy, for Sheridan had far too few troops at hand for the task. He could muster perhaps fourteen hundred infantry for garrison and guard duty, but he had only two regiments of cavalry for field service, the Seventh and Tenth. Of the latter regiment, four companies were

26 Hoig, *Peace Chiefs*, 120–21; U.S. Army, Military Division of the Missouri, *Record of Engagements with Hostile Indians*, 9–12; *Annual Report of the Commissioner of Indian Affairs for the Year 1868*, 68–70; *Annual Report of the Secretary of War for the Year 1868*, 4–5.
27 Senate, S. Exec. Doc. 13, 40th Cong., 3d sess., 9–11.

needed in Indian Territory. But the fuming Sheridan did his best to put every available man in the field.

General Sully at Fort Dodge organized an expedition of nine companies of the Seventh Cavalry and three companies of the Third Infantry to subdue hostiles who had been active along the Arkansas. Two weeks of campaigning south of the river garnered precious little results, and he retired with Indian warriors yipping at his heels and gesturing obscenely to convey their contempt.[28]

The buffalo soldiers hardly had time to cool their saddles. Detachments were necessary to constantly escort stages and trains, to protect workers at the end of track, and to scout along the Smoky Hill, Saline, and Solomon Rivers. In August alone the overworked troopers scouted more than one thousand miles searching for flitting Indian raiders but made no interceptions. September was more of the same until the middle of the month.

At that time Captain G. W. Graham with thirty-six men of I Company struck and followed a trail along the Denver road until they reached Big Sandy Creek. There one hundred Cheyennes were waiting and engaged them in a bitter fight at close quarters. The men of I, in their first encounter and outnumbered badly, fought like cornered wildcats. When the engagement ended at nightfall, eleven Cheyennes were dead and fourteen wounded. Graham reported his loss as one man wounded and eighteen horses either killed or missing.[29]

On September 21 Captain Louis H. Carpenter and H Company left Wallace to "finish what Captain Graham had started." He found no sign of the Indians but remained in the vicinity to secure the road and threw out scouting detachments. It was well that he did so.

Badly in need of additional cavalry, Sheridan requested Sherman to make another regiment available. Meanwhile, he authorized his aide, Major George A. Forsyth, to raise a force of fifty frontier scouts for immediate service. Forsyth experienced no difficulty in recruiting the necessary men at Forts Hays and Harker and arming them with Spencer repeating rifles and revolvers. Lieutenant Frederick Beecher, Third Infantry, was second in

---

28 Sheridan, *Personal Memoirs*, 2:297. An interesting account of the Sully expedition is found in Godfrey, "Some Reminiscences, Including an Account of General Sully's Expedition," 421–23.

29 Organizational Returns, Tenth Cavalry, September 1868; Bigelow, "Historical Sketch"; Post Returns, Fort Wallace, September 1868; Medical History, Fort Wallace, vol. 363.

command, with Dr. J. H. Mooers as surgeon. By September 5 Forsyth and his scouts were at Fort Wallace. Four days later he was marching toward the town of Sheridan, thirteen miles east of Wallace, where Indians had struck a freighter's train.[30]

The trail of the raiders was followed easily. By evening, September 16, it had led the scouts to a small valley along the Arikaree Fork of the Republican River. There they encamped for the night and were prepared to push on next morning. Little did they dream that several of their number would never live through another day.

Near noon on September 22, two buffalo soldiers of H Company were riding westward from Wallace with dispatches for Captain Carpenter, who was then on Sandy Creek some forty-five miles from the post. They were hailed by two bedraggled and footsore men who proved to be scouts from Forsyth's command, Jack Stilwell and Pierre Trudeau.

They bore grim news. On the morning of September 17, hundreds of Indians had struck Forsyth's camp, and savage fighting had raged all day. By evening the command was in desperate straits. Surrounded by hostile warriors, its rations and medical supplies were exhausted, and they were suffering from many casualties. Stilwell and Trudeau, having volunteered to seek aid at Fort Wallace, had managed to make their way safely to the Denver road. The men reported that unless relief reached Forsyth soon, his entire command might be wiped out.

The two scouts then turned toward Fort Wallace while the troopers spurred their mounts on to Sandy Creek and apprised their commander of Forsyth's plight. Carpenter decided to march at once to relieve Forsyth, although not a man in his command was familiar with the country to the north. He had fought with Forsyth in the Shenandoah and in the Wilderness during the Civil War. His troopers were eager for a fight, and if the situation had been described accurately, there was no time to waste.

Before dark on September 23, Carpenter had covered thirty-five miles at an alternate walk and trot with scouts thrown far out. He was on the move again at dawn the next day and, after covering some twenty miles, reached a dry riverbed. A scout of several miles upstream proved unproductive, and the northward march continued. Late afternoon brought the tired

30   George A. Forsyth to Brevet Brigadier General C. M. McKeever, AAG, Department of the Missouri, "Report of the Organization and Operation of a Body of Scouts Enrolled and Equipped at Forts Harker and Hays, Kansas, August 24, 1868," March 31, 1869, Phillips Collection, University of Oklahoma [hereinafter cited as Forsyth, "Report"].

but determined column to a stream flowing through a wide, grassy valley.

Here they found a large Indian trail, and a search soon revealed a number of Indian dead on scaffolds. The bodies were examined, and in every case death had been caused by a gunshot wound. One body was mounted on a platform inside a tipi and wrapped in a fine buffalo robe. The corpse was not disturbed, but Carpenter did carry away a drum that he later gave to the Pennsylvania Historical Society.[31]

Early next morning, as the troopers saddled up, horsemen were seen in the distance, and shortly after five riders came into camp. One of them proved to be Jack Donovan. Another of Forsyth's scouts, he had made his way to Fort Wallace. Finding that most of the garrison had gone in search of Forsyth, he had persuaded four men to return with him. By sheer chance he had come upon Carpenter's command. Fired with an even greater sense of emergency, Carpenter took thirty of his best mounted men and a wagon loaded with hardtack, coffee, and bacon and moved out at a gallop with orders to the rest of the company to follow as rapidly as possible.

Eighteen miles farther north brought the advance to the Arikaree. When movement was seen down the valley, Carpenter and his orderly, Private Reuben Waller, put their horses to a run. In minutes they were at Forsyth's side. Seeing them coming, the intrepid major had grabbed *Oliver Twist* from one of his men's saddlebags to give the impression that he was nonchalantly reading. "Welcome to Beecher Island," was his greeting amid the pitiful sight of his command.

Four men were dead, among them Lieutenant Beecher and Surgeon Mooers. Scout Louis Farley would die that night and another scout later. Fifteen were wounded, including Forsyth, who had been shot through both legs; maggots were having a field day in the wounds. The stench from dead bodies, men, and animals was so overpowering that Carpenter's first move was to transfer the survivors a good distance away and then attend to their needs. Dr. Jenkins Fitzgerald wanted to remove one of Forsyth's legs at once, since he saw signs of blood poisoning.[32] The major protested so vehemently that the good doctor only shook his head and warned that a life was better than a leg.

---

31 Ibid.; Brevet Colonel L. H. Carpenter, "The Story of a Rescue," *Winners of the West* 11 (February 28, 1934). Carpenter thought the body was that of Roman Nose, a prominent Cheyenne warrior, but apparently it was the corpse of another Cheyenne named Killed by a Bull. See Grinnell, *Fighting Cheyennes*, 280.

32 Carpenter, "Story of a Rescue"; Dixon, *Hero of Beecher Island*, 86.

Next day, September 26, Captain H. C. Bankhead, Fifth Infantry with Graham's Company I of the Tenth and detachments of the Fifth and Thirty-eighth Infantry arrived after a forced march from Fort Wallace. Carpenter and his buffalo soldiers had done all that they could in the field. The follow-ing day the united commands set out for Fort Wallace.[33]

Meanwhile, Sheridan's request to Sherman for additional cavalry brought results. Seven companies of the Fifth Cavalry were transferred from the southern states to Fort Harker and placed under the temporary command of Major William B. Royall until an officer of greater rank, Brevet Major General Eugene A. Carr, could gain release from staff duties in the Depart-ment of Washington and join the regiment. The Fifth was ready for the field by October 1. Although Carr was still absent, Royall left Harker on that date to search for a large war party thought to be encamped along Beaver Creek.

Royall searched over a wide area and then went into bivouac along Prairie Dog Creek. From this point detachments fanned out in all directions to follow trails that seemed to lead everywhere. On October 14, while most of the command was so engaged, the Cheyennes hit the camp, killed one trooper, wounded another, and ran off twenty-six horses of H Company. A frustrated Royall concentrated his command and marched to Buffalo Tank on the Kansas Pacific, having done little more than provide the Cheyennes with some amusement and some excellent horses.

On October 12 General Carr reached Fort Wallace, anxious to join his regiment. The next day he left the post, escorted by Captain Carpenter, Captain Graham, and Companies H and I of the Tenth. The column marched due north for the Beaver, struck that stream on October 15, and turned downstream searching for Royall. No sign of him was found either that day or the next.

On the morning of October 17, Carpenter sent Lieutenant Myron Amick with ten troopers and scout Sharp Grover, who had been with Forsyth, toward Shortness Creek to look for Indians while the main body continued

33 Carpenter, "Story of a Rescue"; Private Reuben Waller, formerly of Troop H, Tenth Cavalry, "Forsyth's Fight," *Winners of the West* 2 (August 1925); Brady, *Indian Fights and Fighters,* 102–7; Medical History, Fort Wallace, vol. 363; Bigelow, "Historical Sketch"; *Army and Navy Journal* 6 (October 3, 1868): 98; Forsyth, "Report"; Organizational Returns, Tenth Cavalry, September 1868. Louis Henry Carpenter was a native of New Jersey who enlisted as a private when the Civil War came and rose to the rank of lieutenant colonel in the Fifth Cavalry with brevets for gallantry at the Battles of Gettysburg and Winches-ter. He joined the Tenth Cavalry as a captain in July 1866 and enjoyed a long and distin-guished career. One of the finest officers on the frontier, he retired as a brigadier general in October 1899. See Heitman, *Historical Register,* 1:284.

on down the Beaver. At nightfall Carpenter encamped with the stock inside
a wagon corral, and soon thereafter Amick returned to report that there was
no sign of Royall. Grover, however, had discovered the single tracks of a
running Indian pony crossing the rear of Amick's line of march—if Indians
were in the vicinity, they had no doubt been warned that soldiers were near.

Carr, now doubting that his missing regiment was along the Beaver,
decided to return to Fort Wallace. Early on the morning of October 18, however, Captain Graham volunteered to make a short search farther downstream while the rest of the command packed up for the return march.
Graham and two troopers trotted away. He had gone no more than a few
hundred yards when a small party of warriors rushed to cut him off from
the main body. Graham and his troopers spurred for the creek with bullets
snapping past their ears while Amick and thirty men charged the Indians
and drove them off.

When Graham and Amick rejoined, the whole command moved off,
crossing to the north side of the Beaver. As they did some two hundred Indians came up to the south side of the stream, and gunfire flamed from both
sides. Carpenter, content to duel at a distance, continued his march, with H
on the flanks and front and I covering the rear. Shortly after midday the
Indians disappeared, only to return half an hour later with hundreds of reinforcements. They attacked the column on the front, flanks, and rear. Fearful of being caught in the creek bottom, Carpenter turned off and took his
stand on a small knoll. He formed his wagons in the shape of a horseshoe,
with the mules facing inward, while the troopers rode inside, tied their
mounts, and formed outside in open order.

The Indians charged at once but were repulsed by seven-shot Spencers,
leaving three of their number within fifty feet of the wagons. They then
circled, firing into the wagons but suffering additional casualties as the
buffalo soldiers maintained a steady, accurate fire. No longer green troops,
H and I could hold their own with any troops in the army. As the afternoon
wore on, the Indians drew off, and Carpenter moved down to water at the
Beaver and encamp.

"Wolves" howled around the camp all night, but there were no further
attacks. When morning came, the command set out for Fort Wallace, which
it reached on October 21. Carpenter had marched 230 miles in nine days,
killed ten Indians, and wounded a larger number. His own loss was
three men wounded, and only one of these, Private John Daniels of H, was
seriously injured. Sheridan personally commended the buffalo soldiers

of H and I and recommended Carpenter for a Medal of Honor. As for Eugene A. Carr, men with whom he had refused to serve had saved his "hair," and he corrected his earlier opinion.[34]

Sheridan himself had not been idle. He now understood more clearly than ever, in light of the events at Beecher Island, the danger, as one scholar notes, "of using small, mobile ranger units to fight Indians."[35] Plans were under way for a large decisive campaign against the warring tribes. By October, arrangements were set to move the peaceful tribes to Fort Cobb to keep them from harm. General Sherman had appointed Brevet Major General W. B. Hazen, Sixth Infantry, to conduct the Kiowas and Comanches from Fort Larned to Cobb. When these Indians failed to appear at the appointed time, an anxious Hazen set out alone for Fort Cobb. He feared that the Kiowas and Comanches might have joined forces with the hostiles.

Meanwhile, pending Hazen's arrival, Captain Alvord, commanding M Company of the Tenth at Fort Arbuckle, was ordered to Cobb to care for any Indians who might have gone there. Alvord arrived in mid-October and to his astonishment found that several hundred Indians had preceded him—sufficient to press sorely on his available supplies.

After taking care of their immediate needs, Alvord organized a small scouting force comprised of friendly Indians and a few white scouts to locate and keep him informed of the movements of the various tribes. In this way he soon learned that the main body of the Kiowas and Comanches was nearby and had not engaged in the recent hostilities. Nonetheless, they were sullen and restless. When Alvord requested troopers, Companies L of the Tenth and E of the Sixth Infantry were sent from Fort Arbuckle. The men erected crude picket shelters for themselves and roofed several crumbling adobe structures to protect the supplies.

Hazen arrived early in November and held councils with many of the chiefs and headmen of the Kiowas and Comanches. He disliked what he considered their arrogant attitude. When he learned later in the month that many of the Cheyennes and Arapahos had arrived along the Washita River within easy striking distance of Fort Cobb, he sent for additional reinforce-

34 Organizational Returns, Tenth Cavalry, October 1868; Medical History, Fort Wallace, vol. 363; Brady, *Indian Fights and Fighters,* 124–35; Bigelow, "Historical Sketch"; *Annual Report of the Secretary of War for the Year 1868,* 19; "The History of the Fifth United States Cavalry from March 3, 1855, to December 31, 1905," File 1102491, AGO, RG 94 NA; King, *War Eagle,* 81–85. Carr joined his regiment at Buffalo Tank a few days later and on October 25–26 fought a hot but indecisive skirmish with the Cheyennes at Beaver Creek.
35 Dixon, *Hero of Beecher Island,* 87.

ments. Companies D and M of the Tenth were soon on hand. Hazen could now protect his position and, in addition, supply Sheridan with valuable information regarding the location of the hostile camps.[36]

While Alvord and Hazen dispensed supplies and forwarded information, Sheridan completed plans for an unprecedented and daring winter campaign to conquer a peace with the Cheyennes and Arapahos. Vast stores were accumulated at Forts Dodge, Lyon, and Arbuckle, and a four-pronged plan of attack, based on converging columns and close cooperation between and among commanders in the field, was devised.

A "main column" was organized under Brevet Brigadier General Sully consisting of eleven companies of the Seventh Cavalry under Lieutenant Colonel George A. Custer, five companies of infantry, and the Nineteenth Kansas Volunteer Cavalry under Governor S. J. Crawford. Acting as "beaters in," to drive the Indians into the path of the main column, were three commands. One of eight companies of cavalry and infantry, under Brevet Lieutenant Colonel A. W. Evans, would march east from Fort Bascom, New Mexico. A second led by General Carr would push southeast from Fort Lyon. The third, under Brevet Brigadier General W. H. Penrose, would precede Carr from Fort Lyon and effect a junction with him along the North Canadian.[37]

The role in the winter campaign assigned to the badly scattered buffalo soldiers of the Tenth was diverse. D, L, and M remained at Fort Cobb to keep a watchful eye on the Indians assembled there. E operated out of Fort Arbuckle; A, C, H, and I guarded the Kansas frontier; and B, F, G, and K moved to Fort Lyon to join Penrose along with one troop of the Seventh Cavalry.[38]

Penrose's command, the first to take the field, left Fort Lyon on November 10 with forty-three days' rations and "Wild Bill" Hickok as a scout. Supplies thereafter would be drawn from a depot that Carr would establish along the North Canadian. All went well at first, but five days out a heavy snowstorm struck the command, forcing Penrose to encamp in a barren area with no wood or even buffalo chips for a fire. Twenty-five horses in the rear

36 Organizational Returns, Tenth Cavalry, October–November 1868; Hazen, "Some Corrections," 300–10; Senate, S. Exec. Doc. 13, 40th Cong. 3d sess., 22–23; *Annual Report of the Commissioner of Indian Affairs for the Year 1868*, 388–96; Alvord to Hazen, October 30, 1868, Sherman-Sheridan Papers, Phillips Collection, University of Oklahoma, Norman; Hazen to Sherman, November 10, 1868, ibid.

37 Sheridan, *Personal Memoirs*, 2:309; *Annual Report of the Secretary of War for the Year 1868*, 44–45; Senate, S. Exec. Doc. 7, 40th Cong., 3d sess., 1. An excellent overview on Sheridan's military objectives and the degree to which he was an innovator can be found in Hutton, *Phil Sheridan and His Army*, 50–55.

38 Organizational Returns, Tenth Cavalry, November 1868.

guard gave out in the heavy going and had to be shot. Despite bitter cold and snow, however, the command pushed on toward the North Canadian, its trail littered with dead animals. On November 17 alone, fourteen horses died.

Penrose slogged on, with temperatures pushing well below zero, until he reached San Francisco Creek on December 6. No signs of Indians had been observed. The half-frozen troopers ranged out in small scouting parties with no results except severe frostbite to themselves. The men were reduced to half rations, and there was no forage for the animals. Unless Carr arrived soon, the command would be in desperate straits. Nevertheless, the buffalo soldiers remained cheerful as they rubbed frozen feet and hands and fashioned makeshift footgear from the hides of dead animals to replace boots that had fallen apart.

Carr was also having his troubles. Although he had left Fort Lyon on December 2 in clear but cold weather, three days later a howling blizzard had struck the column, freezing four men to death and causing the loss of more than two hundred head of cattle that were to supply fresh meat for both Carr and Penrose. Carr fought his way slowly through mountainous drifts, worrying increasingly about the fate of Penrose and the possibility of not being able to locate him in such weather.

These doubts were resolved on December 21 when Carr's chief scout, "Buffalo Bill" Cody, met two buffalo soldiers out searching for Carr. Two days later the commands were joined along the San Francisco. Penrose's troopers, reduced to quarter rations, were slowly starving, and more than two hundred of their animals had perished from hunger. Carr established a supply depot and, after selecting about five hundred of the strongest men, set out for the Canadian and reached it on December 28.

He remained there until January 7, 1869, when news came that the main column under Custer had struck the Cheyennes a devastating blow along the Washita and that Evans, on Christmas Day, had soundly whipped a large band of Comanches along the North Fork of Red River. In a written statement, Penrose both praised and sympathized with the officers and men in his command. Through their endurance and perseverance they had forced "a large force of the enemy" into the Seventh Cavalry's path, thereby assuring their defeat. He extended to them his "kindest, heartfelt thanks" and his best wishes for success in all their future endeavors.[39]

39 Ibid., November–December 1868; Armes, *Ups and Downs,* 280–86; Cahill, "Indian Campaign and Buffalo Hunting"; "History of the Fifth Cavalry," 181; King, *War Eagle,*

Four companies of the Tenth had thus made a considerable contribution to the success of Sheridan's winter campaign. The four companies in Kansas, moreover, had on occasion met the enemy. A detachment of ten troopers from Captain Nicholas Nolan's Company A under Sergeant Augustus Wilson, scouting out of Larned, overtook a small party of hostiles on November 19 and in a twenty-mile running fight killed two of them. Late in the month the indefatigable Carpenter with H and I scoured a large area south of the Arkansas, but the group was forced to return after encountering on December 4 a blizzard that permanently disabled two troopers.[40]

Late in January Carpenter was in the field again with H and I along with two companies of the Fifth Infantry under Captain Bankhead. The command searched the country between the Big Sandy and the Republican, the same area over which Carpenter had marched to Forsyth's relief. No Indians were encountered, but the men themselves supplied enough fireworks when a few of the buffalo soldiers tangled with white infantrymen. Unfortunately, Doctor Fitzgerald had to amputate one trooper's arm. Captain Byrne and twenty-five men of C Company from Fort Dodge had better luck. On January 29 they overtook a party of Pawnee horse thieves, killed seven of them, and wounded one. Byrne's loss was two men wounded.[41]

Meanwhile, to the south the winter campaign was coming to a successful conclusion, and this course of events served to move the whole of the Tenth Cavalry to Indian Territory. The previous year had been a difficult one. Eight companies of the regiment had scarcely been out of the saddle, and the winter had been harsh. Many of the men had scurvy, which the surgeon at Fort Wallace attributed to "hardships and privations of arduous winter scouts which were frequent with often little time intervening for purposes of recuperation . . . and a monotonous pork diet." Little wonder the men looked forward to a change and the possibility of a home in a comfortable garrison for a time.[42]

87–93. For a good account of the oft-told Battle of the Washita, see Godfrey, "Some Reminiscences, Including the Washita Battle." Evans's campaign is described in Rister, "Colonel A. W. Evans' Christmas Day Indian Fight."

40 Armes, *Ups and Downs,* 287–88.

41 Organizational Returns, Tenth Cavalry, November 1868; Post Returns, Fort Wallace, November 1868; Medical History, Fort Wallace, vol. 363.

42 *Army and Navy Journal* 6 (February 6, 1869), 397; Medical History, Fort Wallace, vol. 363; "Engagements and Casualties during the War of 1868–1869, against Hostile Indians in the Department of the Missouri," n.d., SLR Relating to the Ninth and Tenth Regiments, U.S. Cavalry.

General Benjamin H. Grierson
Courtesy of Fort Davis National Historic Site, Fort Davis, Texas

Kicking Bird, a Kiowa chief
Courtesy Western History Collections, University of Oklahoma Libraries
Photograph by William S. Soule

Satanta
Courtesy Western History Collections, University of Oklahoma Libraries
Photograph by William S. Soule

Kiowa Indians camped in a wooded area, 1869, near Fort Sill, Oklahoma

Courtesy Western History Collections, University of Oklahoma Libraries

Photograph by William S. Soule

An Army of Occupation

The columns of George Custer, George Evans, Eugene Carr, and W. H. Penrose in a fine display of teamwork had inflicted a severe defeat on the Cheyennes at the Washita in November 1868. Early in December, General Sheridan, accompanied by Custer and the main column, left Camp Supply, recently established near the junction of the North Canadian River and Wolf Creek, and marched to the Washita. There he turned downstream, driving before him some Kiowas under Satanta and Lone Wolf. Distrustful of these chiefs and determined to weaken leadership among hostile bands, Sheridan placed them both under arrest before reaching Fort Cobb.

At Cobb he found most of the Comanches awaiting him and, using the captive chiefs as bait, soon forced the Kiowas to come in and surrender. But the Cheyennes and Arapahos remained out. Some wished to surrender, others were fearful of a trap, while still others were prepared to carry on the war. Many months of campaigning and negotiation would be required before these proud people were on their reservations.[1]

Sheridan disliked the location of Fort Cobb. Like Fort Arbuckle, it was ill situated with respect to the Kiowa-Comanche reservation and too far

---

1 Utley, *Frontier Regulars*, 153–54. Camp Supply was established on November 18, 1868, as a base of operations for troops of the main column in Sheridan's winter campaign. It was an important post for more than a decade as a focal point for operations against the Southern Cheyennes and Arapahos. See Carriker, *Fort Supply*, 124–25.

removed to afford effective protection for the Texas frontier. He desired a
new post to replace both Arbuckle and Cobb. In discussing possible sites
with Colonel Benjamin Grierson, who had arrived from Fort Gibson, Sheridan asked about the colonel's reconnaissance in May to Medicine Bluff
Creek.

Grierson still considered that place as ideal and was ordered to visit the
site once more to ascertain if there would be enough grass for the animals
and to make a thorough inspection and report. Grierson, W. B. Hazen, a
number of other officers, and journalist De B. Randolph Keim set out at
once, escorted by forty buffalo soldiers of D Company under Lieutenant
William E. Doyle.

The party reached Medicine Bluff on the morning of December 29, and
a daylong inspection reaffirmed Grierson's earlier impressions and delighted
his companions. The clear, trickling water of Medicine Bluff and Cache
Creeks assured a pure and ample supply, the whole area was covered by a
rich carpet of grass, wild game was seen everywhere, and the rugged beauty
of the Wichita Mountains promised an abundance of building material.
Grierson was back at Fort Cobb the following day, and his report to Sheridan caused the latter to decide to move immediately to the new site and to
construct a permanent post there.[2]

Heavy rains delayed departure for a week, and even then the long column
of troops and wagons sloshed through a sea of mud and water. Swollen
streams added to the difficulty, and four days passed before all the troops
reached "Camp Wichita."[3] The men set to work immediately erecting temporary shelters, the troopers of the Tenth constructing their "homes" from
condemned tentage, brush, and mud. Supplies expected from Fort Arbuckle
had not arrived because of the condition of the road between that post and
Camp Wichita. Grierson at once sent Captain George T. Robinson and the
men of E Company to put the road in good condition. Working swiftly, the
troopers threw a 135-foot span across Beaver Creek and cleared trees and
underbrush. By the end of February 1869, supplies were flowing without
difficulty between Arbuckle and the new post.[4]

2 Keim, *Sheridan's Troopers*, 231–32; Sheridan to Sherman, January 8, 1869, Sherman-
Sheridan Papers, Phillips Collection, University of Oklahoma, Norman; Organizational
Returns, Tenth Cavalry, December 1868, AGO, RG 94, NA.
3 Keim, *Sheridan's Troopers*, 247–52. This name was selected because it was the site
of an old Wichita Indian village.
4 B. H. Grierson to Alice Grierson, January 20, 30, 1869, GP-ISHS.

Meantime, General Hazen and Agent A. G. Boone, recently appointed, moved the Kiowas and Comanches from Fort Cobb and settled them near Camp Wichita. Sheridan lectured their chiefs for past transgressions, and after securing their promises that they would behave themselves in the future, he released Satanta and Lone Wolf. There was still little indication that the Cheyennes were ready to take up reservation life, though contacts with the Arapahos indicated that these people were ready to surrender. Sheridan assigned Custer and the Seventh Cavalry the task of rounding up the Cheyennes and returned to his headquarters at Fort Hays.[5]

To Grierson and the Tenth, Sheridan gave a new role. Headquarters would move from Fort Gibson to Camp Wichita, and the regiment would serve as "an army of occupation" among the Kiowas, Comanches, Southern Cheyennes, and Arapahos as these tribes settled down to reservation life. It was not an enviable assignment as the next six years were to prove.

When Grierson moved his headquarters to Camp Wichita in March, four companies of the regiment were already there and two more were on the way. The remaining six companies were to garrison Camp Supply as rapidly as they could be moved from Kansas. From these posts the Tenth had to oversee thousands of Indians; drive out white trespassers, whisky peddlers, and horse thieves; furnish escorts for stages, supply trains, and the mail; and build an entire fort from scratch.

Work began immediately on the new post. After dismantling an old sawmill at Fort Arbuckle and moving it to the new site, fatigue details cut logs in the Wichita Mountains, opened rock quarries, dressed the stone, and began the construction of quarters, stables, and storehouses. All of this was backbreaking work. Construction slowed in late March and April as a steady flow of Cheyenne and Arapaho bands came in, surrendered, were fed, and then escorted to Camp Supply. By early summer, however, most of this traffic had ended, and Grierson believed that peace would prevail.[6]

5 Custer made two expeditions from Camp Wichita against these Indians and managed to induce most of them to move toward the reservations without a fight. See George A. Custer, *My Life on the Plains; or, Personal Experiences with Indians* (New York: Sheldon, 1875). A scholarly and interesting account of this phase of the Cheyenne campaign is in Berthrong, *Southern Cheyennes,* 334–44. Tall Bull's band of Cheyenne "irreconcilables" fled north, but they were cornered at Summit Springs, Colorado, by General Carr and defeated decisively. See Price, *Across the Continent.*

6 Post Returns, Fort Sill, March 1869, AGO, RG 94, NA; Alvord to Grierson, February 14, 1869, GP-ISHS; B. H. Grierson to Alice Grierson, February 7, 1869, ibid.; Grierson to the AAG, Department of the Missouri, April 3, 1869, SLR Relating to the Ninth and Tenth Cavalry, AGO.

There were others who shared Grierson's views, particularly the Society of Friends. When Ulysses S. Grant was inaugurated as president on March 4, 1869, he launched a new Indian policy. He proposed to reform the Indian Bureau, long a political hotel where party faithful were housed without reference to qualifications. To achieve this objective, Grant called upon the religious denominations of the country to nominate candidates to supervise the agencies and in this way to bring interest and integrity into the Indian service.

This plan became known as the "Quaker policy," for the most enthusiastic response came from the Society of Friends. Eager, peace-loving, and industrious Quakers were soon filling roles as agents to most of the Indian tribes, among them Lawrie Tatum for the Kiowas and the Comanches and Brinton Darlington for the Southern Cheyennes and Arapahos.

If the Indians were now to be "killed with kindness," the role of the military had to be redefined. After lengthy discussions between the secretaries of war and the interior, they agreed that Indians on the reservations would be under the exclusive control of their agents, who might, if the need arose, call upon the military for assistance. Indians off the reservations would normally be regarded as hostile.[7]

Grierson was in accord with the new policy and gave it his full support. In his talks with chiefs and headmen, many of whom he invited to dinner, he learned that they and their families were often in dire straits. Annuities frequently gave out between issues, and their people went hungry for days. In those circumstances hunger forced them to leave the reservation to hunt game. He could do little, but wherever possible, he tried to help.

Often Grierson gave Indians an order on the post bakery for bread, and half a century later old Indians were still asking for "that good army bread." He also came to believe that the solution to the Indian problem was simple: supply them with plenty of nourishing food, furnish them with good quality annuities, and keep all promises made them. In his view, "Without strait [sic] forward manliness, generosity and integrity the case is hopeless."[8]

7 Loring B. Priest, *Uncle Sam's Stepchildren: The Reformation of United States Indian Policy, 1865–1887* (New Brunswick, N.J.: Rutgers University Press, 1942), 44–47; *Annual Report of the Commissioner of Indian Affairs for the Year 1869*, 5.

8 Nye, *Carbine and Lance*, 111; Tatum, *Our Red Brothers*, 30–31; Benjamin H. Grierson, undated note [1869], Benjamin Grierson Letters and Documents, Southwest Collection, Texas Technological University, Lubbock, microcopy of manuscript 343A, Benjamin H. Grierson Collection, Edward Ayer Manuscript Collection, Newberry Library, Chicago, Ill.

The Tenth's commander learned quickly to like and respect Agent Tatum, who shared his concerns that Congress keeps its promise to American Indians. In fact, as Tatum later recalled, one warrior told him, "when they made their last treaty they got a large amount of annuity goods and a liberal supply of provisions." Since then, they had suffered. Thus, they told him that "the only way that they could get a large supply of annuity goods was to go out onto the warpath, kill some people, steal a good many horses, get the soldiers to chase them awhile, without permitting them to do much harm, and then" would come the payoff. The government would "give them a large amount of blankets, calico, muslin, etc., to get them to quit!"[9]

In that context, then, it is not surprising that Grierson soon faced trouble. He and his regiment were in a virtual straitjacket when the reservation Indians chose to misbehave. Tatum's charges, as well as those of Darlington, gave little trouble during the remainder of 1869—while on the reservations. But small bands of Kiowas and Comanches constantly left their camps and headed south across the Red River to strike at the hated Texans. There the implacable Kwahadis from the Staked Plains, who spurned all attempts to bring them to the reservations, joined them. The fall of 1869 was thus a bloody one on the Texas frontier.[10]

For the time being at least, Grierson and his troopers continued their construction work and spent some time preparing for field duty when the need arose. There was more of the former than the latter, however, and Grierson grumbled over poor showings on the firing range and complained that discipline was only "fair." In at least one case it was somewhat less than that. In August the name of the new post was changed to Fort Sill, and Private Benjamin Kewconda of E Company celebrated the occasion by getting drunk and disorderly in an Indian camp near the post.

When arrested he shouted that Grierson and all the officers of the Tenth were a "bunch of God-damned sons-of-bitches." He may or may not have changed his opinion after being "tied up."[11] Reflecting the harsh discipline

9   Tatum, *Our Red Brothers*, 30.

10   Grierson to Tatum, September 30, 1869, Military Relations, Kiowa Files, Indian Archives Division, Oklahoma State Historical Society, Oklahoma City; *Annual Report for the Department of Texas, 1869*, 2.

11   "Charges and Specifications Preferred against Benjamin Kewconda, Private, E Company, Tenth Cavalry," August 1869, SLR Relating to the Ninth and Tenth Regiments, U.S. Cavalry, AGO, RG 94, NA; Organizational Returns, Tenth Cavalry, August–September 1869. Fort Sill was named for Brigadier General Joshua Sill, who was killed at the battle of Stones River, Tennessee. See Frazer, *Forts of the West*, 124.

in the army, this meant that a trooper was seated on the ground with knees up, feet flat, and arms bound to the front. A stick was then pushed across his arms and under his knees, rendering him completely helpless, and a piece of wood was commonly used as a gag. Normally such punishment lasted about half a day.[12]

Since Grierson ran a "dry" post, Kewconda's escapade caused a search for the source of his inspiration. A Sergeant Gibbs of E Company found a number of kegs of whisky buried just outside the post, and ownership was traced to a couple of teamsters with a four-wagon train. Grierson had the kegs broken up and the men and wagons escorted to Van Buren, Arkansas, for trial.[13]

Early in October, Grierson and as many of his troopers as could be spared from extra duty took their first tour of the reservation. The column consisting of the "effectives" of Companies B, D, L, and M—a total of sixty men— marched west to Otter Creek and then southwest to the North Fork of Red River. After a bit of exploration and feasting on wild game, the command moved northeast and visited a large Comanche camp on Rainy Mountain Creek. The Indians extended a warm welcome and gave assurances of future good behavior.

Grierson undoubtedly hoped that the Indians were sincere. He had no desire to war against them and would do so only if their actions forced him to take punitive action in return. Satisfied with his first excursion, Grierson returned to Fort Sill. For officers and men it was a welcome release from the monotony of garrison duty and a much needed acquaintance with the country in which they would operate for many years.[14]

Little else interrupted the daily routine until the end of the year, when Lieutenant Doyle apparently found stimulation equal that of Kewconda's. When he met Lieutenant Thomas Lebo of C Company and the commissary officer, Captain Norman Badger, Doyle called them both sons of bitches, went to his quarters, loaded a carbine, and told Lieutenant Russell Day that he intended to kill Badger "before I sleep." He failed to find Badger that day, but the next morning he was still on the rampage and again accosted Lebo and offered to fight a duel.

When the longsuffering Lebo refused, Doyle called him a "God-damned

12 See Whitman, *The Troopers*, 93.
13 Alice Grierson to Louisa Semple, November 23, 1869, GP-ISHS.
14 Post Returns, Fort Sill, October 1869; Organizational Returns, Tenth Cavalry, October 1869.

coward" and then fired the carbine at Captain Robert Gray, who tried to mediate the dispute. Fortunately the shot went wild and post guards arrived in time to prevent further trouble. A court-martial suspended Doyle from rank and pay for six months and confined him to the post for the same period. The frontier army was no place for the sensitive or the weak at heart.[15]

Grierson's pride and joy, the regimental band—despite the loss of some instruments in a fire at Camp Wichita—did much to soften the rough work and loneliness at Fort Sill. Evening concerts "under the stars" were keenly anticipated and much enjoyed by the officers and men. It was thus that the tune "Auld Lang Syne" welcomed in the new year, but the notes had scarcely died away before trouble rumbled in the distance.[16]

The regiment was ill prepared to cope with any large-scale Indian difficulty. Death, disease, disability, and desertion had cut the total enlisted strength to fewer than eight hundred by the fall of 1869. When those sick, confined, or on extra duty were deducted, Grierson could field no more than five hundred men. As 1870 opened, some three hundred raw recruits arrived at Fort Sill and Camp Supply, bringing the regiment near to full strength, but it was many months before these men were capable soldiers.[17]

Green troopers were not the only difficulty, however. Captain Louis Carpenter at Camp Supply with his hard-bitten veterans of H Company complained in a letter to Grierson that the Tenth was "getting mean and wornout horses of the Seventh Cavalry." Some of these trail-weary nags died within days of reaching the post. In Carpenter's view, "Since our first mount in 1867 this regiment has received nothing but broken down horses and repaired equipment as I am willing to testify to as far as my knowledge goes."[18]

Old mounts, old equipment, and untried men notwithstanding, there was a challenging task ahead, as the burly Kiowa chieftain Satanta was quick to provide. Early on the afternoon of January 11, 1870, about forty miles south of Camp Supply, Satanta and a large force of Kiowa warriors stampeded a trail herd of three hundred Texas cattle. The drover, Jacob Hershfield, and fourteen cowboys were pushed back to their wagons, where the Indians took all their sugar, bacon, flour, coffee, and tobacco, as well

15 General Court-Martial Orders No. 48, Headquarters, Department of the Missouri, March 29, 1870, GP-ISHS.

16 Glass, *History of the Tenth Cavalry,* 18; Alvord to Grierson, February 14, 1869, GP-ISHS.

17 Organizational Returns, Tenth Cavalry, September 1869–January 1876.

18 Carpenter to Grierson, May 27, 1870, GP-ISHS.

as $150 in cash. The timely arrival and intervention of Chief Kicking Bird of the Kiowas probably saved the lives of Hershfield and his men. Five hours were required to round up the cattle. Hershfield might just as well have spared himself the efforts, for Satanta again stampeded the herd. None was recovered.[19]

When news of Satanta's raid reached Camp Supply, Brevet Colonel A. D. Nelson, Third Infantry, commanding the post, sent Major M. H. Kidd with A, F, I, and K Companies of the Tenth to drive the Kiowas back on their reservation. On the way Kidd stopped off at the Cheyenne camp of Chief Whirlwind, who told him, "You don't have half enough men for the job." Whirlwind believed that the appearance of troops in the Kiowa camps would precipitate a war. Kidd continued on to Kicking Bird's camp, however, and there received assurances of good behavior sufficient to cause him to turn back without a fight. The major felt the appearance of his troopers had produced a "salutary effect" on the Kiowas.[20]

Kidd had avoided serious trouble, but as spring came and passed, rumors of war sifted steadily into Fort Sill and Camp Supply. Grierson decided that a demonstration in force might be in order, but so great was the demand for detachments of the Tenth for other duties that a major concentration of the regiment proved unfeasible. White horse-thieves were a constant nuisance, and since the restrictions of the Quaker policy did not prevail in such cases, Grierson's troopers managed to make that occupation an extremely hazardous one.

On May 6 a party of thieves stole 139 mules from a government train at Bluff Creek, Indian Territory, and made for Texas with their haul. Lieutenant William Harmon and five men of M Company went in pursuit. Two days later in Montague Country, Texas, Harmon overtook five men driving the mules and pressed them so hard that they abandoned one hundred of the animals near Clear Creek in Cook County. After a chase of eighteen more miles, Harmon brought his quarry to bay in a wooded ravine, killed one of them, and captured the other four. On questioning his prisoners, Harmon learned that they were expecting three others to join them. Harmon awaited the threesome, captured them without a fight, and recovered two wagons,

19 Jacob Hershfield to Lieutenant John Sullivan, January 11, 1870, SLR Relating to the Ninth and Tenth Regiments, U.S. Cavalry.
20 Grierson to the AAG, Department of the Missouri, May 20, 1870, SLR, AGO, RG 94, NA; Brevet Colonel A. D. Nelson to the AAG, Department of the Missouri, January 18, 1870, ibid.

three horses, and four mules. He then marched to Fort Arbuckle with his prisoners, 127 government mules, three horses, and two wagons.[21]

The troopers at Camp Supply were the first to feel the annual summer upswing of Indian activity. Early in May a small party of warriors stole some stock near the post and defied all efforts of Captain Nicholas Nolan and A Company to find them. A much stronger war party attacked a wagon train north of Supply the same month, ran off all the mules, and killed a man before Carpenter and old-reliable H Company came to the rescue and drove the Indians off.

On the last day of the month, thirty-five Arapahos hit the mail station along Bear Creek about forty miles south of Fort Dodge on the Camp Supply road, killed two privates of the Third Infantry, and inflicted eight arrow wounds on their sergeant as the little detachment fought to save the station. Major Kidd with A and K drove off the Indians and brought the critically wounded sergeant into Dodge.[22]

In June, Indian war parties grew bolder. On June 8 one hundred hostiles attacked a government train from Fort Dodge escorted by Lieutenant J. A. Bodamer and twenty-five men of F Company. A hard-riding buffalo soldier broke through the encircling Indians and raced to Camp Supply for aid. Nolan and A Company galloped to the rescue, but when they reached the scene Bodamer had fought off the attackers and killed three of them. Corporal Freeman and Private Winchester suffered slight wounds.[23]

Kiowas had made most of these attacks, but on June 11 a formidable body of Comanches decided to test the mettle of all the buffalo soldiers at Camp Supply. They first attempted to run off the cavalry horses, but failing in that, they lingered long enough to skirmish for an hour with all five companies then at the post. They paid for their audacity with six dead and ten wounded, and the Comanches were never again quite so curious about the fighting qualities of the Tenth. Shortly after this fight the troopers received another boost in their morale when Lieutenant Colonel John W. Davidson of their own regiment replaced Colonel Nelson as the new commander at Camp Supply.[24]

21 *Army and Navy Journal* 7 (May 21, 1870): 622.

22 Post Returns, Camp Supply, May 1870; Organizational Returns, Tenth Cavalry, May 1870; Brevet Colonel W. G. Mitchell to General John Pope, June 6, 1870, SLR.

23 Post Returns, Camp Supply, June 1870; Organizational Returns, Tenth Cavalry, June 1870.

24 Organizational Returns, Tenth Cavalry, June 1870; Post Returns, Camp Supply, June 1870.

Grierson and his troopers at Fort Sill were having their problems as well. On June 12 an inveterate Kiowa raider, White Horse, ran off seventy-three mules from the quartermaster's corral at Sill. Captain J. W. Walsh and Companies D and E were quick to pursue but lost the trail in a maze of fresh buffalo tracks. Other Indian prowlers, along with lurking white thieves, kept detachments on the move in the vicinity of the post and Tatum's agency. These, however, were minor annoyances compared to Kiowa and Comanche activity in Texas.[25]

In May and June, war parties from these tribes struck heavily along the North Texas frontier, killing fifteen persons in Jack County alone. Fresh from his coup at the quartermaster's corral, the redoubtable White Horse crossed the Red into Texas, killed Gottlieb Koozier, and took his wife and six children as captives. In the opinion of Colonel James Oakes, Sixth Cavalry, commanding at Fort Richardson, the Kiowas were making all-out war on Texas, and it "should be stopped." Oakes professed to believe that the Indian agent at Fort Sill was actually arming the Indians with late-model weapons and implied that Grierson and the Tenth were doing little or nothing to stop the raids. Texas newspapers echoed these charges and vented their wrath on both Tatum and Grierson.[26]

These accusations were unjustified and unfair, and Brigadier General John Pope, Sheridan's successor as commanding general, Department of the Missouri, was quick to defend Grierson and his troopers. He pointed out the handicap under which they worked:

> Indian reservations and the Indians upon them are wholly under the jurisdiction of the agents in charge who are alone responsible for the conduct of the Indians, and for the protection of the rights of persons and property both of the Indians and of white men on Indian reservations. The military forces on or near such Indian reservations are placed there solely to assist the Indian agents to preserve good order on the Reservations.
>
> Under no circumstances except specific orders from Depart-

25 Post Returns, Fort Sill, June 1870; Organizational Returns, Tenth Cavalry, June 1870; Nye, *Carbine and Lance,* 107.

26 Oakes to the AAG, Department of Texas, September 10, 1870, SLR; *Austin Daily Journal,* May 14, 1871; Post Returns, Fort Richardson, Texas, May–June 1870. The Indians were not so well armed as charged, and most of their weapons were obtained in trade with the comancheros of New Mexico. See Haley, "Comanchero Trade."

ment Headquarters or higher authority will any commander of troops assume jurisdiction or exercise control over reservation Indians or their agents, nor originate nor execute any act of their own volition in regard to affairs on such reservations.[27]

Within these severe limitations Grierson did what he could. All through the summer he kept patrols along the Red River, but a few troopers, no matter how alert, had little chance of intercepting bands that could cross at dozens of places along many miles of river. More than this he could not do unless called upon by Agent Tatum. As for that harassed Quaker, he slowly lost faith in the peace policy and at length asked Grierson to station troops at the agency on issue day. This had some effect, for Tatum was able to recover thirty-seven mules White Horse had stolen as well as the captive Kooziers. Tatum's superiors, who had little if any understanding of conditions on or off the reservation, deplored even this limited reliance on the military.[28]

Raids and depredations declined as fall arrived, and Grierson resumed construction work at Fort Sill. But there were vexing problems within the regiment. Captain Charles Cox of K Company was court-martialed for drunkenness on duty, selling government property, breach of arrest, and conduct unbecoming an officer and a gentleman. Cox was dismissed from the service, fined five hundred dollars, and sentenced to three years' imprisonment. His fate now became a matter of public notice, and it was "deemed scandalous for an officer to associate with him."[29]

Captain G. W. Graham of I, an officer with a fine combat record, was dismissed for selling government property. Tempestuous Captain George Armes of F also suffered court-martial on an impressive list of charges. Captain Edward Byrne of C Company ran afoul of Grierson in an argument over the former's prerogatives as temporary commander at Fort Arbuckle and was shortly mustered out of the army.[30]

It was a time of trial for the troopers as well. Malaria swept through the

---

27 General Orders No. 28, Headquarters, Department of the Missouri, War Department, LR, File 1305-1871, AGO, NA [hereafter cited as File 1305-1871].

28 Grierson to the AAG, Department of the Missouri, August 7, 1870, SLR; Organizational Returns, Tenth Cavalry, June–August 1870; Tatum, *Our Red Brothers*, 42–44.

29 SLR 1870 Relating to Captain Charles G. Cox, Tenth Cavalry, SLR, 1870–74, AGO, RG 94, NA; Organizational Returns, Tenth Cavalry, August 1870.

30 Organizational Returns, Tenth Cavalry, August 1870; B. H. Grierson to Alice Grierson, July 30, 1870, GP-ISHS.

ranks and this, combined with typhoid and a wretched diet, caused twelve deaths. Sergeant Frank Skidrick of I died of an accidental gunshot wound, Sergeant Boyd Daniel of L drowned in Cache Creek, and Private George Watkins of I was shot and killed by another trooper. The manner of Watkins's demise was a rare one, for the men normally got on well together. Fistfights were far more common in settling disputes, although these could be sanguinary affairs if the antagonists were wearing "drinking jewelry"— horseshoe nails bent into a ring with the head up.[31]

But Grierson had his command prepare for the worst from the Indians, and it was well he did so, for the Kiowas and Comanches did not wait for spring to raid in Texas. They struck again in January 1871 and in the process killed a bona fide hero, Brit Johnson, a black frontiersman who had managed the recovery of a number of captives from the Comanches at great risk to himself. Johnson and three companions were hauling supplies from Weatherford to Fort Griffin when an overwhelming force of warriors attacked them on January 24. The four men killed their horses for a breast-work and were slain only after a desperate fight. Johnson's corpse was horribly mutilated, the stomach split open, and the body of his little pet dog stuffed inside.[32]

Peaceful chiefs told Tatum that many small parties were in Texas, and reports of raids came steadily into Fort Sill. Grierson blamed part of the trouble on railroad-surveying parties, whose appearance upset the Indians. But he believed a long delay in the arrival of annuities was the prime difficulty. Whatever the causes, the situation grew steadily worse, and in March a thoroughly disillusioned Tatum requested Grierson to continue patrolling along the Red River to stem the tide of marauders.[33]

Grierson sent Companies L and M to the mouth of Cache Creek to scout the Red River line, but it was a hopeless task. The entire regiment would have been insufficient to guard all the many crossings and turn back the swift-riding bands.

Meanwhile, General Sherman had been bombarded with letters, telegrams, and resolutions from Texas citizens and their legislature complain-

31 Organizational Returns, Tenth Cavalry, October–December 1870; Rickey, *Forty Miles a Day*, 57–59.

32 Wilbarger, *Indian Depredations in Texas*, 581–82; Porter, "Negroes and Indians on the Texas Frontier," 155–56.

33 Tatum to Enoch Hoag, March 18, 1871, Depredations, Kiowa Files; Grierson to the AAG, Department of the Missouri, September 1871, Annual Report, LR, File 1305-1871; Tatum to Grierson, March 25, 1871, Depredations, Kiowa Files.

ing of Indian raids and depredations and demanding greater protection. Doubtful that conditions were as bad as painted, Sherman nevertheless decided to make an on-the-spot inspection. On April 28, 1871, he arrived in San Antonio and four days later set out for the frontier, accompanied by Inspector General Randolph B. Marcy, two other officers of his staff, and a picked detachment of seventeen troopers of the Tenth Cavalry as an escort.

The little party visited Forts McKavett, Concho, and Griffin, hearing much but seeing nothing of Indian activity. On May 18 they arrived at Fort Richardson, their tour of the Texas posts completed. Sherman's doubts had not been resolved, although Inspector Marcy, who had surveyed the same region years earlier, pointed out that there were fewer people along the route than had been the case prior to the Civil War.

Sherman's doubts were soon erased. Early on the morning of the nineteenth, a bloodstained teamster named Thomas Brazeale staggered into Fort Richardson with the story of a raid. About midafternoon of the previous day, a party of one hundred or more Indians had attacked a ten-wagon train on the open prairie about twenty miles west of Jacksboro. According to Brazeale, seven of his eleven companions had been killed. He and four others had escaped into nearby timber.

Sherman at once ordered Colonel Ranald S. Mackenzie, Fourth Cavalry, who had replaced Oakes as commanding officer at Richardson, to take every available man at the post and run down the raiders. Mackenzie was on the march at noon with one hundred and fifty men and reached the scene of the attack early in the evening during a driving rainstorm. Six bloated and mutilated bodies were discovered, and a seventh was found chained to a wagon pole and burned to a cinder. Five dead mules were found, but forty-one were missing. Leaving a small detachment to bury the dead, Mackenzie pushed on in an effort to overtake the war party, but rain and mud made progress difficult.[34]

An angry Sherman set out for Fort Sill, where he arrived on May 23. Wasting little time with formalities, the general, accompanied by Colonel Grierson, called on Lawrie Tatum and told him about the attack on the train. He

34 Post Returns, Fort Richardson, May 1871; "Extracts from Inspector General R. B. Marcy's Journal of an Inspection Tour while Accompanying the General in Chief during the Months of April, May, and June 1871," Phillips Collection, University of Oklahoma, 186–91; Sherman to Mackenzie, May 19, 1871, LR, File 1305-1871; Report of Assistant Surgeon J. N. Patzki, ibid.

then asked the horrified agent if he knew of any Indians who had recently raided in Texas. Tatum was not certain but felt sure he could find out. The Indians would be in for their rations in a few days, and he could question them at that time.

On Saturday, May 27, the Kiowas came to the agency, and Tatum called the chiefs into his office, told them about the raid on the train, and asked if they knew who had done it. A boastful and belligerent Satanta rose immediately, berated Tatum for the many wrongs the Kiowas had suffered, accused him of cheating the Indians, and demanded guns and ammunition. He then bragged that he had led the raid and that Chiefs Satank, Eagle Heart, Big Tree, and Big Bow had accompanied him. Instructing his employees to go ahead with the rations issue, Tatum excused himself and penned a hurried note to Grierson relaying the information Satanta had given him and asking that the guilty Indians be arrested.

Tatum then went in person to see Sherman and Grierson, whom he found on the porch of the latter's headquarters. They decided to call a council in front of Grierson's house at which time the guilty parties would be arrested. Orders were issued swiftly to the buffalo soldiers to go to the stables, saddle, and mount. At a given signal the companies would take up designated positions to prevent escape. In addition, a dozen troopers were stationed inside Grierson's house behind shuttered windows facing the porch.

Hardly had these preparations been completed when Satanta arrived. He had heard that a big Washington officer was at the post, and he "wished to measure him up." Under questioning from Sherman, the chief readily admitted his part in the raid, but as he saw the general's temper rising, he first altered his story and then rose and started for his pony. Grierson's alert orderly drew his pistol immediately and ordered Satanta to sit down—an order he obeyed with alacrity. Some twenty Kiowas, among them Satank, then arrived for the council.

Sherman informed them that the guilty chiefs were under arrest and would be sent to Texas for trial. Satanta flew into a rage and clutched at the revolver under his blanket, but at this instant Sherman gave a command and the shuttered windows flew open, revealing a dozen buffalo soldiers with carbines cocked and leveled. Satanta subsided at once.

The signal was now given to the troopers in the stables. The gates opened and D Company, led by Lieutenant R. H. Pratt, trotted into position in line on the left of Grierson's quarters while Captain Carpenter and H positioned itself on the right. Captain Robinson's E formed two detachments, one covering the rear of the house and the other moving to the front. For the Indians on the porch there was no escape. Another detachment under Lieutenant L. H. Orleman, consisting of ten men from each of the companies, moved quietly into position across the parade ground and behind a large body of Indians who had gathered there to watch the proceedings on the porch.

At this point Lone Wolf rode up from the trader's store, where he, Big Tree, and several others had been helping themselves to wares they fancied. Lone Wolf dismounted, carrying two Spencer repeaters and a bow and arrows. As he advanced toward the porch, he tossed the bow and arrows to one warrior, a carbine to another, and then with the remaining carbine at full cock, he faced General Sherman. It was a delicate moment. A shot could have made the porch a slaughter pen, but Grierson's cold courage saved the day. He grabbed Lone Wolf's carbine and at the same time shouted to interpreter Horace Jones to tell the Indians that violence would not save their chiefs. It was sound advice, and fortunately the jittery Indians accepted it and the crisis passed. Without more ado, Satanta and Satank were escorted to the guardhouse and put in irons.

A summons was sent to Big Tree and Eagle Heart, and when they failed to appear, Lieutenant Woodward, Lieutenant Pratt, and D Company were ordered to the trader's store to take them. When they reached the store, Woodward dismounted and with a detail entered to make the arrest. Big Tree was behind the counter passing out goods when he saw the troopers enter. With no wasted motion he dashed to the rear of the store, pulled his blanket over his head, and plunged through the glass window. Once outside he raced across a fenced field. Pratt sent his troopers at a gallop along the sides of the fence, hemmed in the flying chieftain, and forced him to surrender. In a matter of minutes he joined Satanta and Satank in the guardhouse. Eagle Heart, on his way to answer the summons, saw Big Tree's arrest and, thus forewarned, escaped.

Meanwhile, the Indians Orleman had been watching began edging away and, when called upon to halt, opened fire. The only casualty was Private Edward Givins of D Company, who was hit in the leg by an arrow. The troopers returned fire, killing one Indian, but the rest escaped in a wild stampede. Other Kiowas who had remained in their camps joined them in a mad dash toward the Wichita Mountains.

The council on the porch now drew to a close. Sherman told the chiefs that Satanta, Satank, and Big Tree would be held in arrest and that the forty-one mules from the wagon train must be returned within ten days. When the Indians assented, the troopers opened ranks and permitted them to return to their people.[35]

With the wagon train affair thus solved, Sherman left for Fort Gibson, escorted by Carpenter and a proud H Company. He was impressed with the post that Grierson and his men were constructing, deeming it one of the best he had ever seen.[36]

Colonel Mackenzie, whose pursuit of the raiders had bogged down in the mud, came into Fort Sill on June 4 and made preparations to return the Indian prisoners to Jacksboro, Texas, for trial. On June 8 two wagons were driven to the guardhouse, and a cursing, struggling Satank was forced into one of them, guarded by a corporal and two privates. Satanta and Big Tree climbed meekly into the second wagon, with one trooper watching each of them. The column then set out on the Fort Richardson road. What followed is told simply in a letter from Grierson's young son Charles to his aunt:

Fort Sill, June 9, 1871

DEAR AUNT:

Yesterday General Mackenzie's command left here with the Indian prisoners for Texas. Satank said that he was not going to Texas at all, that he was going to kill somebody. He attempted to put his threat into execution by stabbing the corporal that was sitting in the wagon with him and he was shot in 3 or 4 places. When the soldiers were shooting at Satank, some of them shot the teamster making a long wound on the head. The other Indians made no fuss at all. Today Captain Robinson is going to the mouth of Cache Cr. with the remainder of his company.

Affectionately yours,
C. H. GRIERSON[37]

---

35 Pratt, "Some Indian Experiences," 210–11; Sherman to Sheridan, May 29, 1871, LR, File 1305-1871; Sherman to Townsend, May 28, 1871, ibid.; "Extracts from Inspector General R. B. Marcy's Journal," 195–97; Organizational Returns, Tenth Cavalry, May 1871; Post Returns, Fort Sill, May 1871; Pratt, Battlefield and Classroom, 44–46; Tatum, Our Red Brothers, 116–18.

36 Sherman to General Pope, May 24, 1871, SLR.

37 C. H. Grierson to Louisa Semple, June 9, 1871, GP-ISHS.

Mackenzie got the remaining two chiefs safely to Fort Richardson, where they were turned over to civil authorities for trial. Both were sentenced to hang, but pressure, largely from Quakers and including Agent Tatum, caused Governor Edmund J. Davis to commute their sentences to life imprisonment. Sherman was disgusted, for earlier he had warned that if the chiefs were set free, "no life from Kansas to the Rio Grande will be safe, and no soldier will ever again take a live prisoner."[38]

For the buffalo soldiers, the capture and arrest of Satank, Satanta, and Big Tree added an exciting episode to the history of the Tenth Cavalry, but it was more than that. The troopers had carried out their orders with crisp coolness and disciplined restraint. A moment's loss of nerve or an instant's "trigger-itch" could have launched a bloodbath. Neither had occurred, and only two maddened Kiowas had lost their lives. The climax to the wagon train affair was a tribute to the officers and men of the regiment.

Although the Kiowas captured most of the attention in the spring and early summer of 1871, the Cheyennes were also a source of concern. Kiowas constantly visited the Cheyenne camps, urging war, but with the exception of a few young warriors, they gained few adherents. Agent Darlington worked carefully and diligently to keep the Indians at peace, and Colonel Davidson cooperated fully. Rumors of war persisted, however, and in May, when more than three hundred of the Cheyennes left the reservation, it was feared they had joined the Kiowas. Lieutenant J. A. Bodamer, sent out with F and K to locate the absentees, found them encamped along San Francisco Creek. Since they had not listened to the Kiowas, Bodamer had no difficulty in persuading them to return to the reservation.[39]

The Comanches were another matter. Along with the Kiowas, they had been raiding frequently in Texas. Grierson strengthened his river patrols, though with little success. On the afternoon of May 30, a band of thirty-five Comanches attacked a small party of prospectors just south of the Red River and within six miles of the picket post Grierson had established at the mouth of Cache Creek. John Hoxey of Macomb County, Michigan, was killed and scalped, but his companions escaped to the river and made their

38 Sherman to Townsend, May 28, 1871; Post Returns, Fort Richardson, June 1871; Wilbarger, *Indian Depredations in Texas,* 122; Tatum, *Our Red Brothers,* 122; Headquarters, Department of Texas, Special Order No. 185, September 12, 1871, LR, File 1305-1871.
39 Organizational Returns, Tenth Cavalry, May 1871; Post Returns, Camp Supply, May 1871; Darlington to Davidson, July 10, 1871, LR, File 1305-1871; Berthrong, *Southern Cheyennes,* 359–62.

way to the camp on Cache Creek. Lieutenant T. J. Spencer immediately sent a courier to Fort Sill for reinforcements and then, with only twelve men of L Company, swam the rain-swollen Red River and took up the pursuit. The Indians had apparently recrossed, however, and Turner lost the trail.[40]

Meanwhile, the Indian Bureau revised somewhat the peace policy. Henceforth, the military would be permitted to enter the reservation to pursue raiders and to recover stolen property. The Tenth, nonetheless, still operated under severe restrictions. It could not take action outside the reservation against Tatum's Indians unless in "hot pursuit" of raiders. The role of an army of occupation was beginning to prove wearing for the men of the Tenth. There was enough latitude, however, for Grierson to combine with Mackenzie and his Fourth Cavalry to strike the Kiowas if they failed to return the stolen mules and to seek out and bring in the Kwahadis, who had never been on the reservation and who were bringing so much woe to the Texas frontier.[41]

In July Grierson concentrated nine companies of the Tenth at Fort Sill. A and F remained at Camp Supply, while C was escorting a party of Atlantic and Pacific Railroad surveyors to Santa Fe. A campaign of three weeks was planned, and arrangements were made for a rendezvous with Mackenzie at Otter Creek.

On August 10 Grierson and Mackenzie reached camp along Otter Creek and made final plans. Five days later, in extremely hot weather, the two long columns set out, with Mackenzie moving up the Salt Fork and Grierson the North Fork of Red River, with the intention that both would go as far west as McClellan Creek. The march was grueling. The country was broken and rough, the streams gypsum impregnated, and temperatures soared over one hundred degrees, causing great suffering among men and animals. And it was all for naught. On August 24 Grierson received word from Tatum that the Kiowas had returned the forty-one mules, and he turned back to Fort Sill, leaving four companies in charge of Captain Louis Carpenter at the camp along Otter Creek to await Mackenzie's return.

Mackenzie came in on September 1 thoroughly disgusted since he had not seen a single Indian. Perhaps his efforts were not entirely wasted, for he

40 Organizational Returns, Tenth Cavalry, May 1871; *Army and Navy Journal* 8 (July 1, 1871): 731.

41 Secretary Delano to Commissioner E. S. Parker, June 20, 1871, LR, File 1305-1871; Grierson to the AAG, Department of the Missouri, September 21, 1871, ibid.

was rewarded in a different respect. The resourceful Carpenter, equal to any occasion, had a full-course dinner prepared for Mackenzie and his staff. One of Mackenzie's officers remarked that his commander was most impressed, especially with the prune pie, on which he commented, "prune pie! prune pie! Well I'll be damned."[42]

The troopers at Fort Sill experienced more excitement than those in the field. On the night of August 10, two civilians named Edwards and Neal and three troopers, all confined in the guardhouse, cut a hole in the floor, dropped down into the basement, and escaped through the rear entrance. The sergeant of the guard heard the noise but ran first to the prison room, and the escapees got a lead. Four of the guards started in pursuit and fired a number of shots, but none took effect. A mounted detachment took up the chase, but early next morning the three errant troopers returned and gave themselves up. Edwards and Neal made good their escape.

A week later the sawmill caught fire, and a bucket brigade of sixty men turned out to douse the flames. Most of the woodwork was destroyed, but repairs were made quickly and the mill was running again by the time Grierson returned from the field.

C Company had, meantime, returned from Santa Fe with a story that cast a pall over the garrison. En route, Lieutenant Robert Price, new to the company, had permitted himself to quarrel with Privates York Johnson and Charles Smith. In a fit of rage, Price shot both men to death. He remained in arrest in Santa Fe when the company returned to Sill but was released in the fall and allowed to resign from the army. The affair was a shock to the regiment, for the officers and men normally enjoyed a close relationship.[43]

There was a killing of a less serious nature at Fort Sill that torrid summer of 1871. Alice Grierson explained in a letter to her husband: "Tucker—the soldier who has taken care of Captain Walsh's and our cows so long, shot one of ours, three days ago, because she would not come home just as he

42 Organizational Returns, Tenth Cavalry, July–August 1871; Robert K. Grierson to Louisa Semple, August 3, 1871, GP-ISHS; Carpenter to Grierson, September 15, 1871, ibid.; Carter, *On the Border with Mackenzie*, 142–43; Alice Grierson to Charles Grierson, August 15, 1871, GP-ISHS; Post Returns, Fort Sill, August 1871; B. H. Grierson to Alice Grierson, August 11, 1871, GP-ISHS; Grierson to Tatum, August 14, 1871, Military Relations, Kiowa Files.

43 Organizational Returns, Tenth Cavalry, June–September 1871; Major G. W. Schofield to Grierson, August 12, 1871, GP-ISHS; Lt. Samuel Woodward to Grierson, August 30, 1871, ibid. Lieutenant Price, a graduate of West Point, was assigned to the Tenth Cavalry in June 1870 and resigned April 27, 1872. Heitman, *Historical Register,* 1:807.

wanted her to. She had to be killed, the butcher made beef of her. The soldier says he will pay for her."[44]

This was by no means the first time that Alice Grierson had interceded on behalf of the buffalo soldiers. Ever since she and the three Grierson children, Charlie, Robert, and Edith, then eleven, six, and one respectively, had joined Colonel Grierson at Fort Leavenworth in mid-November 1866, she had been protective of the black soldiers. In large measure, her stance arose from her background as the daughter of abolitionists who had opened their Youngstown, Ohio, home in the 1840s to fugitive slaves. Later her father, John Kirk, had assisted blacks with legal fees following the passage of the Fugitive Slave Act of 1850.[45]

That upbringing and her proclivity for deferring to no one when it came to speaking her mind left her acutely sensitive to any sign that black soldiers were being discriminated against, especially by white officers or their wives. At Fort Gibson in July 1868, she had interceded on behalf of a buffalo soldier when the wife of Captain Henry Alvord had sought disciplinary action against a soldier for what Mrs. Alvord saw as insubordination. Later the following spring, Alice had championed the cause of Mat Moss, a buffalo soldier who had killed another trooper and was in the guardhouse. In her view he had acted in self-defense and needed to be released as quickly as possible.[46]

Alice Grierson was unusual, if the recorded comments of other officers' wives speak for the majority of such women. Elizabeth Custer had been at Fort Riley in the summer of 1867, when companies of the Thirty-eighth Infantry had manned the post while the Seventh Cavalry was involved in the Hancock campaign on the Great Plains. She described the situation there as "a reign of terror to us women, in our lonely, unprotected homes." In her opinion the black infantrymen were "boisterous, undisciplined creatures" and "monkey acrobats" who desecrated the parade ground. Frances Roe, the wife of Lieutenant Fayette Roe of the Third Infantry, made similar comments in letters to relatives from Camp Supply in 1873 and argued that the appearance of black sergeants with authority over white privates was, in her opinion, a "good cause for desertion."[47]

44 Alice Grierson to Ben Grierson, August 31, 1871, GP-ISHS.

45 John Kirk to Alice Kirk, October 17, 1844, GP-TTU. See also *Mahoning Free Democrat*, September 29, 1853, May 24, 1854.

46 Alice to Ben, July 5, 1868, GP-ISHS; Alice Grierson to Ben Grierson, March 1, 1869, ibid.

47 Elizabeth Custer, *Tenting on the Plains; or, General Custer in Kansas and Texas*, 320–21; Roe, *Army Letters from an Officer's Wife*, 77–78, 103–4.

With the return of the mules and the march of two strong columns into the western reaches of the reservation, Grierson and Tatum hoped that the Kiowas would stay away from Texas, but strong patrols were kept moving along the Red River to turn back bands attempting to slip into the state. Most of the Kiowas were quiet, at least temporarily, but close friends and relatives of Satank and Satanta sought revenge. On September 22 they killed and scalped two of Tatum's herders, Patrick O'Neal and John Johnson, within sight of the post. Three days later Grierson received word that a small band, presumed to be Kiowas, had ambushed three troopers of B Company as they scouted along the Red River and mortally wounded bugler Larkin Foster. A strong detachment had pursued the slayers, but the trail had been lost.[48]

As usual, raids and depredations eased off with the coming of winter. By the early spring of 1872, restless Kiowa raiders like White Horse and Big Bow soon joined the Comanches, again marauding in Texas. The buffalo soldiers maintained their ceaseless patrols along the Red, but to little avail. On the reserve both tribes behaved reasonably well, but efforts by the Five Civilized Tribes at their annual conference, held at Okmulgee in midsummer, to persuade their plains neighbors to adopt the "white man's road" were scorned. A visit to Washington by several of their prominent chiefs under the auspices of the Indian Bureau had little effect. In fact, the visit proved a serious mistake. The commissioner of Indian affairs, in a flush of enthusiasm, promised the release of Satanta and Big Tree on March 1, 1873.[49]

Raiding in Texas was a "legitimate" and "honorable" occupation to Tatum's Indians, but this was not the sole source of their inspiration. Whisky peddlers and unlicensed traders sneaked across the Kansas border, established "ranches," and supplied both liquid encouragement and weapons for Indian raiders. Comancheros from New Mexico hovered on the western borders of the reservations, trading arms and ammunition for stolen cattle and horses. Many undesirables, the off-scourings of the frontier, were attracted to the territory by railroad construction and were ready to steal or murder anything on foot, including Indians and their herds. Ever a problem, these vultures that accompanied westward movement so increased their activities that Grierson and his troopers had great difficulty in coping with them.

48 Grierson to the AAG, Department of the Missouri, September 25, 1871, SLR; Organizational Returns, Tenth Cavalry, September 1871.
49 *Annual Report of the Commissioner of Indian Affairs for the Year 1872,* 99; Tatum, *Our Red Brothers,* 125; *Army and Navy Journal* 10 (October 26, 1872), 165.

In an effort to deal more effectively with such people, Grierson moved his headquarters to Fort Gibson in June 1872, along with four companies of the regiment. With two companies under Davidson at Camp Supply and six companies at Fort Sill commanded by Major G. W. Schofield, he believed the "intruder" problem could be handled more effectively. A concerted effort resulted in the arrest and expulsion of hundreds of these vermin, but punishment was often so trivial that it encouraged the same characters to reappear time and again. A typical case was the experience of Lieutenant Pratt and Company D at Camp Supply.[50]

In January 1873 John D. Miles, who had succeeded Brinton Darlington (after the latter's death) as agent to the Southern Cheyennes and Arapahos, complained to Davidson that there were five "ranches" selling whisky to his Indians on the northern border of the reservation. He wished these places broken up and their owners arrested. Davidson ordered Pratt to take a detachment and carry out the agent's request. With temperatures well below zero, Pratt and twenty troopers, bundled in their heaviest winter gear; two wagons; and an Indian guide left to find the ranches.

A severe and cutting north wind made the march a miserable one, but it also confined the peddlers to their cabins. Thus, Pratt rounded up fifteen intruders; a large quantity of foul whisky; late-model rifles, revolvers, and ammunition; and considerable stores of sugar, coffee, and bacon, as well as buffalo robes and cattle, which the Indians had traded. In extreme cold, Pratt and his men convoyed peddlers, supplies, and cattle back to Camp Supply. Thirteen buffalo soldiers were hospitalized at once for severely frost-bitten hands and feet. They must shortly have wondered about the necessity for their suffering. The peddlers were sent for trial to Topeka, Kansas, where each was fined ten dollars and sentenced to a month in jail.[51]

When spring arrived a change of command occurred in the Tenth. Grierson was ordered to St. Louis as superintendent of the Mounted Recruiting Service, and Lieutenant Colonel Davidson took command of the regiment. An able though erratic officer, Davidson was jealous of Grierson's popularity with the officers and men; unlike his tolerant predecessor, Davidson was

50 Major John Bigelow, Jr., "Historical Sketch, Tenth United States Cavalry, 1866–1892," U.S. Army Commands, RG 98, NA; Organizational Returns, Tenth Cavalry, June 1872; Post Returns, Fort Sill, June 1872.

51 Post Returns, Camp Supply, January 1873; Organizational Returns, Tenth Cavalry, January 1873; Pratt, *Battlefield and Classroom*, 49–53.

a strict disciplinarian. Almost immediately, he forced the resignation of Grierson's old staff but the adjutant general overruled him on the grounds that Grierson's assignment was a temporary one. The good of the service would not be promoted by a staff overhaul of a transitory nature. Davidson gained nothing from his maneuver but the enmity of many of his officers.[52]

Enlisted men as well soon knew that a new regime reigned. New regulations that forbade the men to gamble in the barracks forced them to resort to pushing up the ceiling boards and gambling in the attic. Anyone who walked on the grass while crossing the parade ground was subject to immediate arrest. Ironically, the first culprit was Davidson's son. According to one officer at the post, Mrs. Davidson gave her husband "hell" when guards arrived with their offspring in tow.[53]

Temporarily, Davidson could afford some time in improving deportment at Fort Gibson, for he assumed command of the regiment during a period of comparative quiet. In the fall of 1872, Mackenzie and his Fourth Cavalry had struck the Kwahadis of the Staked Plains a heavy blow, and for the first time, these Indians had come into the reservation. Mackenzie captured more than a hundred of their women and children and held them as hostages to secure Comanche good behavior. During the early months of 1873, therefore, the Texas frontier enjoyed a period of almost unprecedented peace.[54]

The "honeymoon" did not convince Agent Tatum that the peace would last. He feared that when Satanta, "a daring and treacherous chief," was released, the result would be disastrous for "innocent and unsuspecting parties." Utterly disillusioned with the judgment of his superiors and the Friends Indian Committee, his immediate supervisors among the Quakers, he resigned in May 1873. James Haworth, who was in thorough accord with

52 Colonel J. B. Fry, AAG, Military Division of the Missouri, to General Augur, December 31, 1872, SLR, Department of Texas, 1873, AGO, NA; Davidson to the AG, April 1873, LS, Tenth U.S. Cavalry, U.S. Army Commands, RG 98, NA.

53 Flipper, *Negro Frontiersman*, 3–4. Davidson was a graduate of West Point and served in the Mexican War. He had extensive service in the West prior to the Civil War, for he served as a captain in the First Dragoons, which in 1861 became the First Cavalry. By February 1862 he was a brigadier general of volunteers and became chief of cavalry, Military Division of the West, in 1864. At the end of the war, he was a brevet major general with numerous citations for gallant and meritorious service. He accepted a lieutenant colonelcy in the Tenth Cavalry in December 1866 and remained at that rank until he left the regiment in 1879. Davidson died of injuries when a horse fell on him in 1881. Heitman, *Historical Register*, 1:355–56.

54 Carter, *On the Border with Mackenzie*, 377–78; *Army and Navy Journal* 10 (November 16, 1872): 213; *Annual Report for the Department of Texas, 1873*, RG 94, NA.

the peace policy and had none of Tatum's confidence in the military, succeeded him. As one of his first acts as agent, he dismissed the detachment of soldiers guarding the agency.[55]

Military authorities, sharing Tatum's gloom, ordered Davidson to move his headquarters from Fort Gibson back to Fort Sill and temporarily concentrate most of the regiment there. Davidson was pleased with the move, not only from the standpoint of strategy but also in the interest of "regimental efficiency." He had not served with many of the companies and proposed to look them over with a rigorous eye. It is doubtful that so great a concentration on one post achieved the efficiency Davidson had in mind, for a quarrel among the officers over quarters provided gossip for the garrison for months to come.

Lieutenant William Foulk accused Captain T. A. Baldwin, Captain William Kennedy, and Major Schofield of persecuting him and of making uncomplimentary remarks about his family. When Baldwin went to Foulk's quarters to soothe over the dispute, Mrs. Foulk flailed at him with a horsewhip and their two sons, "holy terrors" on the post, threw books at him.

Most of the officers supported Baldwin, and a number signed a resolution not to associate with Lieutenant Foulk. Davidson solved the problem by managing a promotion for Foulk, giving him command of D Company, and transferring the new commander, his company, and his family to Fort Griffin, Texas. The arrival of the two Foulk children at the latter post probably signaled a new wave of on-post terrorism, for they seem to have dedicated their young lives to the cause of promoting adult misery.[56]

The shift of the Tenth to Fort Sill and later the transfer of several companies to Texas was dictated by the need not only to strengthen frontier defenses in that state and along the Red River but also to interlink the companies of the Ninth Cavalry with those of the Tenth in the interest of more "homogeneous" garrisons as regarded color. The dictates of frontier defense thus joined hands with the mandates of racial prejudice.

Shortly after Davidson's arrival at Fort Sill, Major John Hatch, on orders from Brigadier General C. C. Augur, commanding the Department of Texas,

55 *Annual Report of the Commissioner of Indian Affairs for the Year 1873*, 219; Tatum, *Our Red Brothers*, 160.

56 Organizational Returns, Tenth Cavalry, April 1872; Davidson to the AAG, Department of Texas, March 28, 1873, SLR, Department of Texas, AGO; Lieutenant William L. Foulk to the AAG, Department of Texas, March 18, 1873, ibid.

arrived on a tour of inspection. He found morale and spirit high among the troopers, although many new recruits needed training. But Hatch was astounded when he viewed the horses and equipment. Many of the mounts were castoffs from the Seventh Cavalry, others had been in the artillery service, and some were so old they had been ridden during the War of the Rebellion. F Company had only forty-eight serviceable horses, and all but three were over fifteen years of age. The troopers had taken excellent care of these ancients, but Hatch was convinced a future campaign might founder if dependent on these hoary steeds.

Hatch discovered other problems. Most of the equipment was very old, though again, well cared for. F Company had saddles more than three years old, while Captain Nolan's A was using thirty saddles that had long since been condemned, and the men were worried about harming their horses' backs. The artillery was so old that Hatch did not believe a single piece would stand more than a shot. Ammunition too was in short supply, which was just as well for the artillery, but Captain Kennedy's G Company had only twenty-five rounds of carbine cartridges per man; few of the other companies were much better off. Horses, new equipment, and adequate ammunition were essential at once.

Hatch's report was but an echo of complaints officers and men of the Tenth had been making for years. The army was understaffed and spread out over a vast expanse, and undoubtedly other regiments experienced similar problems obtaining adequate mounts and supplies. Still, the Tenth at this time had more than its share of deficiencies. Even its regimental standard had been made by the men and was faded and worn. Higher headquarters had never seen fit to supply the regulation silk-embroidered standard despite the Tenth's good, if not spectacular, record. Discipline, moreover, was excellent, and desertions had steadily declined to the point that the rate was among the lowest of any unit in the army. Courts-martial for drunkenness, a curse in the frontier army, were lower than for comparable white units. Given the many handicaps, Grierson's "orphans" had done rather well. They would do even better.[57]

---

57 Dobak and Phillips, *Black Regulars*, 106–8; Maj. John Hatch to the AAG, Department of Texas, April 2, 1873, SLR, Department of Texas; Chauncey McKeever, AAG, Department of Texas, to Davidson, May 17, 1873, ibid.; Captain Nolan to Chief Ordnance Officer, Department of Texas, May 28, 1873, ibid.; Davidson to Chief Quartermaster, San Antonio, Texas, June 13, 1873, LS, Tenth U.S. Cavalry.

In April and May 1873, seven companies were transferred to Texas posts: E, I, and L marched to Fort Richardson; C and D to Fort Griffin; and A and F to Fort Concho. For these troopers and their officers, the days of "occupation" were over, and they were free for campaigning and policing activities wherever it might be necessary. But if they expected a warm welcome from the Texans, they were swiftly disillusioned. The citizens of a former slave state in the throes of Radical Reconstruction were hardly likely to welcome anyone in a blue uniform, much less so if that uniform encased a black frame.[58]

Jacksboro, adjacent to Fort Richardson, was typical of the wild little frontier towns that grew up in the vicinity of army posts. It boasted a population of about two hundred, many of them drifters, gamblers, prostitutes, and thieves. Twenty-seven saloons ministered to the needs of a thirsty population. Among the more popular establishments were the Gem, Emerald, Island Home, and Jimmy Nolan's Dance House. Mackenzie's Fourth Cavalry had its troubles while at Richardson. Company B had burned down a house of prostitution because one of their buddies had been killed there and threatened to burn the whole town. Fighting between citizens and the buffalo soldiers was frequent, and as one observer put it, "Jimmy Nolan's . . . was resonant with sound and frequently the scene of an inquest."[59]

But it was not always fighting and friction; in fact, more often it was cooperation. Detachments of six to ten troopers were on constant escort for contractors' trains and stages and were kept busy assisting civilians in running down rustlers and maintaining law and order. A representative item in reports to department headquarters ran: "April 22, 1873. Corporal John Wright, Company 'L,' 10th Cavalry, with two (s) privates, fully armed and equipped, mounted, furnished with rations . . . left Post for Weatherford, Texas for the purpose of assisting Deputy Sheriff in taking to that place one Reddy Draper, an escaped criminal, the Sheriff having reported himself unable to perform the duty without military protection." For the troopers at Forts Griffin and Concho, life differed little from that of their comrades at Fort Richardson. Griffin had its Flats and Concho its Saint Angela, and

58 Organizational Returns, Tenth Cavalry, April–May 1873.
59 Hatch to the AAG, Department of Texas, April 4, 1873, SLR, Department of Texas; H. McConnell, *Five Years a Cavalryman, or Sketches of Army Life on the Texas Frontier, 1866–1871* (Jacksboro, Tex.: J. N. Rogers, 1889; reprint, Norman: University of Oklahoma Press, 1996), 160–61.

either could just as easily have been spelled "Trouble." As the post surgeon at Fort Griffin put it, when payday came he knew "killings would occur."[60]

Trouble of a different kind and in plenty was brewing in Indian Territory. The Kiowas remained in their camps during the spring and summer, angry at the failure of the federal government to return Satanta and Big Tree in March as promised but held in check by pledges that the chiefs would be released in the fall. Small Comanche parties, however, slipped into Texas despite efforts of some of their chiefs to restrain them, and when the government returned the captive Comanche women and children in June, the lid was off. From Fort Griffin, Lieutenant Colonel George Buell, Eleventh Infantry, commanding the post, reported, "the Indians . . . have been quite troublesome this month and . . . I have run my cavalry about down." Captain Charles Viele of C and Captain Foulk of D and their buffalo soldiers could certainly agree with the post commander, for in June alone they had scouted nearly a thousand miles.[61]

At Fort Sill Agent Haworth stoutly insisted that his Indians were not raiding, but Davidson distrusted the agent and had no faith in the peace policy. In July he sent out Companies B, H, and M under Captain Carpenter to scout along the Red and in the Pease River country of Texas. While encamped along the Pease, hostiles fired into the camp, and Carpenter found many trails leading from the reservation into Texas. This was enough for Davidson. He prepared to take all five companies at Sill, march along the southern line of the reservation, and "hit anything that came out."[62]

On August 19 Davidson left Fort Sill with G, H, K, and M. Captain John Vande Viele's B remained at the post because of the poor condition of its horses. The column marched west along the Red to Gilbert's Creek, where Companies E and I under Captain Baldwin, operating out of Fort Richardson, joined the command. The westward march continued without incident until August 28, when Groesbeck Creek was crossed. There a fresh grave was found with a crude headstone on which was engraved "Hank Medley, killed

60   Col. H. Clay Wood to the AAG, Department of Texas, May 5, 1873, SLR, Department of Texas; Medical History, Fort Griffin, Texas, vol. 103, Medical History of Posts, AGO, RG 94, NA.

61   Buell to the AAG, Department of Texas, June 15, 1873, SLR, Department of Texas; Organizational Returns, Tenth Cavalry, June 1873. The troopers at Forts Richardson and Concho were on almost constant scout during the entire summer.

62   Davidson to the AAG, Department of Texas, July 25, 1873, SLR, Department of Texas; Organizational Returns, Tenth Cavalry, July 1873.

by Indians August 25, 1873." A detachment soon located Medley's companions, members of a surveying party. The party chief, a Mr. Maddox, reported
that Medley had gone hunting and was killed by eight Indians before his
companions could come to his rescue.

Davidson pushed on until he reached the hundredth degree of longitude
and then turned north across the Salt Fork, Elm Fork, and North Fork of
the Red before turning eastward to Fort Sill, which his force reached on
September 14. The scout had covered some four hundred miles, and Davison had firmly concluded "that these Indians confine themselves to no
particular belt of operations, but shoot straight from wherever their camps
happen to be into Texas, that the reservation is a 'city of refuge' for these
marauders, that hunting for any enemy who has the eye of a hawk, and the
stealth of a wolf over the arid plains and salty sandy beds of streams, I have
traversed, is like hunting needles in hayricks, and that an effective method
of meeting this condition of affairs, while the Government is feeding and
clothing reservation Indians, is to dismount them, and make them answer
a daily roll-call."[63]

To the north Agent Miles was watching the growing restlessness of his
Southern Cheyennes with increasing apprehension. This proud and turbulent people had given no real trouble since 1871, but Kiowa and Comanche
couriers were constantly in their camps urging the warpath and occasionally inducing some of the young men to raid with them. And despite all
Miles's efforts, whisky dealers were demoralizing the Cheyennes. Late in
March 1873 a party of warriors attacked a group of U.S. surveyors near
Camp Supply, killing E. N. Deming, the crew chief, and three of his assistants. The bulk of the Cheyennes remained peaceful, however, but many of
the young men were raiding by the summer and fall, and Miles was unable
to stop the steady flow of liquor to them.[64]

At Fort Sill Agent Haworth was also fearful. Satanta and Big Tree were
still in a Texas prison and the Kiowas were on the point of becoming
unmanageable. Release of the chiefs, promised by the Indian Bureau as no
later than March 1, 1873, had struck a snag. Governor Davis of Texas had

63 Davidson to the AAG, Department of Texas, September 16, 1873, SLR, Department
of Texas; Lieutenant S. L. Woodward to Grierson, August 18, 1873, GP-ISHS; *Army and
Navy Journal* 11 (October 4, 1873): 117; (December 20, 1873): 292.

64 *Annual Report of the Commissioner of Indian Affairs for the Year 1873*, 220–23; T. H.
Barrett, U.S. Surveyor, to Miles, March 8, 1873, Cheyenne-Arapaho Files, Indian Archives
Division, Oklahoma State Historical Society, Oklahoma City.

refused to turn them loose. Finally, however, yielding to pressure from President Grant, Davis agreed to return the chiefs to their people, but with conditions attached. Satanta and Big Tree were brought to Fort Sill under military escort early in September and confined in the guardhouse. Governor Davis arrived on October 3 with several members of his staff and was greeted by E. P. Smith, commissioner of Indian affairs, and the superintendent for the plains tribes, Enoch Hoag.

Davis wished a formal council with the Kiowas to inform them of the terms under which he would release the chiefs, and arrangements were made at once for a meeting at the post on October 6. In view of the impatience of the Kiowas and a fear of violent reaction to any delay in the release of the chiefs, Davidson took every possible precaution to quell trouble if it arose. Every buffalo soldier at Fort Sill was on the alert, fully armed and equipped, with his mount saddled and ready for instant action.

At the appointed time the Kiowas assembled and listened with growing anger to Davis's demands. In effect, they would have to become farmers, permit spies in their midst, surrender their arms, and conduct themselves as white men before their chiefs were returned to them. Even then their chiefs would be subject to immediate seizure and imprisonment if any raids occurred. The council broke up when Indian pleadings failed to move Governor Davis.

Commissioner Smith, Superintendent Hoag, and Agent Haworth all converged on the governor to persuade him to soften his terms, call for another council, and release the captive chiefs. Adamant at first, Davis finally yielded, and a second council was called for October 8. Meanwhile, in the Kiowa camps a decision had been reached to regain their chiefs by force if necessary. Tension ran high, and the buffalo soldiers and their officers maintained a round-the-clock vigil.

When the council met, Davis surprised everyone by agreeing to let Satanta and Big Tree go and asked for the surrender of five Comanches, known to have been raiding in Texas recently, to civil authorities for punishment. On this note the council ended, and the danger of a blood bath on the post was averted.[65]

---

65 *Annual Report of the Commissioner of Indian Affairs for the Year 1873,* 219; Campbell, "Down among the Red Men," 638–39; Battey, *Life and Adventures,* 199–200; Hoag to Haworth, August 12, 1873, Trial of Satanta and Big Tree, Kiowa Files; Davis to Davidson, August 14, 1873, ibid.

Buffalo soldiers in a familiar
role—riding shotgun on a
Concord Stage Coach
Courtesy of Buffalo Soldiers Research
and Re-enactors of Maryland

General William T.
Sherman, commander
of the Military Division
of the Missouri
Courtesy National Archives

Tenth Cavalry on Parade
Courtesy of Buffalo Soldiers Research and Re-enactors of Maryland

Colonel Benjamin H. Grierson and party at Medicine Bluff, near Fort Sill, Oklahoma, 1869 or 1870. The photograph probably was taken by William S. Soule, who became official post photographer for Fort Sill in 1869 and held the post for six years.
Courtesy U.S. Army Artillery and Missile Center Museum, Fort Sill

Colonel Benjamin H. Grierson, commander of the Tenth Cavalry
Courtesy National Archives

That same day Smith, Hoag, and Haworth met with the Kiowas and Comanches at the agency to remind them of the necessity for turning over the raiders Governor Davis had demanded. After much angry discussion, a young Comanche chief, Cheevers, agreed to lead a few warriors and a detachment of troops in search of the raiders. Smith gave him thirty days to get results.

Cheevers with nineteen warriors came to Fort Sill, and on October 12, with Captain P. L. Lee and fifty picked troopers, set out to find the offending Comanches. The expedition was a wild-goose chase, for Cheevers led Lee over a wide area of northwestern Texas with no results. Not an Indian had been seen when the little column plodded wearily back to Fort Sill.[66]

At first the Indian Bureau took a firm line with the Indians. The five Comanches must be turned over or rations and annuities would be withheld. The threat backfired. Many small bands immediately left the reservation to raid in Texas, but a few days later the bureau changed its mind and made the distributions. The vacillation had been a costly one when coupled with the long delay in releasing Satanta and Big Tree. Davidson and his regiment had nothing to do in influencing these floundering switches in policy, but the results would keep the buffalo soldiers in the saddle almost constantly for many long months.[67]

Weary troopers at Forts Richardson and Griffin could have told the Indian Bureau that far more than five Indians had been giving them sleepless days and nights for weeks. Colonel Buell, commanding at Griffin, reported that he was virtually helpless to stop widespread raiding. His only cavalry consisted of Captain Viele's C Company and Captain Foulk's D Company, and every man in both units was pursuing hostiles. There were no additional troopers to respond to the calls for aid that poured into his post since E, L, and I were operating out of Richardson without respite and badly in need of remounts. Colonel W. H. Wood, commanding at Richardson, wrote department headquarters that these three companies were "about worn out" and that he could mount a total of only 116 men largely because of "unserviceable horses."[68]

---

66 Battey, *Life and Adventures*, 211–12; Campbell, "Down among the Red Men," 639; Organizational Returns, Tenth Cavalry, October 1873; Davidson to Lee, October 9, 1873, SLR, Department of Texas.

67 Woodward to Grierson, December 5, 1873, GP-ISHS; Battey, *Life and Adventures*, 229.

68 Buell to the AAG, Department of Texas, August 8, 1873, SLR, Department of Texas; Wood to the AAG, Department of Texas, September 3, 1873, ibid.

Colonel Davidson at Fort Sill was certain large-scale field operations were imminent, yet his regiment was in dire need of more than three hundred horses along with much new equipment. Seventy-seven mounts had been received in August, but of these only twenty-one were "suitable . . . for soldiers who are expected to pursue and overtake Indians." It was not until almost the end of the year that the buffalo soldiers received some "fair" horses along with new .45-caliber Springfield carbines and Colt revolvers.[69]

Throughout the fall and early winter, Indian raiders took scalps, cattle, and horses along the Texas frontier. Colonel Wood at Fort Richardson complained that he had never known Indians to be so "numerous, desperate or persistent." Nor were they the only source of trouble. White thieves were also active and often raided Indian pony herds, ensuring retaliatory action in Texas. It was a severe challenge to a badly scattered regiment, riding poor horseflesh, and many raiders, both Indian and white, often escaped, though not always. Between September and December 1873, detachments of the Tenth recovered nearly twelve hundred head of stolen animals, killed four white horse thieves and captured seventeen others, had a dozen brushes with Indian war parties, and inflicted an undetermined number of Indian casualties.[70]

During the winter of 1873–74, two events occurred that had far-reaching consequences, contributing to a major Indian war and ending completely the role of the Tenth as an army of occupation. On December 9 Lieutenant C. L. Hudson, Fourth Cavalry, and a detachment of forty-one men intercepted a party of Indian raiders on the West Fork of the Nueces River. In the fight that followed, nine Indians were killed. The war party consisted of an elite group of young Kiowa and Comanche warriors from the reservation. Among the dead were Tau-ankia, son of Lone Wolf, and Gui-tain, son of Lone Wolf's brother, Red Otter.[71]

69 Major Schofield to Davidson, August 17, 1873, ibid.; E. D. Townsend, AG, to General Sherman, December 24, 1873, ibid.; Davidson to Schofield, October 9, 1873, LS, Tenth U.S. Cavalry.

70 Wood to the AAG, Department of Texas, October 10, 1873, SLR, Department of Texas; Wood to the AAG, Department of Texas, November 1, 1873, ibid.; Organizational Returns, Tenth Cavalry, October–December 1873; Wood to the AAG, Department of Texas, November 30, 1873, SLR, Department of Texas; Lieutenant T. C. Lebo to Wood, October 21, 1873, ibid.; U.S. Army, Military Division of the Missouri, *Record of Engagements with Hostile Indians*, 37.

71 Lieutenant Hudson to the PA, Fort Clark, Texas, December 15, 1873, LR by the Office of Indian Affairs, Kiowa Agency; *Army and Navy Journal* 11 (January 3, 1874): 324; *Austin Weekly Democratic Statesman*, December 25, 1873; Nye, *Carbine and Lance*, 182–83.

When news of this fight reached the Kiowa camps in January 1874, the whole tribe went into mourning. Lieutenant Woodward wrote Grierson from Fort Sill that Lone Wolf burned nearly everything he had, killed many of his ponies, and "slashed himself all up."[72]

Disaster also struck the Comanches. Winter raiding had been so extensive that Davidson stationed most of his troopers in stockaded camps on a line between Forts Sill and Griffin. In this way he could move more swiftly to hit raiding parties. Failing to intercept them, he still could relay information far more quickly to Buell at Fort Griffin regarding the probable direction in which the Indians were heading. The new system soon brought dramatic results.

Late in January, Buell received information that a party of Comanches had stolen some stock and were headed in the direction of the Double Mountains, about one hundred miles west of his post. With Captain P. L. Lee, Lieutenant R. H. Pratt, and fifty-five buffalo soldiers of D and G Companies and guided by eighteen Tonkawa Indian scouts, Buell left Griffin in search of the raiders. On February 5 he found his quarry in the valley of the Double Mountain Fork of the Brazos River and in a running fight killed eleven warriors and recovered sixty-five animals.[73]

The twin blows of Hudson and Buell brought a burning desire for revenge to the camps of the Kiowas and Comanches. Many of the warriors could think of nothing but war, and their couriers found ready ears in the lodges of the Southern Cheyennes. The spring winds of 1874 brought with them all the elements of a major war.

72 Woodward to Grierson, February 24, 1874, GP-ISHS.
73 Davidson to the AAG, Department of Texas, March 20, 1874, SLR, Department of Texas; Post Returns, Fort Griffin, February 1874; Organizational Returns, Tenth Cavalry, February 1874; Medical History, Fort Griffin, vol. 103.

The Ninth in Texas

While the buffalo soldiers of the Tenth Cavalry labored to keep the peace between and among various groups on the central plains, Colonel Edward Hatch and the Ninth Cavalry performed their duties in West Texas and along the meandering Rio Grande. For eight long years they sweated, bled, and died to make life and property secure on one of the most turbulent and strife-ridden frontiers in the history of American westward advance.

The movement of the Ninth west to Forts Davis and Stockton in the summer of 1867 was accompanied by initial orders to protect the mail and stage route between San Antonio and El Paso, search out and defeat raiding Indians or Mexicans, and maintain law and order on the troubled Rio Grande border. It was no mean assignment for a single regiment, particularly one whose early history had been extremely troubled.

Merely patrolling the vast region in their charge was a well-nigh impossible task. Soldiers confronted hundreds of miles of brush jungle along the Rio Grande; vast areas of plain, desert, and mountain where water was often scarce or entirely absent; and other terrain that was unusually rough and broken. Temperatures ranged from above one hundred degrees in summer to well below freezing in winter; and violent and sudden changes were the norm. But the Ninth faced more formidable challenges than those posed by weather and terrain.

Texans, hostile to all Indians, had driven the peaceful tribes from the region north of the Red River before the Civil War. Given the sparse Anglo settlement in West Texas, that region was, more than ever, open to bands of Mescalero Apaches. For centuries they had ranged widely from Chihuahua and Coahuila in Mexico to the Rio Grande and the Pecos River. Now, as newcomers moved into West Texas, the Mescaleros often swept down from their camps in the Guadalupe Mountains to seize cattle and to menace stages, wagon trains, and unwary travelers.

Kiowa and Comanche warriors flowed into West Texas from the north, and they also roamed freely. The Comanche had long competed with residents of northern Mexico for pasturage and water holes for their pony herds. During the Civil War these "Lords of the Southern Plains" had increased their raids on Mexico, and afterward they saw no reason to discontinue that practice. Consequently, they were spreading terror from the Red River to the Rio Grande and for hundreds of miles into Mexico when the Ninth arrived. It was no accident that Fort Stockton was located at Comanche Springs astride the "great Comanche War Trail." This well-trod highway for the warrior elite ran from the shallow waters of the Arkansas to the haciendas of Durango.[1]

Indian raiding was not one-way traffic. Mexican Kickapoos, as refugees from the United States, remained embittered over losing their homeland and harbored implacable hatred toward those who lived north of the Rio Grande. They joined the Lipans, a group of fierce Apaches who also bore longstanding enmity toward the Anglo settlers on the northern side of the river. Together these two groups raided remote areas of Texas with, according to one historian, unsurpassed "viciousness, vindictiveness and destruction of life and property" against those they identified as their enemies.[2]

Marauding Indians, Mexican or American, were only one problem, however. The Republic of Mexico, born of revolution and torn by half a century of sporadic civil war, spawned almost countless bandits and revolutionar-

---

1 Hagan, *Quanah Parker*, 9. Fort Stockton was established on March 23, 1859, to protect the San Antonio–El Paso stage route. Named for Commodore Robert Stockton, U.S. forces abandoned it in April 1861 and Confederate troops occupied it briefly and then burned it. Hatch and four companies of the Ninth reoccupied the site on July 7, 1867, and began the work of reconstruction. Stockton was finally abandoned on June 30, 1886. Frazer, *Forts of the West*, 162; Organizational Returns, Ninth Cavalry, July 1867, AGO, RG 94, NA.

2 Gibson, *Kickapoos*, 210.

ies. Often, the difference between the two was a matter of semantics, and many of them, by reason of birth or convenience, made their homes on the North Mexico frontier. There the weak and languid arm of the Mexican federal government posed no threat to their activities. They had many sympathizers among the Hispanic population on the American side of the river, which they crossed and recrossed at will, often killing, thieving, or organizing as need and whim dictated.[3]

The activities of these groups brought affairs on the Rio Grande to a state of near anarchy for more than twenty years, but the woes of the Texas frontier, and thereby the problems of the Ninth Cavalry, did not end here. Riffraff abounded north of the river, ever ready with gun, knife, rope, and branding iron to ply any trade that afforded an easy and illegal dollar. And lurking in the background was the shadowy and elusive comanchero with his trade goods, whisky, guns, and ammunition to reward those who stole cattle and horses for him. There was a steady and lucrative market for these animals in New Mexico Territory, and A. B. Norton, superintendent of Indian affairs for New Mexico, in his annual report for 1867 described the territory as "filled with Texas cattle."[4]

Such challenges were enough to occupy fully every soldier in Texas. But of three regiments of cavalry in the state, only one, the Ninth, was assigned exclusively to the frontier. Not more than half of four regiments of infantry were available for such service. For too long, ranking officers such as Generals Sherman and Sheridan refused to believe conditions were as bad as thousands of frontier petitioners painted them. Besides, Texas was undergoing the throes of Reconstruction, and many troops were needed in the interior of the state.[5]

In the face of almost overwhelming responsibilities, the untried Ninth also contended with a problem that compounded the difficulties of their tasks. Citizens on the frontier might rage and storm, demand and plead for greater protection, but they gave scant comfort and support when that protection arrived in the form of a black soldier. Raiding Indians, Mexican bandits and revolutionaries, pistol-happy border scum, and stealthy

3 Parkes, *History of Mexico,* 242–50; Brevet Major General J. J. Reynolds to the AG, U.S. Army, October 1869, *Annual Report for the Department of Texas, 1869.*

4 *Annual Report of the Commissioner of Indian Affairs for the Year 1867,* 194–95.

5 *Annual Report of the Secretary of War for the Year 1866,* 15. Sheridan's view was that there certainly had been depredations on the frontier, "but they are not very alarming." The other cavalry regiments assigned to Texas were the Fourth and Sixth.

comancheros might wipe out cattle herds and hundreds of lives, but they did not suffice to wipe out the poison of racial prejudice in most instances.

There was too much to be done, however, for Hatch and his troopers to waste time complaining. Forts Stockton and Davis required complete rebuilding. Details were soon cutting logs, making adobe bricks, constructing sinks, and erecting quarters and corrals. Initially, Lieutenant Colonel Wesley Merritt hired additional civilian labor to expedite progress at Fort Davis, but by 1868 the Quartermaster Department would overrule that decision as too costly and curtail the funds available. By then, enlisted men would still be sleeping in tents. A year later they would have only two barracks with dirt floors where six companies could lay their weary bodies on bedsacks filled with straw, tossed across slats on bunk irons. The rest would still be residing in tents.

Other comforts were and would remain lacking. Food, poor in quality and lacking in variety, usually consisted of coffee, bread, beans, and beef, with molasses, cornbread, and sweet potatoes added to spice up the evening meal. In July 1867 the beans that arrived at Fort Davis were inedible even after "twenty-four hours of uninterrupted boiling," according to Merritt, and the soldiers' diet included no vegetables.[6]

Beyond plain and sometimes less than nourishing meals, the men at Davis and Stockton, as well as most other western posts, endured the effects of abysmal sanitary facilities. As late as 1878, Assistant Surgeon John Hall reported that the privies at Fort Stockton—which numbered two for every four companies and contained "broken and leaky" sinks located in the midst of filth—were totally inadequate for the number of soldiers on post.[7]

During 1867, the task of reconstructing the West Texas posts and making them more habitable and healthy progressed slowly, for more than half the troopers were constantly in the field. So active were Indian raiders that, from

6 Hutcheson, "Ninth Regiment of Cavalry," 282; Post Returns, Fort Stockton, July–August 1867, AGO, RG 94, NA; Organizational Returns, Ninth Cavalry, August–September 1867. Fort Davis, located near Limpia Creek in Presidio County, was established in October 1854 to protect the San Antonio-El Paso road. Named for Jefferson Davis, then secretary of war, the post was evacuated by U.S. troops in April 1861. Indians and Mexicans used the buildings from time to time but also damaged them. Merritt and six companies of the Ninth reoccupied the fort in July 1867 and rebuilt it completely. Though isolated, the general climate and healthfulness made it a desirable post at which to serve. Frazer, *Forts of the West*, 148; Joseph H. Toulouse and James R. Toulouse, *Pioneer Posts of Texas* (San Antonio: Naylor, 1936), 151–54. For information on the reoccupation of Fort Davis and its problems obtaining adequate food supplies, see Wooster, *History of Fort Davis*, 193, 197.

7 Barnett, *Ungentlemanly Acts*, 56–57.

the first, heavy herd guards and lookouts on high ground were necessary to prevent these matchless thieves from running off the horses. Scouting detachments were in the saddle from dawn to dusk probing along the Pecos, Concho, and Devils Rivers, while others patrolled the San Antonio–El Paso road, escorted trains and stages, and guarded the mail stations to the east and west.[8]

Green troopers and officers unfamiliar with the country had little success in intercepting marauding Indians. Further, for a time at least, small raiding parties seemed to prefer a quick hit-and-run strike for taking cattle and horses or the killing of a lonely shepherd. News of such small-scale activity was slow to reach the isolated posts, and pursuit was all but useless. As summer faded into fall, however, the Indians grew bolder. Late in October a revenge-bent party of Kickapoos drew blood from the buffalo soldiers. They ambushed and killed Corporal Emanuel Wright and Private E. T. Jones of D Company as they escorted the mail from Camp Hudson to Fort Stockton. On December 5, more than one hundred Mescaleros attacked the stage eastbound from El Paso; killed Private Nathan Johnson, a member of the escort; and in a running fight wounded four horses. The Apaches did not give up the chase until the stage came within sight of Eagle Springs Station, where Captain Henry Carroll and Company F, who were encamped nearby, drove them off.[9]

Near the end of the year, a force of Kickapoos, Lipans, Mexicans, and some white renegades, estimated at nine hundred strong, attacked the bivouac of Captain William Frohock and K Company at old Fort Lancaster, some seventy-five miles east of Fort Stockton. It afforded the buffalo soldiers their first opportunity to face their foes "toe to toe," and they responded with grim enthusiasm. A vicious three-hour fight left K Company in possession of the field after killing twenty of their attackers and wounding a large number. Three herd guards, Privates Andrew Trimble, William Sharpe, and Eli Boyer, who had been taken by surprise, roped, and dragged away, were missing and presumed dead.[10]

8 Organizational Returns, Ninth Cavalry, August–September 1867. Companies A, B, E, and K were at Fort Stockton; C, D, F, G, H, and I were at Fort Davis; and L and M remained at Brownsville.

9 Ibid., October 1867; General George Thomas, AG, to the Secretary of War, February 20, 1868, SLR, AGO, RG 94, NA.

10 Organizational Returns, Ninth Cavalry, December 1867; Post Returns, Fort Stockton, December 1867; *San Antonio Weekly Express,* January 9, 1868; J. Lee Humfreville, *Twenty Years among Our Hostile Indians,* (New York: Hunter, 1889), 178. The remains of

The fight at Fort Lancaster proved the virtues of hard work, discipline, and a sense of purpose and should have removed any doubts concerning the combat effectiveness of the Ninth's black troopers. Certainly there were none in the minds of those who fought them on that cool, clear, December day or in the minds of Hatch and his officers. Others—in white regiments and in the higher echelons of command—remained unconvinced.

Although raiding Indians showed a decided reluctance after Fort Lancaster to indulge in pitched battles with troopers who showed such relish for fighting at close quarters, there was no letup in their hit, steal, and run tactics. To counter these thrusts more effectively, Hatch moved L and M Companies upriver from Brownsville to Forts Duncan and Clark. Fort Quitman, along the river northwest of Fort Davis, was reoccupied by a strong detachment under aggressive Major Albert P. Morrow. With all companies of the regiment in position to coordinate their operations, Hatch planned a vigorous offensive when spring arrived. In February 1868, however, he was appointed assistant commissioner of the Freedmen's Bureau for Louisiana and placed on detached service. Lieutenant Colonel Merritt replaced Hatch as commander of the Ninth.[11]

Merritt was eager to carry out the plans of his predecessor, but the spring and summer of 1868 found the region alive with small war parties that stretched to the limit the strength and endurance of his command. A year of campaigning had changed the face of the Ninth. It was now a tough, hard-hitting unit, but intercepting the flitting marauders was almost as difficult as getting a firm grasp on a group of ghosts. When hard pressed, the raiders almost invariably turned and fled across the Rio Grande into Mexico. From the other side, they thumbed their noses at the frustrated troopers, forced to halt at the river's edge.

Trimble, Sharpe, and Boyer were found three months later near the scene of the fight. Fort Lancaster was established in August 1855 along Live Oak Creek near its junction with the Pecos. Named for Captain Stephen Lancaster, First Infantry, it was abandoned in 1861 and was never reactivated, although troops often camped there after the Civil War. Frazer, *Forts of the West.* 183.

11 Organizational Returns, Ninth Cavalry, January–April 1868; Hatch to the AG, October 31, 1868, SLR. Morrow rose through the ranks during the Civil War from a sergeant in the Seventeenth Pennsylvania Infantry to lieutenant colonel, Sixth Pennsylvania Cavalry, with citations for conspicuous gallantry in action. In July 1866 he accepted appointment as captain in the Seventh Cavalry but transferred to the Ninth with the rank of major in March 1867. He served with the regiment for the next fifteen years and was one of its ablest officers. He retired in 1892 as colonel of the Third Cavalry. Heitman, *Historical Register,* 1:729.

Kickapoo war parties threatened to devastate whole counties. In one swoop into Atascosa County, they killed three men and drove off four hundred head of horses. Within three months they had killed five more citizens and stolen another three hundred head of animals in the same county. A ranchers' posse caught up with them only to be badly whipped and routed. Duval, Schlicher, and Uvalde Counties were equally hard hit. Mescalero and Comanche raids were almost as devastating.[12]

It was too much for one regiment. The Ninth was spread too thin, their enemies were far too numerous, the region simply too vast, and the international boundary too porous for effective defense. Not all of the raiders escaped unscathed, however. On September 26 two hundred Apaches struck a train near Fort Stockton, ran off all the stock, and wasted no time in heading for sanctuary across the Rio Grande. With orders from Merritt to spare neither men nor horses, Lieutenant Patrick Cusack, sixty-one men of A Company, and ten civilian volunteers took up the pursuit.

They found the trail without difficulty and followed it into the wild and broken country southeast of Stockton. The search ended in the rugged Santiago Mountains, where Cusack overtook his quarry and, though badly outnumbered, attacked at once. In a running fight of five miles, the buffalo soldiers soundly whipped the Apaches, killing twenty-five, wounding as many more, and recovering two hundred animals and two captive Mexican children. Cusack's only casualties were two men wounded.[13]

The lieutenant praised all his men as worthy of receiving citations for gallantry, but he singled out three men from C Company as outstanding: Ross Alsie, John Harrison, and Lewis White, all of whom had been released from the guardhouse for the scout. White was especially praiseworthy. An arrow had severely wounded him in his side early in the fight, and he had lost his horse when it had been shot from under him, but he had nonetheless "remained in the foremost of the fight." Although none of the men received official recognition and White was not given the Medal of Honor he deserved, a reporter in the *San Antonio Herald,* which was generally unfriendly toward black troopers, expressed appreciation. He wrote, "All honor to . . . the brave soldiers who so thoroughly did their duty."[14]

---

12 Wilbarger, *Indian Depredations in Texas,* 633; Gibson, *Kickapoos,* 212–13; House, H. Exec. Doc. 13, 42d Cong. 3d sess., 5:1–3.

13 Organizational Returns, Ninth Cavalry, September 1868; *Army and Navy Journal* 6 (October 10, 1868): 114.

14 Kenner, *Buffalo Soldiers and Officers of the Ninth Cavalry,* 53–54.

The raids eased somewhat as winter came on but were renewed early in 1869 and continued throughout the year. Between January and April, fierce Kickapoo raids in Bexar, Frio, Uvalde, Zavala, Medina, and Atascosa Counties cost the lives of sixteen persons, the loss of hundreds of horses, and thousands of dollars in other property. With the advent of summer, Kiowa and Comanche warriors raced down from their reservation in Indian Territory, leaving havoc in their wake. Burnett, Comanche, Johnson, Parker, and Tarrant Counties especially suffered.[15]

The men of the Ninth rode their mounts hard over thousands of dusty miles in blistering heat, pursuing war parties that seemed everywhere and yet nowhere. The usual result was a bleak sentence or two such as appeared in the post returns for Fort Concho in July 1869: "Indians ran off mail mules and government horses from mail station at head of the Concho July 29. Pursuit by Captain Gamble, Company 'B' Ninth Cavalry with detachment failed to overtake the Indians."[16] General Joseph J. Reynolds, commanding the Fifth Military District, reported that the troops were on continuous scout and "all that is possible for their number to do has been done to protect the people and property of the frontier counties."[17] This was cold comfort to the overworked buffalo soldiers, who longed to come to grips with their elusive foes. Reinforcements were on the way, however, and the Twenty-fourth Infantry began taking up positions at Forts McKavett, Clark, Concho, Stockton, Davis, and Quitman. Their presence supporting the cavalry permitted a concentration of forces strong enough to achieve success.[18] In September their dogged persistence finally brought concrete results.

Emboldened by their successes, a strong war party of Kiowas and Comanches committed depredations in the vicinity of Fort McKavett along the San Saba River and headed north for the reservation. Captain Carroll and Captain Edward Heyl with ninety-five men of B, E, F, and M Companies and a detachment of the Twenty-fourth Infantry took up the pursuit. The trail was lost, supplies ran low, and the command was forced to halt at

15 "Report of Felonies Committed by Indians in the Fifth Military District," *Annual Report for the Department of Texas, 1869; Annual Report of the Secretary of War for the Year 1869*, 144–45. In Texas 384 murders were committed during this single year, although not all of these resulted from Indian attacks.

16 Post Returns, Fort Concho, Texas, July 1869.

17 *Annual Report of the Secretary of War for the Year 1870*, 41. Reynolds points out in his report that the troops were also busy with construction work—lumbering, quarrying stone, making adobes, burning brick and lime, and driving wagons.

18 Fowler, *Black Infantry in the West*, 23–24; Carlson, "*Pecos Bill*," 47.

Fort Concho to refit. But Henry Carroll could find Indians as well as any officer on the frontier, and he had no intention of giving up the search. Once resupplied, he returned to the pursuit with renewed determination.

Pushing north from Concho, Carroll regained the trail, which led to the headwaters of the Salt Fork of the Brazos and a camp of nearly two hundred lodges. The eager troopers barely had time to clench their teeth on a generous chunk of chewing tobacco before Carroll gave the order to charge. The blare of bugles and the thunder of hoofs were enough for the Indians, who sought safety in wild flight. For eight miles, shouting, cursing, and exultant buffalo soldiers chased the panic-stricken Comanches and pulled up only when their mounts had given out. They had struck their foe a heavy blow. More than a score of Indians had been killed or wounded, and their entire camp and all its equipage was captured and destroyed. It was a weary but elated column that reached Fort McKavett forty-two days and six hundred miles after their departure from that post. Captain Carroll praised his men collectively, noting that most of them "had never seen an Indian before," but they had still displayed "excellent behavior." But he failed to single out one buffalo soldier. Lieutenant George Albee, by contrast, had repulsed an early Comanche charge with two buffalo soldiers. Later Albee received a Medal of Honor. The two troopers who fought beside him were equally responsible for repulsing the enemy at a critical stage in the encounter. They went unnamed and unhonored, their bravery taken for granted.[19]

Hatch, meanwhile, had returned from detached service and established his headquarters at Fort Davis. Distressed over the lack of success in curbing Indian raids but encouraged by Carroll's strike, he decided on an all-out campaign to drive the Kiowas, Comanches, and Mescaleros from the region

19 Post Returns, Fort McKavett, September–October 1869; Organizational Returns, Ninth Cavalry, September–October 1869; *Army and Navy Journal* 7 (November 27, 1869): 224; Kenner, *Buffalo Soldiers and Officers of the Ninth Cavalry*, 54–55. Carroll was a New Yorker who enlisted in the army in 1859 and rose through the ranks. Commissioned a second lieutenant in the Third Cavalry in May 1864, he was promoted to first lieutenant in April 1866. He joined the Ninth Cavalry as a captain in January 1867 and remained with the regiment for eighteen years. He retired from the service as colonel, Seventh Cavalry, in May 1899 after forty years in the regular army. Heitman, *Historical Register,* 1:286. Fort McKavett, located near the source of the San Saba River, was the third Texas post to be completely rebuilt by the men of the Ninth. It was established in 1852 and named for Captain Henry McKavett, Eighth Infantry, killed during the Mexican War. It was abandoned in March 1859, and Confederates occupied it during the Civil War; U.S. troops did not reoccupy it until March 1869 to curb Indian raids. Companies F and M, Ninth Cavalry, began the work of reconstruction. Frazer, *Forts of the West,* 154–55; Organizational Returns, Ninth Cavalry, March 1869.

under his care. Detachments from six companies of the Ninth were concentrated at Fort Concho under Captain John Bacon, G Company. On October
10 Bacon led his command out of Concho and marched to the site of old
Fort Phantom Hill along the Brazos. There a detachment of the Fourth
Cavalry and twenty Tonkawa Indian scouts joined him. Then, with 198 men
at his back, he moved upriver near the headwaters and went into camp.

Bacon intended to send out scouting parties on the morning of October
28, but five hundred Kiowa and Comanche warriors spared him the trouble
by attacking at sunrise from all sides. For the second time in two years, hostile
Indians boldly assaulted a camp of buffalo soldiers. For the second time they
found themselves in a hornets' nest. In a bitter and at times eyeball-to-eyeball
struggle, the Indians were whipped and forced to flee. But neither Bacon nor
his troopers were satisfied, and they set out to find the Indian encampment.
Their efforts were rewarded near midafternoon on October 29, when their
fierce charge scattered the demoralized braves in all directions. Bacon placed
the Indians' loss at forty killed and seven women and fifty-one horses
captured. His own casualties were eight wounded, none fatally.[20]

December and January brought bitter cold weather, but Hatch pressed
his campaign relentlessly. On January 20, 1870, Captain Francis Dodge of
D Company with two hundred men from A, C, D, H, I, and K Companies
marched northwest from Fort Davis to carry the war into Mescalero country. While slogging through rain and sleet, the column came upon a Mescalero rancheria "in the most inaccessible region of the Guadalupe Mountains."
As the troopers approached, the Apaches fled and took refuge on a nearby
peak. Dodge had the men dismount and begin the ascent at once.

Precarious footing and heavy Indian gunfire slowed the march, but the
troopers pressed on and gained the summit as night fell. The Apaches fled
and the exhausted buffalo soldiers slept on the peak. Next morning the
troops counted ten Apache dead and concluded that others had been carried
away during the night. Dodge rounded up twenty-five ponies; destroyed a

---

20 Hatch to the AAG, Department of Texas, November 7, 1869, SLR Relating to the
Ninth and Tenth Regiments, U.S. Cavalry, AGO, RG 94, NA; Post Returns, Fort Concho,
November 1869; Post Returns, Fort McKavett, November 1869; *Army and Navy Journal*
7 (December 4, 1869). Fort Concho was a home for the buffalo soldiers of both Hatch and
Grierson. Established late in 1867, it was located at the junction of the North and South
Concho Rivers on the site of present San Angelo. Because of its strategic location, it
became one of the most important of the Texas frontier posts. Frazer, *Forts of the West*,
147. See also Haley, *Fort Concho and the Texas Frontier*.

large number of robes, bows and arrows, and other supplies; and after a search of the immediate vicinity, retraced his steps to Davis.[21]

It was a bad winter for the Apaches, for as Dodge fell upon them in the Guadalupes, the enterprising Bacon struck another Mescalero camp some seventy-five miles southwest of Fort McKavett. He captured the camp and chased the occupants for fifteen miles before turning back to destroy the lodges, all camp equipment, and six hundred beautifully dressed hides. In addition, his troopers drove eighty horses and mules back to McKavett.[22]

Hatch was not content to rest on his laurels. Once the weather moderated, he proposed to launch a campaign in the Guadalupe Mountains designed to ferret out the remaining haunts of the Mescaleros and stop raids on the Texas frontier from that quarter. This assignment he gave to Major Morrow, stationed at Fort Quitman. Morrow left that post on April 3 with ninety-one men of H and I Companies and, in summerlike heat and dust, marched upriver to El Paso, where Mexican guides were employed. There the command turned almost due east and set out for Pine Spring in the Guadalupes, the site agreed upon for a supply camp and a rendezvous with reinforcements from Forts Stockton and Davis.

If Morrow hoped to catch the Mescaleros off-guard, he was disappointed. On April 9, while encamped in the Cornudas Mountains, Private John Johnson of I Company accidentally fired the grass. Racing flames spawned huge columns of smoke, "alarming all the Indians in the country."[23] Consequently, the column moved on to Pine Spring with an "escort" of smoke signals accompanying it on all sides.

The rendezvous was reached on April 11, and work began at once to construct a base camp. Some of the wagons had not come up, however, and Corporal Ross of I was ordered to take the back trail and urge the laggards on. He had gone scarcely a mile from Pine Spring when three Mescaleros

21 Hatch to Brevet Colonel H. Clay Wood, AAG, Department of Texas, February 2, 1870, SLR. Dodge, a native of Massachusetts, rose through the ranks and was a captain in the Second Cavalry when the Civil War ended. He accepted appointment as a first lieutenant in the Ninth Cavalry in July 1866 and was promoted to captain in July 1867 and to major in January 1880, at which time he transferred to the Department of the Paymaster General. On March 22, 1898, nearly twenty years after the fight, he was awarded the Medal of Honor for his gallantry in the Milk River battle against the Utes in September 1879. Heitman, *Historical Register*, 1:376.

22 Post Returns, Fort McKavett, January 1870; *Army and Navy Journal* 7 (February 19, 1870): 422.

23 Morrow to the AAAG, Subdistrict of the Presidio, June 1, 1870, SLR.

Tenth Cavalry buffalo soldier
Courtesy National Archives

tried to interrupt his errand. Immediately Ross dropped his bridle, spurred his mount to a full run, and drove at his foes with carbine flaming. He killed one warrior and sent the remaining two scurrying for safety. Ross then located the tardy wagons and brought them into camp.

On April 12, Lieutenants Gustavus Valois and M. B. Hughes reached Pine Spring with sixty men. Next morning at dawn, Morrow was under way, marching northeast to the scene of Dodge's fight in January and then plunging into the heart of the Guadalupe Range. Canyon after canyon was scoured, and in nearly all, abandoned rancherias were found. Morrow reported:

> The guides knew nothing of the country we were now in but ... again took up the trail and after marching four or five hours found myself back in the camp of the night before. In this march we passed about two hundred recently occupied lodges. . . . Our guides, although the best in the country, were completely lost and baffled by the multiplicity of trails running in every direction crossing and retracing. They finally succeeded in finding a trail leading down what appeared an impassable ravine, the horses and pack mules had to be lifted down over the rocks. One or two fell into crevices and could not be extricated. Toward evening we came across a rancheria of 75 lodges which the Indians abandoned at our approach leaving a large amount of mezcal bread, about a hundred gallons of an intoxicating beverage brewed from the maguey and other commissary supplies, a great number of hides, robes, dressed and green skins, baskets, ojos, and all sorts of utensils and furniture pertaining to an Indian village.[24]

This camp was in sight of the Sacramento Mountains of New Mexico, and Morrow bivouacked at Cuervo Springs on the evening of April 21. The men were in woeful condition. Their boots had fallen to pieces and most were barefoot, their clothing was in tatters, and half the command was dismounted, so great had been the loss of horses. For two days the troopers mended their rags, made moccasins for bruised and bloody feet, and gained as much energy as they could from hardtack and bacon.[25] Morrow moved

24 Ibid.
25 Ibid.; "Journal of the March of Indian Expedition as Kept by Brevet Colonel George A. Purington, Captain 9th Cavalry, from April 3, 1870 to May 26, '70 Inclusive," ibid.

out again on April 23, marched to the Penasco River, and then turned eastward to his supply camp at Pine Spring.

After a brief rest, Morrow struck directly southwestward, skirted the eastern base of appropriately named Sierra Diablo, and headed for Rattlesnake Spring. There the advance surprised a small party of Mescaleros, who fled without offering any resistance and left the troopers in possession of thirty lodges and twenty-two horses. When extensive scouting turned up nothing more of significance, Morrow moved on to Fort Quitman after fifty-three days in the field. Few Indians had been killed, but scores of lodges had been destroyed along with great quantities of stores. Mescaleros would never again feel entirely secure in their old retreats in the Guadalupes. Their raids on the Texas frontier diminished, and the Ninth could claim a victory.

In his official report Morrow had nothing but praise for the performance of his troops. They had "marched about 1,000 miles, over two hundred of which was through country never explored by troops, drove the Indians from every rancheria . . . , destroyed immense amounts of . . . food, robes, skins, utensils and material and captured forty horses and miles. I cannot speak too highly of the conduct of the officers and men under my command, always cheerful and steady, braving the severest hardships with short rations and no water without a murmur. The negro troops are peculiarly adapted to hunting Indians knowing no fear and capable of great endurance."[26]

Morrow's appraisal of the buffalo soldiers received no little reinforcement from the heroics of tiny Sergeant Emmanuel Stance of Captain Carroll's F Company, stationed at Fort McKavett. On the morning of May 20, Stance and ten troopers left the post for a scout toward Kickapoo Spring, some twenty miles to the north. Halfway to their destination they saw a party of Indians driving a herd of horses. Stance formed his men in line and, charging at a dead run with Spencers blazing, routed the astonished Indians and captured nine horses. He then proceeded on to Kickapoo Spring and encamped for the night.

The next morning Stance decided to return to his post with the captured animals. He and his troopers had traveled only a short distance when he spied a party of warriors preparing to attack a small train. Once more Stance charged, forced the Indians to flee, and captured five more horses. But the Indians were not quite ready to call it a day. They soon reappeared at

---

26   Morrow to the AAAG, Subdistrict of the Presidio, June 1, 1870.

Stance's rear and opened fire at long range, but the sergeant would have none of this. He wheeled about and "turned my little command loose on them . . . and after a few volleys they left me to continue my march in peace."[27] This was Stance's fifth successful encounter with Indians in two years, and this time Captain Carroll was unstinting in his praise. The result was a Medal of Honor for the redoubtable sergeant.[28] Stance's career, so promising at this point, would prove to be long and controversial.

Although considerable success had been achieved against the Mescaleros, the Kiowas, Comanches, Kickapoos, and Lipans remained a sore problem. At Fort Davis a fuming Hatch believed his regiment could make short work of the problems the latter two tribes caused if he could only pursue their raiding parties to their villages in Mexico. In October he submitted a plan to General Reynolds for a winter campaign with this objective in view. The Ninth would take the field with every effective trooper that could be mustered; advance toward the Rio Grande on a broad front, driving every Indian they could find before them; and crossing the river, cooperate with Mexican troops in gaining an overwhelming and decisive victory.

Hatch's proposal was sound and won the swift approval of his superiors. Just as swiftly it struck a diplomatic snag. Mexican officials professed their willingness to cooperate but notified Thomas Nelson, U.S. minister to Mexico, that foreign troops could operate on Mexican soil only with the express consent of the Mexican Congress. That body would not convene until April 1871. This situation revived Hatch's plans for a winter campaign in 1870, but any future cooperation such as he envisioned was shunted aside as well when a suspicious Mexican Congress on April 29, 1871, refused entry of American troops to Mexican soil even if in "hot pursuit" of raiders.[29]

A high price had already been paid for lack of cooperation along the river frontier, and as Hatch was pleading for combined action, a grisly affair just south of the border should have lent great force to his proposal. Apaches attacked Charles Keerl, his wife, and a party of seven, killing all but one and leaving the dead mutilated. Keerl's head and that of his wife were severed, and her head was placed upon his shoulders. Belated efforts by Mexican

27 Sergeant Emanuel Stance, F Company, 9th Cavalry, to the PA, Fort McKavett, Texas, May 26, 1870, ibid.

28 Stance to the AG, Washington, D.C., July 24, 1870, ibid. This was Stance's letter of acceptance for his reward.

29 Hatch to the AAG, Department of Texas, October 4, 1870, ibid.; Thomas Nelson to Hamilton Fish, Secretary of State, April 29, 1871, ibid.

forces under Colonel Joaquin Terrazas, commanding in Chihuahua, failed to run down and punish the guilty tribesmen. It was only one of many such affairs that had occurred in the past and lay in the future.[30]

Hatch, meanwhile, was relieved of any immediate concern for affairs in West Texas. In December 1870 he was ordered to St. Louis as superintendent of the Mounted Recruiting Service, and command of his regiment once more fell to Lieutenant Colonel Merritt. It was many months before Hatch again returned to the Texas frontier.[31]

Although a lack of decisive victories over elusive Indian foes, who still fought tenaciously for control of what they saw as their homeland, was frustrating to Hatch, Merritt, and their men, one salient fact did not escape them. They had scouted, pursued in, and mapped areas troops had never before penetrated. The information thus gained would certainly shorten the time required to pacify the region and bring warring elements under control. And in the summer of 1871, a routine affair sent troopers of the Ninth into one of the last portions of West Texas Indian hostiles still regarded as safe.

On the evening of June 16, bold Indian raiders ran off forty-three animals from the herd of Company A, Twenty-fourth Infantry, as they bivouacked at Barella Springs between Forts Davis and Stockton. Lieutenant Colonel William R. Shafter, Twenty-fourth Infantry, commanding at Davis, with a detachment of buffalo soldiers set out for Barella, where Captain Michael Cooney and A Company of the Ninth joined him.[32] On June 21 Shafter, six officers, seventy-five troopers, and two guides set out on the Indian trail and followed it northeast to the Pecos.

From the Pecos the trail led north into the virtually unknown White Sands region, where Shafter managed to find water after a two-day search. Trails led through the sand in every direction, and for ten searing days the dogged colonel and his tough black troopers plowed back and forth along a maze of trails, suffering intensely from thirst and heat. Finally, with the command at the point of utter exhaustion, Shafter marched back to Fort Davis.

The immediate results of the march were meager. An abandoned village

30 *Galveston News,* April 13, 1871.
31 Organizational Returns, Ninth Cavalry, December 1870; Post Returns, Fort Davis, January 1871.
32 William Rufus Shafter, a Michigan native and Medal of Honor winner, emerged from the Civil War as a brigadier general. In 1869 he became lieutenant colonel of the Twenty-fourth Infantry and remained in that position until he accepted the colonelcy of the First Infantry in March 1879. See Heitman, *Historical Register,* 1:876.

of some two hundred lodges was destroyed. There had also been some long-range skirmishing with the elusive Comanches, and one woman had been captured, along with a few horses and mules and a small quantity of powder and lead. Ample evidence had also been discovered that the "Sands" was a place of barter for the comancheros. The real significance of the dreary search, however, lay in the destruction of a myth—that soldiers could never operate in such country. The buffalo soldiers could, and never again would an Indian or a comanchero close his eyes with any guarantee of unbroken sleep in the once mysterious White Sands.[33]

Despite increased military activity and the penetration of old sanctuaries, Indian raiders continued to plague ranchers and their herds. In late August they stole three hundred head near Fort McKavett, and detachments of F and M of the Ninth set out in pursuit. On September 1, Lieutenant John L. Bullis, Twenty-fourth Infantry, and four troopers of M, while scouting some distance from the main column, came upon three Indians driving the stolen cattle. Bullis attacked immediately and soon found himself in possession of the herd—but not for long. The initial three raiders returned with reinforcements numbering fifteen. For an hour and a half, Bullis and his intrepid four skirmished, charged, retreated, turned, and fought again, eventually retiring with two hundred head of cattle still in their possession.[34]

By year's end the Ninth had experienced nearly five years of the harshest kind of service with no respite. Most of the men had not seen their homes since enlistment, and efforts of their officers to secure extended furloughs for them were denied—at a high cost in veterans when enlistments expired. Their stations were among the most lonely and isolated in the country. Their mere service at such posts should have merited honorable mention. For the first few years, poor meals were almost constant companions of black troopers. The post garden at Fort Davis had failed to produce vegetables three out of the past five years. By 1871, however, meals were improving. This was largely because troopers were tending a five-acre garden that was producing "all kinds of vegetables including Irish and sweet potatoes and melons."[35]

Still the surgeon at Fort Concho saw little improvement and complained that the food remained inferior to that provided at other posts. The bread

33 Shafter to H. Clay Wood, AAG, Department of Texas, July 15, 1871, SLR.
34 Post Returns, Fort McKavett, September 1871; *Army and Navy Journal* 9 (December 2, 1871): 243.
35 Wooster, *History of Fort Davis,* 199.

was sour, the beef of poor quality, and the canned peas unfit to eat. Also lacking were the staples common at other forts—molasses, canned tomatoes,
dried apples, dried peaches, sauerkraut, and onions. The butter was made of
suet, and there was only enough flour for the officers. Certainly the worn-out
troopers coming in to Concho after days or weeks in the field had no antici-
pations of enjoying a sumptuous repast as a reward for their efforts.[36]

As for the education and uplift that the army through its chaplains was
supposed to provide, the Ninth was so widely dispersed over seven forts in
West Texas that any attempt to provide systematic education was hopeless.
Moreover, as one authority notes, the regiment's two chaplains, John C.
Jacobi and Manuel Gonzales, "were in such bad health (or so uninterested)
that they spent two-thirds of their time on sick leave."[37]

Opportunities for recreation in the soldiers' off-hours were singularly
lacking at their posts, a grave problem given the boring nature of much of
the construction work that consumed their days when they were not in the
field. Not until the mid-1880s, however, would the army seek to improve
leisure-time activities as a way of improving military morale. Until then,
soldiers of the Ninth might find time for some off-duty hunting or fishing,
although their participation in baseball and track-and-field contests,
increasingly popular among infantrymen by the early 1870s, was too time
consuming for them at this point in their history. And though black soldiers
had reputations for lower rates of alcoholism than other men in the western army, boredom drove some to overindulge in spirits or into furtive
games of monte or other gambling, which was forbidden in their barracks.

Off-post recreation, of the unwholesome and dangerous sort, was available in the sordid little towns that blossomed around the posts, but a black
soldier had no cause to seek trouble—it was awaiting him. If a trooper was
unfortunate enough to lose his life in a clash with a white citizen, his
comrades could hardly expect that justice would be served. One citizen,
John Jackson, a settler near Fort McKavett, murdered a black infantryman,
Private Boston Henry, in cold blood; long eluded the law; and in the process
shot and killed Corporal Albert Marshall and Private Charles Murray of
Captain Carroll's F Company. When finally apprehended and brought to
trial, a jury quickly set him free.[38]

36 Medical History, Fort Concho, vol. 404, Medical History of Posts, AGO, RG 94, NA.
37 Kenner, *Buffalo Soldiers and Officers of the Ninth Cavalry*, 14–18.
38 Dobak and Phillips, *Black Regulars*, 84, 146; Organizational Returns, Ninth Cavalry,
February 1870; Haley, *Fort Concho and the Texas Frontier*, 264.

Discipline remained severe. A buffalo soldier in the Ninth could expect little mercy at the hands of a court-martial, even for trivial offenses. Drunkenness while on duty, for example, brought a dishonorable discharge and one year at hard labor. Privates George Perry and Richard Talbot, both of Company I, received that same sentence for, in Perry's case, purloining a jar of candy from a saloon, while Talbot had stolen one dollar from a civilian. Private William Tolliver of Company A took a catnap on guard duty and paid for his leisure with a stint of six months in the post guardhouse. Private John Curtis of H spent two months at hard labor for telling his sergeant to "go to hell" when ordered to help feed the company horses.

Incidents that involved women at frontier posts were more complicated, given the fears of black male sexuality that lurked beneath the surface. When Private Andy Clayton of H was charged with entering the quarters of laundress Mrs. Lydia Brown, drawing a knife, and threatening, "I cut you if you don't undress and let me sleep with you," the verdict favored Clayton. Two prosecution witnesses failed to appear at the trial, and another soldier in Company H testified that Clayton had been ill and on his bunk the night he purportedly accosted Lydia Brown. Thus the court found Clayton not guilty.[39]

In 1872, however, the wife of Lieutenant Fred Kendall shot and killed a man crawling in her bedroom window while her husband was on detached duty. The dead man was Corporal Daniel Talliferro of the Ninth Cavalry. The officers and their wives at Fort Davis concluded that Talliferro had intended to rape Mrs. Kendall, although he might have been intent on robbery. Whatever the dead man's motivation, the event was a severe setback for the buffalo soldiers. As one historian notes, the incident "marked the nadir of officer-enlisted man relations."[40]

He might have added that it was also a setback to the buffalo soldiers' standing with civilians and their common desire to win respect. Many whites, exhibiting the racial prejudice common at that time, believed that black men lusted after white women and would give vent to their desires if they were not strictly controlled. That unfortunate belief—a projection of white fantasies and bias—fueled the misgivings that many whites still harbored regarding the question of allowing blacks to serve in the armed forces. Military service meant that, clad in army blue, they carried a U.S. Army–issued weapon and sat astride a U.S. Army–issued horse.

39 Cases tried by a general court-martial at Fort Concho, Texas, July 1874, SLR Relating to Texas, AGO, RG 94, NA; Stallard, *Glittering Misery*, 110.
40 Kenner, *Buffalo Soldiers and Officers of the Ninth Cavalry*, 58–59.

Once these soldiers moved into the field, violent death was always near at hand. Even then, despite the risk to their lives and their many military accomplishments, prejudice often robbed them of recognition and some-times even of simple justice.

Taken as a whole, such conditions could have demoralized any regiment, yet morale in the Ninth Cavalry remained high. Desertion, the curse of the frontier army, dwindled steadily to the point that the regiment's rate was the lowest of any unit on the frontier. Proud, tough, and confident, the Ninth was the equal of any similar combat unit in the country. It needed to be, for its most trying years were still ahead.[41]

Conditions along the Rio Grande, turbulent and bloody for years, wors-ened in the 1870s. Control by the Mexican government was loose at best, and its border states of Tamaulipas, Nuevo León, Coahuila, and Chihuahua were fertile breeding grounds for revolutionary activity, particularly as Porfirio Diaz and his followers undermined and then overthrew the govern-ment of Sebastián Lerdo de Tejada in 1876.[42] Border chieftains with large ambitions were numerous, and their activities were often indistinguishable from outright banditry. Their lust for blood, pillage, and cattle theft was seldom if ever satiated, and thus, these leaders were a menace to their own countrymen and to citizens of the United States.

To make a bad situation worse, the river country was plagued with young desperadoes who had fought in the Civil War, become accustomed to vio-lence, and according to one observer, "had carried the habit into civil life." Gambling, stealing, killing, and drinking were a way of life, and often these men combined in such numbers as to overawe civilian authorities. If they had qualms about killing one of their own kind, they had none about killing a Mexican. They qualified their common brag concerning the number of their victims by indicating they were not counting Mexicans. This feeling was shared in reverse by many a Mexican "hardcase" who felt that killing a Texan merited a medal.[43]

By 1872 the activities of bandits, desperadoes, and revolutionaries, when combined with those of marauding Indians, drove law-abiding citizens and state officials to the brink of despair. Losses in cattle and horses ran into the

41 House, H. Exec. Doc. 1, 45th Cong., 2d sess., pt. 2, p. 49.
42 See Knapp, *Sebastian Lerdo de Tejada;* Parkes, *History of Mexico,* 283–84.
43 Governor Richard Coke of Texas to President Grant, May 29, 1875, LR, Affairs on the Rio Grande and Texas Frontier, Consolidated File 1653, AGO, RG 94, NA [hereafter cited as File 1653].

thousands; ranches were looted and their owners shot down. Post offices and customhouses were systematically robbed, and murders so frequent as to be commonplace. Many officials charged with enforcing the law were either in league with the lawbreakers or too fearful of reprisals to make the effort. If culprits were apprehended, prosecutors were afraid to prosecute and juries unwilling to convict. Little wonder that Governor Richard Coke could write to President Grant that he feared the whole country between the Nueces River and the Rio Grande would be depopulated.[44]

Brigadier General C. C. Augur, who in November 1871 succeeded General Reynolds as commanding general, Department of Texas, now faced this ugly situation. Aware that the spring of 1872 would bring Indian braves pouring south from the reservations in Indian Territory in search of buffalo—especially if the promised annuities were slow or not forthcoming, as they so often were—Augur made the best possible disposition of the troops available to him. The whole of the Fourth Cavalry under Colonel Ranald S. Mackenzie was sent to West Texas, while Merritt was ordered to rotate the companies of the Ninth counterclockwise southeastward so as to bring the bulk of the regiment along the line of the Rio Grande. Supporting the cavalry were the Twenty-fourth and Twenty-fifth Infantry. Thus disposed, the troops formed a vast fourteen-hundred-mile arc stretching from just south of the Red River to near the mouth of the Rio Grande.[45]

On April 16, 1872, in obedience to these orders, Merritt and his staff, the regimental band, and Companies A and H, left Fort Stockton to take up headquarters at Fort Clark. On the afternoon of April 20, the command reached Howard's Well along the San Antonio El Paso road to find the still-smoldering remains of a contractor's train. Bodies of men, women, and children were strewn about, some of them burned to a cinder. All the animals of the train were missing.

Captain Cooney with Company A took up the pursuit immediately, with Lieutenant F. R. Vincent and H close behind. The trail led into a valley, up which both companies advanced in parallel ranks. Many of the men were raw recruits, and the veterans gave instructions while on the march. Shortly, the Indians responsible were found entrenched on steep rocky slopes. The troopers began the ascent but were greeted with a withering volley that

44 Ibid.; "Report of the AG of the State of Texas for the Year 1875," ibid.; N. H. Davis to Inspector General R. B. Marcy, May 14, 1875, ibid.
45 *Annual Report of the Secretary of War for the Year 1872*, 54–55; Organizational Returns, Ninth Cavalry, January–April 1872.

killed or wounded nine horses. Cooney's mount fell, pinning its rider, then rose and started dragging him. Only quick action by trumpeter William Nelson and Private Isaac Harrison saved their commander's life.

Cooney withdrew, had the men dismount, and then advanced to fight on foot. Once more the attempt was made to climb the rugged slopes, and once again the Indians leveled a heavy fire. Lieutenant Vincent was shot through both legs and bled profusely, but wishing to set an example for his green troopers, he refused to leave the field. Darkness fell, and still the stubborn foe held their positions. With water exhausted and ammunition running low, Cooney was forced to order a retreat to Howard's Well, with four troopers carrying the dying Vincent in a blanket.

In camp was Marcella Sera, captured during the attack on the train, who had made her escape during Cooney's fight. More than one hundred Indians had struck the train with devastating force and overwhelmed the defenders. Eight men had been tied to wagon wheels and burned to death. Sera, the lone captive, had been forced to watch while her husband, small child, and mother suffered agonizing deaths. The woman told Merritt that four Indians had been killed in the attack and that Cooney had killed six more. She believed, mistakenly as it turned out, that the war party had come from Mexico.

Next morning, Merritt buried eleven bodies and believed others had been burned to ashes. This grim task accomplished, he had little other choice than to move on to Fort Clark, for rations were barely sufficient to see the command to that post, ammunition was nearly exhausted, and he was encumbered by a large quantity of baggage.[46]

The repulse at Howard's Well gave rise to charges, based on unfounded rumors, which the *San Antonio Herald* promulgated. Despite the earlier

46   Merritt to the AAAG, Department of Texas, April 29, 1872, SDLR, AGO, RG 94, NA; Captain Cooney to PA, Fort Clark, Texas, May 9, 1872, ibid.. The raiders were Kiowas and Comanches under White Horse and Big Bow. Affidavit of Marcella Sera to Lieutenant Patrick Cusack, June 20, 1872, ibid. Michael Cooney was one of the ablest company commanders in the Ninth. A native of Ireland and a professional soldier, he enlisted in the regular army in 1856 and was a private in the Sixth Cavalry at the outbreak of the Civil War. He rose to a captaincy in the Fifth Cavalry by the end of the war and was commissioned a first lieutenant in the Ninth Cavalry in July 1866. He remained with the regiment until December 1888, when he transferred to the Fourth Cavalry with the rank of major. Heitman, *Historical Register,* 1:325. Lieutenant Vincent, a Missourian, rose through the ranks to a captaincy in the Missouri State Cavalry during the Civil War. He was appointed second lieutenant in the Ninth in June 1867 and promoted to first lieutenant in July 1869. Heitman, *Historical Register,* 1:967.

comment of praise, it objected to the presence of black soldiers in Texas and now carried allegations that eight buffalo soldiers had deserted and had joined the Kiowa attack, while the black troopers generally had "behaved badly." Four years later the newspaper would print the unfounded allegation that the black troopers had fought only after their officers had drawn their pistols.[47]

Following Howard's Well, raids and depredations increased, but despite the truly valiant attempts of the Ninth to catch those responsible, interceptions were rare. Merritt was convinced that Mexican citizens aided both bandits and Indians. The pattern seldom varied. Raiders struck, his troopers pursued a trail taking the most direct route to the Rio Grande, and there pursuit had to stop. According to Merritt, the Mexicans never seemed to bother the thieves.[48]

On occasion there was a bit of good fortune. In August Captain Dodge and a detachment of D Company were returning to Fort Stockton after escorting a herd of cattle to the Seven Rivers country of New Mexico. Near the post they discovered a fresh trail and after a short pursuit closed quickly upon an Indian camp. The warriors fled, leaving all their property behind. With great gusto the troopers destroyed twenty tepees and all their contents with the exception of one item for each man—Indian bonnets, which they wore gaily as they trotted into Fort Stockton.[49]

Ill feeling and lack of cooperation hurt law-abiding citizens on both sides of the river. In December 1872 a band of American renegades attacked the small village of Resurrección in Mexico. As soon as the news reached Fort Clark, Lieutenant Cusack and a strong detachment marched to the west bank of the Rio Grande opposite the village and managed by signals to induce the alcalde to come down to the riverbank. Cusack tried to obtain information about the raid by shouting across the river, but the alcalde's reply was so sarcastic that Cusack felt himself accused of having inspired the attack.[50]

Revolutionaries were an increasing headache to the Ninth and kept patrols constantly on the lookout. Captain C. D. Beyer with Company C, working out to Fort McIntosh, should have received a decoration from the Mexican government for his efforts. He seemed to have a "nose for revolu-

47 Kenner, *Buffalo Soldiers and Officers of the Ninth Cavalry,* 57.
48 Merritt to the AAAG, Department of Texas, November 29, 1872, SDLR.
49 *San Antonio Weekly Express,* August 27, 1878; Organizational Returns, Ninth Cavalry, August 1872.
50 Cusack to the PA, Fort Clark, Texas, December 2, 1872, SDLR.

tionaries" and consistently located, arrested, and disarmed rebel leaders and their followers. In December he gathered up seven officers and thirty-seven privates in one swoop and learned that their commanding officer was in Mexico with an equal number of men. Beyer haunted the area for a week and had the pleasure of picking up a colonel and forty enlisted men.[51]

General Augur probably spoke for every officer and man of the Ninth when he noted in his annual report for 1872: "The labor and privations of troops in this Department are both severe. The cavalry particularly are constantly at work, and it is a kind of work too that disheartens, as there is very little to show for it. Yet their zeal is untiring, and if they do not always achieve success they always deserve it. I have never seen troops more constantly employed."[52]

"Constantly employed" was an apt description of the buffalo soldiers. There were no indications of any change, for conditions along the Rio Grande did not improve, and Augur shifted five companies of the Ninth still farther downriver.

Colonel Hatch returned to his regiment in March 1873 and established headquarters at Ringgold Barracks. Companies B, C, G, H, and L were quartered at Ringgold with detachments thrown out for miles along the river guarding crossings. Of necessity, the other companies of the regiment were scattered at Forts Concho, Stockton, Davis, and McKavett to fend off Kiowa and Comanche war parties and to keep the El Paso road open.[53]

Less than half a regiment supported by a few companies of infantry was woefully inadequate to cope with the Rio Grande troubles, while conditions on the northwestern frontier of Texas remained far from satisfactory. Augur, after conferences with General Sheridan, transferred the Fourth Cavalry to Fort Clark. In April, during a meeting with General Sheridan, Colonel Mackenzie was given carte blanche to cross the Rio Grande if in his opinion circumstances warranted such action.[54] On May 16 Mackenzie received word that a fresh trail had been discovered near the river. He set out at once from Fort Clark with six companies of his regiment, eighteen Seminole Negro scouts under Lieutenant John L. Bullis of the Twenty-fourth Infantry, and a few civilians.

51 *Annual Report of the Secretary of War for the Year 1872,* 58.
52 Ibid., 59–60.
53 Organizational Returns, Ninth Cavalry, March 1873.
54 For an account of this exchange, see Pierce, *Most Promising Young Officer,* 124–25.

The trail led to the Rio Grande, which was crossed, and the pursuit continued into Mexico. Early on the morning of May 18, Mackenzie surprised and destroyed three Indian villages, killing nineteen warriors and capturing forty women and children, the Lipan chief Castillitos, and sixty-five ponies. Mackenzie was back at Fort Clark before surprised Mexican officials could intercept him. Strong protests by their government failed to move President Grant, who supported his vigorous commander.[55]

Augur reported optimistically that Mackenzie's raid had done much to quiet the Rio Grande frontier, but this was not so. A single raid, nineteen dead Indians, and a few captives scarcely brought a new order of things. If so, the buffalo soldiers—who had longed to make just such a raid—failed to feel or perceive it. There were many times more than nineteen hostile Indians, bandits, and white renegades menacing the border. Certainly there were more than enough to keep the troopers in the saddle from morning until night. And they were still not permitted to cross that frustrating ribbon of water to overtake their tormentors.[56]

For two more long, grim, and frustrating years, Hatch and nearly half his regiment sought to bring peace and order to a tortured border. They did succeed in cutting down on cattle losses and breaking up bands of outlaws, but conditions remained so bad as to defy description. The country for thirty miles back from the river was a brush jungle, and the population lived on either side of the Rio Grande as convenience or necessity suited them. Small parties organized, stole, killed, plundered, and swiftly dispersed. Such lawlessness was almost impossible to prevent, and spies were everywhere reporting on the location and movement of troops. In this witch's brew, the raiding Indian was never far away.[57]

Detachments of the Ninth could not be everywhere, but to their everlasting credit they tried. Patrols moved from ranch to ranch, from river

55 Carter, *On the Border with Mackenzie,* 416; Mackenzie to the AAG, Department of Texas, SDLR. See also Pierce, *Most Promising Young Officer,* 125–37. Ringgold Barracks, headquarters for the Ninth for more than two years, was situated a short distance below Rio Grande City. Established in 1848, the post was named for Captain Samuel Ringgold, Third U.S. Artillery, who was killed at the battle of Palo Alto during the Mexican War. Federal troops evacuated it in March 1861 and reoccupied in June 1865. The name was changed to Fort Ringgold in December 1878. Frazer, *Forts of the West,* 158–59.

56 C. C. Augur to the AAG, Military Division of the Missouri, September 30, 1873, SDLR. Some historians have gone overboard about the importance of the Mackenzie raid, even indicating it brought a new era along the border. See Haley, *Fort Concho and the Texas Frontier,* 210–13.

57 Major James Wade, Ninth Cavalry, to the AAG, Department of Texas, File 1653.

crossing to river crossing, in constant motion. Others were stationed at or near the small border towns, where according to one observer, the "deputy collectors could not stay a day without troops at those places."[58] When raiders were caught, there was no guarantee of punishment, for local juries showed a decided preference for a verdict of "not guilty."

The Ninth's effectiveness was in no small measure hampered by harassment from local officials who disliked anything in a blue uniform, particularly if blacks wore that uniform. Moreover, some Texas citizens viewed blacks as less than human. In one instance in December 1873, a detachment of buffalo soldiers near Fort Concho was the target of gunfire. Merritt, who investigated the matter, determined that the fire came not from Indians but from Texas cowboys. Earlier he had seen drunken cowboys in the same location riding "below the camp at full speed, yelling and firing their arms. It is a way," he noted, "they have, when under the influence of liquor, of amusing themselves."[59]

Nor were the officers of the Ninth immune from harassment. Among minor nuisances at Fort Ringgold were professional gamblers who infested the post on paydays to relieve the men of their earnings. Hatch was determined to stop the practice and in December 1874 had post guards bring one member of the gambling fraternity, a Mr. James Johnson, to his office. Hatch delivered a tongue-lashing and ordered this dubious pillar of the community off the post.

Promptly, a Starr County grand jury indicted Hatch for "false imprisonment," and he was forced to retain a lawyer to quash the indictment. The attorney general's office refused to countenance payment of the legal fees. Hatch later found himself faced with a suit by his erstwhile legal counsel for five hundred dollars.[60]

Far more serious was an affair the following month. On the evening of January 26, 1875, Sergeant Edward Troutman and four privates of G Company, on patrol out of Ringgold, encamped near the Solis ranch house some sixteen miles from their post. As the troopers prepared their supper, bullets whistled near their heads. Believing the shots had come from the ranch house, Troutman approached and questioned a number of men lounging about. He received evasive answers, noticed the men were all heavily armed, and returned to his camp.

58 Ibid.
59 Quoted in Kenner, *Buffalo Soldiers and Officers of the Ninth Cavalry,* 59.
60 AG to the Secretary of War, January 7, 1875, SDLR.

After discussing the situation with his fellow troopers, Troutman ordered them to mount and move off. They had traveled only a short distance when they were fired upon from ambush. A vicious short-range fight ensued in which Privates Jerry Owsley and Moses Turner were killed. Privates Charley Blackstone and John Fredericks managed to escape into the brush, and Troutman fought his way out of the ambush and returned to Ringgold. The sergeant believed his patrol had killed at least one man and wounded several others.

Early the next morning, an angry Hatch with sixty troopers from Companies B and G and Deputy Sheriff T. Davis marched to the scene of the attack and found the horribly mutilated bodies of Owsley and Turner. In a shack nearby the uniforms and other equipment of the slain men were found. Hatch then moved on to the ranch house and "arrested every suspicious character I could find." Two of those arrested were suffering from bullet wounds. A grand jury at Rio Grande City indicted nine Mexicans for the murders, but only one was tried and quickly acquitted. The remaining eight were permitted to go free.[61]

The affair did not end there. Troutman, Blackstone, and Fredericks, in Rio Grande City to testify for the prosecution, found themselves under arrest and indicted for murder of one of their attackers. Shortly thereafter, Hatch and Lieutenant J. H. French were also indicted—for burglary. They had illegally entered the shack from which they had taken the effects of the murdered Owsley and Turner! Starr County, Texas, took excellent care of its own.

Hatch, French, and the three troopers were eventually cleared of the charges against them but were forced to employ legal counsel and obtain a change of venue to do so. According to their attorney, Stephen Powers, malice in the area toward Hatch and his men was very great, and their indictments stemmed from "gratification of purely local prejudice."[62] If the army high command drew a "water line" for the Ninth, it was also true that the people of the border drew a "color line."

Under such conditions matters could only grow worse, and a report of Captain Francis Moore of Company L was typical of many:

61 Hatch to the AAG, Department of Texas, January 26, 1875; ibid.; Major James Wade to the AAG, Department of Texas, May 12, 1875, File 1653.

62 Attorney Stephen Powers to Major J. G. Boyle, U.S. District Attorney, November 27, 1875, File 1653. A tragic aftermath of this affair occurred at Fort Stockton on April 26, 1876. Private Charley Blackstone shot and killed Private John Fredericks, apparently in a quarrel over attorneys' fees borrowed to secure their release from the murder indictments of the year before. Organizational Returns, Ninth Cavalry, May 1876.

EDINBURG, TEXAS, March 1st, 1875

To the Post Adjutant
Ringgold Barracks
Sir:

On the evening of the 27th instant about 7 P.M. the Sheriff of this county applied to me for a detachment of men to proceed to the ranch of Fulton, about 9 miles below here, a Mexican having just come in and reported that he had seen men firing and running in and around his house and store. I immediately saddled up and with 14 men accompanied the Sheriff arriving at Fulton about 8:45 we found a group of frightened Mexicans, who reported that six men (Mexicans) had attacked the store about dark killing Mr. Fulton and his assistant, a Mexican. The body of the clerk was lying just at the door shot through the head, and Fulton's body about 200 yards distant, also shot through the head. He had evidently run from the store when he had had a struggle with the robbers from one of which he had seized a pistol and wounded one. They robbed his person and with their wounded comrade crossed the river near the ranch. It is not known how much money was taken, a small sum was found in the drawers of a counter, which was probably forgotten in their haste.

It is the general impression that one or more of Fulton's employees were accessories, as there were 7 or 8 men in and around the premises at the time of the attack who tell very contradictory stories, although all of them deny any knowledge of the perpetrators. I placed a detachment of one noncommissioned officer and six privates at the disposition of the Sheriff to assist in taking care of the murdered man's goods. I also offered him as many men as he might require to assist him in making arrests.

Very Respectfully,
Your obedient servt.
FRANCIS MOORE
Capt. 9th Cavalry
Commdg.[63]

---

63 Moore to the PA, Ringgold Barracks, Texas, March 2, 1875, File 1653.

On April 2, Mexican bandits crossed the Rio Grande in great force, surrounded the border town of Roma, and began looting. It required Captain Beyer and his entire Company C to drive them off and free the town. Two weeks later another band struck Carrizo, Texas; murdered the postmaster, D. D. Lovell; robbed his store of seven thousand dollars; and plundered the office of the deputy collector. Once again a detachment of the harried Ninth went in pursuit and was closing fast with the bandits when it was forced to halt on the banks of the Rio Grande.[64]

Shortly after this affair, however, the Ninth gained some measure of revenge and satisfaction, even if indirectly. A body of Mexican bandits carried out a successful cattle raid and was driving a large herd to the river when Captain L. H. McNelly and a company of Texas Rangers on Palo Alto prairie near Brownsville overtook them. McNelly and his men killed twelve of the raiders and recovered more than two hundred head of cattle. A strong relief force of bandits crossed the river to attack the rangers but found itself facing two companies of grim buffalo soldiers and retired quietly to the south side of the Rio Grande.[65]

At this point, Brigadier General E. O. C. Ord replaced General Augur, with instructions not to disperse his troops in small detachments but to keep them at posts in at least company strength. Sherman believed that Ord should call upon sheriffs and local citizens to form posses and send word immediately to military posts as quickly as they discovered that raiders were in the vicinity. Sherman had a lot to learn about cooperation from citizens along the river.[66]

Governor Coke had a more realistic view of how to cope with the situation. He pleaded with President Grant to permit troops to cross into Mexico in pursuit of raiders and punish them wherever caught. Ord agreed with Coke but received unequivocal instructions that no troops were to cross the Rio Grande without express permission from Washington.[67]

Meanwhile, disgusted with lack of local cooperation along the lower river, Secretary of War William Belknap telegraphed Governor Coke that if civil authorities did not stop harassing federal forces, he would remove all troops

64   J. L. Hayes, Customs Collector, to the Secretary of Treasury, May 13, 1875, ibid.; Organizational Returns, Ninth Cavalry, April 1875.
65   Statement of J. P. O'Shaughnessy, June 16, 1875, File 1653.
66   Sherman to Ord, May 1, 1875, ibid.; Ord to the AAG, Military Division of the Missouri, September 10, 1875, ibid.
67   Coke to Grant, May 29, 1875, ibid.; Ord to the AAG, Military Division of the Missouri, November 5, 1875, ibid.

"from that locality." And to lend weight to the threat, Hatch was ordered to transfer his headquarters to Fort Clark and "draw in" outlying companies from Fort Ringgold. These moves preceded a transfer of the Ninth Cavalry from Texas. Sheridan wrote his superiors that the time had come to give officers and men of the regiment some relief. For eight years they had garrisoned the worst posts on the frontier and carried out their duties under the most trying conditions. As a result, Hatch received orders in September 1875 transferring the regiment to the District of New Mexico. The Eighth Cavalry took its place along the Mexican border and soon had the privilege denied the men of the Ninth— permission to cross the Rio Grande in "hot pursuit" of marauders.[68]

68 Belknap to Coke, May 18, 1875, ibid.; Sheridan to Townsend, May 22, 1875, ibid.; Sheridan to Belknap, June 5, 1875, ibid.; Organizational Returns, Ninth Cavalry, September 1875.

The Red River War

The peace, or Quaker, policy of President Grant had failed by 1874, if not before. Many factors had weakened its chances for success. Certain that their culture was superior and with the power to enforce their views, officials of the United States demanded that the Plains Indians and Apaches give up their way of life and live on reservations, where they were expected to become settled Christian farmers.

At the same time, the Grant administration tragically never made the reservation a decent or livable place. Many Indian leaders—such as the late Black Kettle and individuals such as Bull Bear and Tall Bear, who had all signed the Medicine Lodge treaties—sincerely wanted to reach accommodation with the newcomers who demanded their land. They saw that the old ways, which often included stealing horses or livestock as a way of registering protests or, more importantly, as a means of adding to their families' meager rations or diminishing food supply, were becoming increasingly dangerous. But the failure of the U.S. government to keep its word and supply the promised annuities negated their efforts toward ameliorating the differences that arose from cultural misunderstandings and Euro-American ethnocentrism.[1]

The warrior culture among these Indians added to the problems. The Comanches, especially, were "loose knit," and their leaders could not, as one

1 Hoig, *Peace Chiefs*, 83–103; Lamar and Truett, "Greater Southwest and California," 101–3.

authority notes, "restrain young men seeking war honors to establish their credentials in a society that judged a man by the size of his pony herd and the number of scalps collected and coups he had counted."[2] In that mix the ever more rapid destruction of the buffalo as hunters made use of the proliferating railroads angered the Indians of the Great Plains. The loss of the herds spelled the doom of their old way of life. Consequently, growing resentment led to renewed raiding, which convinced many U.S. citizens that the peace policy was a failure. In their view Indians who left their reservations deserved punishment rather than understanding or kindness.

Making matters worse, and despite the continuing efforts of Indian agents and the military's constant vigilance, bootleggers smuggled large quantities of whisky into the Indian camps, and it flowed like water in the spring of 1874. Unlicensed traders, utterly indifferent of consequences, sold late-model arms and ammunition to the Indians in exchange for buffalo robes, cattle, and horses. Arms and whisky in an Indian camp formed an explosive mixture, providing both a stimulus and a means for giving vent to long-standing and smoldering hostilities.[3]

As if that were not enough, white horse-thieves drove the Indians, who prized their ponies and depended on their herds for hunting, almost to the point of frenzy. Agent James Haworth wrote Superintendent Enoch Hoag that the stock stolen by his charges in Texas did not greatly exceed that stolen by Texans from his Indians. Agent John Miles believed that white thieves were the major source of unrest among the Cheyennes and that a raid on an Indian pony herd invariably led to a counter raid by outraged tribesmen.[4]

Predictably, as their ponies grew stronger on the rich plains grass, Comanche and Kiowa raiders left the reservation to raid in Texas. They also served notice on the buffalo soldiers by firing into their stockaded camps along the Red River. When the practice became a habit, a wrathful Lieutenant Colonel John Davidson wrote department headquarters requesting permission to pursue the snipers into the reservation. The request was approved subject to the injunction that great care would be taken to ensure than no innocent Indians suffered. Another string that had fettered the

2 Hagan, *Quanah Parker,* 9.
3 George W. Fox, Indian trader, to Davidson, April 2, 1874, Depredations, Kiowa Files, Indian Archives Division, Oklahoma State Historical Society, Oklahoma City; J. S. Evans to Haworth, April 27, 1874, LR by the Office of Indian Affairs, Kiowa Agency, NA; Battey, *Life and Adventures,* 236.
4 Haworth to Hoag, February 23, 1874, LR by the Office of Indian Affairs, Kiowa Agency; *Annual Report of the Commissioner of Indian Affairs for the Year 1874,* 236.

effectiveness of the Tenth Cavalry had been removed, and the buffalo soldiers were now actively engaged in a series of policing activities that were increasingly arduous for them and their officers.[5]

War parties that raided over hundreds of miles along the Texas frontier often engaged in sniping. Davidson kept his troopers on constant scout and in pursuit of the snipers, as did Lieutenant Colonel George Buell at Fort Griffin. Their initial success in curbing the problem was meager. Captain J. B. Vande Viele's B Company scouted more than five hundred miles in a single month in a vain attempt to corner small bands of hostiles. Captain A. S. B. Keyes, who replaced Captain Foulk as commander of D Company, scoured the Double Mountain country, but the Indians evaded him. Extensive scouts by F and G from Griffin proved fruitless. It was almost worthy of a celebration when L Company struck a small party at the Big Wichita River and recovered a number of stolen horses.[6]

Lieutenant Colonel Wesley Merritt, at Fort Concho with Companies A, D, E, F, and K of the Ninth Cavalry, reported that every trooper able to mount a horse was in the field. He needed more cavalry desperately, but with the critical state of affairs along the Rio Grande, he could not call on Colonel Edward Hatch for additional support. Stepped-up activity from white cattle-rustlers, emboldened by the new opportunities now that the available cavalry was pursuing Indian raiders, complicated Merritt's problems. Lieutenant Patrick Cusack with a detachment of A Company and a citizens' posse from Brownwood had broken up one gang of thieves, and detachments under Sergeants Allsup and Morgan had recovered some stolen stock. But more men were needed to curb the rustlers effectively.[7]

Early in May, an embittered Lone Wolf and a large party of warriors eluded the river patrols and set out to recover the body of Tau-ankia, slain in the fight with Lieutenant C. L. Hudson the previous winter. After finding the remains, the Indians were returning north when they were spotted by a

5 Davidson to the AAG, Department of Texas, April 15, 1874, SLR, Department of Texas, AGO, RG 94, NA.

6 Organizational Returns, Tenth Cavalry, May 1874, AGO, RG 94, NA. Keyes, a native of Massachusetts, rose through the ranks during the Civil War and was promoted to second lieutenant on July 5, 1864. He remained in the service after the war and held the rank of first lieutenant in the Twelfth Infantry until his transfer to the Tenth Cavalry in April 1870. Promoted to captain in December 1873, he remained with the regiment until October 1892, when he transferred to the Third Cavalry. Heitman, *Historical Register,* 1:595.

7 Lieutenant Cusack to the PA, Fort Concho, Texas, February 28, 1864, SDLR, AGO, RG 94, NA; Merritt to the AAG, Department of Texas, December 3, 1873, SLR, Department of Texas.

detachment of Fourth Cavalry under Major H. C. Bankhead and pursued in the direction of Fort Concho. There the Indians obtained fresh horses by stealing twenty-three animals from the herd of Company D, Ninth Cavalry, encamped near the post. Thus mounted, Lone Wolf escaped to the reservation. Detachments under Lieutenants Cusack and M. B. Hughes of the Ninth and Major Bankhead of the Fourth, however, had pursued him so hotly that he was forced to abandon the body of his son. The mission accomplished nothing for the chief except to increase his burning desire for revenge.[8]

Meanwhile on the Cheyenne reservation, white horse-thieves provided the match to explode that Indian powder keg. They stole forty-three prize ponies from the herd of Chief Little Robe. The chief's son set out with a small party of warriors to recover the stock. Failing to find the thieves, they ran off horses and cattle near Sun City, Kansas, to replace their losses. A detachment of the Sixth Cavalry pursued them, and in the skirmish that followed, Little Robe's son was wounded severely. Seeking retaliation, a large body of warriors came to their agency. They reassured the white employees that they would not be harmed, and then after shaking hands, according to one account, "rode off and began killing people."[9]

Late in May the Comanches held a sun dance on the North Fork of Red River. Many Kiowas and an impressive delegation of Cheyennes and Arapahos were also present. They were harangued by a Comanche medicine man, Isatai, who urged a war of revenge on the whites, and his words found ready ears. Most of the Comanches and Cheyennes, and some of the Kiowas, smoked the war pipes, while those who desired to remain at peace moved hastily toward their agencies.

From the sun dance the war parties moved forth to strike the Texas and Kansas frontiers. The Cheyennes killed three men near Medicine Lodge, Kansas, attacked several parties of buffalo hunters along the Canadian River, and placed the Camp Supply–Fort Dodge road under virtual siege. Kiowa and Comanche raiders had every trooper in Indian Territory and West Texas in the saddle and riding hard to fend off attacks.[10]

8 Lieutenant Orleman, Tenth Cavalry, to the PA, Fort Richardson, May 1, 1874, Military Relations, Kiowa Files; *Army and Navy Journal* 11 (June 20, 1874): 708; Captain C. A. Wickoff, Eleventh Infantry, Fort Concho, to Commanding Officer, Fort Sill, May 22, 1874, Military Relations, Kiowa Files.

9 Quoted in Mooney, *Calendar History of the Kiowa*, 199; Berthrong, *Southern Cheyennes*, 383; *Annual Report of the Commissioner of Indian Affairs for the Year 1874*, 233.

10 Haworth to Hoag, May 9, 1874, LR by the Office of Indian Affairs, Kiowa Agency; Battey, *Life and Adventures*, 302–3; *Annual Report of the Commissioner of Indian Affairs*

On June 27 several hundred Comanche, Kiowa, and Cheyenne warriors sought to wipe out a party of buffalo hunters at Adobe Walls on the Main Canadian in the Texas Panhandle. Driven off by accurate rifle fire, they lost nine warriors while killing only three of the hunters. The Cheyennes had better luck nearer their agency, where they killed five men in the first three days of July and caused a frightened Agent Miles to appeal to Davidson for troops. Davidson ordered Lieutenant M. M. Maxon and Company M to the Cheyenne agency. A courier from Fort Sill to the Wichita agency at Anadarko, where Acting Agent J. Connell feared an attack, however, diverted him and his troopers. Miles, without troops for defense, gathered up his employees and made fast tracks for Fort Dodge, where he telegraphed both Commissioner Smith and military authorities apprising them of the outbreak.[11]

The Comanches and some Kiowas, beaten by the buffalo hunters at Adobe Walls, relieved their frustrations with devastating raids into Texas. Lone Wolf achieved the most spectacular success on the afternoon of July 12. With a medicine man, Maman-ti, and about fifty warriors, he ambushed and badly shot up a party of Texas Rangers in Lost Valley northwest of Fort Richardson. One of the rangers managed a daring getaway and reached the post. Captain T. A. Baldwin with I Company galloped to the rescue and reached the scene early on the morning of July 13, but the Indians had drawn off, leaving two rangers dead, two wounded, and twelve horses killed.[12]

Colonel Buell at Fort Griffin sent every trooper at his post after the raiders. Captain P. L. Lee with G, Captain William Kennedy with F, and Lieutenant R. H. Pratt with D cooperated in a five-day search for the hostiles, but the Indians had flown and their trail was lost.[13]

The next day—July 13—Comanches attacked a wood camp less than a dozen miles from Fort Sill. A detachment of the overworked Tenth arrived

for the Year 1874, 220; Haworth to Hoag, June 3, 1874, LR by the Office of Indian Affairs, Kiowa Agency; Post Returns, Camp Supply, June 1874; Organizational Returns, Tenth Cavalry, June 1874; Buell to the AAG, Department of Texas, June 11, 1874, SLR, Department of Texas; *Annual Report of the Secretary of War for the Year 1874,* 30.

11 Davidson to Lieutenant M. M. Maxon, July 6, 1874, SLR, Department of Texas; Leckie, *Military Conquest,* 190–93; Mooney, *Calendar History of the Kiowa,* 203; B. K. Weatherell to Enoch Hoag, July 4, 1874, Depredations, Kiowa Files; *Annual Report of the Commissioner of Indian Affairs for the Year 1874,* 233–34.

12 Webb, *Texas Rangers,* 312–13; Post Returns, Fort Richardson, July 1874, AGO, RG 94, NA; Interpreter Phil McCusker to Lieutenant M. M. Maxon, July 30, 1874, LR, File 3300-1874, AGO, NA [hereafter cited as File 3300-1874].

13 Medical History, Fort Griffin, vol. 103, Medical History of Posts, AGO, RG 94, NA; Post Returns, Fort Griffin, July 1874; Organizational Returns, Tenth Cavalry, July 1874.

in time to deprive the hostiles of fifty-two head of freshly stolen stock and to bury one man who had been killed and scalped. When two more men were killed next day at Elm Spring Station, Davidson, over the protests of Agent Haworth, took decisive action. He telegraphed department headquarters for more cavalry and issued the following general order:

HEADQUARTERS POST OF FORT SILL, I.T.

July 17, 1874

General Orders
   No. 46.

The hostile bands of Comanches, Cheyennes, and Kiowas having committed depredations and murder upon government employees within the Reservation, and within a few miles of the Post, some marked line must be drawn between the hostile and friendly portions of those tribes. In order then that troops and others may be able to distinguish those who are friendly—all such Indians must form their camps on the east side of Cache Creek at points selected by the Agent.

No Indian hereafter will be permitted to approach this post nearer than the Agency, and must come in to the Agency from the east side of Cache creek.

When friendly Indians desire to visit the Post Commander they must come from the direction of the Agency, and with a messenger from the Agent stating the Chief and the number of his party.

J. W. DAVIDSON
Lieut. Col. 10th Cavalry
Bvt. Maj. General USA[14]

Despite the gravity of the situation, an incident on the evening this order was issued provided considerable amusement for the garrison. Horace Jones, the post interpreter, paid a visit to the trader's store and spent several hours drinking with some old cronies. One of Davidson's sentries, a raw recruit fresh from the depot in St. Louis, interrupted his weaving return to the post. He challenged Jones and refused to let him pass. When the inter-

14 General Order No. 46, Fort Sill, July 17, 1874, Military Relations, Kiowa Files. For a summary of Indian depredations near Fort Sill, see Davison to the AAG, Department of Texas, July 20, 1874, LR, File 3144-1874, AGO, NA.

preter indignantly asked why, the trooper replied, "I am sorry, but the new post order says you cannot enter the post unless accompanied by an Indian." A suddenly sobered Mr. Jones made a trip to the guardhouse and provided what was undoubtedly a profane explanation of his visit before being allowed to proceed to his quarters.[15]

The scope of hostile action, so great that it assumed the proportions of a general war, forced the War and Interior Departments to agree on a common policy to cope with the situation. On July 21 General Sherman telegraphed General Sheridan that a decision had been reached. Reservation lines were to be disregarded and hostile Indians pursued and punished wherever they could be found. Great care, however, was to be taken to ensure that the innocent were separated from the guilty. The former were to be enrolled and concentrated at their agencies for their own protection. Sheridan forwarded these instructions to Generals Pope and Augur, and Commissioner Smith so informed the Indian agents.[16]

Davidson received orders on July 26 to proceed immediately with enrollment of the "friendlies" at Fort Sill. The process was completed on August 8. Few Comanches came in, so most of that tribe was regarded as hostile. An overwhelming majority of the Kiowas were enrolled, although the reliability of many was subject to question. Virtually all the Kiowa-Apaches remained at peace. The Arapahos submitted quietly to registration at the Cheyenne agency, but of some two thousand Cheyennes, fewer than three hundred remained on the reservation. Acting Agent Connell at Anadarko had little difficulty enrolling the Wichitas and affiliated tribes but was concerned over Comanche and Kiowa hostiles who lurked in the vicinity.[17]

A few days after enrollment closed, a number of Comanche chiefs sent word to Davidson that they wished to come in. Only one, Assanonica, and his people received permission as all the others, including Big Red Food, a Nokoni, had taken part in the attack on the buffalo hunters at Adobe Walls. These "outs" proceeded forthwith to join the other "out" Comanches near

15 Nye, *Carbine and Lance*, 202.
16 Sherman to Sheridan, July 21, 1874, LR, File 2815-1874, AGO, NA [hereafter cited as File 2815-1874]; Woodward to Grierson, August 8, 1874, GP-ISHS; *Annual Report of the Secretary of War for the Year 1874*, 41; Acting Commissioner of Indian Affairs H. R. Clum to Haworth, August 15, 1874, Depredations, Kiowa Files; Enoch Hoag to Agent Richards, Wichita Agency, July 21, 1874, ibid.
17 Davidson to the AAG, Department of Texas, August 10, 1874, File 3300-1874; *Annual Report of the Commissioner of Indian Affairs for the Year 1874*, 238; Haworth to E. P. Smith, August 17, 1874, LR by the Office of Indian Affairs, Kiowa Agency.

Anadarko. This development made Davidson uneasy, for if these Indians mixed with the friendlies at that agency, he was faced with a delicate situation that might bring great harm to many peaceful Indians.

Shortly, conditions at Anadarko became explosive. Some enrolled Kiowas killed six men in two days near Fort Sill. Many of them, fearing army retaliation, left the agency and joined the hostiles under Lone Wolf. The latter were demanding rations from Connell, stealing food from his Indians, and ignoring his pleas to leave.[18]

Connell consulted with Captain Gaines Lawson, commander of Company I, Twenty-fifth Infantry, the only one manning the post. Both agreed that reinforcements were necessary and the quicker the better. Lawson, therefore, sent an urgent appeal to Davidson. The latter, receiving Lawson's message at six o'clock on the afternoon of August 21, began preparations at once. By ten o'clock that evening, C, E, H, and L under Captains Charles Viele, George T. Robinson, Louis H. Carpenter, and Captain Thomas Little were armed, mounted, and ready to march. Davidson led them out of the post and headed swiftly for Anadarko.

Near noon the next day, Davidson crossed the Washita and entered the agency grounds. The river curled to the south at this point, forming a large arc, which was closed on the north by a range of wooded bluffs. Within this rough rectangle the agency buildings were scattered badly. The agent's house, shops, school, and stables were all under the bluff and a mile from the river. On the bluff to the northwest was the agency sawmill, while Shirley's store was to the northeast. The commissary and corral were near the river.

August 22 was Saturday and issue day at the agency. Most of the Wichitas, Caddos, Pawnees, Delawares, and Penateka Comanches were in or near the commissary, while the camp of Big Red Food was not more than two hundred yards away and close to the Penateka camp. Connell sent at once for Big Red Food, and when the chief arrived Davidson told him that he and his warriors had been given every opportunity to enroll, that they had not done so, and that enrollment had been completed. Now they must surrender, turn over their weapons, and move back to Fort Sill as prisoners of war.

At first the chief was reluctant, but after some urging by Tosh-a-way, a

---

18 Davidson to the AAG, Department of Texas, August 10 1874, File 3300-1874; Haworth to Smith, August 25, 1874, LR, File 3490-1874, AGO, NA [hereafter cited as File 3490-1874]. *Annual Report of the Secretary of War for the Year 1874,* 41. Prominent among those who enrolled and then left for the Wichita Agency were Satanta and Big Tree.

friendly Penateka, he agreed to Davidson's demands. Under escort by Lieutenant Samuel Woodward and forty troopers, he went to his camp to gather
up the weapons. There an argument developed over the surrender of bows
and arrows that the chief wished to retain for hunting purposes. Woodward
hesitated, and then sent a trooper to Davidson for guidance. In the interim
some of Lone Wolf's Kiowas, who were close by, began taunting Big Red
Food and his Nokonis, asking them if they were women and if they intended
allowing a few buffalo soldiers to disarm them.

The chief, no coward, found the jibes too much. Suddenly he gave a loud
whoop, leaped from his pony, and escaped into the brush while a volley
from the troopers whistled around his ears. Hostile Kiowas and the Nokonis returned the fire and the battle was joined. Lawson's infantry, acting
under Davidson's orders, moved at once toward the agency sawmill to cut
off any Indians trying to escape up the Washita, while the latter faced his
companies toward Big Red Food's camp and advanced.

But Davidson found himself in an awkward position. Friendly Indians
were fleeing in all directions, and, having no desire to harm them, he hesitated to open fire. Yet as his troopers moved forward, Kiowa warriors, who
had taken positions behind the commissary and corral, fired into them from
the rear, wounding Sergeant Lewis Mack of H and Private Adam Cork of E.
Some horses were also hit, and Davidson, after swerving his command
abruptly into the thick timber along the river, dismounted to fight on foot.[19]

Captain Little with L moved out and drove the Kiowas from the commissary and corral. Most of these Indians, however, circled Little's right flank,
crossed the river, and headed for the farm and home of a Delaware named
Black Beaver. Carpenter with H Company pursued these Indians, charged,
and routed them, but not before they had killed four men who were in the
fields cutting hay and two more near Black Beaver's home. Davidson
regrouped his command and moved swiftly to protect the agency, now
threatened by a mass of warriors who had gained the bluffs and gutted
Shirley's store. The troopers reached the agency in time to prevent an attack.
As dusk fell, Viele with C Company cleared the bluffs and brought an end
to the day's fighting. During the night Davidson posted detachments at
Shirley's, the commissary, and the agency cornfield. Others destroyed the
camp of Big Red Food and dug trenches on the south side of the river.

19 Davidson to the AAG, Department of Texas, August 27, 1874, File 3490-1874; Augur
to Sheridan, September 13, 1874, ibid.

Lieutenant Henry Flipper
Courtesy of Fort Davis National
Historic Site, Fort Davis, Texas

Colonel William R. Shafter
Courtesy of Fort Davis National
Historic Site, Fort Davis, Texas

General Philip Sheridan
Western History Collections
University of Oklahoma Libraries

Encampment of Tenth Cavalry battalion
Courtesy National Archives

Captain Louis H. Carpenter,
Tenth Cavalry
Courtesy National Archives

Captain Theodore A. Baldwin,
Tenth Cavalry
Courtesy National Archives

Lieutenant Colonel Wesley Merritt,
Ninth Cavalry
Courtesy National Archives

The Indians had not been idle. By early morning nearly three hundred had gathered to recapture the bluff and were beginning the ascent. Captain Carpenter took E, H, and L and drove these warriors off just as they reached the top. Frustrated, the Indians fired the dry grass in an effort to burn the agency. The troopers started counter fires and with much hard work saved the buildings.

The "fire fight" ended the battle of Anadarko. Davidson had four troopers and six horses wounded. He believed that fourteen Indians had been "shot off their horses" and at least four ponies had been killed.[20]

The affair at Anadarko served to clear the air on a number of matters. At least two of these proved shocking to the Indians. The presence of a Quaker agent was no longer a guarantee of immunity, and an agency was no sanctuary in time of bad behavior. A few buffalo soldiers freed from restrictions were nothing to be trifled with—they could fight, and they fought very well. They had not wavered when fired on from the rear. Little's men had advanced on the corrals in steady, even files, Carpenter's H had charged with zest, and Viele's C had ascended and cleared the bluff in a manner that would have pleased even Sherman.

The fight also served to separate clearly the hostile and friendly bands. When news of the fighting reached Fort Sill, nearly all the Indians stampeded, but within less than a month most of them returned. The hostile Kiowas and Comanches moved toward the western reaches of Indian Territory or onto the Staked Plains to join the Kwahadis. The warring Cheyennes were nearby on the edge of the plains and more than two hundred miles southwest of their agency. It was the army's task to find, defeat, and drive these Indians back to their reservations. Once this project had been accomplished, they were to be disarmed and dismounted and their leaders punished.[21]

Sheridan, Augur, and Pope had completed their plans for the campaign in July 1874. Lines separating the Departments of Texas and Missouri were

20 Davidson to the AAG, Department of Texas, August 27, 1874; Augur to Sheridan, September 13, 1874; J. Connell to Miles, August 25, 1874, Military Relations, Cheyenne-Arapaho Files, Indian Archives Division, Oklahoma State Historical Society, Oklahoma City. Connell believed Satanta to be among the Kiowas firing on the troops from the commissary and corral. An excellent account of this fight from the Indian perspective is Nye, *Carbine and Lance*, 206–10.

21 *Annual Report of the Secretary of War for the Year 1874*, 42; Davidson to the AAG, Department of Texas, August 27, 1874; Sherman to Sheridan, July 21, 1874; *Annual Report of the Commissioner of Indian Affairs for the Year 1874*, 234.

to be disregarded and the reservations invaded if necessary. Five strong columns were to converge on the Indians from the north, south, east, and west in a continuing operation until a devastating defeat had been inflicted. One column under Colonel Nelson A. Miles would march south from Fort Dodge toward the headwaters of the Red River, while another commanded by Major William R. Price would move eastward from Fort Bascom, New Mexico, and effect a junction with Miles. A third command under Colonel Ranald Mackenzie would sweep the Staked Plains northwest of Fort Concho and establish contact with Miles. The buffalo soldiers formed the backbone of the remaining two columns. One of these, largely of Ninth Cavalry under Lieutenant Colonel Buell, was concentrated at Fort Griffin, and the other organized at Fort Sill by Colonel Davidson. Buell and Davidson were to operate between Miles and Mackenzie and drive the hostiles westward into their paths.[22]

All five commands were scheduled to take the field in August, but the trouble at Anadarko and a delay in receiving supplies detained Buell and Davidson. It was not until early September that they were ready to march. Meanwhile, the columns of Miles, Price, and Mackenzie had proceeded as planned.

Miles set out on August 14 and in torrid weather pushed far southward to the Salt Fork of the Red River. There, on August 30, he overtook and drove a large body of Cheyennes out onto the Staked Plains. His command was too used up and supplies too low to follow them, so he retraced his steps to the Canadian and established a supply camp at that stream as well as others along the Washita and Sweetwater. From these camps he kept a number of small columns in constant motion and prevented any Indians from escaping to the north.

Price accomplished very little. He left Fort Bascom on August 28 and reached Miles on September 7 as the latter was falling back to the Canadian. He then moved northward to find his train, which he had earlier sent toward the Antelope Hills. On September 12 he stumbled into a mass of Kiowas and Comanches near the Dry Fork of the Washita and fought to a standstill.

22 Pope to Sheridan, July 27, 1874, SLR, Department of Texas; Miles to the AAG, Department of the Missouri, March 4, 1875, File 3490-1874; *Annual Report of the Secretary of War for the Year 1874*, 40; Post Returns, Fort Sill, August–September 1874; Post Returns, Fort Griffin, August–September 1874; Woodward to Grierson, August 12, 1874, GP-ISHS.

From this fight Price marched on to the Canadian, where he merged his force with that of Miles.[23]

The operations of Miles and Price assisted Mackenzie in scoring a spectacular success. The latter left Fort Concho on August 23 and set out to scour the Staked Plains northwest of that post. On September 25 his scouts located a large Indian camp in Palo Duro Canyon along the Prairie Dog Town Fork of the Red River. Mackenzie found a trail leading into the canyon, effected a complete surprise, and routed a large force of Kiowas, Comanches, and Cheyennes, many of whom had taken refuge there from Miles's columns. Mackenzie inflicted few casualties, but he captured and destroyed huge quantities of supplies as well as a pony herd of more than one thousand animals. Until the end of the year, his command remained in the field scouting the breaks of the Red River and the headwaters of the Brazos.[24]

Buell left Fort Griffin on September 1 and marched for Fort Sill, which he reached a week later. There he completed the organization of his command and loaded supplies on thirty wagons drawn by six-mule teams. He moved out of Sill on September 24 and five days later established a supply camp along the North Fork of the Red River a few miles above the mouth of Otter Creek. At the supply camp, final plans were made, and the command divided into two battalions. Major Albert P. Morrow commanded the first, consisting of Companies A, E, F, and K, Ninth Cavalry, while Companies A and E, Tenth Cavalry, formed the second under Captain Nicholas Nolan. Each battalion had a few Tonkawa scouts, and two companies of the Eleventh Infantry guarded the train.

On the morning of October 3, the columns got under way with twenty-five days' rations. Each trooper carried forty rounds of carbine and twenty rounds of pistol ammunition. The only equipment allowed consisted of an overcoat, a poncho, a shelter tent, and one change of socks and underwear carried on the horses. Almost immediately fresh pony tracks were found,

23   Miles's command consisted of Companies A, D, F, G, H, I, L, and M, Sixth Cavalry, and Companies C, D, E, and I, Fifth Infantry—some 750 men. On September 9 the same hostiles who fought Price hit and badly mauled his supply trains. Price had four companies of the Eighth Cavalry, two howitzers, and a few Navaho scouts. For details, see Miles to the AAG, Department of the Missouri, March 5, 1874, File 3490-1874; and Price to the AAG, Department of the Missouri, September 23, 1874, File 2815-1874.

24   Mackenzie had eight companies of the Fourth Cavalry, four companies of the Tenth Infantry, one company of the Eleventh Infantry, and about thirty Tonkawa Indian scouts. His campaign is well described in Carter, *On the Border with Mackenzie,* 473–506. For official reports, consult File 2815-1874.

and shortly thereafter a small party of warriors was sighted and pursued. The Indians made their escape but lost two horses in the process.

Five days of uneventful marching followed, but late on October 8 one of the Tonkawa scouts came in to report that he had "shaken hands with a Comanche some twenty mile toward the south." Buell pushed on with greater speed, and before the day ended his advance overtook and killed a Kiowa warrior who was spying on the column. The trails led toward the Salt Fork of the Red River. On the afternoon of the ninth, a small party of warriors was sighted well to the front. Captain Ambrose Hooker with E of the Ninth charged them at a gallop and killed one warrior before the others vanished in the breaks along the Salt Fork. When the rest of the command came up, a deserted Indian camp of fifteen lodges was found and destroyed.

Here Buell waited impatiently for his train to come up, for signs indicated a large body of Indians was within striking distance. When the wagons finally arrived the following day, the decision was made to cut loose from them in order to march as swiftly as possible. Early on October 11 the pursuit was taken up. The command pushed relentlessly through the rough breaks and canyons along the Salt Fork and then northwest to the edge of the Staked Plains, where a deserted camp of seventy-five lodges was destroyed. The trail now led across the plains toward the headwaters of McClellan Creek and grew rapidly in size as small parties joined from both flanks. The track was also easy to follow since it had been littered with abandoned camp equipage and worn-out ponies as the fleeing Indians sought to shake off their dogged foe.

On the morning of October 12, Buell expected to find the Indians and either bring them to bay or drive them into either Miles or Mackenzie. By midafternoon, however, he came upon a huge but abandoned camp of 475 lodges. By torching the village, he destroyed all of the Indians' tents, clothing, food, and utensils, making it far more likely that, even if they were not caught, homelessness and starvation would force them onto a reservation.[25]

In the meantime, the Indians were undoubtedly heading for the Canadian, but the command was nearly out of supplies and the horses were nearing exhaustion. Buell encamped and conferred with Morrow and Nolan. Both were loath to give up the chase without a decisive action; their rugged troopers were full of spirit and eager to push on. Thus, they continued the

25 Robert Utley views this scorched-earth policy as the post–Civil War army's application of the principles of total war. See Utley, *Cavalier in Buckskin*, 57–38.

pursuit while couriers rode hard for Fort Sill to request that a train with forty days' rations be dispatched at once.

The column moved on northward, but on the evening of October 13, the couriers returned with disturbing news. A party of twenty-five warriors had intercepted and pursued them, and they were fortunate to get back to the main body with their hair. Buell was thoroughly alarmed. Indians might well have overwhelmed his lightly guarded train, which was far to the rear. There was no other choice than a forced night march along the return trail, and before daybreak the train was found. Much to the relief of all, it had not been attacked.

Private Williams of E Company, Tenth Cavalry, and one of the scouts were sent into Fort Sill with the request for rations. The command now plodded back to the camp of the night before. Hardly had the animals been turned out to graze when firing was heard to the rear, and Buell was informed that his scouts were engaging a party of comancheros. This report proved false, for in the poor evening light, the Tonkawa scouts had actually opened fire on one of Miles's detachments. The screech of a howitzer shell over their heads informed them of their error.

From the officer commanding the detachment, Buell learned of Miles's position, which was to the front and right along the Canadian and about two days' march. Buell had driven several hundred Indians into Miles, and both were now following the same parties. He pressed on with horses so weak the men were forced to walk at least half the time and reached the Canadian on October 16. The Indians had scattered in all directions. Buell sent the Tonkawas to locate the main body and ordered Major Morrow to be ready with one hundred picked men to take up the chase if the hostiles were found.

A bewildering maze of trails defied the best efforts of the scouts, but indications were that many of the Indians had curled around the column's left flank and fled back southward. Buell at this point was three hundred miles from his base and in desperate need of forage and rations. A courier hastened down the Canadian seeking Miles while the command followed as rapidly as the condition of the animals would allow. Considerable difficulty was encountered in locating Miles, who proved to be on the Washita, and his camp was not reached until October 24.[26]

26 Buell to Miles, October 18, 1874, File 2815-1874; Buell to the AAG, Department of Texas, November 8, 1874, ibid.

With his needs partially satisfied, Buell wasted no time in ceremony but threw out his scouts and marched south to the Sweetwater, where the broken-down animals were sent on to the supply camp at the Salt Fork. While at the Sweetwater, Captain Viele with C Company of Davidson's column came in. Buell now learned that a large body of Indians had surrendered to Davidson at Elk Creek about forty miles to the front and that scouting reports indicated still other Indians were moving toward the Wichita agency to surrender.

Buell saddled up at once and marched to Elk Creek, where a large trail was struck leading east. Major Morrow with A, D, and E of the Ninth was detached to follow the trail and make certain it was made by the band that had surrendered to Davidson. The rest of the column continued on south until it met a supply train on November 4. The command reorganized while taking a much-needed rest. By November 16, however, Buell was on the move again with eighty buffalo soldiers, while the remaining men went in to Fort Sill.

Buell's intention was to scout the headwaters of the Red River, but he soon encountered "as severe weather as I have ever experienced" and was forced to hole up along the banks of the Salt Fork. The storm subsided somewhat on November 22, and he sent a detachment under Lieutenant Gustavus Valois to scout along the Red while the main column continued along the Salt Fork. Next day a deserted village of twenty-two lodges was found, along with a quantity of horsemeat. The harried Indians had been reduced to killing and eating their ponies. After destroying the village, pursuit was undertaken in the face of a heavy snowstorm, which soon turned to driving rain and stinging sleet. Doggedly, the column pushed on, turned northward, and headed for Miles's supply camp.

But Buell and his troopers were reaching the limits of their endurance, and as the weather grew steadily worse, they soon found themselves fighting to advance in the teeth of a howling blizzard. It was too much; the buffalo soldiers were not clothed for this kind of weather, and many of them were almost bootless. The column was forced to turn back to the supply train, which they found only after a considerable search on December 3. Shortly thereafter, Valois came in with his men badly frostbitten and the animals completely used up. He had gone well up the Red when the storm struck and turned him back.

Buell had demanded and gotten an almost superhuman effort from his black troopers, and he could ask no more. He broke up the expedition and moved in to Fort Griffin. In his official report, Buell, ever sparse with praise, gave the buffalo soldiers a well-earned accolade: "I cannot give them too much credit for manly endurance without complaint."[27]

Buell's expedition was a devastating blow to the Indians. Although their casualties included only two warriors, the expedition—an example of the principles of total war applied to American Indians—had destroyed nearly six hundred lodges, tons of supplies, and much camp equipment. The grim, relentless pursuit broke down scores of Indian ponies and, more important, the will to resist of hundreds of Kiowas, Comanches, and Cheyennes. Totally impoverished, they had no choice but to come on to the reservation. The campaign contributed materially to the success of Mackenzie, Miles, and Davidson, yet curiously it received little notice. This treatment may have been strange to Buell, but it was an old story to the cheerful and willing buffalo soldiers. These soldiers were determined to prove that they were second to no other men in their country when it came to performing their duties and exhibiting fortitude and courage.

The fight at Anadarko and the necessity for providing an adequate garrison at the Wichita agency delayed Davidson for nearly three weeks. Not until September 10 was the Fort Sill column ready to move. It consisted of Companies B, C, H, K, L, and M, Tenth Cavalry; three companies of the Eleventh Infantry; a section of mountain howitzers; and forty-four Indian scouts under Lieutenant Pratt. Forty-six wagons carried a three weeks' supply of rations and forage.[28]

The long column marched northward to the Washita, which was found "bankfull" from recent rains. Davidson's plan was to follow the twisting course of the river northwestward and locate any Indians who might be between his command and that of Miles. If this action proved unproductive, he intended to search along the North Fork of the Red River and McClellan's Creek. His force also might scout the eastern base of the Staked Plains in the hope of driving hostiles into Mackenzie's arms or catching any that Mackenzie might be driving eastward.

27 Buell to the AAG, Department of Texas, February 24, 1875, SLR, Department of Texas; Organizational Returns, Ninth and Tenth Cavalry, September–December 1874; *Army and Navy Journal* 12 (December 26, 1874): 308.

28 Woodward to Grierson, August 12, 1874, GP-ISHS; Post Returns, Fort Sill, September 1874; Organizational Returns, Tenth Cavalry, September 1874.

Davidson marched westward on September 12 with scouts and detachments thrown far out in order to sweep an area forty-miles wide. No trails or Indians were seen until September 17, when Pratt's scouts captured a lone Kiowa with three head of stock. Two days later a detachment found one of Miles's camps at the Sweetwater, and Davidson moved his whole command to that point and bivouacked while couriers rode out to Miles, who was then along the Washita. Miles came in on September 22 and conferred with Davidson, while the men of the command "washed up and refitted."

From this camp Davidson turned south and crossed the North Fork of the Red, while Pratt and his scouts probed the heads of that stream and McClellan Creek. On September 25 Pratt found a large herd of buffalo and had his scouts kill a number of them to supply the command with fresh meat. As he was moving off to rejoin Davidson, a lone Indian was sighted some distance to the rear and was quickly pursued, overtaken, and captured. He proved to be a Cheyenne who had mistaken the pony tracks of Pratt's scouts for those of his own people and had ridden virtually into the column before discovering his mistake.[29]

For a week Davidson's troopers toiled south along the edge of the Staked Plains and into the breaks of Mulberry Creek and Red River "through some of the most broken country I ever saw," according to Davidson's report. When no trace of Indians was found, Captain Caleb Carleton with about two hundred troopers was detached to locate Buell and Mackenzie. A forty-eight-hour search proved fruitless, and Carleton rejoined the main command. By this time the men were on half-rations, forage was exhausted, and the grass scarce, so Davidson decided to turn toward Fort Sill. On October 2, while marching eastward along Red River, a band of Kiowas was surprised and pursued, but the troopers' worn-out animals were too weak to close the gap, and the Indians escaped. The march continued to Herd Creek, about seven miles south of Fort Sill, and the men went into camp to rest and refit. Davidson had little to show for his efforts but fifty-eight dead horses and mules. A tragic footnote was added to the campaign on October 16, when 1st Lieutenant Silas Pepoon of B Company, in a fit of despondency, shot and killed himself.[30]

29 Pratt, *Battlefield and Classroom*, 68–69.
30 Davidson to the AAG, Department of Texas, October 10, 1874, SLR, Department of Texas; Organizational Returns, Tenth Cavalry, October 1874. Pepoon was one of the original cadre of officers assigned to the Tenth.

By October 21 Davidson, resuming operations, marched northwest to Fort Cobb, where he turned due west and advanced on a broad front. Results were obtained almost immediately. In the Pond Creek area, Captain Carpenter with H and L Companies captured forty-five Kiowas and fifty horses without a fight. On October 24 Major G. W. Schofield with B, C, and M surprised a large camp of Comanches on Elk Creek and forced their surrender after a slight skirmish in which Private Alfred Pinkston of M killed a "Kiowa warrior in personal combat."[31] Schofield had captured a number of chiefs, including Big Red Food of Anadarko fame, as well as sixty-four warriors, 250 women and children, and the entire pony herd of two thousand animals. These Indians, fleeing the tenacious Buell and nearing exhaustion, had run squarely into Davidson.[32]

From Elk Creek the command continued westward in excellent weather with the troopers in high spirits. Wild game was abundant, and veritable banquets of wild turkey, antelope, and deer replaced the usual bacon, beans, and hardtack. The honeymoon was brief, however, for difficult days were just ahead.

To his front Miles had a number of columns searching for Cheyenne hostiles. On November 6 Lieutenant Henry Farnsworth with twenty-eight men of H Company, Eighth Cavalry, while scouting toward McClellan Creek, ran afoul of one hundred Cheyenne warriors and succeeded in breaking loose only after one of his men had been killed and three wounded. Davidson and Miles established contact through couriers and moved to find the Cheyennes. On the morning of November 8, as the Sill column was searching the breaks of the North Fork of McClellan Creek, heavy firing was heard to the front, and a hastily abandoned Cheyenne camp of seventy-five lodges was soon found and destroyed.[33]

In an effort to overtake the Indians who had clashed with Miles, Davidson ordered Captain Viele to take 120 of the best men, Lieutenant Pratt, and

31 Davidson's command was the same as in his first campaign, with the exception of K Company, whose animals were in such bad condition as to prevent the unit from taking the field; F Company took the place of K. For Pinkston, see Organizational Returns, Tenth Cavalry, October 1874. See also Post Returns, Fort Sill, October 1874.

32 Davidson to the AAG, Department of Texas, October 30, 1874, File 2815-1874; Organizational Returns, Tenth Cavalry, October 1874.

33 Davidson to General Augur, November 23, 1874, File 2815-1874; Farnsworth to Price, November 7, 1874, ibid.; *Army and Navy Journal* 12 (November 14, 1874): 212. The body of Private William Dencham of Farnsworth's command was found and buried by a detachment of buffalo soldiers on November 10. See Pratt, *Battlefield and Classroom*, 75.

fifty scouts and pursue as swiftly as possible. At first the trail led out on the Staked Plains in a northwesterly direction but then turned sharply toward the southwest. By late afternoon Pratt's scouts sighted the Cheyenne rear guard, and a long chase began. Viele was unable to close with his foe, although rifle fire was exchanged at long range.

Nightfall brought pursuit to a halt, but at daybreak the command was on the trail again and stayed with it until nearly evening, when Viele felt compelled to abandon the chase. The horses were giving out after a march of ninety miles in two days, rations and forage were nearly gone, and a cold north wind was blowing. There was nothing to do but plod wearily back on their out trail.[34]

The weather turned bitter cold, and sleet and snow pelted Davidson's column as it pushed slowly northward in the teeth of the storm to the Sweet-water. More than two dozen troopers were disabled with frostbite, one hundred of the animals froze to death, and supplies were fearfully low. In such a condition little could be accomplished, and Davidson turned back to the North Fork of the Red and then eastward toward Fort Sill, with men and animals suffering intensely from the cold. The post was reached on November 29. Before a warm fire, Davidson could look back with consid-erable satisfaction on his operations. Nearly four hundred members of hostile bands had been captured, several score lodges and much camp equipment had been destroyed, two thousand animals had been taken, and all without the loss of a man. The troopers had performed admirably under the most trying conditions.[35]

While hundreds of hostiles had been captured and other hundreds had moved in and voluntarily surrendered either at Fort Sill or at the Cheyenne agency, many remained out. Early in December the buffalo soldiers of the Ninth and Tenth Cavalry made a final effort to drive in these last holdouts. Major Schofield took the field on the morning of December 7 with K, M, and D Companies of the Tenth and Company C, Eleventh Infantry. Enough supplies were carried to maintain a scout of twenty-five days.

Schofield marched north to the Wichita agency and then turned west-ward up the Washita searching for trails. Nothing of any significance was

34 Davidson to Captain Carlton, November 17, 1874, File 2815-1874; Organizational Returns, Tenth Cavalry, November 1874; *Army and Navy Journal* 12 (December 12, 1874): 276; Pratt, *Battlefield and Classroom*, 76–77.

35 Davidson to Augur, November 23, 1874; Organizational Returns, Tenth Cavalry, November 1874; Lieutenant Pratt to the AAAG, Fort Sill Column, November 29, 1874, File 3490-1874.

discovered until December 18, when a hastily abandoned Cheyenne camp of fifteen lodges was found. Captain Keyes with Company D and ten men of Company M were detached to pursue these Indians while Schofield pushed on toward the Canadian.

Keyes overtook the Cheyennes at Kingfisher Creek fewer than twenty miles from their agency, capturing fifty-two men, women, and children and about fifty animals. Schofield scouted for more than two hundred miles in a vast arc between the Canadian and the Washita but found nothing. He took time out to allow the troopers a turkey shoot on Christmas Day and then set out for Fort Sill, arriving on December 31.[36]

Major Morrow, who had been at Fort Sill with A, D, and E of the Ninth since mid-November, left the post on December 4 and marched to Buell's supply camp at the North Fork of the Red, where he obtained three weeks' rations. He then set out for the main Red River and searched far upstream in intense cold. The scout was unproductive, and he turned to the Pease River for one final look under constant hammering by rain and snow. When fifty-four of his sixty mules froze to death, he called it quits and marched into Fort Concho.[37]

There was little here to comfort the half-frozen soldiers, and Post Surgeon William Buchanan filed a complaint with the post adjutant. The men had "just returned from a fatiguing campaign," yet there was little for them to eat. The bread was heavy and sour; the meat poor in quality; and canned peas furnished as "fresh" were of Swiss origin, very old, and poisoned by the tin and solder. There were no crackers, molasses, sugar, cheese, canned pears, or sauerkraut. Equally discouraging, the roofs of the barracks leaked and the doors and porches needed repair. According to Buchanan, all these conditions were to be "regretted."[38]

For all practical purposes, the Red River War was over by the beginning of 1875, although Davidson and Miles continued to harass the Cheyennes and round up small parties of beaten and destitute Kiowas and Comanches. On March 6 the main body of Cheyennes reached their agency and surrendered. Thereafter, only the Kwahadis of the Staked Plains remained out, and in June they too came in peacefully and surrendered at Fort Sill. Sheridan summed up the war in a letter to Sherman. "This campaign was not only

36 Schofield to the PA, Fort Sill, December 31, 1874, File 3490-1874.
37 Morrow to the AAG, Department of Texas, January 23, 1874, ibid.
38 William Buchanan to the PA, Fort Concho, Texas, February 28, 1875, SLR, Department of Texas.

very comprehensive, but the most successful of any Indian campaign in this country, since its settlement by whites."[39]

Sheridan should have been pleased. He could criticize little in the operations of Mackenzie and Miles. The columns of Buell and Davidson had scouted more miles, captured more Indians, and had destroyed more lodges and property than any other regiments in the war. By now, Satanta and Big Tree were incarcerated, for they and their followers had surrendered early in the war at the Cheyenne agency. Satanta had been sent back to the penitentiary at Huntsville, Texas, where, despondent over his loss of freedom, he would take his own life in October 1878. Other prominent Kiowas and Comanches who were imprisoned included Lone Wolf, Woman's Heart, Bird Chief, White Horse, Red Otter, and Maman-ti of the former tribe and Pe-che-wan, Buck Antelope, Dry Wood, and Little Prairie Hill of the latter.[40] Lone Wolf and Maman-ti would spend their imprisonment in Fort Marion in St. Augustine, Florida, far from the plains they loved and which they mourned as their cherished homeland.

Meanwhile, the process of dismounting, disarming, and imprisoning ringleaders of the outbreak had gone on apace. All went smoothly until April 1875, when serious trouble occurred at the Cheyenne agency. This affair was sheer tragedy for the Cheyennes and at the same time provoked a bitter controversy among officers of the Tenth that cast a shadow over the outstanding effort of the regiment during the war. All but two companies of buffalo soldiers had been transferred to Texas in March—Captain Keyes and Captain S. T. Norvell with Companies D and M remained at the Cheyenne agency to assist the garrison there under Lieutenant Colonel Thomas H. Neill in watching over large numbers of Cheyenne prisoners of war.[41]

On the afternoon of April 6, a small detachment of Fifth Infantry under Captain Andrew Bennett brought a few prisoners to the agency blacksmith to have leg irons fitted. Nearby, a group of Indian women taunted the warriors as they were shackled. It was more than young Black Horse could bear. He kicked over the blacksmith and dashed madly for the Cheyenne

---

39 *Annual Report of the Secretary of War for the Year 1875*, 58; *Annual Report of the Commissioner of Indian Affairs for the Year 1875*, 269; Pope to Sherman, February 23, 1875, File 3490-1874; Davidson to the AAG, Department of Texas, February 3, 1875, SLR, Department of Texas.

40 Robinson, *Satanta*, 193–94; Lieutenant Pratt to Davidson, March 12, 1875, SLR, Department of Texas.

41 Organizational Returns, Tenth Cavalry, February 1875.

camp. The guards called out to him to halt, but when he continued to run, they fired and killed him instantly. Some of the shots struck lodges in the Cheyenne camp and brought a volley of arrows that wounded two of Keyes's troopers who had just reached the scene. The fire from the camp was returned and the Cheyennes stampeded.

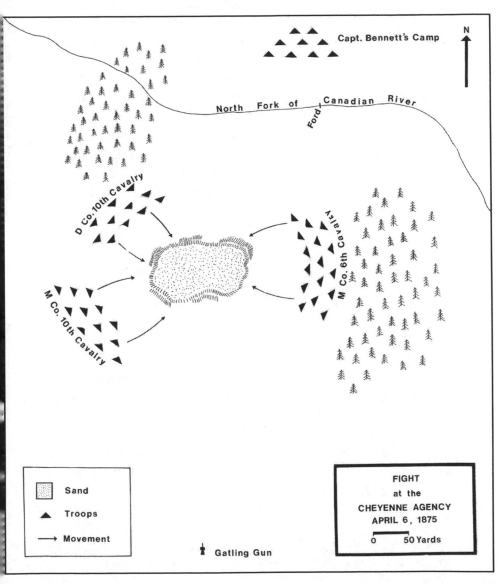

Fight at Cheyenne Agency

Between 100 and 150 warriors with a few women and children fled to an elevated sand hill on the south side of the North Fork of the Canadian; dug up arms and ammunition, apparently buried there prior to surrender; and entrenched themselves. Neill immediately ordered Captain William A. Rafferty, Sixth Cavalry, with M Company to dislodge the Indians. Shortly thereafter he sent Keyes and Norvell to assist him.

According to Neill's official report, Rafferty arrived on the east side of the sand hill in advance of Norvell and Keyes. He ordered his men to dismount, hold their fire, and advance. The Indians waited until the soldiers had approached within a short distance and then fired a volley into M Company, driving it back. When Keyes and Norvell arrived, their men moved to the southwest side of the hill and opened fire.

It was near midafternoon when Neill arrived and surveyed the battleground. Long-range rifle fire was getting nowhere, so he ordered a mounted charge. A courier from Norvell and Keyes brought word that the terrain on their front made a mounted charge impracticable, and Neill had a Gatling gun brought up to spray the Indian position at four hundred yards. He then ordered a charge on foot, but only Rafferty's men advanced, and the attack failed. The Gatling gun again swept the sand hill and again a charge was ordered, but accurate Indian fire held off the troops until nightfall.

Neill called off the troopers and prepared for an early morning assault with every soldier at the agency, but the Indians fled during the night, and a pursuit of nearly four hundred miles by a detachment from D and M of the Tenth failed to overtake them. Lieutenant Austin Henely, Sixth Cavalry, took up the chase with sixty troopers from Fort Wallace. On April 23 Henely surprised the Cheyennes, who had encamped along the North Fork of Sappa Creek in Kansas. Some of the Indians managed to escape, but nineteen warriors fought until killed along with eight women and children who remained with them.[42]

Back at the Cheyenne agency, Neill's report on the fight at the sand hill raised a storm of controversy. It contained high praise for Rafferty and the troopers of the Sixth and gave credit to Lieutenant Edward P. Turner of Keyes's company for leading a charge. It had not one word of commenda-

42 Neill to Lieutenant Colonel R. Williams, AAG, Department of the Missouri, April 7, 1874, SDLR; Lieutenant Henely to Major Hambright, Commanding at Fort Wallace, April 25, 1875, File 3490-1874. In addition to the twenty-seven Cheyennes killed by Henely's men, seven more were killed in the fight at the sand hill.

tion for the buffalo soldiers, in fact quite the opposite. Twice, according to Neill, he had ordered a charge, and twice the men of Norvell and Keyes had failed to support Rafferty. Lieutenant Turner supported him and orally charged that Keyes was a coward and the troopers of D and M a bunch of "god-damned Moacks who wouldn't fight; there was no charge in them."[43]

Captain Norvell was quick to counter both Neill and Turner. D and M had marched to the Cheyenne agency in February 1875 after a hard campaign with no more than thirty men to each company. While there, they did not receive adequate shelter or clothing and at times were without rations. The men had not complained, however, and had performed their duties with customary cheerfulness. When the fight broke out and the Cheyennes fled, he and Keyes had marched swiftly toward the sand hill and, moving to Rafferty's left, had taken a position south of the hill and at a rough right angle from Rafferty.

Once in position, the companies dismounted and started to advance on foot when a courier arrived from Neill ordering them to fall back and mount, which they did. But then Norvell and Keyes had decided that a mounted charge was not practicable due to the nature of the terrain and so informed Neill. Orders were then received to advance on foot, and the men pushed forward, but the Indian fire was accurate, a number of men were hit, there was no cover, and the advance stalled.

At this time the Gatling gun opened fire, and the rounds came so close to D and M that Norvell felt momentarily that he was being fired upon from the rear. Orders for another charge were received and the troopers of all three companies shouted and moved forward, but two men in Norvell's company were shot down instantly, and the other troopers had great difficulty in making headway in the deep sand to their front. Captain Keyes, not Lieutenant Turner, with a few men had succeeded in getting within sixty yards of the Indian position before being pinned down. Short-range firing had continued until dark, when Neill ordered a general withdrawal.[44]

In concluding his report, Norvell demanded recognition for the buffalo soldiers. No such recognition was ever forthcoming, and higher headquarters apparently accepted Neill's version of the fight. Years later, Corporal Perry Hayman of Norvell's company wrote his version of the struggle at the

43 Neill to Williams, April 7, 1874, SDLR; Norvell to the AAG, Department of the Missouri, May 15, 1875, ibid.
44 Norvell to the AAG, Department of the Missouri, May 15, 1875.

sand hill. "As the first set of fours crossed the river, the Indians opened up on us and Corporal George Berry was wounded. We charged them. . . . While rolling around on the ground (when ordered to take cover) my rifle," he added, "got some sand in the breech. I had to take a stick to clean it out, and in doing so I got in full view of the Indians. It was here that I got shot in the right side. I laid down behind a stump, and again those Indians fired a number of shots, but" fortunately for him, "none of them hit me. Some came so close to me that they threw sand in my face. . . . I stayed there until dark, and then I managed to crawl away from my hiding place." When pursuit was undertaken on the morning following the fight, Hayman related, "I crawled out of my tent and wanted to saddle my horse, but the captain made me go to the hospital."[45]

In light of Hayman's story and in view of the casualties incurred, Norvell's demand for recognition deserved a better fate. Rafferty's company had five men wounded but only one severely. Keyes's D had eight men hit, five seriously, while Norvell's M had three wounded, one of them mortally. Of sixteen men wounded, eleven were among the buffalo soldiers, and they suffered the only fatal wound as well. For troopers who had refused to fight and "had no charge in them," they had certainly managed to get in the way of a disproportionate amount of lead.[46]

In fact, the contributions the buffalo soldiers had already made throughout their service were grossly unrecognized. At this point only Emanuel Stance had received the Medal of Honor. After the Red River War, twenty-

45 Quoted in Rickey, "Negro Regulars."

46 Casualties in D Company of the Tenth were Sergeant Richard Lewis and Privates John Green, Robert Logan, David Saddler, Jacob Slimp, Ephraim Smith, Benjamin Smith, and Sammy Vincent. Norvell's M had Private Clark Young killed, Corporal Perry Hayman and Private George Berry wounded. Organizational Returns, Tenth Cavalry, April 1875. Neill's report indicates nineteen men were wounded, with five of these in Rafferty's company, but the returns cited above do not bear out these figures. Norvell and Keyes preferred charges against Lieutenant Turner, and Colonel Grierson, who returned to the regiment in April, felt the case merited a general court-martial in justice to the Tenth, but the judge advocate general refused to hold an inquiry. Grierson to the AAG, Department of Texas, June 3, 1875, SLR, Department of Texas; Captain C. D. Emory to the AAG, Department of Texas, June 12, 1875, ibid. Captain Stevens Thomson Norvell rose through the ranks in the Civil War and was commissioned a first lieutenant, Fifth Michigan Infantry, in February 1863. He was assigned to the Tenth Cavalry as a captain in December 1870 and was promoted to major in March 1890. He ended a long career in 1898 as a lieutenant colonel in the Ninth Cavalry. Heitman, *Historical Register,* 1:753. Turner was a center of controversy until he resigned from the army in June 1878 after eight years of service. Heitman, *Historical Register,* 1:974.

five soldiers who had served in the Fourth and Sixth Cavalry and the Fifth Infantry would receive that honor. Although Seminole Negro scout Adam Payne would receive a Medal of Honor for courageously defending himself and four other scouts against twenty-five Comanches on the Staked Plains, not one black cavalryman would be singled out for that award. Moreover, later histories of the conflict would, for the most part, ignore the buffalo soldiers' contributions.[47]

Nonetheless, whatever the lack of appreciation then or later, the black troopers had done their duty and done it well. Changes were now in store for them. D and M would soon be transferred to Texas to join the rest of their regiment in completing the work their comrades in the Ninth had begun. They would continue mapping the terrain, building the roads and telegraph lines, and keeping the peace in the vast and lonely reaches of the United States' borderland with Mexico.

47 Schubert, *Black Valor*, 33–34; Kenner, *Buffalo Soldiers and Officers of the Ninth Cavalry*, 162.

The Tenth in West Texas

Colonel Benjamin Grierson, after more than two years as superintendent of the Mounted Recruiting Service, resumed command of the Tenth Cavalry on April 30, 1875, with headquarters at Fort Concho. He found the regiment badly scattered. Six companies composed the garrison at Concho, two others were at Fort Griffin with Lieutenant Colonel Davidson in command of the post, two more were at Fort McKavett, and one each at Forts Davis and Stockton. In addition, the regiment was woefully undermanned and poorly mounted. Some measure of relief was needed after the rigors of the Red River War for rest, refitting, and recruitment, but conditions on the Texas frontier permitted no such luxury.[1]

Small parties of "out" Comanches were active in the vicinity of Forts Concho and Griffin, the Kickapoos and Lipans continued to harass settlers and ranchers along the Rio Grande, while depredations by hostile bands of Mescalero and Warm Springs Apaches were on the increase. White and Mexican bandits were, with little restraint, relieving owners of their herds, and Mexican revolutionaries remained a source of concern. Needs notwithstanding, the Tenth plunged into this maelstrom of violence and lawlessness, while Grierson pleaded with General E. O. C. Ord for at least two

1 Organizational Returns, Tenth Cavalry, April 1875, AGO, RG 94, NA.

hundred more troopers and the animals to mount his regiment properly.[2]

Bold white horse-thieves got quick attention from the Tenth. Five men clumsily disguised as Indians attempted to run off part of the herd of Captain T. A. Baldwin's Company I encamped near Fort Concho. Fortunately, alert guards engaged them in a gunfight, put four of the thieves to flight, and captured one with a smoking pistol in his hand. The prisoner was turned over to civil authorities at Saint Angela, but a tolerant jury released him.

Near Fort Griffin another gang had more success. It stole a number of ponies belonging to friendly Lipan Indians living adjacent to the post. Lieutenant George Evans, E Company, with four troopers investigated the theft, and with a Lipan serving as guide, soon found the trail. It led southeast to the pasture of a man named Cooksie, and there they found one of the stolen animals. Cooksie proved most helpful. He had no idea how the pony got into his pasture, but the thieves were undoubtedly a party of men who had recently passed his place and gone to the village of Picketville.

Inquiries at Picketville revealed no such party of men, and Evans returned to Cooksie's by a circuitous route and found another stolen pony tethered in some thick brush. Shortly thereafter Cooksie was encountered riding a horse that the Lipan identified immediately as one that they were looking for. Cooksie wasted no time in conversation but spurred at a dead run into some heavy brush with the troopers at his heels. He escaped, however, and apparently kept right on running. Evans learned later that Cooksie and some companions had decided to leave the country.[3]

Small war parties of Comanches were also busy gathering up horses at outlying ranches and, when pursued, fled into the trackless wastes of the Staked Plains. Few such raiders could be overtaken, although on occasion they paid for their audacity. On May 6, 1875, an alert patrol under Sergeant John Marshall of Company A intercepted a party of eight Indians near Catfish Creek, killed one, and scattered the others in a running fight of seven miles. The following day on the North Concho, Lieutenant Thad Jones and

<hr />

2 Grierson to the AAG, Department of Texas, May 5, 1875, SLR, Department of Texas, AGO, RG 94, NA. Grierson had a total of 650 men and even fewer horses. Many of these animals were old, broken down, or otherwise unserviceable.

3 Captain Baldwin to the PA, Fort Concho, Texas, May 28, 1875, ibid.; Lieutenant Evans to the PA, Fort Griffin, Texas, June 18, 1875, SDLR, AGO, RG 94, NA.

a detachment of H Company overtook a small party and recovered thirty-three head of stock.[4]

These raids were on a small scale, but the swift-hit-and-rapid-run tactics kept post commanders busy trying to fend off the attacks, which often gained the troopers nothing more than exhausted mounts and bad tempers. The activities of a few Comanches were demanding far too much time and energy, and in May General Ord decided to settle this business once and for all. Since Grierson was unfamiliar with the country, Lieutenant Colonel William Shafter was ordered from Fort Duncan to Concho to organize an expedition for the purpose of sweeping the Staked Plains of hostile bands. Shafter was also given an additional task. The westward flow of settlement was lapping at the edges of the plains, and his orders required that he "show in detail, the resources of the country passed over, looking to its adaptability for cultivation and stock-raising," and to pay special attention to the location of bodies of water.[5]

Buffalo soldiers formed the backbone of Shafter's force. When preparations were complete, the command consisted of six companies of the Tenth, two companies of the Twenty-fourth Infantry, and one company of the Twenty-fifth Infantry. In addition, Lieutenants John L. Bullis and C. R. Ward now led a body of Seminole and Tonkawa scouts. The former were the mixed-blood descendants of Seminole Indians and the black slaves who had intermarried with them in Florida. After the United States had removed most of the Seminoles to Indian Territory, many of the Seminole Negroes, as they were called, had crossed the border to live in Mexico. Since 1870 they or their descendents had been returning to the United States to offer the army their service as scouts.

Secretary of War William Belknap authorized their employment in this capacity since they knew the haunts and ways of the Kickapoos and Lipans who had caused so much trouble on both sides of the Rio Grande. Although the black Seminole scouts resembled the buffalo soldiers, several of them wore Indian war bonnets decorated with buffalo horns along with their blue uniforms. Accompanying the now more colorful and varied command were sixty-five wagons drawn by six-mule teams and a pack train of seven

4 Sergeant Marshall to the PA, Fort Concho, May 12, 1875, SLR, Department of Texas; Lieutenant Jones to the PA. Fort Concho, Texas, May 7, 1875, ibid.

5 AAG, Department of Texas to Shafter, June 30, 1875, SLR Relating to Texas, 1875–76, AGO, RG 94, NA. See also Carlson, *"Pecos Bill,"* 72–75.

hundred mules that carried supplies for a four-month campaign. An additional herd of steers would provide a ready supply of fresh meat.[6]

The long column left Fort Concho in the steaming heat of July 14, 1875, and headed northwest for the Fresh Fork of the Brazos, some 180 miles away, to establish a supply camp. A week later at Rendlebrock Springs, about midway between the North Concho and the Colorado Rivers, Shafter detached Captain Nicholas Nolan with A and C Companies of the Tenth, with twenty days' rations, to scout toward the west and rejoin the main command at the supply camp.

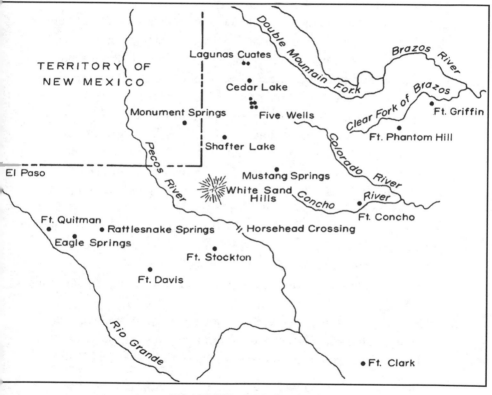

SHAFTER CAMPAIGN

6 Shafter to the AAG, Department of Texas, September 29, 1875, SLR Relating to Texas; Post Returns, Fort Concho, July 1875, AGO, RG 94, NA; Organizational Returns, Tenth Cavalry, July 1875. Companies of the Tenth were A, C, F, I, G, and L under Captains Nolan, Viele, Kennedy, Baldwin, Lee, and Little. For information on the Seminole Negro scouts, see Schubert, *Black Valor*, 28–29.

Nolan pushed west to Mustang Springs, which he reached on July 27, and the next morning picked up the trail of a lone pony leading northwest. The trail grew larger as other riders fed into it, and by early afternoon the scouts sighted a large body of Indians to their front. Nolan made "all possible haste," but all he found for his pains was a deserted camp. Another mile and a half brought a second and larger village, which the Indians had also abandoned, along with most of their supplies. Nolan halted and destroyed both camps, which contained seventy-four lodges, cooking utensils, robes, saddles, and a six months' supply of food. It was late afternoon by the time the work of destruction had been completed, and Nolan decided to encamp and resume pursuit early the next morning.

Dawn brought a hard rain that held the column up until well past noon, when pursuit was again undertaken, but after a slogging march of eight miles, Nolan gave up hope of overtaking the fleeing Indians. From a muddy bivouac he sent a report by courier to Shafter, and the following morning he set out northeast for the supply camp at the Fresh Fork of the Brazos, which was reached August 6. Shafter was pleased with Nolan's destruction of the camps but much upset over what he regarded as a lack of vigorous pursuit. Ten days later, with the approval of General Ord, Shafter relieved Nolan of his command and ordered him to Fort Concho to await a court-martial.[7]

On August 5 Shafter left his supply camp with G, I, F, and L Companies of the Tenth and a detachment of the Seminole and Tonkawa scouts. Rations were carried on pack mules, and a single wagon was used for medical supplies and to carry the sick. The intention was to run down the Indians Nolan had encountered, but it marked the beginning of one of the most demanding marches ever made by the buffalo soldiers—or any soldiers for that matter.

The route was almost due west for some one hundred miles to a lake called Casas Amarillas. Shafter had hopes of striking the Indians at this prominent watering place. No Indians were found, however, and Shafter

> took a southwest course, hoping to find water sufficient in holes on the prairies, which I did for two days; but at the expiration of the 3rd day's march, finding no water I had either to strike for the Pecos or turn back. I determined to make for the Pecos, and

7 Nolan to Shafter, August 1, 1875, SLR Relating to Texas; Shafter to the AAG, Department of Texas, August 5, 1875, ibid.; the AAG, Department of Texas, to Shafter, August 16, 1875, ibid. See also Carlson, *"Pecos Bill,"* 77–79.

did so the next night, marching in the two days and one night seventy seven miles, with water but once (a heavy shower of rain). From there I went down the Pecos as far as HorseHead Crossing, and after resting my stock a few days and getting rations from Stockton, I left the Pecos on the 5th of September at Pecos Falls, forty miles above HorseHead Crossing, on my return across the plains to Supply Camp which I expected to reach in ten days.[8]

Ten days turned into twenty. As Shafter turned northeast and skirted the White Sand Hills, he failed to find water and had to turn westward into New Mexico by forced marches to reach Dug Spring on September 13. There a large Indian trail was found leading north, and Shafter followed it, although "we had but six days rations, and the heat, dust, sand and want of water had told greatly on the stock."[9]

Shortly after midnight, however, a party of warriors numbering about thirty came in on Shafter's back trail and fired into G Company. The guards returned fire immediately, and the hostiles scattered with no harm done on either side. At daybreak Shafter was in pursuit with forty-five selected troopers and followed the trail for twenty miles to an abandoned camp and a very large spring. The rest of the command was brought up and spent the better part of a day burning lodges and other camp equipage. Simultaneously, a detail went to a nearby hill and erected a stone marker seven and one-half feet high and visible for miles in every direction to serve as a beacon to guide the thirsty traveler to Monument Spring.

Meanwhile, the Indians had scattered in all directions, and Shafter decided to give up the chase. Rations were very low, the animals badly worn, and his base was 200 miles away. These considerations turned the column northeast toward the supply camp, which was reached on September 25 after an absence of fifty-two days and a march of more than 860 miles through country of which "nothing was known before by troops." Twenty-nine horses were the only casualties. In Shafter's absence Captain Charles Viele with A and C Companies of the Tenth had crossed the Staked Plains to Portales, New Mexico. After returning to the supply camp for rations, they

8 Shafter to the AAG, Department of Texas, September 29, 1875. See also Carlson, "Pecos Bill," 79–80.

9 Shafter to the AAG, Department of Texas, September 29, 1875. See also Carlson, "Pecos Bill," 80–81.

had pushed north to Palo Duro Canyon to scout that old hostile "winter resort," but the troopers found no sign of Indians.[10]

Shafter remained in camp until October 12 resting his stock and reoutfitting his tattered troopers before moving southwestward to the Double Mountain Fork of the Brazos. There he detached Captain Baldwin with F and I to scout through the Mucha Que country and on south to Sulphur Springs and Big Spring. Baldwin reached Big Spring after a march of 340 miles accompanied by much suffering, which included one stretch of thirty-eight hours without water. After giving his durable troopers a brief rest, he fanned out patrols to the south and west.

Shafter also moved south to Double Lakes, where he left one company of infantry, and then on southwest to Laguna Sabinas (Cedar Lake), a large lake but too salty for drinking purposes; good water was found, however, by digging near the edge. Bullis with his Seminole scouts had preceded Shafter and found a large Indian encampment, but the Indians had escaped. He had captured twenty-five ponies, fifty sacks of mesquite beans, about four thousand pounds of buffalo meat, many buffalo hides, lodge poles, and cooking utensils, all of which he had destroyed.[11]

From Laguna Sabinas the trail was followed some thirty miles south to "Live Large Wells." The Indians had passed on south, and Shafter detached Lieutenant Andrew Geddes, Twenty-fifth Infantry, with Companies G and L of the Tenth and the Seminole scouts "to follow the trail as long as possible." The colonel, meanwhile, turned westward and marched sixty-three miles to Monument Spring, where he arrived on October 23.

Geddes took the order literally and pursued the fleeing Indians with dogged determination as they turned southeast, west, and then south again to throw him off. He refused to be shaken, however, and on November 2 he overtook his quarry within sight of the Rio Grande and charged. Since most of the warriors had left the camp, he encountered and killed only one warrior, captured four women and a small boy, and destroyed the camp. It was a trail-weary command that turned back to Fort Clark for a brief rest and then marched on to Fort Concho, where the troopers arrived on

10 Shafter to the AAG, Department of Texas, September 29, 1875; Organizational Returns, Tenth Cavalry, September 1875. Shafter's scout convinced him that the Staked Plains were clear of Comanches and that the Indians both he and Nolan had encountered were Apaches from New Mexico. See also Carlson, "Pecos Bill," 81–82.

11 Shafter to Colonel J. H. Taylor, AAG, Department of Texas, October 19, 1875, SLR Relating to Texas; Carlson, "Pecos Bill," 83. Bullis came upon the Indian camp on the night of October 17.

November 27. They had covered more than 650 miles of very rough country since leaving Shafter at Laguna Sabinas.[12]

At Monument Spring Shafter found a large Indian trail on October 24 and followed it to the White Sand Hills, where he decided to turn back, for the trail pointed in the direction of Baldwin's area of operations. Returning north to Laguana Sabinas, Shafter sent Lieutenant T. C. Lebo with A Company to Casas Amarillas. No Indians were found, but a lake was discovered that, not inappropriately, was named Lebo's Lake. When the detachment returned, Shafter marched back south and joined Baldwin at Big Spring on November 8. Five days later the command moved northeast to Tobacco Creek, established a new supply camp, and on the fifteenth began another sweep across the Staked Plains to Monument Spring, which was reached after six days of hard marching. Turning back east, Shafter reached the "five wells," where he received orders from Ord to break up his expedition and return to Fort Duncan.

Shafter's expedition, whatever its frustrations, turned roaming Indians away from the plains. More importantly, it provided the first thorough exploration of the Staked Plains and forever dispelled the myth that this region was barren land devoid of water and unfit for development or economic activity.

The colonel's report and accompanying maps would surely have warmed the heart of a Staked Plains Chamber of Commerce had such existed. From Rendlebrock Spring north to the Fresh Fork of the Brazos was slightly rolling country with excellent grass and considerable mesquite—wonderful cattle country. North of Casas Amarillas was "an excellent place for sheep or horses." For nearly sixty miles east of the White Sand Hills was high, rolling prairie with fine grass. Shafter was cautious concerning water but indicated there were several good springs near the edge of Double Lakes, and at Laguna Sabinas water could be obtained from dug springs.[13]

The report, widely circulated and read, spawned a swift movement of

12 Major A. P. Morrow to the AAG, Department of Texas, November 10, 1875, SLR Relating to Texas; Organizational Returns, Tenth Cavalry, November 1875; Shafter to the AAG, Department of Texas, January 4, 1876, SLR Relating to Texas. See also Carlson, "Pecos Bill," 83–86.

13 Shafter to the AAG, Department of Texas, January 4, 1876. Shafter's report, as indicated, had considerable influence on southern plains settlement, but the adjutant general was apparently not impressed, for he approved a deduction of fifty-two dollars from Shafter's pay for authorizing Captain Baldwin and I of the Tenth to expend two thousand rounds of ammunition "in hunting to provide food and improve aim." See also Carlson, "Pecos Bill," 87.

cattlemen, sheepherders, and homesteaders to claim and settle this last great home of the Southern Plains Indians. But if the report had praise for much of the country over which Shafter had campaigned, it was silent in this regard on the officers and men who accompanied him. Except for Captain Nolan it neither condemned nor praised—it all but ignored them. Few incoming settlers knew, and perhaps even fewer cared, that over the trails they trod a tattered, patient, and bone-weary buffalo soldier had gone before.[14]

While half the regiment fought killing heat, thirst, and dust over hundreds of miles with Shafter, the remaining companies of the Tenth were hard at work. A detachment of thirty troopers was detailed for construction work on the U.S. Military Telegraph Line to connect Fort Concho and Fort Griffin. Others provided the essential escort to surveying parties of the Texas and Pacific Railroad, stages, trains, and cattle herds.

The greatest activity and concern, however, was directed toward the Rio Grande, where conditions all but defied improvement. In the spring of 1876, guerrilla bands of Porfiristas and Lerdistas fought for control of the northern Mexican frontier, with the losing parties frequently crossing to the American side of the river for sanctuary. There they were not averse to robbery and murder to recoup losses of arms, animals, and supplies. With these diversions combined with continuing raids of Mexican Indians and bandits, there was more than enough activity to keep every available soldier in almost constant motion.[15]

Troops were too few to guard the many river crossings, and scattered patrols proved ineffective. Pursuit of brigands and raiding Indians rarely produced results, for escape, as in past years, required the mere crossing of the river. A change of policy was essential if peace was to prevail along the border, and in the spring of 1876 it came. General Ord was instructed to use his discretion in allowing troops in his department to continue pursuit

14 Shafter to the AG, USA, January 6, 1876, Correspondence, AG, Document File 1876, AGO, RG 94, NA. Frederick W. Rathjen notes that 1876 is usually seen "as the beginning year of permanent Panhandle settlement," which occurred after the military conquest of the southern plains following the Red River War. See *Texas Panhandle Frontier*, 229. Writings such as Shafter's report were also important.

15 Parkes, *History of Mexico*, 283; *Annual Report of the Secretary of War for the Year 1876*, 26; Captain L. H. Carpenter to the PA, Fort Davis, December 2, 1875, SDLR. Carpenter voiced an old complaint—Mexican authorities encouraged, tolerated, and provided ready markets for loot brought back by raiding Indians from Texas—and he urged a more aggressive policy.

across the Rio Grande. Revolutionary bands crossing to the American side were to be rounded up as quickly as possible, arrested, disarmed, and interned until such time as they were prepared to give parole that they would not attempt to organize on U.S. soil or disturb the peace of their native country.[16]

Mexican Indians soon learned that a new day had dawned. Kickapoos and Lipans had reaped a considerable harvest of cattle and horses in the spring and early summer of 1876, and in May 1877 they taunted the buffalo soldiers by quick thrusts within virtual gunshot of Forts Davis and Stockton. Efforts to overtake these raiders proved futile, for they always had a head start in the inevitable dash for the Rio Grande and safety. It was enough for General Ord—the time had come to "use his discretion." In July he ordered Colonel Shafter at Fort Duncan to form a strong column and attack a large camp of marauding Indians known to be in the vicinity of Saragossa (Zaragoza), Mexico.[17]

Shafter quickly assembled a force consisting of Companies B, E, and K, Tenth Cavalry, Lieutenant Bullis and a party of Seminole scouts, and detachments of the Twenty-fourth and Twenty-fifth Infantry. The command marched upriver and, some twenty-five miles above the mouth of the Pecos, splashed across the Rio Grande into Mexico. It was a long-awaited opportunity for the buffalo soldiers and one that might not have materialized had General Ord not been so hard-pressed for cavalry. In his annual report Ord wrote: "I must remark, however, that the use of colored soldiers to cross the river after raiding Indians, is in my opinion, impolitic, not because they have shown any want of bravery, but because their employment is much more offensive to Mexican inhabitants than white soldiers."[18] A buffalo soldier might have replied that the attitude of Mexican citizens along the river left much to be desired in any case.

Shafter's column pushed southwestward for five days before he called a halt. There were growing fears that a Mexican force might cross the back

16 AG to Commanding General, Department of Texas, March 10, 1876, LR, Affairs on the Rio Grande and Texas Frontier, Consolidated File 1653, AGO, RG 94, NA [hereafter cited as File 1653]; House, H.R. 96, April 4, 1876, 44th Cong., 2d sess.; Sheridan to Townsend, April 18, 1876, File 1653; *Annual Report of the Secretary of War for the Year 1876*, 493.

17 House, H. Exec. Doc. 1, 45th Cong., 2d sess., pt. 2, p. 81; Medical History, Fort Davis, Texas, vol. 9, Medical History of Posts, AGO, RG 94, NA; Wallace, "John Lapham Bullis," 82. See also Carlson, *"Pecos Bill,"* 88–90.

18 House, H. Exec. Doc. 1, 45th Cong., 2d sess., pt. 2, pp. 80–81.

trail and cut off a return to the river. The colonel proposed that the Americans encamp, and Bullis with the Seminoles, Lieutenant George Evans, Tenth Cavalry, and twenty picked troopers march on to the Indian village.

Bullis and Evans needed no urging. In just twenty-five hours they covered 110 miles and located the village of twenty-three lodges some 5 miles from Saragossa. At dawn on July 30 the village was assaulted. After the first volley a savage hand-to-hand fight—clubbed carbine against thrusting lance—swirled among the lodges. In minutes it ended with the Indians in full flight, but they left fourteen dead warriors, four of their women, and ninety horses behind. Bullis, with only three wounded, quickly destroyed the village and retreated to Shafter's camp pursued by a force of Mexican regulars close on his heels. The united command then marched back to the Rio Grande and crossed. Here the only loss to the command occurred when Trooper Joseph Titus of Company B drowned.[19]

The buffalo soldiers quickly followed up the strike at Saragossa. Captain Lebo with B, E, and K crossed the river on August 4 and headed for the Santa Rosa Mountains. An eight-day march led to a small Kickapoo haven of ten lodges. That site was destroyed, and sixty horses and mules were captured. Following this success, Grierson put virtually his entire regiment into the field. B, E, K, and M scoured the area around the Pecos and Davis Rivers and then moved into the Guadalupe Mountains, scattering small bands in all directions. A, D, F, and L, operating out of Fort Concho, scouted more than a thousand miles between July and the end of the year. With the Tenth on an all-out hunt, it was now difficult for an "honest" thief to make a living. Not until December did the companies come in for a much needed rest.[20]

In partial compensation for a year of constant field operations, Grierson gave a Christmas party for the entire garrison at Fort Concho. The regimental band, ever a source of pride and satisfaction, provided the music while officers and men feasted on sandwiches, turkey, buffalo tongue, olives, cheese, biscuits, sweet-and-sour pickles, candy, raisins, pears, apples, and four kinds of cake—all washed down with gallons of coffee. Such food was a rare treat for any soldier but most especially for buffalo soldiers at such

19 Shafter to the AAG, Department of Texas, August 3, 1876, File 1653; Wallace, "John Lapham Bullis," 83; Porter, "Seminole Negro-Indian Scouts," 370; Organizational Returns, Tenth Cavalry, August 1876. See also Carlson, "Pecos Bill," 90–94.

20 Organizational Returns, Tenth Cavalry, July–November, 1876; Post Returns, Fort Concho, Fort Clark, Fort Davis, and Fort Stockton, August–November, 1876.

isolated posts, where fruits and desserts such as cakes were scarce since eggs were hard to come by. The entire post, stationed in what Grierson's brother, John, called "the most God-forsaken part of Uncle Sam's dominions," needed the respite. Frontier duty was proving wearing on not only men but officers as well, for Alice Grierson wrote her son Charlie, then attending the Military Academy at West Point, that "the officers drink a great deal more here than at Ft. Sill or Fort Gibson."[21]

If the winter rest was sweet, it was also of necessity short. The under-manned Tenth was the only cavalry regiment in the whole of West Texas. With an authorized strength of 1,202 men, Grierson could count not more than 900 on hand as the new year opened. So few men could at best provide a porous defense for hundreds of miles of frontier. Porfirio Diaz had defeated Lerdo after a year of civil war, but followers of the latter remained active along the Rio Grande, as did bandit chieftains who defied all efforts of the new government to bring them to heel. The Kickapoos and Lipans, although hard hit, still conducted small-scale raids. Disgruntled Mescaleros from their reservation at Fort Stanton, New Mexico, joined them. And restive Comanches—suffering from hunger since former warriors were loath to take up farming on the reservation—were out on the Staked Plains looking for game to supplement their always inadequate annuities.[22] Efforts of the buffalo soldiers to meet and defeat these adversaries resulted in a mixture of triumph and tragedy.

On January 10, 1877, Lieutenant Bullis and his Seminole scouts teamed up with Captain A. S. B. Keyes and ninety troopers of B and D at Fort Clark for another march into Mexico after the Kickapoos and Lipans. A "hastily aban-doned" camp was found and destroyed in the Santa Rosa Mountains. The north bank of the river was regained without a loss.[23] In February and March, detachments of the Tenth made frequent dashes into Mexico with little result other than finding abandoned camps. F Company, however, suffered a sore loss in the Santa Rosa Mountains when gallant Sergeant

---

21 Alice Kirk Grierson to Robert Grierson, December 31, 1876, GP-ISHS; John Grier-son to Ben Grierson, November 23, 1874, GP-TTU; Alice Grierson to Charles Grierson, December 28, 1875, ibid.

22 House, H. Exec. Doc. 1, 45th Cong., 2d sess., pt. 2, p. 33; Parkes, *History of Mexico*, 284; Organizational Returns, Tenth Cavalry, January 1877; Medical History, Fort Concho, vol. 404; Hagan, *Quanah Parker*, 19.

23 Wallace, "John Lapham Bullis," 83; Organizational Returns, Tenth Cavalry, January 1877. See also Carlson, *"Pecos Bill,"* 97.

Sandy Winchester was accidentally shot and killed. Winchester had been a member of F since its organization and had participated in the regiment's first action against the Cheyennes in Kansas on August 2, 1867.[24]

The swift forays of the buffalo soldiers kept the Mexican Indians constantly on the move and reduced the number of raids, but the Mexican government, alarmed at the growing frequency of these incursions, protested vigorously. The protests were ignored, and in May the U.S. minister to Mexico, J. W. Foster, telegraphed Secretary of State William Evarts that the Diaz government was sending forces under capable officers to the frontier to assist in curbing lawlessness.[25]

The initial effort of the Mexican troops was directed toward stopping revolutionary activity. On June 10 they attacked a party of Lerdistas above the mouth of Davis River, and when the latter fled to the north side of the Rio Grande, the government troops crossed and attacked them on American soil. Captain Joseph Kelley with E Company, on patrol near San Felipe, rode immediately to the site of the attack, where he arrested and disarmed fifty Lerdistas. Mexican federal troops had crossed to their side of the river before he arrived.[26]

Small parties of bedraggled Lerdistas continued to cross into Texas. On August 5 Major G. W. Schofield, while scouting out of Fort Duncan with a detachment of the Tenth, surprised and captured forty-four revolutionaries, forty-three horses, and a large quantity of arms and ammunition. With the twin blows of Kelley and Schofield and increasing pressure from Diaz troops, enthusiasm for revolution suffered considerable erosion.[27]

The Kickapoos and Lipans still managed to evade the ceaseless patrols and to depredate in Texas. On June 21 a small party of Lipans crossed near San Felipe and rode northeastward into Edwards County. Near Camp Wood they surprised farmer John Leary, who was taking a siesta beside his wagon. The Indians opened fire, wounding Leary in the wrist, but with the courage of a cornered tiger, he pulled his revolver and cocked it by pushing the hammer against the wagon bed. In this manner he drove off his attackers, but they ran off a horse. The raiders continued northward, steal-

24 Organizational Returns, Tenth Cavalry, January–March 1877.
25 J. W. Foster to William Evarts, May 28, 1877, File 1653.
26 General Sheridan to General Townsend, June 12, 1877, ibid.; Organizational Returns, Tenth Cavalry, June 1877.
27 AAG, Military Division of the Missouri, to General Townsend, August 8, 1877, File 1653.

ing stock in both Kerr and Kimble Counties before turning back toward their camps in Mexico.[28]

Detachments of buffalo soldiers working both up and down the Rio Grande from Fort Duncan failed to intercept the Lipans. The success of this raid encouraged others, and when the Mexican government failed to respond to calls for more energetic action against these hostiles, General Ord authorized another large-scale expedition into Mexico. Lieutenant Bullis with his Seminoles and Captain Lebo with a battalion of buffalo soldiers gathered at Pinto Creek near Fort Duncan. The Rio Grande was crossed on September 28, and the command set out for the headwaters of San Diego Creek, where a Lipan village was discovered. The attack was launched at once, but the Indians wanted no part of a fight and fled helter-skelter. Torches were applied to lodges and equipment, and by September 30 Bullis and Lebo were back in the camp on the Pinto.[29]

Two weeks later Bullis and his scouts were on the move again, searching along the Devils and Pecos Rivers. Finding nothing, Bullis returned to the Rio Grande and crossed on October 28. A trail was found almost immediately and followed to a large canyon near the Santa Rosa Mountains. The Indians, who were driving out a herd of horses as Bullis arrived, opened fire. After a hot skirmish, Bullis was forced to retire, for the warriors were too numerous for his small body of scouts. He set out for Fort Clark, where he joined forces with Captain S. B. M. Young, Eighth Cavalry, then ready to take the field with a detachment of his regiment, and Company C, Tenth Cavalry, under Lieutenant William Beck.

Young, Bullis, and Beck left Clark on November 10 with the intention of crossing the river and marching "across that point of Mexican territory extending north in what is known as the 'Big Bend.'" The column found the going extremely rough, on one day covering only six miles as men and horses were forced to step carefully and ropes were tied to the pack mules to prevent a fall off precipitous trails. Despite the precautions, eleven animals did slip and were lost along with nearly all the medicine and supplies. No one thought of turning back, however, and a warm trail leading toward Mount Carmel was found on November 28.

28 Statement of John M. Leary, June 21, 1877, ibid.; Faltin and Schriener to Dr. Peterson, July 22, 1877, ibid.; Organizational Returns, Tenth Cavalry, June–July 1877.

29 AAG, District of the Nueces, to Captain Lebo, September 13, 1877, File 1653; Organizational Returns, Tenth Cavalry, September 1877; Porter, "Seminole-Negro Indian Scouts," 374.

CAMPAIGN AREA
of the
TENTH CAVALRY 1880

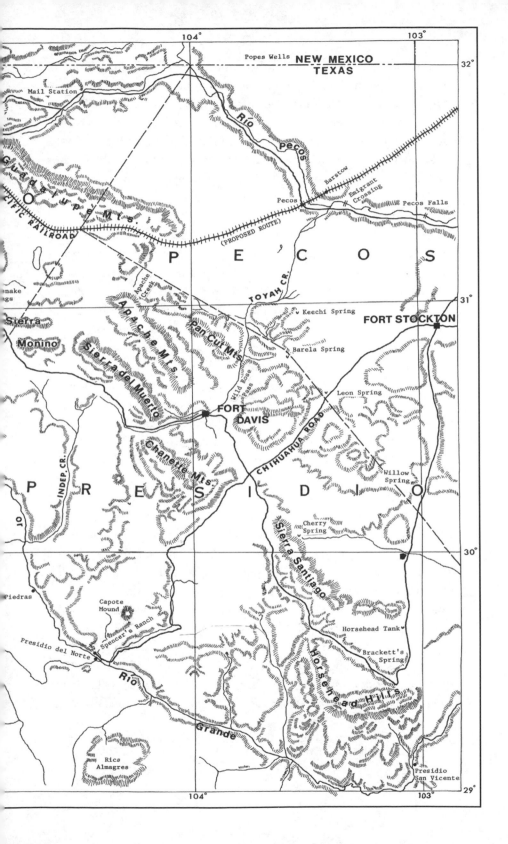

Cold so bitter it froze water in the canteens struck, but the command pushed on with the buffalo soldiers suffering intensely since they "were without great coats." Their grim persistence was rewarded, for the Indians were overtaken in a steep canyon near Mount Carmel. The warriors turned to make a stand, and a blazing fight raged briefly before the Indians broke and fled, with troopers and scouts in hot pursuit. Eventually, the Indians were lost in the broken country, and Young recalled his scattered force to round up twenty-three animals and destroy a large quantity of robes, hides, dried meat, saddles, and ropes.

This task accomplished, the return to Fort Clark began. The men were soon half-frozen, for their clothing was in tatters and there was no escape from the bone-chilling cold. The post was a welcome sight on December 3, and the command received one of Shafter's rare commendations: "Officers and men were exposed to very severe weather and having only pack animals were necessarily restricted to the small allowance carried on the saddle. The country scouted in was exceedingly difficult, more so than any part of Texas, officers and men deserving great credit for the patience, fortitude and energy, they exhibited on this scout, they are to be complimented on its successful issue."[30] Campaigning on the Rio Grande frontier had ended for the year on a note of achievement. Meanwhile, far to the north, other troopers of the Tenth had been busy with hostile Comanches and Mescaleros. In so doing, they had produced one of the starkest dramas in the history of the southern plains.

In the spring of 1877, a strong band of Comanches under Black Horse left their reservation and fled west to the Staked Plains. Angered at the alarming scarcity of buffalo, they made life precarious for numerous parties of buffalo hunters. On April 9 Captain P. L. Lee with G Company left Fort Griffin to search for them. On May 4 he located and attacked a Comanche camp at Lake Quemado, Texas, killed four warriors, and captured six women and sixty-nine horses. First Sergeant Charles Baker was shot in the breast and mortally wounded during this action. A detachment of I Company out of Fort Richardson also scouted more than a thousand miles for these Indians, but without result.

Small parties of Mescaleros were also engaged in raiding activities. In the spring and early summer, bands attacked several stage stations along the

---

30 Captain S. B. M. Young to the AAAG, District of the Nueces, December 18, 1877, File 1653; Lieutenant Bullis to the PA, Fort Clark, Texas, December 22, 1877, ibid.

San Antonio–El Paso road, and Sergeant Joseph Claggett with a detachment of H Company from Fort Davis pursued one group into the Guadalupe Mountains before losing its trail. Claggett was convinced that the Indians were from the Mescalero reservation. Lieutenant Charles Ayres, also of H Company, chased a party of warriors in the same direction but lost them when eight of his horses died of exhaustion.[31]

The Tenth was committed too heavily along the Rio Grande to permit simultaneous sweeps against the Mescaleros and Comanches. Grierson instead ordered Captain Nolan, who had escaped Shafter's displeasure with a reprimand, to take A Company and punish any marauders he could find on the Staked Plains. On July 10 Nolan, Lieutenant Charles Cooper, and sixty troopers with a four-wagon train left Fort Concho and marched up the North Concho River. The weather was dry and very hot, and on the second day out one of the troopers suffered sunstroke, although he soon recovered. Nolan moved down to the headwaters and then northwest to Big Spring, where he turned due north to the Colorado and across that stream to Bull Creek in present Borden County, Texas. There Nolan found a suitable site and established a supply camp. He also found reinforcements in the form of twenty-eight buffalo hunters who were out looking for the Indians who had stolen their stock.

With the hunters was a veteran guide, Jose Tafoya. He had rendered superb assistance to Colonel Ranald Mackenzie in his campaigns on the Staked Plains, and Nolan welcomed the opportunity to secure his services. Tafoya believed the Indians were at or near Laguna Sabinas due west of the supply camp, and the soldiers and hunters prepared to march to that point. Having no pack mules, Nolan took the eight lead mules from his six-mule teams to carry his rations and forage and sent his wagons back to Fort Concho for additional supplies.

On the evening of July 19, Nolan set out westward with Lieutenant Cooper, forty troopers, and twenty-two buffalo hunters. Sergeant Allsup and nineteen men stayed behind to care for the supply camp. On July 21, as the column made its way along Tobacco Creek, the first Indians were seen. They proved to be a party of Comanches under Chief Quanah Parker. They had a pass from the Indian agent at Fort Sill that Colonel Mackenzie, commanding that post, had countersigned, indicating the chief was on a

31 Organizational Returns, Tenth Cavalry, May–June 1877; Medical History, Fort Griffin, vol. 103; Post Returns, Fort Richardson, May 1877.

mission to induce runaway Indians back to the reservation. Nolan was unhappy, but since "[Parker] and party were liberally supplied with Government Horses, Equipments, Arms, Ammunition and Rations, I did not feel authorized in detaining him."[32] After the Indians left, Nolan marched on to Laguna Sabinas, which he reached on the evening of July 22. But it had been a dry year, and where Shafter had found plenty of water in 1875, Nolan was forced to dig holes and dip out water by the cupful.

The command rested for a day while Tafoya and a few of the hunters scouted south to the Five Wells for signs of Indians or water. They returned the next day, after a waterless trip of thirty hours, to report an Indian trail running northeast toward Double Lakes. Nolan set out on the late afternoon of July 24, preferring to march at night to avoid the searing heat, and reached Double Lakes about noon the following day. No sign of Indians was found, and once again the men were forced to dig for precious water.

The guide, with some of the hunters, rode west to Dry Lake, a distance of about seventeen miles, while Nolan remained in camp. Next morning two of the hunters returned to report that Tafoya had seen a party of forty Indians just west of Dry Lake. Nolan saddled up and marched for that point, arriving about sundown and joining Tafoya. There was no water, but the guide assured Nolan a supply could be obtained about fifteen to twenty miles westward along the trail taken by the Indians. The captain made a fateful decision. He decided to push on in the direction indicated by the guide and continued until nightfall, when a dry camp was made—Tafoya had been unable to find water.

Next morning the trail was followed over gently undulating country dotted occasionally by bunches of stunted mesquite, scrub oak, and patches of grass, over which the thirsty troopers dragged their blankets in hopes of obtaining a bit of moisture for their parched throats. Nolan was forced to call a halt after twenty-five miles. His animals were giving out, and the Indians, apparently aware of the pursuit, had scattered. While the men rested, Tafoya searched for the main trail, which he found, and the weary, thirsty column moved out again, plodding slowly westward into a barren sandy plain.[33]

After a few miles, the heavy going, heat, and lack of water began exacting their toll. One trooper fell from his mount of sunstroke, and others were

32 Nolan to the AAG, Department of Texas, August 20, 1877, LR, AGO, RG 94, NA.
33 Ibid.; Nunn, "Eighty-six Hours without Water," 356.

beginning to straggle. Nolan, now genuinely concerned, asked Tafoya how much farther it was to water. When told it was another six or seven miles, he gave the guide one of his private horses and urged him to lead on as rapidly as possible. The command would follow with as much speed as the condition of men and animals permitted.

Tafoya rode off in a westerly direction and then turned northeast, with Nolan doing his utmost to keep up. This proved impossible, for two more troopers suffered sunstroke. Others were so dehydrated and exhausted that they kept falling from their saddles. Nolan halted briefly, detailed Sergeant William Umbles to stay with the two sick men, picked eight of his strongest men, gave them all the canteens they could carry, and sent them on to follow the guide. It was the last he would see of those eight men for many days.

Nolan limped on for a few more miles and then was forced to bivouac. Shortly after, Sergeant Umbles and the two sick men passed within easy hailing distance but failed to respond to repeated shouts before disappearing into the darkness. Eleven men were now missing, the guide had not returned, and Nolan's plight was becoming desperate.

At daylight on July 28 there was still no sign of Tafoya or the eight troopers, and the buffalo hunters were "scattered over the plains, their ponies gone." Nolan and Cooper, after conferring with the hunters, decided to follow in the direction taken by the guide the day before. After some fifteen miles with no sign of either water or Tafoya, Nolan decided to turn back and make for the Double Lakes, some fifty-five miles to the southeast. The buffalo hunters disagreed—water must be nearby somewhere to the northeast—and they bade Nolan farewell.[34]

Every mile was agony now for Nolan and his troopers. The heat was blistering, exhausted horses were staggering, and the men were constantly falling from them. Discipline became the victim of thirst and fear. Corporal Charles Gilmore deserted after being detailed to care for a trooper who had fainted. When Nolan noticed how badly the little column was straggling, he called a halt to await sundown. Mouths were so dry that no one could swallow bread or mesquite beans, and some of the men were becoming delirious. One of Lieutenant Cooper's horses, completely broken down, was killed and the warm blood drunk to slake partially an all-consuming thirst.

Not until 2:00 A.M. on July 29 could the column begin moving again.

34 Nolan to the AAG, Department of Texas, August 20, 1877; Nunn, "Eighty-six Hours without Water," 357. The hunters reached water at Casas Amarillas late that day.

Officers and men were so weak that three hours had been required to pack and saddle up. Morning brought out the broiling sun to beat down upon half-crazed men. Corporal George Fremont and two other troopers struck off on their own, and forty men had shrunk to twenty-four. Thirst was so overpowering that the urine of both horses and men was sweetened and drunk with relish, which brought momentary relief, then greater suffering. More horses died, and their blood was drunk as tortured officers and men fell, lurched, and staggered another twenty-five miles before sheer exhaustion forced a halt near midafternoon beside some scrub mesquite that gave partial shelter from the blistering rays of the sun.

All now despaired for their lives, but big, rawboned Private Barney Howard summoned the energy to go from man to man giving encouragement and telling cheerful stories. The trooper reminded Lieutenant Cooper of his pretty, dark-eyed wife who awaited him at Fort Concho, and that he must not disappoint her. Barney Howard deserved a medal, but he never received one.[35]

Near sundown Nolan ordered the men to abandon all their rations and surplus property and gird themselves for a last effort. Then the column set out again. But, rather than a disciplined march, it had become an individual struggle to reach life-giving water. Fifteen more agonizing miles brought them at last in little groups to Double Lakes during the early morning of July 30. They had been on the Staked Plains for eighty-six hours without water.[36]

As soon as thirst was quenched, Nolan counted faces. One trooper, Private J. T. Gordon, was missing, and a brief search failed to locate him. The men were in no condition for a thorough scout, and Nolan rested his command until the morning of July 31, when he sent out a detail with two pack mules to return to the last camp, gather up the abandoned supplies, and look for stragglers. While awaiting their return, Nolan spied a long column on the horizon to the north and soon welcomed Captain Lee and G Company, who were scouting out of Fort Griffin. Lee rendered immediate assistance and sent out a strong detachment along Nolan's back trail with plenty of food and water to find any men still lost and to retrieve discarded property. Meanwhile, the detail that Nolan had sent out earlier in the day returned with the abandoned rations, but the troopers had found no stragglers.

On August 1, while the command recuperated at Double Lakes, Corpo-

---

35 Cook, *Border and the Buffalo,* 284–85.
36 Nolan to the AAG, Department of Texas, August 20, 1877.

ral Fremont and another trooper came in. They reported that they had straggled and become lost, all their animals had died, and Private Isaac Derwin, who had also been with them, had perished. Nolan placed both men under arrest as deserters and sent a detail to bring in Derwin's body, but the men failed to locate the remains. Three days later Sergeant Allsup with fifteen men arrived from the supply camp on Bull Creek overjoyed to find their commander alive and safe.

Sergeant Umbles and the two men with him, as well as Corporal Gilmore, had reached the supply camp and told Allsup that Nolan and the rest of the command had become lost and died of thirst. Umbles, Gilmore, and another trooper had then ridden on to Fort Concho to bear the grim news to the garrison, while Allsup had marched at once to find Nolan. The latter immediately sent a courier to Concho to give the lie to Umbles's story and to request that both he and Gilmore be placed in arrest.

On August 5 Nolan broke camp at Double Lakes and, escorted by Captain Lee, marched for his supply camp, which was reached at noon the following day. There he found the eight troopers whom he had sent for water on July 27. Shortly thereafter a relief force from Concho headed by Lieutenant Robert G. Smither and Assistant Surgeon J. H. King arrived, having marched in response to the news Umbles had brought to the post. After rest and treatment, Nolan set out for Fort Concho, where he arrived on August 14.[37]

Nolan's ill-fated expedition cost the lives of four troopers. Privates Isaac Derwin, John Gordon, John Bond, and John Isaacs died of thirst and exhaustion. Twenty-five horses and four mules were also lost. Sergeant Umbles, Corporals Gilmore and Fremont (the post librarian), and Private Alexander Nolan were court-martialed, dishonorably discharged, and sentenced to a year of imprisonment for desertion, although Colonel Grierson had recommended leniency because of the extenuating circumstances involved.[38]

Leniency may well have been in order, for desertion was the most com-

37 Ibid.; Medical History, Fort Griffin, vol. 103.
38 Nolan to the AAG, Department of Texas, August 20, 1877; Organizational Returns, Tenth Cavalry, August 1877; Miles, "Fort Concho in 1877," 49. Nolan was a native of Ireland who joined the regular army in 1852 and was promoted to second lieutenant, Sixth Cavalry, in 1862. He was a first lieutenant at the close of the Civil War and was commissioned a captain in the Tenth Cavalry in July 1866. He remained with the Tenth for sixteen years before transferring to the Third Cavalry in December 1882 with the rank of major. He died less than a year later on October 25, 1883, after thirty-one years of service. Despite many ups and down, he was an able and humane officer. Heitman, *Historical Register*, 1:750.

mon serious offense in the frontier army. For twenty-five years after the Civil War, a third of all men recruited became deserters, and in 1873 the army made an effort to curb the practice by adopting a policy of amnesty for those who surrendered voluntarily. The four troopers of Nolan's Company A fell in this category, and Grierson's request was in accord with then-current policy. In addition, the buffalo soldiers of both the Ninth and the Tenth Cavalry had an outstanding record for faithful service, with a desertion rate well below any other units in the army. For the year 1877, despite the most arduous service in one of the most demanding regions of the country, Grierson's Tenth had a total of 18 desertions as compared with 184 for Mackenzie's famous Fourth Cavalry. Its sister regiment—the Ninth Cavalry—had, moreover, a total of 6 as compared to 172 for the Seventh Cavalry.[39]

The year had been a difficult one in any case at Fort Concho and particularly for Captain Nolan, whose wife had died earlier in the year. Young Lieutenant Hans J. Gasman had returned from a scout to find his infant child, whom he had never seen, dead at the age of six days. One of the telegraph operators had gone insane from loneliness, and Surgeon King's maid had been "eating dirt." Neither Grierson nor his troopers were popular in the nearby village of Saint Angela, the sole source of night life in the immediate area. Grierson described the place as a "resort for desperate characters and . . . mainly made up of gambling and drinking saloons and other disreputable places."[40]

Dreary and dangerous though Saint Angela's "resorts" were for a black trooper, there had been only minor clashes until the fall of 1877. Oddly enough, it was the arrival of a few Texas Rangers that brought serious trouble. Several rangers visited Nasworthy's saloon to drink and dance. When they discovered that some troopers were doing likewise, they pulled their six-shooters and pistol-whipped the soldiers. When the incident was reported at the post, Grierson asked the ranger captain, John S. Sparks, for an apology. Instead, he received the braggart answer that the little ranger company could whip the entire Fort Concho garrison. Fortunately for all concerned, Grierson's temper was equal to the occasion.

The affair did not end there, however, for the angry troopers armed themselves, went back to Nasworthy's, and shot up the place, killing an inno-

39 Rickey, *Forty Miles a Day,* 143, 154; House, H. Exec. Doc. 1, 45th Cong., 2d sess., pt. 2, p. 49.

40 Grierson to the AAG, Washington, D.C., January 12, 1880, LR, AGO; Miles, "Fort Concho in 1877," 29.

cent bystander. Responsibility for this unfortunate turn of events pointed squarely at Captain Sparks, and he left the ranger service.[41]

A few months later more-serious trouble occurred in Morris's saloon, where a party of cowboys and hunters surrounded a sergeant from D Company, cut the chevrons from his sleeves, the stripes from his pants, and had a good laugh over his discomfiture. They did not laugh for very long. The soldier returned to the post and gathered up some fellow troopers. Armed with carbines, they went to Morris's. A blazing gunfight at close quarters followed in which one hunter was killed and two others wounded, while Private John L. Brown was killed and another trooper wounded.

Sparks's replacement, Captain G. W. Arrington, came to the post with a party of rangers intent on arresting First Sergeant George Goldsby of D Company for allowing the troopers to get their carbines. Grierson, however, challenged their authority on a federal post. Meanwhile, Goldsby, a native of Selma, Alabama, had departed for parts unknown. Nine troopers of Company D were indicted for murder and one, William Mace, was given a death sentence, although he later won an appeal. There is no record of any indictment of the others who participated in this affair. The day was still far distant when justice or injustice fell equally on men regardless of race, color, or creed, and the buffalo soldiers had not seen the last of Captain Arrington.[42]

Grierson and his regiment had little time to reflect on an unsatisfactory environment, however, for with the spring of 1878, the old Rio Grande troubles flared with renewed violence. So great was the upswing of revolutionary activity and Indian raiding that Mackenzie replaced Shafter in command of the District of the Nueces. Six companies of the Fourth Cavalry were moved from Indian Territory to add their strength to the border forces.[43]

This move enabled Grierson to withdraw most of his troopers along the lower Rio Grande and concentrate them in his own District of the Pecos. There Lipans, Kickapoos, and Mescaleros were raiding with vengeance. But trouble loomed at Fort Sill, where the reservation Indians were growing restless and sullen over inadequate rations. Thus, it was necessary to shift

41 Haley, *Fort Concho and the Texas Frontier*, 274.

42 *Galveston Daily News*, March 1, 1878; Organizational Returns, Tenth Cavalry, February 1878. Most accounts of this trouble give Goldsby's name as "Goldsbery," which is incorrect. He enlisted as a private in 1867 and by 1872 had risen to the rank of sergeant major. Discharged at the expiration of his five-year term, he reenlisted and had become D Company's first sergeant. Registers of Enlistments in the U.S. Army, 1798–1914, microcopy 233, U.S. Army Commands, RG 98, NA.

43 House, H. Exec. Doc. 1, 45th Cong., 3d sess., pt. 2, p. 87; Organizational Returns, Tenth Cavalry, January 1878.

Nolan's A, Lee's G, and Baldwin's I Companies under Colonel Davidson to that post.[44]

Davidson, his usual temperamental self, soon became engaged in quarreling with his company commanders. Baldwin, Nolan, and Lee were reprimanded for their dress, manner of saluting, and lack of soldierly bearing and constantly reminded that they could be "black booked." Finally, Baldwin exploded in a letter to the adjutant general complaining of Davidson's "tyrannical character" and harsh treatment and asking for a full investigation. Baldwin's request was denied, and his wife took up the cudgels in her husband's behalf and wrote a letter to President Rutherford B. Hayes detailing the mistreatment her spouse had suffered and describing Davidson as "nearly always under the influence of alcoholic stimulant."[45]

In the midst of this heated exchange, detachments of buffalo soldiers pursued their old enemies, the horse thief and bootlegger, with considerable success. The overriding problem at Fort Sill, however, was simply too many hungry Indians. In providing ration allotments for the tribes, the Indian Bureau had made liberal allowance for fresh meat that Indian hunters could supply from the buffalo range. But the once vast herds of buffalo had been virtually exterminated by 1877, and food from this source had dwindled to a vanishing point. There had been no corresponding increase in the ration allotment, and grafting contractors made inroads into an already inadequate supply. The result was thousands of half-starved Indians.

To alleviate this sorry situation and to avoid a possible outbreak, Indian agents permitted small parties of armed Indians, under military escort, to leave the reservation in search of game. The appearance of roving parties of Indian hunters along the northern border of Texas created alarm among farmers and ranchers who feared for their crops, cattle, and hair, although few, if any, could cite more than the loss of a few head of stock. Pleas for protection were sent to Major John B. Jones, commanding the Texas Fron-

44 Organizational Returns, Tenth Cavalry, January 1878. Captain Lee was a popular officer at Fort Griffin and received a letter of tribute signed by twenty-five prominent citizens, which appeared in the *Fort Griffin Echo* of January 10, 1878. Praise for an officer commanding black troops in Texas was rare indeed. In 1878 the Department of Texas was divided into a number of districts—the Rio Grande, the Nueces, the Pecos, and North Texas—commanded (respectively) by Colonel George Sykes, Twentieth Infantry; Colonel Mackenzie; Colonel Grierson; and Colonel H. B. Clitz, Tenth Infantry.

45 Mrs. T. A. Baldwin to President Hayes, October 13, 1878, LR, AGO; Baldwin to the AG, July 28, 1878, ibid.; Judge Advocate General Swain to Davidson, May 21, 1878, ibid.; Baldwin to the AG, September 22, 1878, ibid.

tier Battalion. He, in turn, sent Captain Arrington with C Company of the rangers to the North Texas frontier with orders to kill any armed Indians he could find.

On January 15, 1879, while scouting along the Pease River, the rangers spied a party of Kiowas, who fled as they approached. In a hot pursuit one Indian was killed while the others took refuge in a village of fourteen lodges. Arrington was preparing to charge when a detachment of Nolan's A Company approached and informed him that the Indians were out hunting under their supervision. Arrington complained in his report to Jones that the Indians were not under the control of the troopers, but he admitted he had learned of no depredations except one in which a rancher had lost six head of cattle.[46]

Given the situation, friction between ranger and buffalo soldier was inevitable, and the former needed little excuse. In May a small band of Comanches fled to the reservation with Nolan and A in pursuit. Close behind were two small parties of peaceful Comanches under Black Bear and White Eagle, who were authorized to assist Nolan in rounding up the runaways. Nolan searched along Red River, crossed south to the headwaters of the Pease, and then into Blanco Canyon, where he halted at the store of a Mr. Jacobs. Although white thieves had robbed Jacobs of some horses, new rifles, and one thousand dollars in cash, he had seen no Indians. Presently Black Bear and White Eagle joined Nolan and assisted in scouting the Double Lakes country, where the latter had so nearly lost his life in the summer of 1877. No sign of the Comanches was found, and Nolan felt certain they had gone on west across the Staked Plains to join the Apaches.[47]

Meanwhile, Captain June Peake and a detachment of Company B, Texas Rangers, out on a scout near Big Spring, came upon a party of Comanches butchering some colts and immediately attacked. The Indians, fighting like cornered wildcats, stood off the rangers until nightfall, when they retreated westward. Peake pursued the next day but ran into an ambush that cost the

46 House, H. Exec. Doc. 1, 45th Cong., 3d sess., pt. 2, p. 40; Nolan to the PA, Fort Sill, January 8, 1879, LR, AGO; Arrington to Jones, June 20, 1879, LR, AGO; Webb, *Texas Rangers,* 413. The Kiowas were not guilty of depredations, but in April 1879 they killed a Texan named Earle in retaliation for the killing of one of their tribesmen by the rangers in January. Lieutenant Colonel John Hatch to the AAG, Department of the Missouri, April 18, 1879, LR, AGO.

47 Nolan to the AAG, Department of the Missouri, July 22, 1879, LR, AGO; Lieutenant Colonel Hatch to Commanding Officer, Fort Concho, Texas, May 2, 1879, ibid.

life of Ranger W. G. Anglin and seriously wounded another. So hot was the Indian fire that Peake had to withdraw and leave Anglin's body behind on the field.

The day following Peake's fight, Lieutenant C. R. Ward with a detachment of D Company of the Tenth, scouting out of Fort Concho, struck the trail of the rangers and the Indians and followed it to where Anglin's body lay. The buffalo soldiers buried Anglin where he had fallen, but they lost the trail of the Comanches.[48]

In his report Peake blamed Nolan, Black Bear, and White Eagle for the fight. He charged Nolan with arming the Indians and turning them loose on their promise that they would return to Fort Sill. Instead, they had committed depredations and fought his rangers when they overtook them. Peake's report spawned inquiries from both General Ord and General Pope, but a thorough investigation revealed that Peake was in error. The Indians he had fought were the runaway Comanches from Fort Sill under Chief Black Horse, the same party that Nolan and the Indians with him had been pursuing.[49]

Ranger headquarters remained unconvinced, however, and the stage was set for a fiery clash between Captain Arrington and Colonel Davidson. Reports of large parties of armed Indians along the Sweetwater in the Texas Panhandle brought Arrington and his company north to scout along that stream. They turned up no Indians, but they did encounter Davidson and a detachment of buffalo soldiers. Arrington told Davidson bluntly that he intended to kill any armed Indian he could find, and Davidson, hardly the man to be awed or impressed by a threat, just as bluntly informed the ranger that if he or his men killed an Indian who was causing no trouble, it would bring serious trouble to settlers in the area. Thus he proposed to keep troops in the vicinity to prevent any collision between rangers and reservation Indians.

Arrington reported that Davidson had threatened to fire on him, and the air became extremely tense. Fortunately, no incident arose to provoke further difficulties between two equally determined and stubborn men.

48   Peake to Jones, July 5, 1879, ibid.; Nye, *Carbine and Lance,* 238–39; Organizational Returns, Tenth Cavalry, June 1879.
49   Peake to the AG, State of Texas, September 3, 1870, LR, AGO; Lieutenant W. C. Manning, Twenty-fifth Infantry, to the AAG, Department of the Missouri, February 6, 1880, ibid.

Little wonder, however, that no love was lost between officers and men of the Tenth Cavalry and the Texas Rangers.[50]

While three companies of the regiment were thus engaged in watching over reservation Indians and fighting verbal battles with the rangers, the remaining companies were doing their utmost to make the District of the Pecos a safe place for settlers. It was not easy. In the first four months of 1878, hostile Indians, still angry over encroachments onto what had once been their excellent hunting lands and still facing miserable conditions on reservations, killed fourteen persons in the district. Despite their best efforts, the buffalo soldiers failed to overtake their fleeing parties. With only one man for every 120 square miles, their lack of success was no reflection on Grierson and his regiment, a fact that General Sheridan realized fully. In his annual report Sheridan described the situation accurately: "In all other countries, it is the custom to establish garrisons of not less than a regiment or a brigade, while we have for the performance of similar duties only one or two companies; with us, regiments are rarely if ever together, the posts are generally garrisoned by one, two, or four companies, who are expected to hold and guard, against one of the most acute and wary foes in the world, a space of country that in any other land would be held by a brigade. To do this requires sleepless watchfulness, great activity, and tireless energy."[51]

Given these circumstances, Grierson was convinced that a change in strategy was required in order to cope successfully with the old hit-and-run challenge. Beginning in May and continuing throughout the remainder of 1878 and all of 1879, Grierson kept his troopers continually in the field. Many camps and subposts were established from which the scene of a raid could be reached quickly and with some possibility of overtaking the raiders. Underlying the effort was the determination "to make a vigorous effort to drive the Indians and other marauders out of my District, and prevent them, if possible, from returning to commit further depredations."[52]

In 1878 alone, hard-riding columns under Carpenter, Keyes, Norvell, Lebo, and others patrolled and scouted nearly twenty-five thousand miles,

50 Manning to the AAG, Department of the Missouri, February 6, 1880; Arrington to the AG, State of Texas, June 18, 1879, LR, AGO; Pope to the AAG, Military Division of the Missouri, February 7, 1880, ibid; Webb, *Texas Rangers,* 413–14.

51 House, H. Exec. Doc. 1, 45th Cong., 3d sess., pt. 2, pp. 82, 33.

52 Organizational Returns, Tenth Cavalry, May–December 1878; Grierson to the AAG, Department of Texas, December 28, 1878, File 1653.

opened new roads, and mapped every stream, water hole, and mountain pass that came under their observant eyes. Grierson himself spent much time in the saddle gaining an intimate knowledge of the region in his charge. In October 1878 he left Fort Concho with twenty veteran troopers and rode west to Horsehead Crossing on the Pecos. There he turned upstream to Pope's Well on the Texas–New Mexico border and west again along Delaware Creek and Independence Spring to the Guadalupe Mountains. Wild game abounded, and the command feasted on deer and antelope as the troopers explored Blue River Canyon.

The beauty of the country stirred the sensitive musician's heart: "The Cañon is situated just south of the boundary line of New Mexico, is from eight to ten miles in length, and varies in width from fifty feet or less at the head, north of Guadalupe Peak, to half a mile or more near the mouth of the Cañon which opens to the east. On either side as you enter the mountains rise almost perpendicularly to the height of three thousand feet, and besides the great variety of pine, White Oak, Post Oak, Maple, Ash, Wild Cherry, Elm, Hackberry and Mansenita, abounds . . . frost had set in and the great variety of tints and hues of foliage, from dark green to pure carmine, added greatly to the life and beauty of the magnificent scenery."[53]

From the Guadalupes, Grierson and his twenty troopers cut southwest, skirting the Sierra del Diablo and Carrizo Mountains and riding on to the Rio Grande at Fort Quitman. From this lonely post he moved east to Eagle Springs, where he inspected Captain Viele's C Company, and then marched on to Fort Davis for a look at Carpenter's proud H. On November 5 he set out due south, found and pushed through a gap in the Santiago Mountains, located water where none was expected, and again reached the Rio Grande downriver from San Felipe, about equidistant from Forts Davis and Stockton. After locating a number of fording places, the command marched for Fort Concho, which they reached late in the month after an absence of six weeks.

The intimate knowledge Grierson gained on this long scout, combined with that of his company commanders, provided the avenues for the tough buffalo soldiers to clear their district of raiders before 1879 was out. Officers and men of the regiment could look back on a task well done, and Grierson could reflect on the future of this rugged region. He was convinced it was

53 Grierson to the AAG, Department of Texas, December 28, 1878.

destined to "become a great resort for those seeking health and enjoyment."[54] Many years would pass before this prophecy came true. But in a few short months, the men of the Tenth would be called upon to apply all the skill and knowledge they possessed to meet the greatest challenge of their lives—invasion by the wily and, to their enemies, deadly Apaches.

54 Ibid.

Apaches, Civil Broils, and Utes

The movement of the Ninth Cavalry to the District of New Mexico in the winter and spring of 1875–76 plunged the regiment headlong into the Apache troubles that had plagued the New Mexico–Arizona region for centuries. For over three hundred years the Apaches had fought first the Spanish, who had seized them as slaves for their mines to the south, and later the Mexicans, who by the nineteenth century had placed a bounty on their heads. Following the Treaty of Guadalupe Hidalgo in 1848, which ended the U.S. war with Mexico and gave the Americans vast new territory in the Southwest, the Apaches fiercely resisted U.S. efforts to dispossess them of their homeland and to prevent them from raiding into Mexico.[1]

The Civil War presented the Apaches with a rare opportunity to drive out many of their white tormentors. In retaliation, Brigadier General James H. Carleton, commanding Union forces in the area, conducted an all-out campaign against them and enjoyed some temporary success. The increasing flow of settlement after the war, however, brought renewed hostilities on a greater scale than ever before. Both Indian and white committed grisly atrocities and, as historian Edward Everett Dale observes, "sudden death stalked every trail and lurked behind every rock or clump of cactus."[2]

1 Worcester, *Apaches*, 3–80.
2 Dale, *Indians of the Southwest*, 95; Blount, "The Apache in the Southwest," 24–25; Twitchell, *Leading Facts of New Mexican History*, 2:428–29.

Such was the state of affairs when President Grant launched his Peace Policy. Special peace commissioners led successive missions to Apache country in 1871 and 1872. Vincent Colyer, secretary of the newly created Board of Indian Commissioners, first visited New Mexico and recommended the removal of the Warm Springs Apaches from their reserve near Ojo Caliente to a new location in the Tularosa Valley. After an extensive tour of Arizona, Colyer selected Fort Apache, Camp Grant, and Camp Verde as permanent reservations as well as three temporary ones at Camp McDowell, Beal's Spring, and Date Creek.[3]

Hard on Colyer's heels came Brigadier General O. O. Howard, still head of the Freedman's Bureau but now acting as President Grant's personal representative. Howard, after making a valiant effort, achieved some success in persuading Apaches to move to reduce hostilities. He proved especially effective with the Chiricahua followers of Cochise, who agreed to relocate on a reservation in the mountains near the Mexican border. Howard also enlarged the area Colyer had selected at Fort Apache in order to create two reservations, San Carlos and White Mountain. Finally, he abolished the temporary asylums that Colyer had created.[4]

Despite these efforts, Apache raiding continued, and violence frequently erupted between them and Anglo newcomers. In the fall of 1872, Brigadier General George Crook began an around-the-clock campaign to drive the Apaches into their reservations. A dedicated and able soldier, Crook conducted a grim and unrelenting operation that ended only when most of the hostile Apaches surrendered at Camp Verde on April 6, 1873. Meanwhile, most of the Mescaleros, constantly harassed by troops and victimized by lawless whites, were ready for peace and settled on a reserve near Fort Stanton, New Mexico.[5]

Prospects seemed bright in 1873 for a lasting peace, even though some bands continued their isolated raiding. These too might soon have ceased had those genuinely interested in Indian welfare actually guided policy. Tragically, this was not so. Scheming contractors, delivering goods to the various agencies at the same price, saw opportunities for a windfall if they

3 Lockwood, *Apache Indians,* 184; Dale, *Indians of the Southwest,* 98.
4 Lockwood, *Apache Indians,* 187; Dale, *Indians of the Southwest,* 100.
5 Lockwood, *Apache Indians,* 188–202; Twitchell, *Leading Facts of New Mexican History,* 2:438. Crook was not happy about serving in Arizona Territory, but he won respect and a large measure of trust from the Indians. See Crook, *Autobiography,* 163–80. See also Robinson, *General Crook,* 104–41.

could persuade the Indian Bureau to concentrate the Apaches of Arizona on one reservation. Miners, lumbermen, cattlemen, and homesteaders also saw advantages since they coveted the Indian lands that such a policy would throw open. These interests coalesced into the infamous "Tucson Ring." Led by "greedy contractors" from Tucson, Arizona's territorial capitol, they pressured Washington officials to concentrate the Apaches at San Carlos since it was convenient for their operations. Success, as usual, attended their efforts despite warnings by responsible officials and army officers on the scene that such a policy would prove disastrous.[6]

Concentration was a blow to the Apaches, especially since they were not a tribal people. Instead, they had always organized themselves in smaller bands, which included the Chiricahuas, the Coyoteros, the Mescaleros, the Warm Springs, and the Mimbres, among others. Moreover, tensions and dissension characterized the relationships between these bands and the leaders of the various groups. In that context, concentration would have proven difficult even in an ideal setting. Unfortunately, "the desolate sand waste of San Carlos" was, as novelist Owen Wister describes it, an area of "stone and ashes and thorns, with some scorpions and rattlesnakes thrown in." Understandably, the Apaches detested the location and never accepted it as their homeland.[7] Their misery over finding themselves consigned to this inhospitable and depressing location greatly increased the chances that many of them would run away at the earliest opportunity. Others would break for freedom as soon as conditions or confrontations in this hellhole furnished the additional spark.

The able but arrogant agent John P. Clum, who arrived at San Carlos in 1874, implemented the new policy with a firm hand. He organized an efficient cadre of Indian police and instituted a viable system of Indian self-government for the one thousand Apaches then at San Carlos. In the spring and summer of 1875, Clum transferred more than three thousand Indians from Camp Verde and White Mountain with minimal difficulty. The Indian

---

6 Lockwood, *Apache Indians*, 204–7; Major General J. M. Schofield, Commanding the Military Division of the Pacific, "Annual Report of Operations," LR, Affairs on the Rio Grande and Texas Frontier, Consolidated File 1653, AGO, RG 94, NA [hereafter cited as File 1653]; Colonel August V. Kautz, Commanding the Department of Arizona, to the AAG, Military Division of the Pacific, October 20, 1875, File 1653. Kautz placed the blame for the concentration policy squarely on contractors in Tucson and predicted the policy would lead to war. See also Debo, *Geronimo*, 95.

7 Lockwood, *Apache Indians*, 206; Worcester, *Apaches*, 140, 160–61. The Wister quote is found in Schubert, *Black Valor*, 43–44.

Bureau authorized no additional transfers to San Carlos. Instead, softening its stance, the bureau permitted the Warm Springs Apaches to return to their old reserve near Ojo Caliente in New Mexico.[8]

The uneasy quiet that prevailed along the Apache frontier during the winter and early spring of 1875–76 ended in April. With meat scarce at the Chiricahua agency at Apache Pass, Agent Tom Jeffords told these Indians that they must supplement their supply by hunting. Acting on these orders, a band under Taza—the successor to Cochise, who had died the previous year—set out for a hunt in the Dragoon Mountains. A bitter quarrel divided the band, and a majority led by Taza returned and encamped near their agency. A few under Skinya, Taza's rival, remained in the mountains, and from this group a handful of warriors raided into Mexico and returned with a quantity of gold and silver.

On the morning of April 6, one of Skinya's warriors rode to the Overland Mail Station at Sulphur Spring and exchanged some of the stolen money for whisky with a Mr. Rogers, the station keeper. Next day he returned for more whisky, accompanied by another warrior. Both Apaches were drunk and Rogers, with fear overcoming greed, refused to sell them more. The Indians shot and killed him along with the station cook, a man named Spence. After taking all the whisky and ammunition they could carry, they stole some horses and returned to their camp.

The following morning some of Skinya's warriors, roaring drunk, rode into the settlements along the San Pedro River, killed a rancher named Lewis, rounded up a number of horses, and fled into the San Jose Mountains.[9] News of the murders of Rogers, Spence, and Lewis led to exaggerated reports of a major Chiricahua outbreak, and troops in both Arizona and New Mexico were rushed into the field. A detachment of the Sixth Cavalry located Skinya and his followers on a peak in the Dragoon Mountains, but the troopers, unable to dislodge them, were forced to retire to Fort Bowie. Some six weeks later Skinya and his followers came in to Taza's camp to persuade the latter to take to the warpath but instead met with a blunt refusal. A bloody fight followed in which Skinya and eight of his warriors were either killed or wounded, and the "outbreak" was over.[10]

8 Clum, "Geronimo," 122; E. P. Smith, Commissioner of Indian Affairs, to the Secretary of Interior, June 9, 1875, File 1653; Clum to E. P. Smith, July 31, 1985, File 1653.

9 Lockwood, *Apache Indians*, 214–15; Governor A. K. Safford to the Commissioner of Indian Affairs, April 17, 1876, SDLR, AGO, RG 94, NA.

10 Safford to the Commissioner of Indian Affairs, April 17, 1876, SDLR; Schofield to the AG, April 13, 1876, ibid.

Even though only half a dozen Chiricahuas had been involved in these troubles, Agent Clum was ordered to remove all Chiricahuas from their reservation and take them to San Carlos. The energetic agent accomplished his task in early June. Thus, several hundred Chiricahuas were uprooted and punished for the acts of a few. The Tucson Ring should have provided Skinya with an elaborate funeral, for he had supplied them with another easy victory. The citizens and soldiers of Arizona and New Mexico, however, would pay a high price in blood and terror for that triumph.[11]

Clum had not corralled all the Chiricahuas at San Carlos. Prior to the Skinya episode, some four hundred under Juh and Geronimo had fled to Mexico. There these Apaches raided and committed depredations. Clum later blamed Geronimo for all these acts, thereby giving him a notoriety that was undeserved, according to his biographer, Angie Debo. By the time these hostile Apaches returned to the vicinity of the Warm Springs reservation, where still other Chiricahuas had sought sanctuary to escape removal, the *Arizona Citizen* of Tucson was calling for "steady, unrelenting, hopeless, and undiscriminating war . . . until every valley and crest and crag and fastness shall send to high heaven the grateful incense of festering and rotting Chiricahuas." The climate had deteriorated almost beyond repair in Arizona Territory and southern New Mexico.[12]

This was the state of affairs that confronted Colonel Edward Hatch and his buffalo soldiers, newly arrived from Texas. The Ninth Cavalry was badly scattered and far understrength. Two companies were at Fort Bayard, one at Fort McRae, two at Fort Wingate, three at Fort Stanton, one at Fort Union, one at Fort Selden, one at Fort Garland, and one company—K—had still not transferred from Texas. With an authorized strength of 845 men, Hatch could field scarcely more than half that number. Worse yet, neither officers nor men were familiar with the country.[13]

But Hatch wasted no time on complaints. Detachments were thrown out from the various posts, scouting in all directions, while General John Pope was urged to build a fire under army recruiters to fill the depleted ranks. Pope scarcely needed urging to make every effort to bring the regiment to

11 Lockwood, *Apache Indians*, 216–17.
12 Debo, *Geronimo*, 97.
13 Organizational Returns, Ninth Cavalry, April 1876, AGO, RG 94, NA; House, H. Exec. Doc. 1, 45th Cong., 2d sess., pt. 2, p. 32. Companies A and C were at Bayard; B at McRae; E and I at Wingate; H, L, and M at Stanton; D at Union; F at Selden; and G at Garland. The total enlisted strength at this time was only 456 men.

Victorio
Courtesy Western History Collections, University of Oklahoma Libraries

Geronimo
Courtesy Western History Collections, University of Oklahoma Libraries

An Apache wickiup with two women in front, each holding a basket
Courtesy Western History Collections, University of Oklahoma Libraries

Typical Apache country
Courtesy U.S. Signal Corps, National Archives

full strength, but he was more than indignant at the Indian Bureau for creating what threatened to become a bloody mess. He wrote angrily to General Sheridan that the source of the trouble was simply a lack of food, which the bureau should have supplied. The Ninth had been placed in the almost intolerable position of either forcing the Indians to starve to death on their reservations or killing them if they left.[14]

Meanwhile, the far-flung detachments, though playing no part in the tragic removal of the Chiricahuas at Apache Pass to San Carlos, found more than enough to do in pursuing small parties from the bands of Juh and Geronimo as well as a few Warm Springs and Mescalero Apaches who had left their reservations for raiding. Little success attended these initial efforts, although the relentless Captain Henry Carroll and twenty-five hard-bitten veterans of F Company struck a fugitive band in the Florida Mountains on April 15, killed one warrior, and captured eleven horses.[15]

Hatch, fearing an outbreak of the Warm Springs Indians, journeyed to Ojo Caliente late in April 1876. He found little that was reassuring. The "visiting" Chiricahuas had spread their fears and restlessness among the Warm Springs people. Moreover, some truculent Mescalero warriors had come in from Fort Stanton to enliven affairs. The warriors were heavily armed with late-model weapons, including Springfield carbines and Smith-Wesson revolvers. The chiefs, including the potent Victorio, were openly defiant. They told an indignant Hatch that their people could easily live in Sonora and raid in the United States. Securing food, guns, and ammunition from the Mexicans posed no problem.[16]

The colonel reported to department headquarters that he would keep detachments on constant patrol, thereby in all likelihood curbing all but the most turbulent spirits. These his troopers most surely would have to whip. Hatch proved correct. Virtually ceaseless patrols for the remainder of 1876 kept raiding to a minimum. Searching troopers and hostile Apaches exchanged gunfire at least half a dozen times.[17]

---

14 Organizational Returns, Ninth Cavalry, April 1876; Pope to Sheridan, April 11, 1876, SDLR.

15 Organizational Returns, Ninth Cavalry, April 1876; Hutcheson, "Ninth Regiment of Cavalry," 285.

16 Hatch to the AAG, Department of the Missouri, May 20, 1876, SDLR.

17 Ibid. In September Captain Carroll had a skirmish in the Florida Mountains in which a dozen animals were recovered, but the few remaining encounters produced no losses to either troopers or Indians. See Organizational Returns, Ninth Cavalry, July–December 1876.

It was rough work for the buffalo soldiers. In a land of extremes, one day's march could bring searing desert heat that beat down mercilessly, provoking an aching thirst that often went unslaked for hours. The night often could be spent in lonely vigil on a frosty mountaintop. Through it all, with little time for relaxation, to say nothing of entertainment, the troopers performed their duty willingly and with little complaint. Indeed, desertion in the Ninth had all but reached the vanishing point.[18]

The new year opened on a decidedly different note. Hostile Chiricahuas stepped up their raids, and the more restless young men among the Warm Springs band and Mescaleros slipped away from the reservations to continue their raiding. Late in January 1877 word reached Fort Bayard that a party of forty to fifty Chiricahuas had fought a detachment of the Sixth Cavalry in Arizona and had probably moved eastward into New Mexico. Lieutenant Henry H. Wright with six men of Company C and three Navaho Indian scouts left the post at once to search for these Indians.

The trail was struck and followed into the Florida Mountains, where the Indian camp was located on the morning of January 24. Outnumbered badly, Wright did not attack but sought instead to persuade the Chiricahuas to surrender. Half an hour of talk proved fruitless. Suddenly Wright became aware that the women and children had left the camp, and he and his men were now completely surrounded by Apache warriors. Breaking off the council, Wright ordered his men to push through the encircling Indians. As they did, a deadly fight at close quarters broke out, with weapons fired and then used as clubs. In the center of the melee, Corporal Clinton Greaves fought like a cornered lion and managed to shoot until his carbine was empty. Afterward, he used it to bash his way through the Apaches, thereby permitting his companions to break free. With five of their number dead and more wounded, the Indians fled, leaving the field to Wright and his gallant nine. The troopers, suffering only minor wounds, gathered up six Indian ponies and returned to Fort Bayard. For his role in this affair, Corporal Greaves was awarded the Medal of Honor. Privates Richard Epps, Dick Mackadoo, John Adams, and one of the scouts, José Chaves, were all commended for bravery in action.[19]

18 House, H. Exec. Doc. 1, 45th Cong., 2d sess., pt. 2, p. 49. The Ninth suffered only 6 desertions for the year as compared with 170, 224, 172, and 174 for the Third, Fifth, Seventh, and Eighth Cavalry, respectively. The Tenth Cavalry in neighboring Texas had only 18 desertions.
19 Organizational Returns, Ninth Cavalry, January 1877; *Army and Navy Journal* 14 (May 12, 1877): 18; Memorandum 1555B (EB), February 13, 1879, AGO, RG 94, NA.

Four days later Captain C. D. Beyer with the whole of Company C and Captain Michael Cooney with a detachment of Company A found and followed a trail in the vicinity of Wright's engagement. Soon thereafter, the command came upon a camp of about twenty-five Apaches and attacked at once. The Indians took wing and eluded Beyer but lost all their camp equipage and supplies.[20]

Returning to Fort Bayard, Beyer recommended that Hatch station an officer and twenty men at Fort Cummings. Although it had been evacuated in 1873, trails leaving the Warm Springs reserve could "invariably be found in the valley between Fort Cummings and the Magdelena Mountains." Further, the old post was only twenty-five miles from the Florida Mountains, where parties rendezvoused. Hatch agreed, but he had no troopers to spare and wrote to General Pope requesting that D and L Companies, on duty in the Ute country of Colorado, be returned to New Mexico. Pope refused since they were "the only cavalry in that portion of the Department."[21]

Demands on the Ninth were so heavy that Hatch feared a loss of morale and asked Pope for permission to send the regimental band on a tour of the posts where his troopers were stationed. "The various Companies of the regiment should have the benefit of the Band a portion of the year," he wrote, and Pope consented readily. An evening concert became a rare treat indeed for trail-worn troopers, but Hatch's fears regarding morale were groundless. The men apparently thrived on the rough work.[22]

By early March Geronimo and many of his followers were constantly among the Warm Springs people. The commissioner of Indian affairs ordered Clum to take the necessary steps to arrest these fugitives and to call on the military for assistance if necessary. Clum requested Hatch's cooperation, and the latter readily agreed to send Major James Wade with A, B, and C Companies of the Ninth from Fort Bayard to Ojo Caliente to join with Clum and his Apache police in making the arrests.

Greaves's citation in part read, "for coolness and courage displayed in a hand to hand fight with the Apache Indians in the Florida Mountains of New Mexico, January 24, 1877." See also Schubert, *Black Valor*, 44–47.

20 Organizational Returns, Ninth Cavalry, January 1877; *Army and Navy Journal* 14 (May 12, 1877): 18.

21 Beyer to the AAG, District of New Mexico, January 30, 1877, LR, District of New Mexico, U.S. Army Commands, RG 98, NA; Pope to Hatch, March 31, 1877, ibid.

22 Hatch to the AAG, Department of the Missouri, March 20, 1877, LS, District of New Mexico, U.S. Army Commands, RG 98, NA.

The concentration of forces proved unnecessary, for Clum was able to accomplish his mission on April 21 without undue difficulty. He took a fateful step, however, in deciding to remove all the Warm Springs Apaches to San Carlos as well as the hostile Chiricahuas. It proved a costly mistake, for these Indians, abhorring San Carlos intensely, had no intention of remaining there. Clum's decision marked the beginning of one of the bloodiest chapters in New Mexican history and one of the most trying for the officers and men of the Ninth Cavalry.[23]

The lull before the storm for the Ninth came in the summer of 1877 and brought a welcome respite from almost constant field duty. Monotony never posed a problem, however. White cattle-thieves from Texas kept the Mescalero agency in such uproar that Agent F. C. Godfroy had to call upon Captain George A. Purington and H Company at Fort Stanton for aid in recovering stolen stock.[24] Captain Ambrose Hooker's E Company had its hands full with squatters who began moving into the Warm Springs reservation before the dust settled from the departing Indians. Far to the north, G Company had the unpleasant task of removing unauthorized settlers from the Los Pinos reservation in southern Colorado.[25]

By contrast, Captain Beyer and C Company were enjoying a well-earned rest at Mesilla. They gained the plaudits of the *Mesilla Independent* as having made "an enviable reputation wherever stationed" and always under "perfect discipline."[26] Such unaccustomed praise probably sent the troopers into a pleasant state of shock.

The summer, however, proved trying for Colonel Hatch. Wesley Merritt, lieutenant colonel of the Ninth for a decade, was promoted to colonel and transferred to the Fifth Cavalry in July 1876. An officer whose career was checkered with controversy, Lieutenant Colonel N. A. M. Dudley, filled the vacancy.[27]

23 *Annual Report of the Commissioner of Indian Affairs for the Year 1877*, 34–35. Clum remarks in his report that the "Cooperation of troops under General Hatch and Colonel Wade was perfect." Organizational Returns, Ninth Cavalry, April–May 1877. For a detailed report of the arrest and transfer of these Indians, see Clum, *Apache Agent*.
24 *Annual Report of the Commissioner of Indian Affairs for the Year 1877*, 157; Organizational Returns, Ninth Cavalry, July–August 1877.
25 Organizational Returns, Ninth Cavalry, April–May 1877; *Annual Report of the Commissioner of Indian Affairs for the Year 1877*, 44.
26 *Mesilla Independent*, August 25, 1877.
27 Organizational Returns, Ninth Cavalry, July 1876. Merritt eventually rose to the rank of major general. See Heitman, *Historical Register*, 1:386. Nathan Augustus Monroe Dudley was a native of Massachusetts who joined the Tenth Infantry in March 1855. His

No love had been lost between Hatch and Dudley since 1869, when they had served together on a court-martial in Jefferson, Texas. The two men had disagreed over a matter, the nature of which was never made public. Whatever it was, Dudley was a petty and contentious officer who suffered from a persecution complex, was often at odds with his superiors, and had a strong attachment for alcohol. Dudley was assigned to command the post at Fort Union, and doubtlessly Hatch was determined to keep a close watch on his new lieutenant colonel.[28]

Running true to form, Dudley was soon embroiled in a bitter quarrel with Captain A. S. Kimball, post quartermaster at Fort Union, over the quantity and control of transportation on the post. A difference of opinion over repair of porches along officers' row further exacerbated the controversy, as did Dudley's inability, in a drunken state, to comprehend a report Kimball submitted on the amount of cordwood on hand. On May 30, 1877, while Dudley was conducting an inspection of post transportation, the quarrel flamed into the open when he accused Kimball of fraud and charged Hatch with being a collaborator.[29]

Dudley must have known that he was heading for serious trouble. Nonetheless, he plunged headlong into additional difficulties by engaging in a petty squabble with the post chaplain, Rev. George Simpson, and suspending religious services for the summer. Shortly after, however, he charged to the defense of the chaplain's daughter, Lizzie, by accusing a local doctor, W. R. Tipton, of seducing her and demanding that he make amends or at least that he "restore the good name of the girl."[30]

Sorely tried, Hatch wrote to General Pope requesting Dudley's transfer to another post. The request was refused since his "disposition to be troublesome" would "probably find means to evince itself wherever he might be

---

career in the Civil War was undistinguished, and he emerged as a major in the Fifteenth Infantry. After brief service in the Twenty-fourth Infantry, he transferred to the Third Cavalry. Dudley was promoted to lieutenant colonel and assigned to the Ninth Cavalry on July 1, 1876. Heitman, *Historical Register,* 1:386.

28   Dudley was court-martialed at Camp McDowell, Arizona, in 1871 for drunkenness and conduct unbecoming an officer. For one explanation of the origin of the Hatch-Dudley feud, see Emmett, *Fort Union,* 176. Dudley's explanation was that they "simply didn't get along." Dudley to the AAG, Department of the Missouri, August 30, 1877, LR, District of New Mexico.

29   PA to Captain A. S. Kimball, April 23, 1877, LR, District of New Mexico; E. R. Platt to Dudley, October 31, 1877, LS, Department of the Missouri, U.S. Army Commands, RG 98, NA.

30   Emmett, *Fort Union,* 380.

stationed." Thus, Hatch was advised to deal with him "by strictly defining his duties and requiring rigid observance of them than by removing him to some other point."[31]

Dudley might have escaped further trouble at Union had he, in fact, tended to his duties. Instead, he soon charged that the post surgeon, Dr. Carvallo, was conniving with Hatch to embezzle funds donated to the post hospital. Hatch now lost all patience. He came to Union forthwith, placed Dudley under arrest, and removed him from command of the post.[32]

Hatch wasted no time in filing an impressive list of charges against Dudley with department headquarters. The latter was equally prompt in filing similar charges against Hatch. It was soon clear, however, that Pope wished to avoid a court-martial. He informed Hatch that such proceedings would be inordinately expensive and bring scandal to the service. It would be better "if the interest of the service and the requirements of discipline can be properly maintained, to avoid a trial." Still, Pope promised to send an experienced officer to investigate thoroughly affairs at Fort Union.[33]

Dudley, meanwhile, remained under close arrest. In September J. T. Martin, acting assistant surgeon, U.S. Army, examined Dudley and found him very nervous, "addicted to headaches," and in declining health from confinement to his quarters. Shortly thereafter, Pope ordered Hatch to release Dudley from arrest but to permit him no functions of command until the report of his investigating officer had been received.[34]

Pope's investigation ended in the convening of a court-martial at Fort Union on November 23, 1877. Weeks of testimony ended in Dudley being found guilty of defaming Captain Kimball, of vilifying and prejudicing Hatch, and of conduct prejudicial to good order and military discipline. He was suspended from rank and command and his pay was forfeited for three months. General Pope approved the verdict, but President Hayes did not and ordered the unexecuted portion of the sentence remitted. John C. Dent, post sutler at Fort Union, was an intimate of the lieutenant colonel as well as former President Grant's brother-in-law. Dudley benefited from having friends in high places.[35]

31 E. R. Platt to Hatch, August 11, 1877, LR, District of New Mexico.

32 Dudley to the AAG, Department of the Missouri, August 30, 1877; Emmett, *Fort Union*, 382.

33 E. R. Platt to Hatch, September 22, 1877, LR, District of New Mexico.

34 J. T. Martin to H. Kinzie, Surgeon General, Fifteenth Infantry, September 25, 1877, ibid.; Hatch to Dudley, October 15, 1877, ibid.

35 Emmett, *Fort Union*, 378.

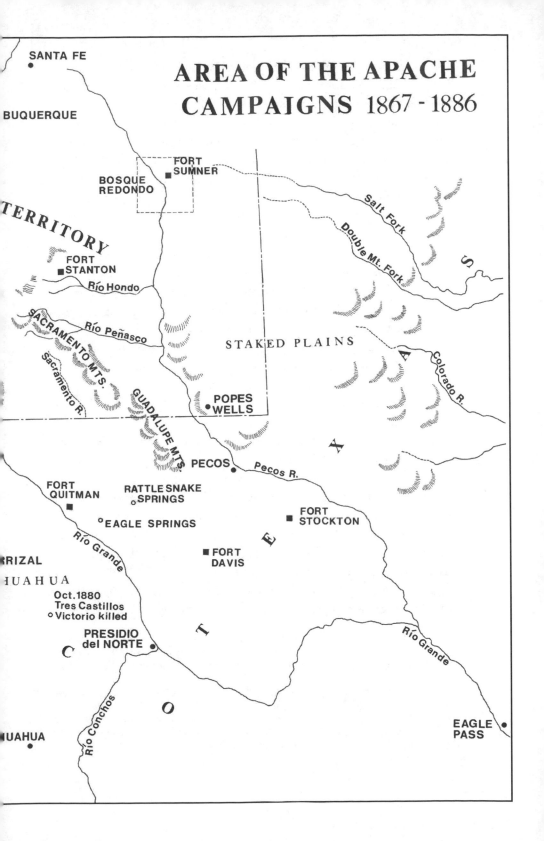

Thus, the Ninth was not free of Dudley. Hatch soon found himself forced to place Dudley in command at Fort Stanton, where shortly he was involved in an affair more serious than any of those at Fort Union.

Meanwhile, the "honeymoon" of the summer of 1877 did not carry over into fall. On September 2, 1877, Victorio and three hundred of his Warm Springs and Chiricahua followers fled the San Carlos reservation. Hatch immediately ordered every available man in his district into the field in pursuit. Four companies of the Ninth plunged into the rugged Mogollon Mountains, and three more searched out of Ojo Caliente while Hooker's E remained on the lookout in that vicinity.[36]

The Indians raided along the Upper Gila, killed a number of persons in outlying ranches, and stole a few horses and mules. Troopers, however, moving swiftly, forced them to retreat into the mountains. The breakout had been ill prepared, and Victorio had little in the way of arms, ammunition, food, or clothing. Swarming detachments kept him in constant motion, and he and his followers were soon in forlorn condition. Many were barefoot, others were naked, and hunger stalked their ranks. Early in October nearly two hundred of them, including Victorio, came in to Fort Wingate and surrendered. Within a few days seventy more came in, while the few remaining "outs" escaped into Mexico.[37]

Victorio told Colonel P.T. Swain, commanding at Wingate, that he and his people would not willingly return to San Carlos; they preferred to return to Warm Springs, for there they wished to be buried. For a time it appeared that this wish might be granted, and escorted by Captains Andrew Bennett and Francis Moore and Companies I and L of the Ninth, they were taken to Warm Springs bereft of arms and horses. But their stay was short, and before October ended they were back at San Carlos once more, although eighty of them, including Victorio, had managed to escape en route.[38]

During the next few months, a trickle of these Warm Springs escapees began arriving at the Mescalero reservations, where Agent Godfroy permit-

36 Organizational Returns, Ninth Cavalry, September 1877; *Mesilla Independent,* September 15, 1877; *Annual Report of the Commissioner of Indian Affairs for the Year 1877,* 20–21. Eight persons were killed in these raids, while troopers and scouts killed thirteen Apaches.

37 *Mesilla Independent,* September 15, 1877; Captain Horace Jewett, Fifteenth Infantry, to the AAG, District of New Mexico, October 8, 1877, LR, District of New Mexico.

38 Swain to the AAG, District of New Mexico, November 1, 1877, LR, District of New Mexico; Pope to Colonel R. C. Drum, AAG, Military Division of the Missouri, October 18, 1877, ibid.; Organizational Returns, Ninth Cavalry, October 1877.

ted them to remain. In February 1878 Victorio and a few followers came to Ojo Caliente and surrendered to Captain Hooker. They were willing to stay in their old homes but refused even to discuss a return to San Carlos. A decision was then made to join them with their kinsmen at Mescalero. This was not to their liking, and they fled to the mountains once again. In June, however, they reappeared, this time at the Mescalero agency, and received Godfroy's promise of good treatment. A short time later their wives and children were brought to them from San Carlos. All outward signs pointed to peace at last with these divided and unhappy people.

The Ninth had been fortunate during this short campaign. Not a single man had fallen to an Indian bullet. But a fatal accident had occurred in the Mogollons, and the aftermath sent a wave of bitterness through the regiment. Corporal James Betters of C Company received a mortal wound when his carbine discharged accidentally. Before his death, Betters asked that he be buried at Fort Bayard, and his wishes were carried out, but Captain Beyer, commanding C, complained bitterly about the manner of interment. The body was laid to rest in the same condition in which it arrived at the post— not even the face was washed. The coffin was placed on a police cart used for carrying garbage and driven by a military convict, "and in this manner, without a flag covering his coffin, without a formal escort, without a single mourner or friend to follow the poor fellows remains to their last resting place was all that remained of this soldier, who had served his country honestly and faithfully for the space of eleven years."[39] Hatch ordered Major Wade to conduct an investigation. He did so but absolved those responsible for the burial because of the condition of the body when it reached Fort Bayard.

The echo of gunfire had scarce died away in the Mogollons, ending the threat of a major war with the Warm Springs Apaches, when a civil dispute in El Paso suddenly erupted into small-scale civil war. For many years people on both sides of the Rio Grande had gathered salt from large deposits some one hundred miles east of El Paso. The area was isolated and thinly settled, and the sharing of salt occasioned no difficulty. After the Civil War, however, more people settled in El Paso and in the little river towns of Ysleta, Socorro, and San Elizario to the south. Thus, ideas of profiting from the sale of salt became attractive.

39 Captain Beyer to the AAAG, District of New Mexico, October 3, 1877, LR, District of New Mexico.

The salt issue became political in the late 1860s when a "Salt Ring" and an "Anti-Salt Ring" formed and supported candidates for local and state offices. The leader of the Anti-Salt Ring was an influential priest of San Elizario, Antonio Borajo, who used his great prestige among the Mexican element to elect A. J. Fountain to the state senate. Borajo's motives, however, were far from pure. He soon proposed that Fountain take possession of the salt deposits and then Borajo would advise his Mexican followers to pay the fees. The profits would be divided equally between him and Fountain. This cozy scheme fell through when Fountain flatly rejected the proposal. Borajo then joined forces with two recent arrivals, Luis Cardis and Charles Howard, to prevent any legislation whatever regarding the deposits.

All went well with the triumvirate for a time. Cardis was elected to the state legislature and Howard became district judge, and the people contin-ued to gather salt as before. But Howard and Cardis quarreled over politi-cal matters, and twice Howard pummeled Cardis in fistfights. Bitter factionalism developed, with Borajo and Cardis leading the Mexican element and Howard heading a small minority composed of a few Mexi-cans and all the Americans.

At this point Howard took the step that led to violent civil strife. In the name of his father-in-law, George B. Zimpleman of Austin, Texas, he now took possession of the salt deposits. With the assistance of a surveyor and John E. McBride, he surveyed the deposits and put up notices that no salt was to be taken without first paying a fee. The Mexican population fumed, and a mob, aroused to fever pitch by Borajo, prepared to lynch Judge Howard. The judge was caught at Ysleta, but his life was spared when Cardis proposed that he be set free, provided that he agree never to return and to post a fourteen-thousand-dollar bond. On October 3, after his release, he left for Mesilla, New Mexico.[40]

Americans in the area feared the fury of the mob, and reports indicated that a large body of Mexicans was gathering across the river to take action with the mob. When news of these developments reached Washington, Hatch received orders to send a detachment to El Paso to protect govern-ment property and to offer sanctuary to those desiring it. In no case were the troops to interfere in civil affairs unless U.S. officials were prevented from

40 Sol Schutz, U.S. Commercial Agent, El Paso, to Second Assistant Secretary of State, October 21 1877, File 1653; Webb, *Texas Rangers,* 347–52; *Mesilla Independent,* October 6, 1877.

carrying out their duties or Mexicans from Mexico intervened. Hatch promptly ordered Lieutenant Rucker and twenty buffalo soldiers to El Paso.[41]

On October 10 Judge Howard returned to El Paso armed with a double-barreled shotgun and set out to find Cardis, whom he regarded as an "infamous monster" and the source of his difficulties. He found his quarry in the store of Samuel Schultz and Brothers and, without a word, riddled Cardis with blasts from both barrels of the weapon. Howard then climbed into his buggy and drove back to Mesilla.[42]

The Cardis slaying outraged the Mexican population, and large groups of heavily armed men roamed the streets of Ysleta, Socorro, and San Elizario. Americans feared a massacre and appealed to Governor Hubbard of Texas for protection. Major John B. Jones of the Texas Rangers came to El Paso, decided at once that the situation was explosive, and organized a ranger company of twenty men under Lieutenant John B. Tays. Apparently satisfied that Tays could keep matters under control, Jones returned to Austin.

Unfortunately, Howard learned early in December that wagons had left San Elizario for the salt deposits. He came to El Paso and, with Tays and the rangers as escorts, left for San Elizario to prosecute the trespassers. Word of Howard's intentions preceded him, and an inflamed mob of more than four hundred men prepared to kill him, rangers notwithstanding. When Howard and Tays reached ranger quarters in San Elizario on the evening of Wednesday, December 12, they were surrounded immediately and forced to hole up inside. Charles Ellis, a local merchant, attempted to reason with the mob, but he was roped and shot, and after his throat was cut, his body was thrown in a pool of water.[43]

Tays managed to get word of his plight to Captain Thomas Blair, Fifteenth Infantry, at Fort Bliss, and Blair marched at once with a detachment of nineteen men. Near San Elizario, however, a strong force of Mexicans stopped him. They informed him that the town's trouble was a purely local matter and that they would fight him if he failed to turn back. Blair's nerve

41 Sheridan to Townsend, October 21, 1877, File 1653.

42 *Mesilla Independent,* October 6, 1877; Webb, *Texas Rangers,* 353; Casey, *Texas Border and Some Borderliners,* 146; Report of Captain Thomas Blair, Fifteenth Infantry, to the AAG, District of New Mexico, December 19, 1877, LR, District of New Mexico.

43 Webb, *Texas Rangers,* 355; Casey, *Texas Border and Some Borderliners,* 147; Carlysle G. Raht, *The Romance of Davis Mountains and Big Bend Country* (Odessa, Tex.: Rahtbooks, 1963), 210–14.

apparently failed him, and he retired to Fort Bliss. Had he pushed on, he could well have saved many lives, for it is doubtful that the Mexicans would have fired on federal troops, thereby assuring swift and decisive intervention from Washington.[44]

Meanwhile, Tays had barricaded the doors and windows of the ranger quarters and cut portholes in the walls. In the building, in addition to Howard and the rangers, were Ranger Campbell's wife and two children; John G. Atkinson, who was a merchant of San Elizario; John McBride; and a Mr. Loomis of Fort Stockton and his black servant.

On Thursday morning the battle opened, and heavy firing continued until the following Wednesday. Then, with three of his rangers dead and two others wounded, and with ammunition, food, and water supplies running low, Tays arranged for a parley under a flag of truce. Mob leaders told the lieutenant they only wanted Howard, and if he was turned over to them, the others were free to leave. Tays refused but on his return informed Howard of the terms, although he also told him that he would be defended to the last man.

As Howard's insistence, he and Tays went out to the mob to talk and were at once seized and disarmed. Meanwhile, on Atkinson's instigation, the other rangers surrendered. A firing squad of nine men swiftly executed Howard. His body was horribly mutilated and thrown into a well. McBride and Atkinson were also shot, and some shouted for the blood of all the Americans, but more-moderate counsels prevailed. The mob then set about systematically looting towns and homes.[45]

Not until fighting was well under way did Governor Hubbard ask for federal assistance, and it was December 15 when Hatch received orders from General Pope to march with every available man to the scene of the rioting. The Ninth was badly scattered, but Hatch soon had nine companies on the march toward El Paso and reached that place himself on December 19. He issued a general field order assuming command of all troops at El Paso and in the immediate vicinity and then pushed on to San Elizario with fifty-four troopers and two howitzers.[46]

44 Blair to the AAG, District of New Mexico, December 19, 1877, LR, District of New Mexico.

45 Ibid.; *Mesilla Independent,* December 22 ,1877.

46 Pope to the AAG, Military Division of the Missouri, February 7, 1878, File 1653; Hatch to Pope, December 22, 1877, ibid.; Organizational Returns, Ninth Cavalry, December 1877. Concentration of the Ninth at El Paso all but stripped the District of New Mexico of cavalry. Only E, I, and K Companies remained at strategic posts.

Hatch found about five hundred rioters "spoiling for a fight." He was ready to oblige but quietly waited for the rest of his command to come up, at which time he intended to "clean them out." It was not necessary. As column after column of scowling, battle-toughened buffalo soldiers, also "spoiling for a fight," trotted into San Elizario, the rioters lost all enthusiasm for a fight or even an argument. They simply faded away. Eleven persons had been killed and an undetermined number wounded, but the total was not complete. The rangers, having recovered their arms with the arrival of the troops, arrested and then shot two Mexicans "for attempting to escape." Hatch investigated the shootings, minutely examined the bodies, and concluded that both men had been bound when shot. He promptly made his position clear to all. Federal troops were there on application of Governor Hubbard to maintain order and protect the lives and property of all citizens, and "outrages in the name and under color of the law and by those who ought to be its representatives and guardians will not be tolerated."[47]

The "Salt War" ended with Hatch's statement. Most, if not all, of the bloodshed and property destruction could have been avoided if a federal officer, Blair, had been less timid and state officials less tardy in requesting necessary assistance. Hatch and his troopers brought an abrupt end to the fighting and prevented a far greater loss of life. As the old year became history and the new one began, Hatch reported that citizens of San Elizario, who had fled their homes during the disorders, were returning and that all was quiet.[48]

Upon his return to district headquarters in Santa Fe, Hatch found numerous complaints on his desk concerning Mescalero raids into West Texas and across the border into Mexico. Agent Godfroy insisted that his Indians were not depredating, but there were hostile bands in the Guadalupe Mountains who should be on some reservation. Dudley, commanding at Fort Stanton, reported that he had investigated conditions at the Mescalero agency and that a few reservation Indians might be raiding. He placed the blame, however, on small bands, or "cut-offs," who were living off the countryside and making mescal.[49]

In June Captain Carroll left Fort Stanton to search the Guadalupes for these Indians with Lieutenant G. W. Smith, fifty-two men of F and H

47 Hatch to Pope, December 22, 1877; Hatch to Pope, December 27, 1877, ibid.; *Mesilla Independent*, December 26, 1877.
48 Sheridan to Townsend, January 2, 1878, File 1653.
49 Godfroy to Dudley, April 22, 1878, SLR, AGO, RG 94, NA; Dudley to the AAAG, District of New Mexico, May 24, 1878, ibid.

Companies, and nineteen Navaho scouts under Lieutenant Wright. The command carried forty days' rations and 150 rounds of ammunition per man. Carroll worked his way through the Guadalupes to Pine Spring, where he met Captain S. T. Norvell, scouting out of Fort Davis with M Company of the Tenth Cavalry. Norvell had marched along the Pecos and as far west as Hueco Tanks before coming in to Pine Spring and had seen no Indians or any fresh trails.[50]

Convinced that the Guadalupes were "clean," Carroll turned west to search the Sacramentos, and near the head of Dog Canyon he discovered a small party of Apaches. In sharp skirmishing three warriors were killed and fourteen horses captured. Moving up the canyon, the troopers struck a larger party, with the warriors fighting a strong rear-guard action to save their women, children, and property. The ascent was very steep, the August heat like a furnace, and a few of the troopers collapsed with heatstroke.

The Indians took refuge on a ledge some eight hundred feet high, fired down at the struggling soldiers, and heaved large rocks at them. Carroll reached the ledge just at nightfall, but the hostiles had fled and scattered. Pursuit proved futile, and Carroll turned back to scout Alamo Canyon. When no Indians were found, he marched back to Fort Stanton.[51]

While Carroll scoured the Guadalupes and the Sacramentos, detachments of the Ninth from Forts Bayard, Wingate, Stanton, and Bliss were contending with hit-and-run raids by Warm Springs and Chiricahua warriors. Catching these crafty hostiles was a tedious and frustrating task, for they skipped nimbly into Mexico when hotly pressed. Often, reports of a raid were two or three days in reaching a post, and by that time pursuit was all but useless. Saddles scarcely cooled in the undermanned Ninth, and Captain Beyer at Bayard wrote Colonel Hatch that so few cavalry were left at the post, he wished permission to mount the regimental band. Hatch approved, and by early August members of the band had exchanged their instruments for Springfield carbines and were scouting in the Hatchet and Florida Mountains.[52]

The Mexican government, complaining bitterly that American Apache

50 Dudley to the AAG, District of New Mexico, July 12, 1878, LR, District of New Mexico; Norvell to the AAAG, District of the Pecos, July 25, 1878, File 1653.
51 Carroll to the PA, Fort Stanton, August 12, 1878, LR, District of New Mexico.
52 Beyer to the AAAG, District of New Mexico, July 31, 1878, File 1653; Hatch to the AAG, Department of the Missouri, August 14, 1879, ibid.

raids amounted to an invasion, lodged an official protest; U.S. troops were not doing enough to stop them. That charge must have caused many a weary buffalo soldier to shake his head and wonder just how much he had to do to earn a few words of praise. But Hatch was not prepared to accept such criticism and complained officially to General Pope. The Indians were obtaining guns and ammunition with ease from Mexican citizens, and cooperation from the Mexican government in the campaigns against these people was conspicuously absent. Major Albert Morrow had gone to Janos in Chihuahua to try to coordinate operations and, in effect, had been run out of town. Vigorous Mexican action could have ended the raids in short order.[53]

While officials of both countries bickered over their respective responsibilities for Indian troubles, restive Mescaleros left the reservation to raid, thereby adding to the death and destruction along the turbulent border. They could scarcely be blamed for these forays. Conditions in Lincoln County, which historian Robert Utley describes as "a frontier backwater," adjoining their reserve, had reached the stage of anarchy. The activities of lawless whites so disturbed the Mescaleros that some of them abandoned their crops and scattered into the mountains. Others yielded to the temptation to depredate. The violence in Lincoln County, meanwhile, involved the already overburdened Ninth in one of the most sanguinary civil broils in the history of the West.[54]

For many years Lincoln County had enjoyed the unenviable reputation of having at least as many crooks, thieves, and murderers per square foot as any other county in the West. This occurred, Utley explains, because "Lincoln was in the 1870s a first-generation frontier community, with infant institutions and the social instability characteristic of new settlements on a remote frontier." Lacking adequate law enforcement agencies, the county attracted both outlaws and "the free-spirited adventurers who peopled every frontier." Making matters worse, many of these individuals, especially those from Texas, brought with them a masculine code of honor that was the basis of the "code

53 John W. Foster to Miguel Ruelas, Minister of Foreign Affairs, March 16, 1879, ibid.; M. de Zamacoma to William Evarts, June 18, 1879, ibid.; Morrow to the AAG, District of New Mexico, August 4, 1879, ibid.; Hatch to the AAG, Department of the Missouri, May 28, 1879, ibid.

54 Utley, *High Noon in Lincoln*, 171; Dudley to the AAG, District of New Mexico, January 23, 1879, LR, District of New Mexico; Louis Scott, American Consul, Chihuahua, to Honorable W. Hunter, Assistant Secretary of State, July 20, 1879, ibid.; *Annual Report of the Commissioner of Indian Affairs for the Year 1878*, 107.

of the West." That code demanded that any insult "real or imagined" must be avenged and that any aggression be answered in kind, not by retreating. If the result was death, so be it, an attitude that was even more widespread given the extensive use of alcohol and the prevalence of firearms.[55]

Late in 1873, civil war was narrowly averted when a number of hard-eyed Texans, including five brothers named Herrold, arrived on the scene to engage in ranching. Shortly thereafter, one of the brothers had the misfortune to quarrel with a deputy sheriff. In the gunfight that followed, he was killed. The surviving brothers were quick to take revenge. On the night of December 20, 1873, they rode into Lincoln, shot up a wedding reception, and killed four men.[56]

The citizens of Lincoln, headed by Lawrence Murphy, James Dolan, and William Brady, organized a vigilante committee—a practice that members of frontier communities often resorted to when law enforcement was weak. They also requested the assistance of federal troops at nearby Fort Stanton. The request was denied, however, for General Pope telegraphed headquarters, District of New Mexico: "Instruct the Commanding Officer, Fort Stanton, to take no action, whatever in any disturbances among the citizens near Stanton, and not on the reservation, until summoned by U.S. officers as a posse, to execute the mandates of the U.S. courts."[57] Fortunately for all concerned, the Herrold brothers decided for reasons of health and longevity to migrate back to Texas.

Far more serious trouble was just over the horizon. The determination of many individuals to amass wealth by any means whatsoever and to protect their riches in the same fashion during the Gilded Age was another element that spawned violence in frontier communities. Lawrence G. Murphy and James J. Dolan, who operated a general store in the town of Lincoln and engaged in small-scale banking and large-scale ranching, dominated the economic life of Lincoln County. They also held a lucrative contract to supply the Mescalero agency with beef and flour—mercilessly and systematically cheating the Indians—and were on intimate terms with Agent Godfroy and with the officers at Fort Stanton. Apparently, however,

---

55 Utley, *High Noon in Lincoln*, 172, 176–77.

56 Keleher, *Violence in Lincoln County*, 13–15.

57 Pope to the Commanding Officer, District of New Mexico, December 30, 1873, LR, File 554-1874, AGO, RG 94, NA; Keleher, *Violence in Lincoln County*, 15. Utley discusses the tendency to resort to vigilante justice in *High Noon in Lincoln*, 173.

Murphy and Dolan were actually little more than agents for the politically potent Thomas B. Catron, attorney general of New Mexico Territory and president of the First National Bank of Santa Fe.[58]

Trouble appeared for this cozy and profitable arrangement in 1876 with the appearance along the Pecos River of a Texas cattle baron, John S. Chisum. Chisum represented formidable competition in the ranching business and, further, in his far-flung operations had encountered legal difficulties with Catron. Chisum soon joined forces with a Lincoln lawyer, Alexander McSween, onetime legal council for Murphy and Dolan. McSween had broken with the partners over disposition of a ten-thousand-dollar life insurance policy upon the death of the insured, Emil Fritz. The firm claimed to be the creditor of the deceased and demanded settlement of the account, while the attorney, an executor of the Fritz estate, refused payment on the grounds that the claim was fraudulent. Murphy and Dolan charged that McSween was an embezzler. When Chisum arrived, the dispute had become a no-quarter legal battle.

Events took an ominous turn in 1877 with the arrival in Lincoln of a wealthy young Englishman, John H. Tunstall. He allied himself with Chisum and McSween and proposed to compete with Murphy and Dolan on all fronts and replace them as the dominant business combine of the county. The stakes were high, feelings bitter, and in the prevailing climate of Lincoln County, both sides resorted to employing accomplished gunmen to further their interests. The inevitable result was a rapid increase in the mortality rate as trigger-happy partisans shot it out with little or no excuse.

So long as only small fry were involved, this state of affairs could have continued indefinitely, but in February 1878 events took a decisive turn. The legal squabble over the Fritz estate resulted in the issuance of attachments on McSween holdings in town, including goods in the new Tunstall store. In the meantime, a deputy with a large posse of known gunmen attached other property in the outlying countryside. While returning to Lincoln, the posse encountered Tunstall riding with a few companions and murdered

---

58 Utley, *High Noon in Lincoln*, 176; Keleher, *Violence in Lincoln County*, 15; Hinton, "John Simpson Chisum," 191–92. The firm was known as L. G. Murphy and Company, with Dolan as principal partner. On April 20, 1877, Murphy sold his share of the business, which then was known as James J. Dolan and Company. Murphy maintained his ranching and livestock activities in Lincoln County. Thus, although the partnership was dissolved, the Murphy-Dolan faction continued to wield influence in the county. See also Billington, *New Mexico's Buffalo Soldiers*, 69–70.

him in cold blood. The other members of the Tunstall party, including William Bonney, known as Billy the Kid, fled for their lives and made good their escape.[59]

Passions ran high in Lincoln County over the Tunstall killing and mounted to a fever pitch when Sheriff Brady proved unwilling or unable to arrest the slayers. Fearing civil war, Governor Samuel B. Axtell hurried to Lincoln and wasted no time in asking President Hayes for military assistance. His sympathies, however, were with Murphy and Dolan, and his message placed full blame for the troubles on Alexander McSween.

Axtell's request was approved at once, and Captain George Purington at Fort Stanton was ordered to support the proper civil authorities in the conduct of their duties. Purington hurried a detachment of twenty-five troopers of Company H to Lincoln but found the situation so confusing he was temporarily at a loss as to how to proceed. Justice of the Peace John B. Wilson issued warrants for the arrest of members of Sheriff Brady's posse, while Brady demanded assistance in rounding up members of the McSween faction. A deputy U.S. marshal named Robert Widenmann argued that he had first claim on the troops. Purington eventually decided that he must protect the women and children of the town. He so notified the leaders of both factions, adding that if they were "spoiling for a fight," they could "withdraw to the mountains and fight to their hearts content."[60]

Apparently since each side was unprepared at this point for open warfare, both decided upon a waiting game. Meanwhile, General Pope solved Purington's dilemma as to the appropriate authorities in Lincoln when he telegraphed Hatch, "Until this conflict of authority ceases, the Sheriff will be considered by you the proper powers to render assistance to when required by him to preserve the peace and sustain the laws." Pope's message thrust the officers and men of the Ninth squarely into the Lincoln County conflict. There was precedent for his instructions, though. A year earlier the buffalo

59   Hinton, "John Simpson Chisum," 194–95; Keleher, *Violence in Lincoln County*, 82–91; *Mesilla Independent*, September 8, 1877; Nolan, *Life and Death of John Henry Tunstall*, 220. Tunstall's friends were some distance away, engaged in a hunt, when the posse halted him. Billy the Kid's real name was Henry McCarty.

60   Purington to the AAAG, District of New Mexico, March 6, 1878, LR, AGO, File 1405-1878, RG 94, NA [hereafter cited as File 1405-1878]. Axtell to President Hayes, March 4, 1878, ibid. George A Purington, a native of Ohio, rose through the ranks during the Civil War to become lieutenant colonel, Second Ohio Cavalry. He accepted a commission as captain, Ninth Cavalry, in July 1866 and served continuously with the regiment until October 1883, when he transferred in the rank of major to the Third Cavalry.

soldiers at Fort Stanton had assisted a sheriff and a posse in action that had led to a shootout with desperado Frank Freeman and other outlaws and rustlers, fighting that claimed Freeman's life. Freeman had shot and wounded a black noncommissioned officer in a bar simply because of his color and then had escaped the sheriff's posse after his arrest.[61] Now, in the present conflict, buffalo soldier involvement tilted the scales; it placed a potent weapon in the hands of Sheriff Brady and indirectly into those of Murphy and Dolan.

Since a roundup of Tunstall's killers would have required Brady to arrest members of his own posse, he made no effort to do so. Before long Tunstall's friends took matters into their own hands. In March, Richard Brewer, a neighbor of the slain man, organized a posse, which included Billy the Kid and, with the warrants issued by Justice of the Peace Wilson, set out to find the murderers. They soon located and arrested Frank Baker and William Morton, known to have participated in the killing of Tunstall. En route to Lincoln with their prisoners, the posse apparently decided Brady would release the captives, and both were shot, along with a member of the posse who had proven to be a spy. The "Lincoln County War" was on in earnest.[62]

On the morning of April 1, while Sheriff Brady and two deputies, George Hindman and J. B. Matthews, walked along Lincoln's main street, a volley of shots from behind an adobe wall in the rear of Tunstall's store killed Brady and Hindman instantly; Matthews narrowly escaped the same fate. Billy the Kid and three other members of the McSween faction immediately were accused of the shooting.

The killings brought Captain Purington, Lieutenant Smith, and Company H to Lincoln. With George W. Peppin, a tool of the Murphy-Dolan crowd, they made several arrests and, without a warrant, searched McSween's home for weapons. Until now the officers at Fort Stanton, outwardly at least, had acted impartially. Purington's actions on April 1, however, indicated leanings toward Murphy and Dolan, a preference that soon became obvious.[63]

61 Pope to Hatch, March 24, 1878, ibid.; Billington, *New Mexico's Buffalo Soldiers,* 68–69

62 Keleher, *Violence in Lincoln County,* 97–98; Sheridan to Sherman, April 5, 1878, File 1405-1878; Purington to the AAAG, District of New Mexico, March 29, 1878, ibid. For one story of Billy the Kid, see Garrett, *Authentic Life of Billy the Kid.* For a more recent work, see Utley, *Billy the Kid.*

63 Organizational Returns, Ninth Cavalry, April 1878; Nolan, *Life and Death of John Henry Tunstall,* 130–311; Keleher, *Violence in Lincoln County,* 110.

April 5 brought still more killings. The Lincoln County commissioners offered a reward of two hundred dollars for the assassins of Brady and Hindman, "dead or alive." The offer stimulated Andrew "Buckshot" Roberts, a Murphy-Dolan partisan, to go bounty hunting. At Blazer's Mill on the Mescalero reservation, he encountered far more than he had bargained for in the form of Richard Brewer, Billy the Kid, and several others. Instantly guns were flaming, and when the shooting stopped, Roberts lay mortally wounded, and Brewer was dead.[64]

Hoping that he could restore order, the county commissioners elected John S. Copeland, a McSween sympathizer, as Brady's successor. Copeland appealed to the new commander at Fort Stanton, the eccentric N. A. M. Dudley, for assistance, and a detachment of twenty troopers of H Company under Lieutenant Smith accompanied Copeland in his efforts to disarm and arrest roving armed bands. The new sheriff apparently made an honest effort, but Governor Axtell, at the instigation of Murphy and Dolan, removed him from office, and George Peppin was appointed in his place.[65]

The increasing demands for troops in the bloody feud caused grave concern in Washington. Pope undoubtedly was uncomfortable over the presence of the unpredictable Dudley at Fort Stanton. He ordered Hatch to require the former to submit "full and frequent reports" on all matters connected with the use of troops in civil matters in Lincoln County. On May 30 Hatch received a telegram from Governor Axtell requesting troops be sent to the vicinity of Roswell, New Mexico, where rustlers were active and had stolen horses belonging to Attorney General Catron. In addition, Axtell desired sufficient troops sent to Lincoln to "disarm all bands of men found there, whether they claim to be sheriffs posse or otherwise."[66]

Hatch honored Axtell's request by sending Company H to Roswell and ordering Captain Carroll with Company F to Lincoln. But he also wrote department headquarters a review of the troubles in Lincoln County and asked for immediate clarification of the extent military participation was required. At the same time he telegraphed Dudley to cooperate with Sher-

64 Keleher, *Violence in Lincoln County,* 113.
65 Ibid., 124; Dudley to the AAAG, District of New Mexico, May 4, 1878, File 1405-1878. It cannot be proved, but there is some evidence to indicate that Dudley, with his penchant for meddling, connived with Murphy and Dolan in the removal of Copeland. See Statement of Corporal Thomas Dale, Co. H, 9th Cavalry, May 1, 1878, Fort Stanton, New Mexico, on the Conduct of Sheriff John N. Copeland, File 1405-1878.
66 Axtell to Hatch, May 30, 1878, LR, District of New Mexico; Pope to Hatch, April 24, 1878, File 1405-1878.

iff Peppin and to furnish escorts for contractors' cattle being driven to the Mescalero reservation, for he feared they might be stolen.[67]

For the moment, however, a deadly calm had settled over Lincoln County. No one was deceived; all knew it to be a period of preparation for the final showdown between Murphy and Dolan and McSween. On June 7 Dudley reported cheerfully that all was quiet. The only request for troops had come from Agent Godfroy for the purpose of stopping the sale of whisky to his Indians in Tularosa.[68]

The calm was ruffled somewhat on June 18, when Sheriff Peppin appeared at Fort Stanton and asked Dudley for troops to assist in making arrests in Lincoln. The request was granted, and Peppin set out with Lieutenant M. F. Goodwin and twenty-seven troopers. En route, however, when twenty heavily armed citizens, among them John Kinney, a notorious gunman, joined Peppin, Lieutenant Goodwin informed the sheriff that he had no intentions of entering Lincoln in such company. The troopers, therefore, remained on the outskirts of town, while Peppin, Kinney, and the others searched for the wanted men. None were found, and Goodwin returned to Fort Stanton. Peppin's efforts were plainly designed to break up a suspected concentration of McSween's forces.[69]

On June 25 Hatch received the clarification he had asked for three weeks earlier. Adjutant General Edward Townsend telegraphed Pope, who in turn informed Hatch, that troops at Fort Stanton would give no further assistance to civil authorities in Lincoln County. An amendment to the 1878 Military Appropriation Bill had altered the army's ability to become involved in policing activities. Congressmen, still angry over the military's role in the South during Reconstruction, which had ended in 1877, had severely limited the army's power to perform posse comitatus duties. Meanwhile, Peppin again came to Dudley for assistance, which was denied. The sheriff persisted, and when he signed an affidavit that his deputy had been unable to serve warrants, Dudley relented and allowed some soldiers to act as escort. Captain Carroll, Lieutenant Goodwin, and thirty-five buffalo soldiers

67 Hatch to Dudley, June 1, 1878, File 1405-1878; Hatch to the AAG, Department of the Missouri, June 1, 1878, ibid. The strife in Lincoln County had disorganized transportation, and the delivery of beef and flour had been disrupted. Reports had also reached Hatch that outlaws planned to burn the agency buildings and steal stock from the Indians. Small wonder that some of the Mescaleros left the reservation to raid.
68 Dudley to Hatch, June 7, 1878, LR, District of New Mexico.
69 Dudley to the AAAG, District of New Mexico, June 22, 1878, File 1405-1878; Lieutenant Goodwin to Dudley, June 19, 1878, ibid.

accompanied Peppin to the Coe Ranch, some twenty-five miles south of Stanton. Once there, however, a courier reached them with orders to return to the post in obedience to orders from district headquarters.[70]

Early in July, tension in Lincoln became nearly intolerable. The showdown was near, and men, women, and children lived in constant fear. Dudley visited Lincoln and learned that both McSween and Dolan were in the field with their forces engaged in a deadly game of hide-and-seek. On July 6 a delegation of twenty-seven Mexican women came to Stanton and begged Dudley for protection "in the name of God and the Constitution." He informed Hatch that the officers and men of the garrison were embarrassed that they had to stand idly by unable to give assistance.[71]

Dudley must have been embarrassed still further when he found that R. C. Drum, assistant adjutant general of the army, had issued General Orders No. 49. Dated July 7, these orders forbade the use of federal troops in aiding civil authorities as a posse comitatus or in executing the laws without the specific consent of the president obtained through military channels. As events soon proved, N. A. M. Dudley was hardly the man to let general orders interfere with sentiment for very long. His actions brought a storm of criticism on the officers and men of the Ninth Cavalry.

On July 15 Alexander McSween with forty-one followers rode into Lincoln and prepared for battle. He stationed some of the men in his home, while others took positions in the houses of sympathizers and at other strategic places. A short time later Peppin, Dolan, and a posse of more than fifty men converged on Lincoln and also took up points of vantage. Then Peppin sent his deputy, John Long, to the McSween house to serve warrants on a number of men there. But as he neared the place, Long was fired on and forced to take cover.[72]

Both sides dug in during the night, and when morning came the battle was joined. A literal rain of lead whistled across and down the streets of

70 AG to Pope, June 25, 1878, ibid.; Dudley to the AAAG, District of New Mexico, June 29, 1878, ibid.; Carroll to the PA, Fort Stanton, New Mexico, July 1, 1878, LR, District of New Mexico. For more information on the army and the extent to which it could perform policing duties, see Billington, *New Mexico's Buffalo Soldiers*, 78–79; and Tate, *Frontier Army in the Settlement of the West*, 93–97.

71 Dudley to the AAAG, District of New Mexico, July 6, 1878, LR, District of New Mexico.

72 Nolan, *Life and Death of John Henry Tunstall*, 374–75; Keleher, *Violence in Lincoln County*, 142; Statement of Deputy Sheriff John Long, July 22, 1878, LR, District of New Mexico.

Lincoln. With neither side able to gain an advantage, Peppin tried to borrow a howitzer from Dudley. The latter refused, but the exchange caused him to send Private Berry Robinson of H Company to Lincoln as a courier.

When Robinson arrived on the edge of town just before dark, four armed and mounted men stopped him and inquired as to his business. When he replied that he was on "government business," they told him he was damned saucy, to which he replied, "I talk no more damned saucy than you do."[73] The men drew revolvers and Robinson chambered a slug in his carbine, but they let him pass. As he neared the McSween house, bullets zipped dangerously close, but he reached Peppin safely.

This minor episode proved decisive in the war. It is doubtful that the McSween people fired deliberately at a federal trooper. They were more likely shooting at members of the posse who were in his vicinity, but Dudley charged that the shots were aimed at Robinson. It was all the excuse he needed to intervene, and his intervention broke the stalemate and gave victory to Murphy and Dolan.

With almost uninterrupted firing, the battle in Lincoln raged into its fourth day. Dudley meanwhile conferred with his officers and decided to march into Lincoln, as he later wrote, "for the sole purpose of giving protection to women and children." But he also added that he believed the McSween faction was wrong in defying Sheriff Peppin and, further, some of its members had fired at Private Robinson.[74]

Having satisfied himself that intervention was warranted despite General Orders No. 49, Dudley saddled every available man of F and H Companies and, taking a howitzer, a Gatling gun, two thousand rounds of ammunition, and three days' rations, marched into Lincoln on July 19. Cautioning his troopers to pay no attention to catcalls and jeers, he rode down the main street and went into camp at the lower end of town. There he issued an invitation to terrified women and children to take shelter with the troops, and many did. This action would seem to have completed Dudley's announced purpose for coming to Lincoln, but it proved to be only a preliminary step.

Summoning Justice of the Peace Wilson, Dudley forced the frightened but reluctant official to issue warrants for the arrest of McSween, Billy the Kid, and others and then assisted the posse in attempting to serve them. The

73 Proceedings of a Board of Officers Convened at Fort Stanton, New Mexico, July 18, 1878, LR, District of New Mexico.
74 Dudley to the AAAG, District of New Mexico, July 20, 1878, File 1405-1878.

tide of battle turned at once. McSween's home was set ablaze, and as the defenders fled the smoke and flames, four were shot down, among them McSween, who died in his own backyard. Six of the men in the house made their escape, including Billy the Kid. The battle of Lincoln was at an end.

The next day Dudley went to the smoldering ruins of the McSween home with an escort of troopers. McSween's body lay where it had fallen, and chickens were pecking at the dead man's face and eyes. Two buffalo soldiers shooed the chickens away, but a dazed Sue McSween, the dead man's widow, vehemently refused Dudley's belated offer of assistance and ordered him off the premises. The corpse, according to Dudley's report, "was placed unwashed in a blanket and box and buried without ceremony."[75] Meanwhile, the drunken and triumphant victors pillaged the Tunstall store and carried off thousands of dollars in merchandise. Dudley made no effort to protect the property and, apparently satisfied that he had done his duty, returned to Fort Stanton.[76]

At district headquarters in Santa Fe, Hatch digested reports of the affair in Lincoln and sent a tart telegram to Dudley that his actions had been illegal and should cease at once. For the next few weeks, activities of the troopers at Stanton were restricted to providing protection for the Mescalero agency from attacks by roving bands of outlaws, but killing, stealing, and general lawlessness continued to plague Lincoln and neighboring Dona Ana County. On October 2 a band known as the Wrestlers attacked the ranch of a man named Bartlett below Fort Stanton, took the wives of two employees, and according to one report, "forced them into the brush, stripped them naked and used them for their pleasure."[77] Dudley sent Captain Carroll and twenty troopers of F Company to the Bartlett ranch, but they were unable to apprehend the outlaws.

Governor Axtell's partisanship in the Lincoln County troubles had, meanwhile, brought a drumfire of criticism that led to his removal on September 30, 1878. His replacement, retired general Lew Wallace, well

75 Ibid. This is Dudley's official report in which he limits his activities to protecting noncombatants and says nothing of any active role in the fighting. A well-researched and objective study of these events can be found in Keleher, *Violence in Lincoln County,* 378–79. For a detailed report, see Charges and Specifications against Lieutenant Colonel N. A. M. Dudley, Commander at Fort Stanton, New Mexico, May 3, 1879, LR, District of New Mexico. For information on Sue McSween, see Utley, *Billy the Kid,* 36.

76 Nolan, *Life and Death of John Henry Tunstall,* 379.

77 Dudley to Hatch, October 3, 1878, File 1405-1878; Organizational Returns, Ninth Cavalry, August–September 1878.

known as the author of *Ben Hur,* at once applied to Hatch for troops to restore order in Lincoln County, and the latter telegraphed Pope for instructions. On October 8 Hatch received an answer. A presidential proclamation ordered those responsible for the lawlessness in Lincoln County and other parts of New Mexico Territory to disperse peaceably to their homes before noon on October 13. Otherwise, military force would be invoked and continued so long as resistance lasted.[78]

Troopers moved swiftly to assist civil officials. Before the month was out, violence had subsided to the point that Wallace issued a general amnesty. It did not include the officers at Fort Stanton. Dudley, always ready to ignite controversy, wrote Wallace an insulting letter. Simultaneously, he engaged in a bitter quarrel with Sue McSween and Huston Chapman, a lawyer and friend of Wallace, whom the widow had employed to settle her late husband's tangled affairs. Sue McSween understandably blamed Dudley for the unfortunate outcome of the fight in Lincoln. Chapman charged in a letter to Wallace that Dudley was "criminally responsible" for McSween's death. Dudley, never at a loss for words, replied by maligning Sue McSween's character.

All this was too much for Wallace, and on December 7 he formally requested Hatch to remove Dudley as commanding officer at Stanton. The latter, in his view, had "excited the animosity of parties in Lincoln County to such a degree as to embarrass the administration of affairs in that locality." After Hatch forwarded the request through channels, it received the approval of both Pope and Sheridan but was denied by General Sherman. Dudley, apparently, still had loyal friends in Washington.[79]

On February 18, 1879, two gunmen of the Murphy-Dolan faction killed lawyer Chapman in front of the Lincoln County Courthouse. Chapman was unarmed and the killing was without provocation. George Kimball, who had succeeded the discredited Peppin, was at Fort Stanton at the time requesting assistance in arresting Billy the Kid and a few companions who were roaming the streets. The sheriff had been unable to find anyone with courage enough to join a posse. Lieutenant Dawson with a detachment drawn from F, H, and M Companies accompanied Kimball to Lincoln, but Billy and his friends had departed. They did find the body of Chapman, still

78 Secretary of War to General Sherman, October 8, 1878, File 1405-1878.
79 Utley, *Billy the Kid*, 100; Wallace to Hatch, December 7, 1878, ibid.; Keleher, *Violence in Lincoln County*, 192, 200–201.

lying where he had fallen, for local citizenry were too intimidated even to approach the corpse. Dawson located a trembling justice of the peace to whom he gave the necessary assistance, and as later reported, "the body was removed to the courthouse."[80]

Chapman's murder brought both Wallace and Hatch to Lincoln. The governor remained in town with a bodyguard of buffalo soldiers, while Hatch went on to Fort Stanton. There, at Wallace's request, he removed Dudley from command and ordered him to Fort Union to await formal charges, primarily that he had conspired to murder Alexander McSween. Captain Carroll replaced Dudley as the commanding officer at Stanton.[81]

On April 14 a grand jury convened at Lincoln and returned some two hundred indictments, most of them against members of the Murphy-Dolan crowd but one against Dudley, charging him with arson in the burning of the McSween home. Two days later a court of inquiry assembled at Fort Stanton to review a host of charges against the lieutenant colonel growing out of his actions in Lincoln on July 19–20 and afterward. Once again Dudley's luck and influence held. A jury in Mesilla acquitted him on the arson charge. After protracted hearings of more than seven weeks, the court of inquiry cleared him of all military charges. His attorney telegraphed exultantly to U.S. Attorney General Charles Devens: "General Dudley triumphantly acquitted yesterday after long fierce trial. Jury out but a moment, great applause by people. It is time prosecutions against him eased. Inform Adj. General."[82] It mattered little that Wallace, Hatch, and Pope all felt there had been a whitewash. Dudley was soon commanding the post at Fort Cummings.

For many months small detachments of the Ninth continued to aid civil officials in running down desperadoes in Lincoln and Dona Ana Counties. This occurred despite Hatch's protest to department headquarters in which he noted, "the troops find this duty disagreeable, as it must expose them to more or less odium and obloquy from the community."[83] He might have added that his obedient and tireless troopers rarely encountered anything

80 Dudley to Hatch, February 19, 1879, File 1405-1878; Dawson to Dudley, February 19, 1878, ibid.

81 Dudley to the AG, March 13, 1879, ibid.; Dudley to General Sherman, March 18, 1879, ibid. In this personal letter to Sherman, Dudley makes much of the fact that Wallace and Hatch came to Lincoln together.

82 Sidney M. Barnes to Charles Devens, November 30, 1879, ibid.; Carroll to the AAG, District of New Mexico, May 3, 1879, LR, District of New Mexico. Carroll's letter contains a summary of affairs in Lincoln County for the week ending May 3 and includes the work of the grand jury.

83 Hatch to the AAG, Department of the Missouri, December 17, 1878, File 1405-1878.

other than "odium and obloquy" from the public, no matter how faithfully they carried out the orders of their officers.

With the close of the Dudley court of inquiry, the Lincoln County War was over, except for running down the remaining hardened outlaws. The energies of the Ninth, however, had never been fully directed toward pacifying that strife-torn county. No more than three companies were ever at Stanton, for others were needed to combat continual Apache raiding. Even when they were engaged in Indian fighting, however, other duties and activities consumed most of their waking hours.

While the buffalo soldiers were in New Mexico, they constructed housing for laundresses and a post hospital at Fort Stanton. They also fought fires at Forts Union and Wingate, as well as one at Stanton and another at Camp Ojo Caliente. Among their other duties, they improved and extended the North Star Road in the territory and performed the dangerous task of escorting the mail through Indian country. Early in their tenure in the territory, the regimental band, at the invitation of the city's music committee, played in Santa Fe for the Fourth of July celebration. Citizens of the capital city, impressed with their music, petitioned General Pope, asking him to reassign the band to nearby Fort Marcy. Pope refused, stating that the musicians belonged to the regiment and had to be stationed at its headquarters.[84]

In 1878–79, trouble with bands of Utes demanded the dispersal of elements of the Ninth to Colorado. The background of the Ute problems in this region was grimly similar to those of other peoples who held lands newcomers found desirable. For many years the state's Utes—White River, Uncompahgre, and Southern Ute bands—had not been in the direct line of white advance. The discovery of gold in 1859 and the Pike's Peak rush had brought the inevitable white influx and a treaty in 1863, which gave the Utes all the territory west of the Continental Divide. Typically, the Indians did not remain undisturbed for long. In 1868 they were forced to make additional cessions and to accept Ouray, an Uncompahgre, as chief of all the Utes.[85]

By the time the Ninth Cavalry had moved to New Mexico in 1876, the Utes were served by three agencies: a northern one at White River, a middle one at the Gunnison and later at the Uncompahgre, and a southern agency near the New Mexican border. White pressure was mounting, and bold squatters were encroaching on Indian lands. In an effort to protect their

84 Billington, *New Mexico's Buffalo Soldiers,* 109–17.
85 *Annual Report of the Commissioner of Indian Affairs for the Year 1868,* 16; Emmitt, *Last War Trail,* 23–24.

homeland, the Utes lashed out at intruders, burning their cabins, stealing their stock, and at times, killing or maiming them. By March 1878 Agent F. H. Weaver, concerned about an outbreak, feared for his life. Lieutenant Gustavus Valois with a detachment of troopers from D Company of the Ninth came to Los Pinos to investigate.

Valois was at the agency when the Utes came in for rations and annuities, sullenly insisting on a four-week supply. After discussing the matter with Valois, Weaver complied. The Indians did not return until the full time had elapsed and then made the same demands. Once more Weaver yielded, but when the Utes came in and wanted still another four-week issue, the agent closed the storehouse and sent for troops.

Major Morrow with D, G, I, K, and M Companies marched to the La Plata River and encamped. There Hatch and Captain A. S. Kimball, who came north from Santa Fe, joined him. The colonel arranged a council with Ignacio, the Southern Ute war chief, and a number of his warriors. All were insolent, and the warriors told Hatch, "we have no ears to hear unless Ignacio agrees."[86] Hatch did not dally. He told Ignacio the troops had come in peace to protect Indians as well as whites, but if the Utes wanted war, it might as well begin immediately. There would be no gifts except bullets from gun muzzles, if necessary. Then, adopting a more conciliatory tone, Hatch indicated that if the Indians desired peace, he would return with a commission to negotiate an acceptable treaty. This proposal satisfied Ignacio, and after a scout along the La Plata, Hatch returned to Santa Fe.[87]

On May 24, 1878, a Ute commission was appointed consisting of Hatch, N. C. McFarland of Kansas, and William Stickney of Washington, D.C., although the latter was soon replaced by Lot M. Morrill of Maine. Tedious negotiations were conducted during the summer, and the Southern Utes agreed to move to the headwaters of the Chama, Navajo, Blanco, Piedra, and San Juan Rivers, thereby relinquishing claim to a strip occupied by settlers. Efforts at a more comprehensive settlement with all the Colorado Utes failed. But in southern Colorado, at least, a possible war had been averted and peace prevailed.[88]

Serious trouble was not avoided with the White River Utes, however.

---

86   Captain A. S. Kimball to the Quartermaster General, U.S. Army, Washington, D.C., June 1, 1878, LR, District of New Mexico; *Annual Report of the Commissioner of Indian Affairs for the Year 1878*, 17.

87   Kimball to the Quartermaster General, June 1, 1878.

88   William Leeds, Acting Commissioner of Indian Affairs, to Hatch, May 24, 1878, ibid.; *Annual Report of the Commissioner of Indian Affairs for the Year 1878*, 170–72.

N. C. Meeker, who became agent to that band early in 1879, quickly aroused bitter resentment when he made strenuous efforts to educate the Utes and convert them into farmers. A crisis came in September 1879 when an Indian named Johnson, a brother-in-law of Ouray, quarreled with the elderly Meeker and beat him severely. With the atmosphere at the agency ominous, Meeker appealed for troops.

In response to this appeal, Major T. T. Thornburgh, Fourth Infantry, left Fort Frederick Steele in Wyoming on September 21 with three companies of cavalry, one of infantry, and a train of twenty-five wagons. Meanwhile, aware that Captain Francis Dodge and Company D of the Ninth were encamped on the Grand River, Meeker also contacted that officer for aid.

Thornburgh's command reached Milk River near the agency on September 29, crossed that stream after watering, and had proceeded only a short distance when several hundred Utes, well concealed on ridges overlooking the trail, opened a withering fire. Several men were killed, and Thornburgh ordered a retreat to the wagons, which had been hastily corralled about two hundred yards from the river. During the retreat, Thornburgh was killed along with a number of his men.

Under heavy attack, the troops unloaded the wagons, made breastworks of the contents, and fought off the Utes, though fighting continued until nightfall. The troops used the respite to dig trenches around the wagons and a pit in the center of the corral for a hospital. Nearly all the horses had been killed, and their carcasses were used to strengthen the breastworks. When this work had been completed, couriers were sent out to seek aid.

At daybreak the Utes opened a galling fire that made any movement about the corral suicidal, and there was no letup on this or the following day. Suffering became acute. Thankfully, a measure of relief was near at hand. Captain Dodge, Lieutenant M. B. Hughes, and thirty-five buffalo soldiers, after a hard ride, reached the Yampa River before dawn on October 2 and halted briefly. Each trooper was issued three days' rations and ample ammunition, the train was parked, and with only one pack mule, Dodge pushed on to the embattled command at Milk River. The corral was reached at daybreak without loss, accompanied by the cheers of the defenders.[89]

The Utes, by contrast, greeted the black soldiers with amazement. They saw them, as historian Robert Emmitt writes on the basis of later Ute testimony, as "something to wonder about and to laugh about—perhaps, some-

89 Burkey, "Thornburgh Battle," 96–108; Organizational Returns, Ninth Cavalry, September–October 1879.

times, to be a little angry with—but . . . nothing to be afraid of." Indeed, the
warriors began crying out, "To-Maricat'z! The black-whitemen! The Buffalo
Soldiers!" Later, the Utes taunted them as "Soldiers with black faces," as they
sang out:

> You ride into battle behind the white soldiers;
> But you can't take off your black faces,
> And the white-face soldiers make you ride behind them.[90]

The battle continued unabated throughout the day. But the ridicule the
Utes heaped on the buffalo soldiers was misplaced. That night Sergeant
Henry Johnson, a veteran of twelve years whose service dated back to the
original formation of the Tenth Cavalry's F Company, inspired regimental
pride. Under heavy fire, he left his rifle pit and made the rounds of the
trenches to see that all was well. Then, on the evening of the fifth day of fighting, Johnson once more climbed from his pit, shot his way to the river, and
returned with a supply of water. This brave soldier became another in a growing list of Ninth Cavalry troopers who would wear the Medal of Honor.[91]

A deadly fire from Ute sharpshooters continued, but couriers, sent out on
the first night of the battle, had gotten through. Colonel Wesley Merritt
marched from Fort D. A. Russell with five companies of the Fifth Cavalry
and reached Milk River on the morning of October 5. As he approached,
the Utes retreated, ending the ordeal of the men in the corral. Fourteen were
dead, forty-three were wounded, and of all the horses and mules, only a
handful were still alive. In Dodge's company only two animals were left. Ute
casualties were uncertain, but the Indians were well concealed and their
losses were undoubtedly light.

Merritt rode on to the agency to find nothing but death and devastation.
Meeker and eleven employees had been murdered and all the women and
children taken captive. Their release was soon obtained, and the White River
Utes faced removal for their deeds. But by then Captain Dodge and a weary
Company D were already marching south. Apaches were again raiding and
depredating in New Mexico, and Colonel Hatch was in desperate need of
every buffalo soldier in the regiment.[92]

---

90 Emmitt, *Last War Trail*, 219–20. See also Schubert, *Black Valor*, 43.
91 Captain M. B. Hughes to the Adjutant, Ninth Cavalry, July 26, 1893, LR, File 5993-
PRD-1890, AGO, RG 94, NA.
92 Burkey, "Thornburgh Battle," 108–9; Beyer and Keydel, *Deeds of Valor*, 2:253–59.

The Victorio War

The policy of Apache concentration paid a frightful and inevitable dividend in late August 1879. Victorio had learned that he was under indictment for murder at Silver City, New Mexico. Fearing either arrest or another forced return to the hated San Carlos reserve in Arizona, Victorio and his Warm Springs Apaches, along with a few restless Mescaleros, fled the Fort Stanton reservation, determined to die before submitting to any new restraints.[1] His actions precipitated the "Victorio War." The causes, however, stemmed from white greed coupled with mistaken Indian policy, which denied the Warm Springs Apaches the right to live on land they loved and required them to dwell on a reservation that they could never accept as their homeland.

The buffalo soldiers and their officers never made Indian policy; rather they carried it out and contended with its results regardless of merit. General John Pope summarized their duty succinctly. He deplored the concentration policy as a tragic mistake, but there was now a war to be fought against Victorio and his people. "The capture," he noted, "is not very probable, but the killing (cruel as it will be) can, I suppose, be done in time."[2]

Victorio had scarcely left the reservation before he cut a swath through sheepherders and their flocks. He left his calling card with the Ninth Cavalry on September 4, when with sixty warriors, he struck like lightning at the

---

1 Thrapp, *Conquest of Apacheria*, 181.
2 *Annual Report of the Secretary of War for the Year 1880*, 1(2):88.

horse herd of Captain Ambrose Hooker's Company E at Ojo Caliente. In minutes, eight troopers guarding the herd were either dead or wounded, and E was less forty-six mounts. Hooker was all but unhorsed at one fell swoop. General Pope quickly, and perhaps unfairly, charged him with "carelessness."[3]

In the next six days the Apaches killed nine citizens, and Colonel Hatch put every company of his regiment into the field. It was the beginning of more than a year of concerted effort by the buffalo soldiers to run Victorio to earth and as grueling a campaign as U.S. cavalry ever undertook.

Scouts from a column under Lieutenant Colonel N. A. M. Dudley consisting of Captain Byron Dawson's B Company and Hooker's E Company found Victorio's trail on September 16. A pursuit of two days brought them to the canyons at the head of the Las Animas River. There, as a strongly entrenched Victorio awaited them, the troopers found themselves trapped under a withering fire. Dudley now faced yet another mess, and one that all his Washington influence could hardly solve for him. His luck held to some degree. Captain C. D. Beyer and Lieutenant William H. Hugo, searching nearby with Companies C and G, heard the heavy gunfire echoing and re-echoing along the canyon walls.

Galloping toward the echoes, Beyer and Hugo joined the fight, but all four companies could not dislodge the Apaches. After an all-day fight that claimed the lives of five troopers, three scouts, and thirty-two horses by nightfall, Dudley ordered a withdrawal. The Ninth's first head-on encounter with Victorio had almost ended in disaster. Thereafter, Dudley's name was conspicuously absent from field reports. Major Albert P. Morrow, a far abler soldier, took command of operations in southern New Mexico.[4]

Morrow, with detachments from B, C, and G and a body of Apache scouts, found Victorio's trail and doggedly pursued it for eleven days until the chief turned at bay on the Cuchillo Negro. Morrow launched his attack at once, and fighting raged from midafternoon of September 29 until ten o'clock in the evening, when both sides cooled their rifles and rested. Next morning, while the troopers swallowed their hardtack and coffee, an Apache sharpshooter killed a sentinel on post overlooking the camp. Fighting

3 Ibid., 86.
4 Pope to the AAG, Military Division of the Missouri, September 24, 1879, LR, Selected Documents Relating to the Activities of the Ninth and Tenth Cavalry in the Campaign against Victorio, 1879–80, File 6058-1879, AGO, RG 94, NA [hereafter cited as File 6058-1879].

erupted immediately, with the troopers pressing their antagonists and finally dislodging them. A two-hour running fight followed, but near two o'clock in the afternoon, Morrow was forced to break off the action and return to the head of the Cuchillo Negro for water. At least three Apaches had been killed, while Morrow lost two troopers and a number of horses.

Pursuit resumed on the morning of October 1, and near sundown the scouts reported that they had located Victorio's camp some four miles to the front. Morrow halted and waited until midnight before positioning his men to strike the Apaches' very strong position at daybreak. When the attack was ordered, however, the Indians had fled into the Mogollon Mountains, thereby saving Morrow and his men from an assault that would have, he reckoned, "cost the lives of half the command."[5]

Morrow, after moving into Ojo Caliente for rations and ammunition, sent to Fort Bayard for reinforcements. When he moved out again on October 5, he was joined on the march by Captain George A. Purington with H Company; Captain Beyer with the rest of C; a detachment of A Company, Sixth Cavalry; and about two dozen Indian scouts. Three weeks of twisting, turning, and grinding pursuit followed, taking its toll of men and horses and eventually bringing the column to Palomas Lake, some four miles south of the Mexican border.

The dogged Morrow, reduced to eighty-one leather-tough buffalo soldiers and eighteen Indian scouts, continued the pursuit, although "horses were dropping every mile." His bulldog tenacity paid off on October 27 when he overtook Victorio near the Corralitas River, but he could not drive him from very strong positions. With his troopers in tatters, rations gone, and most of his animals dead, Morrow had no choice other than to retire to Fort Bayard, where he arrived on November 2. He had been unable to bring off a decisive action, but he had at least driven Victorio from the country. As he noted in his report to the assistant adjutant general, District of New Mexico, dated November 5, 1879, the courage and devotion to duty of Sergeants Thomas Fredericks of H Company and David Badie of B, Corporal Charles Parker of G, and Privates Isaac Holbrook and William Jones of H and L respectively had been especially noteworthy and deserving of praise.[6]

Colonel Hatch wrote to General Pope at this time describing the difficulties involved in fighting such an enemy:

5 Morrow to the AAG, District of New Mexico, November 5, 1879, ibid.
6 Ibid.

Major Morrow's command shows that the work performed by these troops is most arduous, horses worn to mere shadows, men nearly without boots, shoes and clothing. That the loss in horses may be understood when following the Indians in the Black Range the horses were without anything to eat five days except what they nibbled from piñon pines, going without food so long was nearly as disastrous as the fearful march into Mexico of 79 hours without water, all this by forced marches over inexpressibly rough trails explains the serious mortality among the horses. . . . Morrow has over exerted himself to such an extent as to produce a dangerous hemorage [*sic*], long night marches have been made on foot by the troops in their efforts to surprise the Indian camp. Morrow deserves great credit for the persistency with which he has kept up the pursuit and without foot Indians and constant vigilance must have fallen into ambuscades resulting in the destruction of his command. The Indians are certainly as strong as any command Major Morrow has had in action. We always fight in extended skirmish line, the Indian line is always found to be of same length and often longer extending in some actions more than two miles hence the efforts to extend his flanks with the object of surrounding them fails.

The Indians select mountains for their fighting ground and positions almost impregnable usually throwing up stone rifle pits where nature has not furnished them and skillfully devising loopholes.

The Indians are thoroughly armed and as an evidence they are abundantly supplied with ammunition their fire in action is incessant and nearly all their horses and mules they abandon on the march are shot. It is estimated they have killed 600 to 1,000 since the outbreak. . . . It is impossible to describe the exceeding roughness of such mountains as the Black Range and the San Mateo. The well known Modoc Lava beds are a lawn compared with them.[7]

7 Hatch to Pope, February 25, 1880, ibid. Many writers in describing these campaigns stress the large number of troops in the field against Victorio. At this point the Ninth and Tenth Cavalry constituted most of the soldiers in the field and thus totaled twenty-

After shaking off Morrow, Victorio took cover in the Candelaria Mountains for a time. There he rested amid plenty of wood, water, and grass. His warriors, however, found an old and hated enemy easy prey for improving their marksmanship. Fifteen Mexicans from the little town of Carrizal, out searching for cattle thieves on November 7, came upon Victorio's trail. They followed it straight into an Apache ambush that left no survivors. When they failed to return, thirty-five of their fellow citizens set out to find them. They too were ambushed, and eleven of their number killed. The desperate Mexicans sought the aid of Lieutenant G. W. Baylor, who was stationed at Ysleta, Texas, with Company C, Texas Rangers. Baylor, with ten men, accompanied the Mexicans to the scene of the ambush. All they accomplished was the burial of twenty-six bodies.[8]

The devastating blow to the people of Carrizal did, however, stir a lethargic Mexican government to action. General German Trevino, commanding in Chihuahua, raised a large force to fight the Apaches and telegraphed Hatch that the movement of Mexican troops would probably serve to drive Victorio back into New Mexico. He pledged his full cooperation. Trevino was right—January 1880 found Victorio on another slashing raid into New Mexico, and the Ninth once more took to the field.[9]

On January 9 Morrow closed with Victorio near the head of the Puerco River, but the cunning chieftain slipped from his grasp. Then, like a chain of exploding firecrackers, Morrow pursued, caught up, and was fought off on January 17 in the San Mateos and on January 30 and again on February 3 in the San Andrés Mountains. None of these engagements was decisive, and Morrow's loss was three men killed, including Lieutenant Hansell French, and seven men wounded. A month of continuous marching and fighting had exhausted Morrow's command. Forage, rations, and ammunition were also dangerously low, and he turned back to Ojo Caliente to rest and refit.

---

four companies with a normal strength of about 2,000 men, and this is the figure commonly used. This information fails to note, however, that both regiments were far understrength and that Hatch had not more than 400 effectives and Grierson about 550. Thus, the combined strength of both regiments was fewer than 1,000. See Organizational Returns, Ninth and Tenth Cavalry, September 1879–February 1880, AGO, RG 94, NA.

8 Lieutenant G. W. Baylor, Company C, Texas Frontier Battalion, to General John B. Jones, AG, Austin, Texas, December 3, 1879, File 6058-1879.

9 Pope to the AAG, Military Division of the Missouri, January 9, 1880, ibid.; Hatch to Pope, January 13, 1880, ibid.

Meanwhile, Victorio seemed to vanish into thin air, though leaving a trail of dead and dying New Mexicans in his path.[10]

Victorio's success thus far in fending off all forces sent against him brought new recruits to his ranks, including several score fighting men from the Mescalero reservation. Believing that the Mescaleros were not only joining but also feeding and arming Victorio's hostiles, General Pope issued orders to Hatch to march on the Mescalero reservation and disarm and dismount those Indians.[11]

On February 23 Hatch formed all the troops at his disposal into three battalions under Morrow, Captain Hooker, and Captain Henry Carroll. Believing that Victorio was in Hembrillo Canyon in the San Andrés Mountains, Hatch decided on a two-phase operation. His battalions would descend on Victorio from the west, east, and north. Then, having (he hoped) inflicted a decisive defeat on the elusive chief, he would march to the Mescalero reservation, where he would attend to his assigned task.[12]

Morrow left Fort Bayard on March 29 with Companies H, L, and M, Ninth Cavalry, about seventy-five men; a detachment of the Fifteenth Infantry; and a few San Carlos Indian scouts. He marched to Palomas, where he was joined by reinforcements from Arizona—Captain C. B. McClellan, Lieutenants Charles B. Gatewood and Stephen Mills, eighty-five troopers of the Sixth Cavalry, and about forty Indian scouts. The battalion then marched to Aleman on the Jornada del Muerto near the west slope of the San Andrés. Carroll with Companies A, D, F, and G of the Ninth, about one hundred men, moved westward from Fort Stanton to attack from the east, while Hooker with detachments of buffalo soldiers from E, I, and K; twenty men of the Fifteenth Infantry; and some Navaho scouts came down the west slope from the north.

The plan was well conceived and might have worked, but a water pump spoiled Hatch's strategy. Carroll was on the march on April 4 and Hooker two days later. Morrow was scheduled to reach Hembrillo Canyon by daybreak on April 8, but the water pump at Alemán, the only source of water at that desert station, had broken down, and Morrow had great difficulty watering his command. On the evening of April 7, Morrow ordered McClel-

10 Morrow to Hatch, January 18, 1880, ibid.; Hatch to Pope, February 3, 1880, ibid.
11 Secretary of the Interior to the Secretary of War, February 11, 1880, ibid.; *Annual Report of the Secretary of War for the Year 1880*, 1(2):93–98.
12 *Annual Report of the Secretary of War for the Year 1880*, 1(2):109–10; General Field Order No. 1, Headquarters, District of New Mexico, February 23, 1880, File 6058-1879.

In the background, entrance to Hembrillo Canyon, the site of the near disaster to Captain Henry Carroll's command in fight with Victorio
Courtesy of Mark and Patricia Erickson

Captain Thomas C. Lebo, Tenth Cavalry
Courtesy National Archives

Tenth Cavalry at the Battle of Rattlesnake Springs, original painting by Nick Eggenhofer
Courtesy of the artist, the National Park Service, and the Fort Davis National Historic Site

Colonel Edward Hatch,
commander of the Ninth Cavalry
Courtesy National Archives

Captain Henry Carroll,
Ninth Cavalry
Courtesy National Archives

lan and his scouts to make a night march in order to reach the canyon at the appointed time. Meanwhile, he would follow with the main column as rapidly as it could be watered. The delay proved costly.

Early on the morning of April 8, McClellan arrived at Hembrillo Canyon to the sound of heavy gunfire and found Carroll pinned down and virtually surrounded. Carroll's men had consumed tainted water at the onset of their march. Suffering the ill effects of that water and finding another spring dry, they had entered Hembrillo Canyon desperate to quench their thirst. Unfortunately, Victorio and his men awaited them.[13]

McClellan and his scouts swarmed to the attack, but Victorio and his warriors scattered among the rocks and vanished. It had been a close call for Carroll's diminutive battalion. Eight men were wounded, including Carroll, and twenty-five horses and mules had been killed. Indian losses were uncertain; Carroll believed at least three had been killed, while the scouts claimed that twenty had fallen. Whatever the actual score, only one dead warrior was found on the field. A scout through the hills by the entire command on April 9—Morrow had arrived at sundown the previous day— found no sign of the Apaches. Hatch, who had come up with Morrow's battalion, took command of the united forces and set out for the Mescalero reservation to disarm and dismount the Indians at that agency.[14]

Meanwhile, General E. O. C. Ord had received orders from General Sheridan to send the Tenth Cavalry to assist Hatch at the Mescalero agency. Colonel Grierson received his instructions on March 20 and began immediate preparations. Officers and men were eager to carry out the assignment, for small parties of Warm Springs and Mescalero Apaches had been causing substantial difficulty. Between July 1879 and March 1880, Captain Charles Viele's C Company alone had chased raiding Mescaleros more than two thousand miles, while Captain Louis Carpenter, Captain A. S. B. Keyes, and Lieutenant T. C. Lebo with H, D, and K amassed the amazing total of six thousand miles. Although they had inflicted little damage on these flitting bands, they had successfully protected sparsely populated areas from significant depredations.[15]

13 Thrapp, *Victorio and the Mimbres Apaches,* 268–69.
14 Captain C. B. McClellan to the PA, Fort Bowie, Arizona Territory, May 16, 1880, File 6058-1879; Hatch to Pope, April 10, 1880, ibid.
15 Grierson to the AAG, Department of Texas, May 21, 1880, ibid.; "Expeditions and Scouts between August 31, 1879, and September 1, 1880," in *Annual Report of the Secretary of War for the Year 1880,* 134–47; Organizational Returns, Tenth Cavalry, July 1879– March 1880.

Grierson swiftly completed arrangements to protect his district and then set out with Companies D, E, F, K, and L, and a small detachment of the Twenty-fifth Infantry to guard his train. Scouting parties were thrown far out in order to cover a fifty-mile front, and two strikes were made en route to Arizona. Lieutenant Calvin Esterly with troopers from D and L found a trail that led northward through the White Sand Hills. After a three-day pursuit of two hundred miles, ninety of which were without water, his men overtook a band of raiders, killed one, and recovered eight head of stolen stock. Captain Lebo with K found a camp at Shakehand Spring, some forty miles south of the Peñasco River, killed one warrior, captured four Indian women, and recovered a captive Mexican boy, Cayetano Segura, and more than twenty head of animals.[16]

On April 10 the entire command rendezvoused at the Peñasco after finding many trails that "invariably" led toward the Mescalero reservation. From the river the command marched to the Tularosa, where the soldiers found a number of Indian camps and Grierson prepared to attack. A courier, however, arrived from Agent S. A. Russell, F. C. Godfroy's replacement, with the information that these Indians were friendly and were under instructions to move to the agency. After making certain that the Indians were actually on the move, Grierson continued to the Mescalero agency, where he joined Hatch on April 12.[17]

After some discussion with Agent Russell, Hatch and Grierson waited another day until all the Indians had come in before disarming and dismounting them. If the delay was agreeable to Grierson, the disposition of troops and the location of the Indian camps were not. The former were at the agency, while the latter were across the Tularosa on a timbered ridge at the base of the mountains and a good half-mile from the soldiers. Grierson reported:

> I advised the surrounding and complete disarming and dis-
> mounting of all the Indians at the Mescalero Agency, and their
> removal to Fort Stanton, where they would be under direct con-
> trol of the military authorities. The agency had, for a long time,
> been simply a sort of hospital for old, infirm Indians, a com-
> missary for Indian women and children, and a safe refuge and

16 Grierson to the AAG, Department of Texas, May 21, 1880.
17 Ibid.

convenient place for the younger and more active Indians to obtain supplies to enable them to continue their raiding and depredations in Texas and elsewhere. The agency, too, had also become virtually a supply camp for Victorio's band, who, in addition to such means of subsistence, were, by a most remarkable manifestation of generosity on the part of the Interior Department having their families fed and kindly cared for at the San Carlos Agency.[18]

Hatch, however, preferred to leave the Indians alone as long as Agent Russell felt he could handle them. Such leniency, Hatch soon learned, was ill advised. Had Grierson's advice been taken, the lives of many Indians as well as whites would have been spared.

For two days stormy weather delayed any action, and the Apaches came in slowly. The disarming date was set back to April 15, but a count that day showed only 320 Indians present. Russell believed, however, that another day would bring the total to 400. To this delay Hatch also assented, and both set April 16 as the day for disarming and dismounting.

On the morning of April 16, everything seemed in order, and Hatch moved his command west of the agency, while Grierson and his troopers, along with Captain Steelhammer and Company G, Fifteenth Infantry, remained in camp. About 10:00 A.M. they heard firing south of the agency. Grierson mounted his command on the double but soon learned that some of the scouts had intercepted a small party of Indians running off some stock, had killed two of them, and had recovered the animals. Agent Russell was much upset. He claimed that the Indians killed were simply obeying his orders to go out and drive in some strays and that the scouts had made a terrible mistake.

Meanwhile, Hatch and Russell had agreed on a plan of procedure. Captain Steelhammer with his company, along with the agent, would carry out the actual disarming beginning precisely at two o'clock. Grierson and Hatch would hold their troopers in readiness in case trouble erupted. If Steelhammer needed assistance, he was to fire three quick shots.

At the appointed time Steelhammer and Russell left to collect the arms and horses, and all seemed to go well until Grierson noticed a number of Indians, mounted and on foot, ascending the mountain behind their camp.

18 Ibid.

Shortly after came three quick shots. The troopers charged immediately and after lively skirmishing rounded up most of the runaways, but fourteen had been killed and about thirty had made their escape. The remaining Indians, about two hundred fifty, were quickly disarmed and their animals taken from them. They then were marched to the agency corral and placed under close guard.[19]

With duties completed at the Mescalero agency, Grierson and his command scouted "very thoroughly" in the Sacramento and Guadalupe Mountains, rounded up several small parties of Mescaleros, and drove them back to their reservation. Then with detachments ranging over a wide front, he set out for Fort Concho, where he arrived on May 16. The Concho column had marched fifteen hundred miles, captured five women, two children, and fifty head of stock. In the fighting that had ensued, five Indians had lost their lives, but young Cayetano Segura had been returned to his family.[20]

Victorio had not been idle. After the fight in Hembrillo Canyon, he had moved westward across the Rio Grande and into the Mogollons, killing sheepherders, miners, and anyone else who had the misfortune to cross his path. Among the slain was a miner, James C. Cooney, the brother of Captain Michael Cooney, commanding A Company, Ninth Cavalry. The latter had the sad task of personally burying his brother.[21]

Hatch and his Ninth were again embarked on their seemingly unending pursuit of Victorio. At the time of the Mescalero breakout, Morrow's battalion was encamped southwest of the agency to prevent any flight in that direction. When news of the trouble reached him, Morrow moved toward Alamo Canyon and on April 17 overtook a small party, killing three warriors and capturing twenty animals. After a futile scout through Alamo and Dog Canyons, Morrow moved in to Tularosa, where Lieutenant Patrick Cusack, now commanding Carroll's battalion, joined him while Carroll recuperated from his wounds.

Morrow marched southwest by way of White Sands and San Nicolas Spring into the San Andrés Mountains, but his scouts could find no sign of hostiles. The command watered at San Agustin Spring and then turned west to the Rio Grande, and at last the elusive foe was sighted. The horses, how-

19   Sheridan to Townsend, April 20, 1880, File 6058-1879; Grierson to the AAG, Department of Texas, May 21, 1880; *Annual Report to the Commissioner of Indian Affairs for the Year 1880*, 130.
20   Grierson to the AAG, Department of Texas, May 21, 1880.
21   Twitchell, *Leading Facts of New Mexican History*, 2:439.

ever, were so broken down that the gap could not be closed, and Morrow was forced to give up the chase and turn toward Ojo Caliente.[22]

Meanwhile, Hatch with Hooker's battalion cut Victorio's trail and pursued him into Arizona. But the Apaches doubled back into New Mexico and headed in the direction of Old Fort Tularosa, some fifty miles northwest of Ojo Caliente. On the evening of May 13, a lone rider on a lathered horse galloped into the Barlow and Sanders Stage Station with the news that Victorio at that moment was probably wiping out the small settlement adjacent to Old Fort Tularosa. Fortunately, Sergeant George Jordan and a detachment of twenty-five buffalo soldiers of K Company were at the station. Jordan and his men were exhausted after escorting a wagon train of supplies all day, but he mounted his small command and headed for Tularosa, a full day's march away. They agreed to push on "as far as they could."[23]

After an all-night march over rugged and, at times, very steep terrain, Jordan's detachment arrived at the old fort early on the morning of May 14. Thankfully, Victorio had not yet attacked. Wasting no time, the sergeant directed his troopers to reinforce a corral and build a stockade. These tasks completed, Jordan carefully stationed his men, sent out vedettes, and moved the frightened citizens into the stockade. Courage and fast work prevented a slaughter. At dusk when the Apaches struck, a curtain of fire drove them back. When they again attacked, they were fought off with equal vigor.

Moreover, in light of Jordan's fortified position, Victorio concluded that the rest of the regiment was probably nearby. He turned southwest toward the Mexican border, leaving the intrepid sergeant in full control of the stockade. Hatch rode in the following morning, paused only long enough to learn the details, and then pushed on after the fleeing Apaches. For "gallantry in action against hostile Apache Indians at Old Fort Tularosa, New Mexico, May 14, 1880, while commanding a detachment of 25 men repulsing a force of more than 100 Indians under Victoria [sic]," Sergeant Jordan would be awarded the Medal of Honor almost ten years later on May 7, 1890.[24]

Hatch reached Ojo Caliente on May 21, and the next day Morrow also came in. Both commands were badly used up, and Hatch telegraphed Pope: "the trails in the Mogollon and in Arizona are fearfully rough. There is no

22 Morrow to the AAG, District of New Mexico, May 21, 1880, File 6058-1879.

23 Schubert, Black Valor, 74–75.

24 Ibid., 76; See also Hatch to the AAG, Department of the Missouri, May 17, 1880, File 6058-1879; Hutcheson, "Ninth Regiment of Cavalry," 286; Beyer and Keydel, Deeds of Valor, 2:273–76.

grass . . . and no forage to be obtained."[25] In fact, some of the detachments were still straggling in, their back trails littered with the dead animals of pursuer and pursued. Captain H. K. Parker and the Indian scouts were, however, still clinging doggedly to the trail. On May 23 their persistence was rewarded —Parker located Victorio's camp near the head of the Palomas River.

Moving with the utmost caution and stealth, the scouts managed to creep within fifty yards of the unsuspecting Indians. At daybreak the next morning Parker opened fire. The first volley killed a number of men, women, and children, but the Apaches, recovering quickly from the surprise, returned shot for shot. It was a bitter, desperate struggle that ended when Parker ran out of ammunition and water. He withdrew with seventy-five captured animals and left thirty dead Indians at the campsite.[26]

When Hatch received word of Parker's fight, he sent Morrow out at once to take up the trail. Pushing horses and men to their limits, Morrow caught up with Victorio's rear guard on May 30, killed three warriors, and wounded several more. The pursuit continued to the Mexican border, where the troopers were forced to halt and, in helpless rage, watch their old enemy slip from the grasp. Pressure from a vacillating Mexican government had once again compelled Washington to issue orders forbidding violations of the international boundary.

Six days later, however, Morrow dealt the Apaches a sore blow. He intercepted a small party making its way to Mexico, and his troopers killed two and wounded three others. One of the dead was Victorio's son.[27]

The main body of Indians had escaped. Thus, a frustrated Hatch telegraphed General Pope to inquire if something could be done to lift restrictions on crossings into Mexico, particularly if the trail was "hot." In ten days he had the answer—the Mexican government refused to give its consent. Nonetheless, although his foe had escaped, Hatch's campaign was not a failure. Again he had forced Victorio to take a Mexican vacation and had inflicted serious losses in men and animals. The chieftain's effective strength had been reduced to fewer than two hundred men.[28]

25 *Annual Report of the Secretary of War for the Year 1880,* 1(2):109.

26 Hatch to the AAG, Department of the Missouri, May 27, 1880, Military Division of the Missouri, Special File, Victorio Papers, U.S. Army Commands, RG 98, NA [hereafter cited as Victorio Papers].

27 Hatch to Pope, June 1, 1880, File 6058-1879.

28 Hatch to Pope, June 12, 1880, Victorio Papers; Pope to Hatch, June 22, 1880, ibid.; Pope to the AAG, Military Division of the Missouri, June 21, 1880, File 6058-1879.

The brunt of the fighting thus far had fallen on the troopers of the Ninth, and late in May, General Sheridan ordered the Tenth sent to New Mexico. Grierson protested the move. It would leave the West Texas frontier wide open to attack, and he was convinced that Victorio's next move would be there. Ord agreed with him and prevailed upon Sheridan to rescind the order. As it turned out, the colonel had predicted the next phase of the campaign perfectly.[29]

Grierson was not clairvoyant. There were clear indications that Victorio might be looking with some favor on a tour of West Texas. On May 12 a party of eight Mescalero warriors, armed with late-model Winchester carbines, ambushed a party of citizens in Bass Canyon west of Fort Davis, killed James Grant and Margaret Graham, wounded her husband Harry Graham and a man identified only as Mr. Murphy, and stripped their wagons of everything of value. Carpenter with H Company pursued to the Rio Grande and reported that he was convinced the warriors were on their way to join Victorio.

In mid-June a party of Pueblo Indian scouts en route to Fort Davis was hit while passing through Viejo Canyon in the Chinati Mountains, and the chief scout, Simon Olguin, was killed along with most of the horses. Extensive scouting by detachments of the Tenth failed to turn up anything, but the surmise was that the Pueblos had run afoul of hawk-eyed spies from Victorio's camp.[30]

Grierson, meanwhile, had profited from Hatch's experience and decided on a change in tactics. Instead of wearing down his command in long and probably unprofitable pursuits, he proposed to guard the mountain passes and water holes. In this way he either could block the movement of the Apaches through the passes, or failing that, he could deny them water— even an Apache had to stop for a drink.

Posting his troopers accordingly, Grierson left Fort Concho on July 10 and headed west with a small escort and his son Robert, who had arrived for a visit from Jacksonville, Illinois, where he was attending school. If Robert was looking for some excitement, he could hardly have chosen a better time.

29 Sheridan to Townsend, May 26, 1880, File 6058-1879; Grierson to Hatch, May 29, 1880, Victorio Papers; Colonel William Whipple, AAG, Military Division of the Missouri, June 11, 1880, ibid.

30 Grierson to the AAG, Department of Texas, May 18, 1880, LR, AGO, RG94, NA; Carpenter to the AAG, District of the Pecos, June 2, 1880, ibid.; Lieutenant Robert Reed, Tenth Cavalry, to the PA, Fort Davis, Texas, June 28, 1880, ibid.

At Fort Davis on July 18, Grierson received word that Colonel Adolfo Valle and four hundred Mexican troops were on Victorio's trail and believed the Apaches were headed for Eagle Springs, Texas. Continuing west, Grierson reached Eagle Springs on July 23 and learned that Victorio was near Ojo del Pino some fifty miles to the southwest in Mexico, that he had skirmished with Mexican scouts, and that he was on the move to the Rio Grande. Grierson and his party proceeded to Fort Quitman, where he was surprised to find that Valle and his troops were just across the river and badly in need of supplies. Grierson sent provisions to Valle, but he feared that the concentration of Mexican troops had given Victorio easy access to Texas.[31]

Grierson left Quitman on July 29 and headed for Eagle Springs, hopeful that he could intercept the Indians before they could do much damage. While en route, an Indian was seen who fled when fired upon, and it was believed that he was a member of Victorio's advance. A short time later couriers from Captain J. C. Gilmore at Eagle Springs informed Grierson that Victorio had crossed into Texas. Gilmore had received the news from couriers sent by Captain Nicholas Nolan, at the river near Quitman. Led by Lieutenant Henry Flipper, the first and only black officer in the regiment, the couriers had carried the dispatches ninety-eight miles in twenty-two hours.[32]

Faced with this information, Grierson decided to make camp at Tinaja de las Palmas, some fifteen miles west of Eagle Springs and "the only waterhole for a long distance north." Victorio would undoubtedly seek to water there, and Grierson would be directly in his path. But the colonel had only eight men with him, including his son Robert, hardly enough to fight Victorio and scarcely enough to detain him for long. Nevertheless, Grierson and his little band entrenched themselves as best they could high on the side of a ridge near the road. When the eastbound stage came by, Grierson sent word to Gilmore at Eagle Springs to send reinforcements immediately. About midnight, couriers reached Grierson and informed him that the Indians were encamped not more than ten miles from his position. The couriers were hastened off to Fort Quitman with orders for Captain Nolan to come up with A Company as rapidly as possible.[33]

About four in the morning, Lieutenant Leighton Finley of G Company

31 Grierson to Ord, July 24, 1880, File 6058-1879; Grierson to Pope, July 24, 1880, Victorio Papers.

32 Flipper, *Negro Frontiersman*, 16; Flipper, the first African American graduate of West Point, joined the Tenth in 1878.

33 Grierson to Ord, July 30, 1880, File 6058-1879.

with ten troopers arrived to escort Grierson to Eagle Springs. Instead, Grierson posted Finley and his men lower down on the ridge and sent a courier to Gilmore with orders to bring every available man at Eagle Springs to Tinaja and on the double. This done, he settled down to await the sunrise.

At nine o'clock the Indian vanguard came into view, spied Grierson's position, and turned eastward so they could cross the road without a fight. Grierson would have none of this. He ordered Lieutenant Finley and ten men to charge the Apaches and hold them up until the other troops arrived. Finley, carrying out his orders "handsomely," managed to hold the Indians in check. Near ten o'clock the advance guard of Captain Viele and C Company came up, but in the smoke and dust mistook Finley's men for Indians and fired into them. Finley beat a hot retreat with the Indians in pursuit, but fire from the camp drove them off. Viele came up and entered the fight. With the odds narrowing, the Apaches withdrew to a ridge south of Grierson's position, but Viele charged and dislodged them. The warriors then attempted to cross to the north but were driven back in some confusion. At this point dust clouds from the west signaled Nolan's rapid approach. In danger of being cornered, Victorio turned and fled south toward the Rio Grande. It had been a four-hour fight, which cost the life of Private Martin Davis of C Company. Lieutenant S. R. Colladay was wounded and ten horses were killed. The Apaches lost an estimated seven killed and an undetermined number wounded.[34]

Grierson sent out scouting parties immediately to find the Indian camp. It was located on the Mexican side of the river about sixty miles below Fort Quitman. Colonel Valle was notified at once, but instead of marching downriver to attack, he turned northward toward El Paso and away from the scene of action.

Grierson believed Victorio would certainly make another attempt to move northward. It came on August 3, when a patrol under Corporal Asa Weaver of H Company engaged the Indians in a fifteen-mile running fight near Alamo. During the action the mount of Private Willie Tockes of C Company suddenly bucked and ran squarely into a mass of Apaches. When last seen, Tockes had dropped the reins and was firing his carbine right and left before going down under an avalanche of warriors.[35]

---

34 Ibid.
35 Major John Bigelow, Jr., "Historical Sketch, Tenth United States Cavalry, 1866–1892," U.S. Army Commands, RG 98, NA; Organizational Returns, Tenth Cavalry, August 1880.

Certain that Victorio would attempt to get through one of the passes east of Van Horn's Wells, Grierson marched with every available man from Eagle Springs to that point, where he discovered that his wily foe had gone northwest of Van Horn's on the evening of August 4. Grierson knew how to march; he had proved that in his famous raid through Mississippi in 1863 and his less-well-known but more devastating sweep through that state in 1864. He proved his ability again on a torrid August 5, 1880. At 3:00 A.M. he moved out for Rattlesnake Springs, some sixty-five miles northwest, keeping a range of mountains between his command and the Indians. He covered the distance in twenty-one hours, arrived ahead of Victorio, and had ample time to prepare an ambush. Few if any commanders or their troops could boast of having outmarched a band of Apaches.

Early on August 6 Grierson placed C and G Companies under Captain Viele in Rattlesnake Canyon to await Victorio's approach. It was a long wait, but near two o'clock in the afternoon, the Indians were seen approaching. The troopers withheld their fire, hoping to volley at point-blank range. Victorio, cautious and perhaps sensing a trap, halted. Viele's opening fire caused considerable consternation, and the Indians swiftly withdrew out of range. But Victorio needed water and, seeing few troopers, regrouped his warriors and moved to attack. Grierson countered by sending Carpenter forward with H and B Companies, thereby repulsing the Indians and scattering them among the hills and ravines.

At 4:00 P.M. Grierson's train, guarded by Company H, Twenty-fourth Infantry, and a detachment of troopers, rounded a point of the mountains to the southeast and headed for the spring. A strong force of warriors rode to cut off the wagons, but Captain Gilmore beat them off. Near dusk the Apaches made a final effort to reach water but were thrown back in confusion and fled, with Carpenter in close pursuit.[36]

Victorio suffered a decisive defeat at Rattlesnake Springs, but this was not the only blow. Three days earlier Captain Lebo and K Company, on scout in the Sierra Diablo, had struck pay dirt in the form of Victorio's supply camp. After routing the warrior guards, the troopers had captured twenty-five head of cattle, a quantity of maguey bread, a supply of beef on pack animals, and some berries.

Grierson gave Victorio no time to rest. Companies of the Tenth guarded

36   Grierson to the AAG, Department of Texas, August 3, 1880, Victorio Papers; Grierson to the AAG, Department of Texas, August 4, 1880, ibid.; Grierson to Ord, August 14, 1880, ibid.

the water holes and closed the mountain passes to the north, while others pushed the search for Victorio. On August 11 Carpenter and Nolan found his trail west of Fresno Spring and set out in pursuit. Carpenter's horses gave out, but Nolan hung on and chased the fleeing Apaches to the Rio Grande, where they crossed into Mexico. It was Victorio's last appearance on American soil.[37]

Grierson reported that his troopers had killed and wounded at least thirty warriors and more than seventy-five animals. Victorio had been stripped of his supplies and driven from the country. Scouts sent to follow the chief into Mexico had returned with the information that the Indians were making their way slowly to the Candelaria Mountains, hampered by many wounded and with most of their stock broken down. Grierson's losses were three men killed, three seriously wounded, a number with minor injuries, and one trooper, Private Wesley Hardy, missing in action.[38]

Meanwhile, the Mexican and U.S. governments had at last agreed on a cooperative campaign to destroy Victorio. A powerful force was assembled under Colonels George Buell and Eugene Carr to cross into Mexico and take combined action with Mexican troops commanded by Colonel Joaquin Terrazas. Ten companies of Grierson's buffalo soldiers were posted along the Rio Grande to prevent a break into Texas.[39]

Early in October the troops of Buell, Carr, and Terrazas converged on Victorio, and scouts reported that he had taken refuge in the Tres Castillos Mountains. Avenues of escape were quickly closed off, and plans for a final assault were made. On October 9, however, Terrazas informed his American counterparts that the presence of their troops in Mexico was objectionable, and Buell and Carr reluctantly withdrew to the border. Terrazas then moved up, surrounded Victorio's camp, and on the morning of October 14 attacked from all sides. The battle was over by 9:00 A.M. Victorio was dead. Sixty warriors and eighteen women and children were also killed, and sixty-eight women and children taken prisoner; 180 animals were captured. Terrazas reported that only a handful of warriors had escaped his net and evaded pursuit.[40]

---

37 Grierson to Ord, August 14, 1880; Nolan to the Commanding Officer, Fort Bliss, Texas, August 15, 1880, Victorio Papers.

38 Grierson to the AAG, Department of Texas, August 19, 1880, ibid.; Organizational Returns, Tenth Cavalry, August 1880.

39 Pope to Sheridan, September 10, 1880, Victorio Papers.

40 Buell to Hatch, October 18, 1880, File 6058-1879; Terrazas to Buell, October 22, 1880, ibid.

Mexican troops had killed Victorio and most of his warriors, and the war was over. In a very real sense, however, they had only delivered the *coup de grâce*. The real victors were the buffalo soldiers of the Ninth and Tenth Cavalry. They had pursued and fought the great chief over thousands of blood-spattered miles in an unrelenting contest of courage, skill, endurance, and attrition. Twice Hatch had forced Victorio into Mexico and with a modicum of cooperation from Mexican troops could have ended the struggle. When Victorio turned into Texas, he marched into the jaws of disaster.

Grierson's campaign had been a model of its kind and a masterpiece of counter guerrilla warfare. Not an Indian penetrated the settlements; the Apaches were outfought and outmarched, denied access to food and water, and driven pell-mell into Mexico. Beaten, dispirited, and sapped of the will to fight, Victorio was an easy target for the final thrust.

Despite these achievements, the buffalo soldiers received virtually no credit at the time and precious little since. Hatch and Grierson were objects of bitter criticism, and the latter has sometimes been pictured as little more than a buffoon. The men in the ranks more often than not were and have been tailored to fit the stereotype of grinning, fumbling misfits incapable of independent thought or action. But General Pope knew better and, at the close of the campaign, remarked: "It is my duty, as it is my pleasure, to invite the special attention of the authorities to the meritorious and gallant conduct of Col. Edward Hatch, commanding the District of New Mexico, and to Major A. P. Morrow, Ninth Cavalry, and the officers and soldiers under their command, in the difficult and trying campaign against the Southern Apaches. Everything that men could do they did, and it is little to say that their services in the field were marked by unusual hardships and difficulties. Their duties were performed with zeal and intelligence and they are worthy of all consideration."[41]

And General Ord, who lost no love on black troopers, wrote: "I trust that the services of the troops engaged will meet with that recognition which such earnest and zealous efforts in the line of duty deserve. They are entitled to more than commendation. . . . In this connection I beg to invite attention to the long and severe service of the Tenth Cavalry, in the field and at remote frontier stations, in this department. Is it not time that it should have relief by a change to some more favored district of the country?"[42]

41 *Annual Report of the Secretary of War for the Year 1880*, 1(2):93.
42 Ibid., 111.

Rare praise and a worthy recommendation, but General Sheridan did not agree with his subordinate on a change to a "more favored district." There were still more Apaches to fight, and the Tenth Cavalry faced five more years on the Texas frontier.

The Final Years

The death of Victorio and the near annihilation of his Warm Springs band at Tres Castillos on October 14, 1880, did much to bring peace to the Texas–New Mexico region. Still, a remnant survived that was capable of inflicting a painful, if not fatal, sting. A party of thirty warriors, en route to Victorio's stronghold, tarried long enough at the Rio Grande to escape the fate of their comrades. Its members now wanted revenge. At dawn on October 28 they ambushed one of Colonel Grierson's patrols, under Sergeant Charles Perry, on the river below Ojo Caliente, Texas. Firing at point-blank range, they killed Corporal William Backus and Privates Jeremiah Griffin, James Stanley, Carter Burns, and George Mills. When reinforcements arrived, the Indians had departed, taking with them four of the patrol's horses and two of their mules.[1]

For the next few months, small parties of these inveterate raiders, ranging in number from eight to ten, were active enough in southern New Mexico to keep Colonel Hatch and most of his Ninth Cavalry in the field. In January 1881 the stage was attacked near Fort Cummings. The driver, Thomas White, and a passenger were killed, and the mail scattered to the winds. Detachments of Companies C, D, F, and I were unable to run down

---

1 Organizational Returns, Tenth Cavalry, October 1880, AGO, RG 94, NA; Major John Bigelow, Jr., "Historical Sketch, Tenth United States Cavalry, 1866–1892," U.S. Army Commands, RG 98, NA.

the raiders, who fled back and forth across the international boundary. Repeated raids in February, March, and April brought the same results.[2]

More serious trouble was forthcoming. Nana, one of Victorio's lieutenants, had not been at Tres Castillos. More than seventy years old, bitter, implacable, and quite able, he nursed a burning desire to avenge his kinsmen. Carefully he collected a few warriors, guns, and ammunition, and by July 1881 he was ready. Nana with fifteen warriors left his refuge high in the Sierra Madres of Mexico, and General John Pope later described them as "rush[ing] through the country from one mountain range to another like a pack of hungry wolves, killing everybody they met and stealing all the horses they could get their hands on."[3] Nana stopped long enough, however, to recruit about two dozen war-hungry Mescaleros, and with a force of forty warriors, he gave the buffalo soldiers a nightmarish four months of campaigning.

Nana served notice on July 17, when he struck the pack train of Company L near the mouth of Alamo Canyon, wounded one trooper, and made off with three mules. Lieutenant John Guilfoyle with twenty men of L and a body of Apache scouts set out in pursuit. The chase led through Dog Canyon; across the inferno of White Sands, where the hostiles killed three Mexicans; and on into the rugged vastness of the San Andres. There on July 25 Guilfoyle caught up and attacked. The Indians, after sustaining two casualties, Guilfoyle believed, fled, leaving two horses and twelve mules behind.[4]

Nana rode west, crossed the Rio Grande, killed three more citizens, and headed into the San Mateos. Ranchers in the area formed a posse of thirty-six men in the naive belief they could do better than regular troops and marched into the San Mateos to beard the Apaches. They found the trail and followed it into Red Canyon and into an ambush. When the firing was over, one rancher was dead, seven were wounded, and Nana had all their horses. Guilfoyle, following rapidly, caught up again on August 3 at Monica Springs, captured eleven horses, and wounded two warriors, but the rest of the band got away.[5]

2 Hatch to the AAG, Department of the Missouri, January 15, 1881, LR, Selected Documents Relating to the Activities of the Ninth and Tenth Cavalry in the Campaign against Victorio, 1879–80, File 6058-1879, AGO, RG 94, NA; Organizational Returns, Ninth Cavalry, February–April, 1881.

3 *Annual Report of the Secretary of War for the Year 1881*, 117.

4 Ibid., 126; Organizational Returns, Ninth Cavalry, July 1881; Hutcheson, "Ninth Regiment of Cavalry," 286.

5 Organizational Returns, Ninth Cavalry, August 1881; *Annual Report of the Secretary of War for the Year 1881*, 127; Sonnichsen, *Mescalero Apaches*, 192.

Guilfoyle's horses broke down, and it was nine days and two dead citizens later before the Ninth found Nana again. Captain H. K. Parker and nineteen troopers of K Company intercepted the Apaches about twenty-five miles west of Sabinal. The Indians entrenched themselves in near impregnable positions, but Parker, outnumbered two to one, attacked at once. In a hard-fought hour-and-a-half fight, Nana drove off the gallant buffalo soldiers and escaped. Privates Charles Perry and Guy Temple were dead, three other troopers were wounded, and nine horses were killed. Parker cited Sergeants Jordan and Thomas Shaw. Jordan, on the exposed right flank and facing superior numbers, had "held his ground," thereby saving the rest of the command. For his action he was awarded the Certificate of Merit, a valued award since it increased a soldier's pay by two dollars a month. As for Shaw, he had held the "most advanced position" so tenaciously that the Apaches "gave up the attack and retreated." For extraordinary courage in action, he received the Medal of Honor.[6]

On August 16 a hysterical Mexican dashed into the camp of Lieutenant Gustavus Valois and I Company near Cuchillo Negro to report that Nana and his warriors had murdered his family on a ranch nearby. Lieutenant George Burnett and a detachment of fifteen men saddled immediately and set out for the ranch, while Valois and the rest of the company prepared to follow. Burnett reached the ranch to find the horribly mutilated bodies of a woman and three children. The trail was easily found, and reinforced by a few Mexicans, Burnett took up the pursuit. The Indians were overtaken in the foothills of Cuchillo Negro, but as usual, they had taken strong positions among the rocks and crevices.

Burnett deployed in three wings, with himself leading the center, First Sergeant Moses Williams the right, and the Mexicans taking the left. Unable to dislodge the Indians, Burnett attempted to flank them with a handful of men and was nearly surrounded. Trumpeter John Rogers volunteered to go for aid and, under a hail of bullets, managed to reach Valois unhurt. The latter marched swiftly to Burnett's right to flank the Indians from that side, but they shifted quickly and poured a volley into I Company, killing ten horses.

Burnett charged, fought his way to Valois, and the united command fell back to stronger positions. Four troopers failed to hear the order to retreat, and the Apaches moved to cut them off. Burnett, Sergeant Williams, and

6 *Annual Report of the Secretary of War for the Year 1881*, 127; Organizational Returns, Ninth Cavalry, August 1881; Hutcheson, "Ninth Regiment of Cavalry," 286–87; Kenner, *Buffalo Soldiers and Officers of the Ninth Cavalry*, 147–49.

Private Augustus Walley dashed to their rescue, with leaden slugs cutting the air all around. Two of the imperiled men were wounded and unable to move. Burnett and Walley carried them to safety, while Williams and the remaining two troopers covered the retreat. Fighting continued until nightfall, when Nana broke off the engagement and disappeared in the hills. For conspicuous gallantry in action, Lieutenant Burnett, Sergeant Williams, and Private Walley were awarded the Medal of Honor—three more in the growing list of heroes among the officers and men of the Ninth Cavalry.[7]

From Cuchillo Negro, Nana's trail led south, and Captain Michael Cooney with A and Valois with I struggled to close with the clever old warrior and his band. But another blow was in store for the Ninth. In an effort to cut off Nana's escape to Mexico, Hatch ordered Lieutenant G. W. Smith to march from Fort Cummings with a detachment of forty-six men of B and H. For reasons never explained, Smith moved out with only seventeen men. A party of cowboys under rancher George Daly joined him near McEver's ranch, and the Apache trail was followed to Gavilan Canyon.

Smith, fearing an ambush, called a halt. Daly and his untrained crew, however, plunged ahead, and the gallant Smith would not let them go alone. They had hardly entered the canyon before a crashing volley killed both Smith and Daly. The latter's followers took to their heels, leaving seventeen buffalo soldiers to carry on as best they could. Sergeant Brent Woods of B Company took command at this point. He rallied his men and led them in a countercharge up the canyon walls, holding off the Apaches until a detachment of H under Sergeant Anderson arrived. The combined command put the Apaches to flight, and Anderson pursued, "carrying his dead and wounded with him." Although Woods won high praise and lasting gratitude from his men and others in the regiment, turnover in the officer corps and their heavy workload in 1881 meant that thirteen years passed before he received the Medal of Honor he clearly deserved.[8]

Nana and most of his warriors returned to the Sierra Madres after the fight in Gavilan Canyon, but some of them lingered on—too long as it turned out. On the morning of October 4, Apache-wise Captains Carroll and Parker, with F and K Companies, hit the trail of these hostiles on the

---

7 Hutcheson, "Ninth Regiment of Cavalry," 287; Organizational Returns, Tenth Cavalry, August 1881; Beyer and Keydel, *Deeds of Valor*, 2:277–81.

8 *Annual Report of the Secretary of War for the Year 1881*, 127; Beyer and Keydel, *Deeds of Valor*, 2:281; Hutcheson, "Ninth Regiment of Cavalry," 287; Organizational Returns, Ninth Cavalry, August 1881; Schubert, *Black Valor*, 85, 86.

eastern slopes of the Dragoon Mountains and followed it until late afternoon, when the Apache rear guard was sighted. A fifteen-mile running fight
brought the Indians to bay among the rocks, and a sharp engagement of an
hour drove them out. The hostiles then scattered and made for the Mexican
border. F and K had three men and a horse wounded, while Indian losses,
though believed heavy, were uncertain.[9]

Nana's raid capped six years of arduous service for the troopers of the
Ninth in New Mexico, Colorado, and Texas. They had fought effectively and
almost continuously against Apaches, lawless whites, and Mexicans—this
on the heels of eight demanding years on the Texas frontier. General Pope
felt the Ninth was entitled to a much-needed rest, and in November Hatch
was ordered to transfer regimental headquarters from Santa Fe to Fort Riley,
Kansas. Five companies garrisoned this post, with the others taking station
at Fort Elliott, Texas; Fort Hays, Kansas; and Forts Sill, Reno, and Supply in
Indian Territory.[10]

Meanwhile, Grierson and the Tenth were encountering problems of a
different kind. The defeat of Victorio and the growing power of the Diaz
regime in Mexico had gone far toward bringing unprecedented peace to the
West Texas frontier. This favorable turn of events permitted concentration of
the regiment at Forts Concho, Stockton, and Davis, although small detachments maintained patrols along the Rio Grande and in the Guadalupe
Mountains.

Grierson was proud of his buffalo soldiers and with good reason. Their
performance against Victorio could scarcely be faulted. They had marched,
fought, and scouted in the best traditions of the service. Equally, their behavior in camp and station left little to be desired. Desertions in 1880, despite
the most rigorous campaign in the regiment's history, reached an all-time
low of five—the best record by far of any regiment in the country. Other
violations of the military code were also few in number. They included four
cases of theft, one "neglect of duty," one assault and battery, three AWOL,
one "sleeping on post," one "leaving post as sentinel," one "selling of clothing," and two lesser offenses. By contrast, the Eighth Cavalry, stationed adjacent to the Tenth, had exactly twice this number of offenses.[11]

9 Organizational Returns, Ninth Cavalry, October 1881; Hutcheson, "Ninth Regiment of Cavalry," 287.
10 *Annual Report of the Secretary of War for the Year 1881*, 118; Organizational Returns,
Ninth Cavalry, November–December 1881.
11 Organizational Returns, Tenth Cavalry, November 1880; *Annual Report of the Secretary of War for the Year 1880*, 1(2):152. Offenses for troopers of the Eighth included one

A combat record that saved many lives and thousands of dollars in property, as well as excellent behavior, made little or no impression on the citizens of tough little Saint Angela (San Angelo after about 1880–81), and tensions between the town and the Fort Concho garrison remained high. Early in 1881 an incident occurred that finally broke the dam of trooper restraint. Impecunious soldiers sometimes danced or sang for drinks in the saloons. On the night of January 31, Private William Watkins of E Company was so engaged in McDonald's Saloon. Tom McCarthy, a sheepman along the San Saba River, was enjoying the show and buying drinks. When Watkins finally tired and expressed a desire to stop, McCarthy insisted that he continue. When Watkins protested politely, McCarthy pulled his pistol and shot the unarmed trooper through the head.

McCarthy fled the saloon, but on his way out of town, post guards at Fort Concho apprehended him. He was held until the following morning, when he was released into the custody of Sheriff Jim Spears. Instead of jailing the prisoner, Spears permitted him the freedom of the town pending an examining trial. Feelings ran high at the garrison, and on Thursday, February 3, a handbill appeared on the streets of Saint Angela:

> FORT CONCHO, TEXAS, FEB. 3, 1881
>
> We, the soldiers of the U.S. Army, do hereby warn the first and last time all citizens and cowboys, etc., of San Angelo and vicinity to recognize our right of way as just and peaceable men. If we do not receive justice and fair play, which we must have, some one will suffer—if not the guilty the innocent.
>
> "It has gone too far, justice or death."
>
> SIGNED U.S. SOLDIERS[12]

On the evening the handbill appeared, a group of troopers left the post and searched for McCarthy. Spears, however, managed to hide him behind the boardinghouse of a Mrs. Tankersley. Grierson, meanwhile, sent a strong detachment into town to round up the enraged troopers and at the same time promised to see to it that McCarthy was lodged in jail where he belonged.

---

discharge for worthlessness, three for neglect of duty, one for disobedience of orders, four for drunkenness on guard duty, one for quitting the guard, four for sleeping on post, four for being AWOL, four for being drunk and disorderly, and six for minor offenses—not a bad record, but not as good as the Tenth.

12 *San Saba News*, February 12, 1881; Organizational Returns, Tenth Cavalry, February 1881.

Following the examining trial on February 4, McCarthy was ordered held without bond pending action by a grand jury. A detachment from the post accompanied civil authorities to Ben Ficklin, the county seat, to make certain McCarthy was safely lodged in jail. The matter might have ended there except for an unfortunate stroke of fate. McCarthy had a brother, Dave, almost a twin in appearance, who picked that very evening to ride into Saint Angela. He was sighted almost at once, and news reached the men at Fort Concho that Tom McCarthy had been turned loose.

Seething with rage, a large number of troopers armed themselves, marched into town, and relieved their feelings by firing into a number of buildings, including the Nimitz Hotel. According to local sources, more than 150 shots were fired, although no one was killed and only one man was slightly wounded. The troopers dispersed quickly when bugle calls and the roll of drums from the post indicated Grierson was preparing to send sufficient force into town to preserve order.

Thereafter, Grierson kept his men under rigid control, but on February 5 he received a caller. Captain Bryan Marsh of the Texas Frontier Battalion had just arrived with twenty-one rangers. Marsh reportedly informed Grierson that any soldier crossing the North Concho into town during the next ten days would be carried back feet first, and if necessary he and his rangers would storm the post. Grierson's reply was not recorded, but Bryan Marsh, brave man that he undoubtedly was, faced an old soldier whose courage had never faltered in more than twenty years in uniform. Marsh's threat to storm the post was sheer braggadocio. Twenty-one rangers thrown at two hundred veteran buffalo soldiers would have been more in the nature of pouring sausages into a meat grinder than a fight.

Tom McCarthy was indicted for murder in the first degree and transferred to Austin for trial. The jurors had scarcely left their seats before returning with a verdict of "not guilty." Justice supposedly had been served, although the ghost of William Watkins and more than a few officers and men at Fort Concho undoubtedly disagreed.[13]

If there had been whitewash in Austin, the surgeon at Fort Concho made certain there was plenty of it at that post. In May he recommended

> a thorough cleaning of the back yards to officers quarters and
> damp wet places covered with lime, all out buildings should be

13 Marguerite E. Kubela, "History of Fort Concho, Texas," 96; *San Saba News,* February 19, 1881.

carefully cleaned and limed.... The privies should be thoroughly disinfected with sulfate of Iron (which can be supplied from the hospital) and white-washed. If any stables are used in back yards they should be likewise cleaned, disinfected and white-washed. Indeed I should recommend that the quarters occupied by the officers be white-washed.... The privies attached to the barracks should be white-washed and disinfected.... The slop barrels should be white-washed and disinfected.... The slop barrels should be white-washed on the outside and should have a piece of sacking thrown over them which should be ... disinfected with Carbolic acid or permanganate of Potash.[14]

Fatigue details spent many a weary hour in the hot summer of 1881 seeing to it that Fort Concho was properly whitewashed. Without a doubt those efforts were needed. Frontier posts remained notably deficient in sanitation and creature comforts.

The summer also found Lieutenant Henry Flipper in major trouble. The only black officer in the Tenth, and for that matter in the U.S. Army, Flipper had been assigned to Captain Nicholas Nolan's A Company. He was well received by officers and men and proved an excellent soldier. His services during the Victorio War had won plaudits from both Nolan and Grierson, and a bright career seemed assured. Clouds, however, appeared on the horizon when A Company came in to Fort Concho. Flipper found a riding companion in Millie Dwyer, Nolan's sister-in-law and one of the few eligible young ladies at the post. His attentions to her aroused the resentment of some of the other officers. Lieutenant Charles Nordstrom, who wanted Miss Dwyer entirely to himself, was particularly incensed.[15]

When A Company transferred to Fort Davis, Flipper was appointed post acting assistant quartermaster and acting commissary of subsistence. In spring 1881 Lieutenant Colonel William R. Shafter assumed command of the post, and shortly after, Flipper was arrested for embezzling some two thousand dollars and confined in the post guardhouse. Although some officers of the Tenth treated him coldly, most respected him. Captain Nolan was Flipper's close friend and had once described one of Flipper's detractors as "an officer who never smelt powder except on his lady's face." Colonel Grierson was disturbed since he considered Flipper a brave and talented

14 Medical History, Fort Concho, vol. 404, Medical History of Posts, AGO, RG 94, NA.
15 Stallard, *Glittering Misery*, 108–9.

officer. He knew that commissary funds were often in disorder at posts, and he was certain that in Flipper's case it arose from inexperience or carelessness, not dishonesty. Grierson wrote a long letter praising Flipper and asking the court for leniency.[16] Nonetheless, Shafter was a harsh commander. Flipper, knowing that he had lost the funds entrusted to his care, tried to cover up by lying, and in so doing, he only added to his problems.

On June 30, 1882, a court-martial cleared Flipper of embezzlement but convicted him of "conduct unbecoming." After review of the case by the judge advocate general, Flipper was dismissed from the service. When such cases arose regarding white officers, they were usually allowed to replace the money. Flipper maintained that he was the victim of a plot hatched by Colonel Shafter, Lieutenant Nordstrom, and Lieutenant Louis Wilhelm.[17] For the remainder of his long and productive life as an engineer, he struggled to clear his name. Unfortunately, not until 1976, thirty-six years after his death, was the stain on his record removed. Another twenty-two years passed before President William Jefferson Clinton pardoned him posthumously.[18]

In July 1882, headquarters of the Tenth was shifted to Fort Davis, which became the regiment's home for nearly three years. The buffalo soldiers enjoyed a period of quiet, punctured occasionally by pursuit of a band of horse or cattle thieves or the arrest of an outlaw who defied civil authorities. Such activity seldom reached the newspapers or required lengthy official reports but was found in the terse phraseology of the organizational returns:

> TROOP M—Peña Colorado, Texas. Saddler Ross mortally wounded, Sgt. Winfield Scott and Pvt. Augustus Dover wounded in line of duty while attempting to arrest desperado on military reservation—desperado W. A. Alexander was killed resisting arrest.
>
> TROOP C.—Sergeant Pratt and 9 men encamped at Peña Colorado, Texas went in pursuit of horse thieves who stole 14 horses. Sergeant recovered nine head.[19]

16 Captain Nicholas Nolan to Mr. R. N. Price, September 4, 1879, GP-TTU; Grierson to the AAG, Department of Texas, April 5, 1882, MS343A, Edward Ayer Collection, Newberry Library, Chicago Ill. (microfilm, GP-TTU).

17 Charles M. Robinson, III, argues that poor judgment and some lying to try to cover his mistakes made matters worse for Flipper, although he also admits that the lieutenant had racist enemies. See Robinson, *Court Martial of Lieutenant Henry Flipper*, 9–21, 111–14.

18 Flipper, *Negro Frontiersman*, 15–20; Organizational Returns, Tenth Cavalry, August 1881, July 1882. See also Stallard, *Glittering Misery*, 109; "First Black West Point Grad to Get Pardon," *Atlanta Constitution*, February 18, 1999, 4c.

19 Organizational Returns, Tenth Cavalry, September 1882, January 1884.

Sometimes the stark sentences of the surgeon's report revealed much of the loneliness and tragedy that accompanied garrison life at an isolated post: "Died, John Wesley Wiggins 9 10/30 mos—male—negro—a son of Pvt. John Wiggins, Band, 10 Cav." Grierson undoubtedly shared Trooper Wiggins's bereavement. His only surviving daughter, Edith, lay in a post cemetery, having died of typhoid fever at age thirteen in 1878, when the Tenth had been stationed at Fort Concho.[20]

As the above notation indicates, some enlisted men had families living with them at Fort Davis. The 1880 census disclosed that twenty-nine women at the post were there as laundresses, hospital matrons, and maids. Of these, eighteen were black, seven were mulattos, and four were Hispanics. They ranged in age from sixteen to forty-six, but the average was twenty-eight, which placed most of them in their childbearing years.

These records also indicate that fifteen or more were the wives of enlisted men. That was not surprising since, as historian Frank Schubert has noted, the longer men served in the army, the more likely they were to be married, although regulations required them to obtain their commanders' permission before they took their vows. When they did marry, enlisted men's wives often served as laundresses, especially since this position entitled them to housing on post (usually consisting of hovels or, at Fort Davis from 1883 to 1885, an eight-room structure "past repair"), food, fuel, and transportation. With an income of 37 1/2 cents per man per week, and calculating each company at about fifty men and two laundresses per company, these working women could expect to earn about $37.50 per month. That was far more than their husbands made as enlisted men and thus a boon to their families. At the same time, however, being a washerwoman was one of the most backbreaking and arduous occupations individuals could perform, and these women assuredly earned every cent they made.[21]

By 1883, married enlisted men whose wives were not laundresses had access to some housing for their families in an area northeast of the parade ground. In addition, the surgeon's report that year noted that noncommissioned officers and their families were living in "two or three dilapidated adobe huts," which he urged the army to tear down and replace with "decent quarters."[22]

20 Medical History, Fort Davis, vol. 12; Medical History, Fort Concho, vol. 404.

21 Wooster, *History of Fort Davis*, 259–61; Schubert, *Buffalo Soldiers, Braves, and the Brass*, 61–68. Until 1878, laundresses were a part of the military and were carried on the company rosters. See Sibbald, "Camp Followers All," 56–67; Stewart, "Army Laundresses," 421–36.

22 Wooster, *History of Fort Davis*, 263.

Quarters, however, were never adequate, even for officers and their families. The War Department viewed the Indian wars as temporary conflicts that would soon end, but the Indians proved more formidable foes than expected, and as Robert Utley notes, "the 'temporary' posts continued to be used year after year."[23] In that context the housing needs of enlisted men, laundresses, and the families of privates and noncommissioned officers were not high on the list of priorities for improvement. In addition to the depressing quarters, the difficulties of bearing and raising children on lonely frontier posts without family nearby, the rigors of serving in the army for the men, and the hard labor demanded of the women who worked as laundresses, hospital matrons, or maids placed family life under substantial strain for all involved in military life, the buffalo soldiers and their dependents included.

Educating children at frontier posts was still another concern. The officers and their wives often arranged for private tutoring within their quarters for their younger children and then sent the older ones back east to live with relatives while they attended secondary schools. Enlisted men lacked the financial resources to employ tutors or to send their children away. Beginning in 1878, however, army regulations mandated that all posts must provide the children of enlisted men and those of the commanding officer with schooling. At Fort Davis the chaplain taught children during the day in the chapel. Enlisted men who could read and write served in their off-duty hours as his assistants at a salary of thirty-five cents a day.[24]

For many buffalo soldiers, a main concern was achieving at least elementary literacy skills for themselves. Now that campaigning against Indians had subsided, at least in Texas, they had more time to benefit from educational opportunities on post. Their schooling was offered during evening sessions, which like the children's classes were held in the chapel. African Americans—especially those who had once been slaves—saw in education their best hope of achieving mobility for themselves and advancement for their race. After the Civil War, teachers for the Freedmen's Bureau had noticed that some adults even accompanied their children into the classroom, seeking to achieve literacy along with their offspring because

23 Utley, *Frontier Regulars,* 82.
24 Alexander McD. McCook, who became army supervisor of education, had been largely responsible for winning this educational benefit for the children of enlisted men. But mandating schools was not the same as creating them, and 32 posts out of 137 still lacked such schools in 1881. See War Department, *Regulations of the Army of the United States,* 56–58. See also Coffman, *The Old Army,* 323–27.

southern laws had denied them that right as slaves.[25] Likewise, many freed-men who joined the military saw the education available to them in the army as one of the additional benefits of their new occupation.

Chaplain George Gatewood Mullins had begun his service to the black Twenty-fifth Infantry at Fort Davis in 1875 believing that black soldiers were "generally of that abject servile disposition which does just what is absolutely necessary, and nothing more:—eye servants," as he phrased it, "driven to duty by no praiseworthy pride, but fear of punishment."[26] He soon learned that he was wrong.

The regiment had gone almost three years without a chaplain, despite military regulations mandating that each black regiment—as opposed to each post for white regiments—must be assigned a chaplain to supply edu-cational as well as religious services. In addition, Mullins was working initially without adequate supplies or equipment and with little or no encouragement from other officers. Once he gained assistance from the offi-cers and developed a truly stimulating educational program, he uncovered a latent but very real fervor for education among many of the black soldiers at the post. As he wrote with moving sincerity in a report he issued a year and a half later in 1877: "The ambition to be all that soldiers should be is not confined to a few of these sons of an unfortunate race. They are possessed of the notion that the colored people of the whole country are more or less affected by their conduct in the army."[27]

Certainly, if many black soldiers were desirous of gaining an education for themselves, they and their wives were equally dedicated to obtaining schooling for their children.[28] Although the facilities and supplies for classes at Fort Davis and other posts were Spartan at best, schools for blacks throughout the nation, and most especially in southern states, were often totally inadequate. The U.S. Army did not offer an easy way of life. Nonethe-less, ordinary black men and their families in America—particularly those from the South and born into slavery—found it an institution that for all its

---

25 Jones, *Labor of Love, Labor of Sorrow,* 76–77.

26 Fowler, *Black Infantry in the West,* 95.

27 General Orders No. 25, War Department, Adjutant General's Office, August 1, 1866, cited in Fowler, *Black Infantry in the West,* 108 n. 1; Mullins quoted in ibid., 97.

28 Black women were seven times more likely than their white counterparts to work for wages after marriage, often as domestic laborers such as laundresses or maids, as a way of ensuring that their children could gain as much education as possible before entering the workforce. Woloch, *Women and the American Experience,* 232–36. See also Jones, *Labor of Love, Labor of Sorrow,* 222–23.

dangers and drawbacks offered them more opportunities than available anywhere else.[29]

By 1885 the Tenth was no longer essential in West Texas since settlement and law and order, which the regiment had done so much to assist, were more firmly established. Far to the west, however, the Indian wars remained unresolved. Geronimo and his Chiricahua Apaches had bolted their reservation, and troops were badly needed to bring them back. In March, orders came transferring the Tenth to the Department of Arizona. Officers, men, and equipment were concentrated at Fort Davis, and on April 1, for the first time in the history of the regiment, all twelve companies—38 officers and 696 enlisted men—marched together along the tracks of the Southern Pacific Railroad.[30]

At Bowie Station, Arizona, the regiment split up once more. Grierson established headquarters at Whipple Barracks, while the various companies took station at Forts Grant, Thomas, Apache, and Verde. The Apaches had been troublesome recently, but at the moment quiet reigned on the Arizona frontier, and the troopers could look forward to acquiring a leisurely acquaintance with their new stations and the surrounding country. So it seemed in early May 1885, but the men of the Tenth had scarce warmed their bunks before they were in the saddle and riding hard to overtake fugitive Apaches.

The problem in 1885 concerned the Chiricahuas. Years of campaigning had driven a majority of the Apaches into the reservations at San Carlos and Fort Apache, although many hostiles remained at large. Serious outbreaks occurred in 1881–82, however, and General George Crook returned to Arizona in the summer of the latter year. With his customary skill, patience, and resourcefulness, Crook soon restored peace. Still, there remained a grave source of concern—some five hundred Chiricahua and Warm Springs runaways, old Nana among them, were still holed up in the mountains of northern Mexico, ever ready to launch devastating raids into Arizona.

In March 1883 a small band of these Indians under Chatto struck like a hurricane in southern New Mexico and Arizona. In just six days twenty-five persons were killed, one young boy captured, and a number of ranches looted and burned. Then like wraiths the Apaches disappeared across the

29 This is a point that Frank Schubert makes in *Buffalo Soldiers, Braves, and the Brass* and William Dobak and Thomas Phillips weave throughout their work, *Black Regulars*.
30 Bigelow, "Historical Sketch"; Organizational Returns, Tenth Cavalry, March–April, 1885.

border, leaving citizens and troops alike in a state of shock.[31]

Crook immediately gathered a powerful force, including a large body of Apache scouts, crossed into Mexico, and invaded the Sierra Madres. In a three-week campaign of alternate fighting and deft diplomacy, Crook forced the surrender of the Chiricahua irreconcilables. Chatto, Geronimo, Nachez, Loco, Benito, Mangus, and their followers, as well as Nana and his Warm Spring Apaches, agreed to march to the San Carlos reservation, where they were to remain under army control.[32]

The Indians came in slowly, but by spring 1884 they were on the reservation a few miles southwest of Fort Apache. Peace had come at last, but it proved ephemeral. Bickering over Indian policy soon developed between the War and Interior Departments, and Crook asked to be relieved of any responsibility for control over the Apaches in Arizona. Ultimately, the general was sustained and the military remained in control, but the quarrel had penetrated, as it always did, to the lower echelons, and the reverberations reached the wary tribesmen. Nervous and uneasy, many of them were ready to listen to Geronimo, Nana, and others who were urging a return to the Sierra Madres and the old way of life.

On the night of May 17, 1885, after a "tiswin drunk," Geronimo, Nachez, Chihuahua, Nana, and Mangus, with nearly 150 followers, broke from the reservation. Troopers at Fort Apache were in the saddle within an hour but failed to overtake or even ascertain the direction taken by the runaways. Crook threw every available man into the field to hunt them down. By May 20 Grierson had his buffalo soldiers searching in the Black Range, the Mogollons, and the Chiricahua Mountains. Units of the Third, Fourth, and Sixth Cavalry, accompanied by Apache Scouts, searched in all directions but found no trace of the Indians.[33]

The puzzle of the Apaches' whereabouts was solved on June 10. The

31 Twitchell, *Leading Facts of New Mexico History,* 2:441–43. John Gregory Bourke gives first-hand recollections of campaigning with Crook and the problems he encountered when he returned to service in the Southwest in the 1880s. See *On the Border with Crook,* 452–85. See also Bourke, *An Apache Campaign.* Whipple Barracks was located along Granite Creek near Prescott, Arizona. It was named in honor of Major General A. W. Whipple, who was mortally wounded at the battle of Chancellorsville in May 1863. Frazer, *Forts of the West,* 14. Grierson's headquarters remained there until July 1886, when they were moved to Fort Grant.

32 "Report of Brigadier General Crook," in *Annual Report of the Secretary of War for the Year 1886,* 1:147; Lockwood, *Apache Indians,* 279.

33 "Report of Brigadier General Crook," 1:148; Organizational Returns, Tenth Cavalry, May 1885.

hostiles appeared with startling suddenness in Guadalupe Canyon, surprised a detachment of Fourth Cavalry encamped there, killed four troopers, and crossed into Mexico. The trail pointed toward the Sierra Madres, and Crook sent Captains Emmet Crawford, Third Cavalry, and Wirt Davis, Fourth Cavalry, in pursuit with two companies of cavalry and nearly two hundred Apache scouts. To cut off a return to the United States, Crook stationed detachments "at every water-hole along the border" and established a "second line" paralleling the Southern Pacific Railroad. For most of the buffalo soldiers, these dispositions meant seemingly endless days and nights of staring at a waterhole.[34]

For three months Crawford and Davis toiled across the peaks and canyons of the Sierra Madres but failed to bring off a decisive encounter. Their pressure was unrelenting, however, and on September 28 the Chiricahuas fled back across the border, eluded patrols in Guadalupe Canyon, and headed into the Chiricahua Mountains, with Crawford and Davis in close pursuit. The constant harassment was telling on the runaways. Their animals were breaking down, and they might have been cornered had Arizona ranchers not unwittingly provided a convenient means of escape. They were engaged in a roundup and had a large *remuda* at a ranch in White Tail Canyon. The Apaches descended on the herd and "made off with some of the best stock in the country." The Indians, now superbly mounted, easily shook off pursuit and reached the border. Captain Charles Viele with C and G of the Tenth followed their trail all the way to Ascension in Chihuahua, where his animals gave out.[35]

By the end of November, Crawford and Davis were again in the Sierra Madres, and after months of grueling cat-and-mouse, the former located the Indian camp on the Aros River sixty miles below Nacori. On the night of June 10, 1886, Crawford attacked and captured all the stock and supplies, but the hostiles escaped to nearby peaks. During the night Apache couriers came in to inform Crawford that their people desired a conference the following morning to discuss terms of surrender.

At daylight, however, Mexican forces, mistaking the scouts for hostiles, attacked Crawford's camp. Before the ensuing confusion could be cleared up, Crawford was mortally wounded and Tom Horn, an interpreter, was

34 "Report of Brigadier General Crook," 1:149; Organizational Returns, Tenth Cavalry, June–September 1885.

35 "Report of Brigadier General Crook," 150; Organizational Returns, Tenth Cavalry, October 1885; Post Returns, Fort Thomas, October 1885, AGO, RG 94, NA.

shot through the arm. Fortunately, the hostiles remained in the vicinity, and arrangements were made for a meeting with General Crook in the Canyon de los Embudos on March 25.[36]

The conference occurred as planned, and after lengthy discussions the hostiles agreed to surrender and return to the reservation. Crook set out for the border on March 27 with Geronimo, Nachez, Chihuahua, Nana, and 111 men, women, and children, but on the night of March 29, Geronimo and Nachez stole away and fled into the mountains. Twenty warriors and 16 women and children accompanied them. The remaining Apaches, 77 in all, were taken to Fort Bowie and entrained for Fort Marion, Florida, as prisoners of war.[37]

The escape of Geronimo and Nachez upset General Sheridan, who placed much of the blame on Crook's extensive use of Apache scouts, whom Sheridan considered untrustworthy.[38] Crook asked to be relieved, and on April 2, 1886, Brigadier General Nelson Miles replaced him. The task before Miles was clear—to capture or destroy Geronimo, Nachez, and their thirty-six followers as well as the shadowy Mangus and his small band, who apparently had vanished. Miles made careful preparations, including the establishment of twenty-seven heliograph stations for the rapid transmission of messages, but Geronimo struck before plans were completed.[39]

On April 27 he crossed the border and swept through the Santa Cruz Valley, killed a number of cowboys, captured the Peck Ranch, butchered Mrs. Peck and one of her children, and took her husband and thirteen-year-old daughter as captives. Peck, temporarily insane, was soon released, but the Apaches still held the girl as they headed for Mexico. News of the raid reached Captain T. C. Lebo, who was scouting in the vicinity with Company K.[40] Lebo was an able and seasoned commander, and at his back

36 *Annual Report of the Secretary of War for the Year 1886*, 1:9–10.

37 "Report of Brigadier General Crook," 1:152; *Annual Report of the Secretary of War for the Year 1886*, 11.

38 For an excellent and balanced account of the relationship between Crook and Sheridan, see Robinson, *General Crook and the Western Frontier*, 281–85. Robinson notes that Crook was a man who could not accept criticism, even from the commanding general of the army.

39 Bourke, *On the Border with Crook*, 474; *Annual Report of the Secretary of War for the Year 1886*, 12.

40 Angie Debo, Geronimo's foremost and, in the end, sympathetic biographer, maintains that he killed Mexicans because he hated them. But, she argues, "the killings on the American side of the border were a necessary part of raiding." Quoting Nachez, whom she identifies as "Naiche," Debo notes that the two Apache leaders believed: "Anybody who saw us would kill us, and we did the same thing. We had to if we wanted to live." *Geronimo*, 270.

were many veterans of the Victorio War. They found Geronimo's trail and clung to it like leeches. The Apaches tried in every way to throw off these pursuers, but to no avail. For two hundred miles the chase continued, and at last Lebo cornered them on a rocky slope in the Pinito Mountains, thirty miles south of the border in Sonora. On the back trail were thirty horses the Indians had ridden to death.

As K Company dismounted and started up the slope, the men were met with a curtain of lead that killed Private Hollis, severely wounded Corporal Edward Scott, and forced the troopers to take cover. A vicious, short-range rifle duel developed, and Scott lay exposed to enemy fire. Young Lieutenant Powhatan Clarke rose from behind a boulder and, ignoring a hail of bullets, raced to the trooper's side and carried him to safety. Presently the Indian fire slackened and then ceased—Geronimo was on the move again. Lebo hung on for four days until the Fourth Cavalry took up pursuit. For rescuing Corporal Scott, Lieutenant Clarke was awarded the Medal of Honor.[41]

Miles gave the Chiricahuas no rest. Companies of the Tenth and Fourth kept them constantly on the move. On May 15 Captain C. A. P. Hatfield, Fourth Cavalry, with a strong detachment struck the hostile camp near Santa Cruz in Sonora. The blow caused the Apaches to turn northward into Arizona, where they sought refuge in the Dragoon Mountains. There was no respite. Detachments of buffalo soldiers under Captain Steven Norvell and Lieutenants Robert D. Read, Levi Hunt, James B. Hughes, and William E. Shipp pursued without letup. In desperation the Indians fled toward Fort Apache to seek aid from their kinsmen on the reservation. As they came near, however, Captain J. T. Morrison and A of the Tenth intercepted them, stripped them of their horses, and drove them back.[42]

Sorely beset, the hostiles turned toward Mexico, hastened in their flight by troopers working in relays. Once the Indians were over the border, troops and scouts under Captain H. W. Lawton, Fourth Cavalry, took up the chase. For months Lawton trailed his slippery foes but was unable either to capture

41 Glass, *History of the Tenth Cavalry,* 24; Organizational Returns, Tenth Cavalry, May 1886; Miles, *Personal Recollections,* 489. Lebo joined the Tenth in June 1867 and remained with the regiment until 1893, when he transferred to the Sixth Cavalry. He retired in 1901 as colonel of the Fourteenth Cavalry. Heitman, *Historical Register,* 1:622. Clarke, who hailed from Louisiana, graduated from West Point in 1880. He began his service with the Tenth Cavalry as a second lieutenant in 1884, and in 1891 he joined the Ninth Cavalry as first lieutenant. Clarke drowned in July 1893. Ibid., 1:307.

42 *Annual Report of the Secretary of War for the Year 1886,* 1:167–69; Organizational Returns, Tenth Cavalry, May–June 1886.

or to destroy them. His work was not in vain, for it finally convinced the Apaches of the utter hopelessness of ever finding a safe retreat. Word soon reached Miles that they were willing to discuss terms of surrender.

Miles sent Lieutenant Charles B. Gatewood, Sixth Cavalry, to Mexico as a special emissary. Gatewood made contact with Geronimo on the Bavispe River near the end of August 1886. Arrangements were made for a meeting between him and Miles in Skeleton Canyon. There on September 3, the Apaches formally surrendered after receiving assurances that they would remain together even as prisoners of war. They were taken to Fort Bowie, Arizona, and sent by train to two separate locations in Florida: the women and children were placed at Fort Marion, and Geronimo and other warriors were imprisoned in Fort Pickens.[43]

The buffalo soldiers played no role in these final months, although Lieutenant Leighton Finley of the Tenth commanded the scouts under Lawton. They were, however, destined to be principals in drawing the final curtain on the Apache wars.

The vast majority of the Chiricahuas had remained peacefully on the reservation during the breakout, but Washington officialdom wanted these people removed to Florida for imprisonment. It fell to Lieutenant Colonel James Wade, commanding at Fort Apache, and more than half the companies of the Tenth to arrest and transport over four hundred men, women, and children to Holbrook, Arizona, where they too were entrained for Fort Marion. These Apaches had been well behaved since General Crook placed them on the reservation in 1884, and they deserved a better fate, but it was not for the buffalo soldiers to reason why.

43 *Annual Report of the Secretary of War for the Year 1886*, 1:169; Miles, *Personal Recollections*, 529; Lockwood, *Apache Indians*, 301–6. Angie Debo provides an excellent overview of Geronimo's decision to surrender, which she maintains was based on Miles's promise to keep his Chiricahua Apaches together and thus was based on deception. Debo, *Geronimo*, 290–96. Joseph C. Porter interprets Miles as deliberately giving the impression to General O. O. Howard, and thus to President Grover Cleveland, that Geronimo had surrendered unconditionally, which was not true. Porter, *Paper Medicine Man*, 220–22. Robert Wooster notes that mixed communications between Miles and higher authorities governed this surrender, and he also notes that Miles protected the Apaches from mob justice from the white citizenry. Initially, he explains, Miles wanted the Apaches removed to Indian Territory. Wooster, *Nelson A. Miles and the Twilight of the Frontier Army*, 150–56. For an especially balanced account of events regarding the surrender and the separation of Apaches in Forts Marion and Pickens in Florida, despite Miles's pledges to Geronimo, see Kraft, *Gatewood and Geronimo*, 178–204. Tragically, the Apache scouts who had served the army with loyalty were also sent to Florida for imprisonment. See Bourke, *On the Border with Crook*, 485.

One hostile chief remained at large. Mangus and his small band had separated from Geronimo and managed to avoid efforts to run them down. The search continued, however, and on September 18 a detachment of H Company under Captain Charles Cooper found a trail in the White Mountains. A pursuit of more than forty miles over rough and broken country brought Cooper upon a small party of Apaches. After a running fight of fifteen miles, the troopers cornered the Indians and forced their surrender. The net had finally closed over the last holdouts—Mangus, two warriors, and eight women and children. Arizona was pacified except for one last incident.[44]

The disturbance came in March 1890, when a small party of Apaches ambushed and killed a freighter near the San Carlos reservation. A pursuit of more than two hundred miles over rugged canyon-carved country by a detachment of the Tenth under Lieutenant Powhatan Clarke brought the buffalo soldiers close to the Apaches. However, Clarke had no way of knowing exactly where the Apaches were in the maze of canyons until a bullet whizzed by and he and his men saw smoke from a nearby cave, in which the Indians were ensconced and safe from their adversaries.

The Apache advantage ended when someone—in all probability Sergeant William McBryar of K Company—began, according to one report, "firing against a rock almost in front of their cave, thereby spatter[ing] lead and splintered rock in their faces." As the buffalo soldiers prepared to launch a final rush, the Apaches surrendered. Among those later receiving commendations for their role in this action were Sergeants James T. Daniels of the Fourth Cavalry, Apache scout Sergeant Rowdy, Privates William Turner and William Warrent of K Company, Private Charles Taylor of I Company, and Sergeant William McBryar. On May 15, 1890, only ten weeks after this encounter, McBryar, who had been cited for "coolness, bravery and good marksmanship," became the first buffalo soldier in the Tenth Cavalry to receive the Medal of Honor. Others who also received that honor were Sergeants Rowdy and Daniels.[45]

While the Tenth fought the "battle of Saint Angela," pursued horse thieves, and brought in the Chiricahua Apaches, Hatch and the Ninth never got the much-needed rest that General Pope had recommended. They now were involved in clearing Indian Territory of invading and ingenious

44 Organizational Returns, Tenth Cavalry, September 1886; Bigelow, "Historical Sketch"; Miles, *Personal Recollections*, 528–30.
45 Schubert, *Black Valor*, 105–6.

"Boomers." That meant more than four years of near-unremitting and frustrating labor that would bring the Ninth a mountain of abuse as the sole monument to their efforts.

Intruders had long been a sore problem to Indian agents and the military. As early as 1870 Grierson had found it necessary to keep patrols on the lookout, and two years later he moved his headquarters from Fort Sill to Fort Gibson, partly in response to growing intruder activity in that vicinity. By 1876 the problem required attention from Secretary of War George W. McCrary and General Sherman. Three years later intruders were crossing the Kansas line in sufficient numbers to occupy virtually the full attention of a battalion of buffalo soldiers under Captain Nolan. Many of these troopers were undoubtedly relieved when the Victorio War occasioned their transfer to West Texas in June 1880.[46]

Intruder or Boomer activity had been increasing since spring 1879. The immediate source of inspiration apparently stemmed from a widely circulated article that had appeared in the *Chicago Times* issue dated February 15. Written by a Cherokee, Colonel Elias C. Boudinot, the article pointed to fertile and unoccupied lands in the heart of Indian Territory and argued that these potentially productive millions of acres were public domain and therefore subject to settlement under existing homestead laws. Boudinot's message was all that hordes of land-hungry citizens and railroad promoters needed to read. Nor were the possibilities of fat profits from increased trade lost on entrepreneurs in the towns bordering the territory. The goal of these groups was simply to force settlement with or without federal authority.[47]

Rumors of a Boomer invasion led by "Colonel" Charles C. Carpenter in April 1879 caused President Hayes to issue an official warning that the lands in question were not open to homestead entry and any invaders would be expelled by force if necessary. Carpenter breathed fury and defiance, and border merchants did a land-office business in firearms with prospective homesteaders. In considerable numbers they crossed the Kansas line near Coffeyville, but the sight of Nolan's scowling troopers was enough for most of the would-be settlers, and Carpenter's movement collapsed.[48]

David L. Payne, a far abler and more persistent leader, took his place. In

46 Savage, "Role of Negro Soldiers," 26–28.
47 McReynolds, *Oklahoma*, 281–82; Litton, *History of Oklahoma*, 1:358.
48 Litton, *History of Oklahoma*, 1:360–61; Organizational Returns, Tenth Cavalry, April–May 1879.

serving with the Nineteenth Kansas Cavalry in Sheridan's winter campaign of 1868–69, Payne had come away impressed with the possibilities of the country he had traversed. Later he had served as a member of the Kansas legislature and as an assistant doorkeeper of the U.S. House of Representatives. He appeared in Wichita, Kansas, in August 1879 and immediately assumed leadership of the Boomer movement, probably with financial assistance from the Atlantic and Pacific Railroad. In the next five years, Payne launched no fewer than nine attempts to colonize in Indian Territory.[49]

The target area for Boomer efforts was around present-day Oklahoma City, and Payne's initial efforts at establishing a colony were comparatively small. In April and again in July 1880, he eluded patrols and reached the chosen site but was arrested swiftly and ejected from the territory. Payne had little to show for a year of effort except a charge of trespass lodged against him at Fort Smith, Arkansas. Yet Payne thrived on failure, redoubled his activities, and the movement continued to grow.

In summer 1881 small parties of Boomers filtered in from various points along the border in sufficient numbers to require the constant attention of six companies of cavalry. Pope had to borrow D, E, I, and M of the Tenth from General E. O. C. Ord. In November the ubiquitous Payne made a third effort, this time from the Texas line, but he was caught on Cache Creek and expelled with little ceremony. Such was the situation when Pope transferred the Ninth from New Mexico.[50]

Hatch, keenly aware that his regiment faced a tedious and unpopular task, knew that bloodshed was a distinct possibility, in which case he and his troopers would endure a wave of national indignation. He nevertheless set about an unpleasant duty with his customary efficiency and energy. Ceaseless patrols were maintained out of Forts Sill, Reno, and Supply and from the border town of Arkansas City. Four times in 1882 Payne led his followers into the territory, and four times he was promptly arrested and ejected.

Persuasion proved successful at first, but the Boomers, certain their cause was just, became increasingly stubborn and resentful. In August 1882 Lieutenant C. W. Taylor ordered Payne to reload his wagons and move out. When Payne refused, Taylor instructed his troopers, "Yellow Legs" as the Boomers called them, to hitch the teams and load both goods and

---

49   Litton, *History of Oklahoma*, 1:363–69
50   *Fort Griffin Echo*, May 21, 1881; Organizational Returns, Tenth Cavalry, June 1881.

homesteaders into them. Fists flew before the Boomers were overcome, bound hand and foot, and tossed into the wagons as if "they were sacks of shelled corn."[51]

In January 1883 the irrepressible Payne was back again, this time with nine hundred settlers, some of them heavily armed. Lieutenant Charles Stevens and a dozen troopers sighted the long column near the North Canadian on February 7. Stevens attempted to arrest Payne, but the latter failed even to slow his pace. Stevens then sent a courier to Captain Carroll at Fort Reno and fell in beside the wagons. By midafternoon of the following day, Payne's column reached a valley near the North Canadian, and the men set to work at once constructing "Camp Alice."

About five o'clock, however, Payne had far more to contend with than a nervous and uncertain young lieutenant. Captain Carroll arrived with ninety veterans of F and I Companies and came to the point at once. The Boomers could get out of their own accord or they would be "helped out." At the same time, Carroll insisted that he had nothing to do with the laws. He and his troopers were simply performing their duty. Resistance melted before Carroll's gentle firmness. Payne and ten old offenders were arrested and taken to Fort Reno, while the weary buffalo soldiers, who were not totally unsympathetic toward Boomer ambitions, escorted the others to the Kansas line.[52]

Carroll held Payne and his companions for a few days, treated them kindly, and then sent them under escort to Caldwell, Kansas. Kindness did not stop the Boomers. Payne's principal lieutenant, William L. Couch, forced Hatch's troopers to escort him from the territory three times between August 1883 and the end of the year. And Couch could scarcely complain of the treatment he received at the hands of the buffalo soldiers. Often they shared their beans, bacon, and hardtack with him and his followers.[53]

The era of good feeling, such as it was, ended abruptly in spring 1884. Couch brought more than a thousand Boomers to the site of present-day Oklahoma City in April, and they established four large camps along the North Canadian. The men were soon hard at work erecting cabins, building a schoolhouse, and plowing the soil. On April 24 Lieutenant M. H. Day

51 Rister, *Land Hunger,* 111–12; Savage, "Role of Negro Soldiers," 32.
52 "Tribute to Captain Payne," 13–14; Rister, *Land Hunger,* 127–29; Organizational Returns, Ninth Cavalry, February 1883.
53 Rister, *Land Hunger,* 145; Organizational Returns, Ninth Cavalry, October–November 1883.

with seven troopers arrived, found Couch's father plowing a field, and placed him under arrest. The old man resisted, and Day ordered him bound and placed in a wagon.

The lieutenant proceeded to the main Boomer camp and arrested nine leaders, including J. D. Odell. The latter, incensed over the treatment of the elder Couch, put up a fight, and two troopers had the unpleasant duty of subduing and binding him. Next morning, as Day prepared to take his prisoners to Fort Reno, Odell refused to climb into a wagon. Day, in no mood to argue, had the recalcitrant Boomer tied to the vehicle. He could take his choice—either walk or be dragged all the way to the post. The tempers of Boomers and soldiers were beginning to run thin.

By May 7 Day was back with a detachment of twenty troopers and six Indian scouts. He attempted to arrest a number of men at work on the schoolhouse but met with angry resistance. Efforts to seize the workmen touched off a flurry of fisticuffs, and Day momentarily lost his head. He ordered his troopers to fire, but fortunately the buffalo soldiers refused to obey. Day quickly regained his composure. The Boomers, sobered, quietly submitted to arrest; they realized, as did Day, that a bloodbath had been narrowly avoided. Good feeling was gone, however, and only bitterness remained. *War Chief,* the organ of the Boomer movement, revealed the depth of feeling with a blast at an old nemesis, Lieutenant C. W. Taylor, calling the officer "one of a litter of mud turtles born of a Negro woman."[54]

Boomer determination was stronger than ever, however, and in June 1884 David Payne made his final effort. More than fifteen hundred homesteaders crossed the line and settled at Rock Falls. Activity on this scale brought Colonel Hatch personally to the scene. Many of the Boomers were belligerent and ready to fight, and Payne warned Hatch not to bring up troops. The atmosphere was so explosive that the colonel telegraphed his superiors outlining the situation and indicating he felt reinforcements were necessary. He received unequivocal orders to remove the Boomers. On August 5 he delivered an ultimatum—leave before the day was over or he would drive them out. All but a hard core of about 250 left, and L and M Companies quickly removed them and burned all cabins and other buildings.[55]

Payne died suddenly on November 28, 1884, and the mantle of leader-

54 Rister, *Land Hunger,* 149; "Publishing a Newspaper in a 'Boomer' Camp," 368; Litton, *History of Oklahoma,* 1:373.

55 Organizational Returns, Ninth Cavalry, August 1884; Rister, *Land Hunger,* 165–70.

ship fell to William L. Couch. This activist was soon on the move with three hundred settlers and on December 12 encamped at Stillwater Creek. Hatch sent Lieutenant Day and thirty troopers to evict these Boomers, but they ignored his demand for surrender. Day's force was far too small to contend with such numbers, and he withdrew. When Hatch was notified, he hastened to the scene and sent for reinforcement. By January 24 seven companies of the Ninth were on hand, and all were under veteran commanders. Two howitzers and a company of infantry supported the cavalry.

Captain Carroll rode to the Boomer camp and demanded a surrender. It was refused, and Couch sent word to Hatch that his settlers would defend their rights. A lesser man might well have begun a battle, but Hatch was equal to the occasion. He arrived with his troops on Saturday, January 23. On the morning of January 25, he surrounded the camp and cut off all hope of supplies. His action brought a swift end to Couch's recalcitrance. George Conrad, Jr., a former buffalo soldier who retired in Oklahoma City after he left the army, recalled that day. "We formed a line at 9:00 Monday morning and Captain Couch run up his white flag, and Colonel Hatch he sent the orderly up to see what he meant by putting up the flag, so Captain Couch sent word back, 'If you don't fire on me, I'll leave tomorrow.'" Couch's position was obviously untenable. After their wagons were loaded, he led his settlers back to Arkansas City.[56]

The disagreeable and thankless task of driving Boomers from their "Promised Land" ended for Hatch and his buffalo soldiers in June 1885. Regimental headquarters transferred to Fort McKinney, Wyoming, while the companies were assigned to that post and to Forts Robinson and Niobrara in Nebraska and Fort DuChesne in Utah. The long-promised rest had come at last after eighteen years of distinguished service in the Southwest. The Indian wars on the plains were over. The frontier army would now be faced with little more than the routine of garrison life.[57] That and, as it turned out, tension between some commanders and at least some of the buffalo soldiers.

A new generation of men was now serving in the Ninth Cavalry. More assertive than earlier soldiers, they included individuals such as Sergeant

---

56 "George Conrad, Jr.," in *WPA Oklahoma Slave Narratives,* 93; Organizational Returns, Ninth Cavalry, June–July 1885.

57 Organizational Returns, Ninth Cavalry, April 1889.

Joseph Moore, who campaigned to transform John Brown's fort into a historical site at Harpers Ferry. Others who exhibited a new sense of pride in their race were Sergeant John Jackson, who, faced with a threat to his life, had responded by killing the white soldier responsible. Despite this new self-assurance, and perhaps in part because of it, Clarence Stedman, captain of Company F, had allowed and even encouraged his first sergeant, Emmanuel Stance, to mistreat his men. It was a formula for disaster.

The tragedy came on Christmas morning, 1887, when Medal of Honor winner Emmanuel Stance was found dead of a gunshot wound on the road between Fort Robinson and Crawford, the adjacent town. Although Stance had been an outstanding soldier in combat, his insulting language and belligerence in garrison had alienated the soldiers under his command. Suspicions pointed to members of Company F and, most especially, Private Miller Milds. Although Milds was arrested and charged, there was no evidence to convict him because no witnesses came forth. Eventually, he was released, and no one was ever convicted of Stance's murder.[58]

In the years since the Ninth's move from the Southwest, many of the officers and men on the regiment's roll of honor disappeared from the organizational returns. Transfer, retirement, and death took their toll. Morrow, Carroll, Cooney, Dodge, and Parker no longer led their faithful troopers. And on April 11, 1889, Edward Hatch, colonel of the regiment for twenty-three years, breathed his last at Fort Robinson, succumbing to injuries suffered in a carriage accident.[59]

His successor, Colonel Joseph G. Tilford, could review his new command with considerable satisfaction. Many of his company commanders—Day, Hughes, Henry Wright, Taylor, and John Loud—were soldiers of proven ability. Major Guy Henry, with the regiment since 1882, was one of the most distinguished officers in the army.[60] In the ranks, every company had a core

58 Schubert, *Black Valor*, 25–26.
59 Organizational Returns, Ninth Cavalry, April 1889.
60 Ibid. Major Henry, a New Yorker, graduated from West Point in 1856 and was initially assigned to the artillery. During the Civil War he rose to the rank of colonel in the Fortieth Massachusetts Infantry. He served as captain in the First Artillery from December 1865 until December 1870, when he transferred to the Third Cavalry. He joined the Ninth as major in June 1881 and remained with the regiment until January 1892, when he was appointed lieutenant colonel of the Seventh Cavalry. At the end of his military career in 1898, he was a major general of volunteers. Henry was a brilliant officer with seven citations for gallant and meritorious conduct and held the Medal of Honor for his bravery at Cold Harbor in June 1864. Heitman, *Historical Register*, 1:523.

of tough, battle-wise veterans with whom Apache, Comanche, Kiowa, and Cheyenne warriors and outlaws and Boomers were well acquainted. Among the veterans were Medal of Honor heroes—John Denny, George Jordan, Thomas Shaw, Augustus Walley, and Brent Wood—with years of useful service still ahead. In addition, there were the new soldiers who were more acutely aware of racial issues and more likely to take a stand on their own behalf. It was a proud regiment, at least the equal of any in the army. And ahead they would encounter one last opportunity to prove how well they could function compared to other Indian-fighting regiments.

The once proud bands of western Sioux—the Lakota people—former overlords of the northern plains, were now dispossessed of much of their land. Many were also demoralized by the loss of their old way of life, especially since agents had organized Indian police to harass the "non-progressive" elements among them—those who still struggled to maintain and honor their old traditions. To make matters worse, they were confined to shrunken reservations in the Dakotas, where they met little success as farmers on the drought-stricken northern plains, especially since many Indian men still longed to return to the old days of hunting the buffalo.[61] Adding to the suffering of the Lakota peoples, the government had cut off their rations. Little wonder that many were ill and needed medical attention. But as one ethnologist notes, in the cruel winter of 1889–90, "no one seemed to care."[62]

Then came a whisper of hope—a messiah had arrived far to the west. There was great excitement among the Lakota, and emissaries rode westward seeking the truth. When they located the messiah, a Paiute named Wovoka, they learned that ghosts would return in the spring, bringing with them the buffalo and all the other game the white man had slaughtered. When the emissaries returned with this message, the Ghost Dance religion swept like a prairie fire among the Lakotas.[63]

61 Even if they had been enthusiastic farmers, the Lakota would have enjoyed little success when Anglo farmers often proved incapable of holding on to their farms. In many cases the latter had simply given up farming, and those who remained were turning to farmers' alliances that would soon mount a powerful political protest for redress of their complaints. For information on the emergence of the farmers' alliances on the northern plains, see Cherny, *Populism, Progressivism, and the Transformation of Nebraska Politics.*

62 Utley, *Last Days of the Sioux Nation,* 18–59; *Annual Report of the Commissioner of Indian Affairs for the Year 1890,* 123; Hyde, *Sioux Chronicle,* 238.

63 Mooney, "Ghost-dance Religion," 816–21.

Company "K" Ninth Cavalry. Medal of Honor winner Sergeant George Jordan is seated third from left wearing a broad-brimmed hat. Medal of Honor winner Henry Johnson is left of the flag bearer wearing his medal.
Courtesy of Nebraska State Historical Society

ON THE NEXT PAGE:
Company E, Tenth Cavalry, at the close of the Spanish-American War. Medal of Honor winner Augustus Walley is in the last row, second from the right with kerchief around his neck.
Courtesy of Buffalo Soldiers Research and Re-enactors of Maryland

Brigade drill of Tenth Cavalry soldiers
Courtesy National Archives

Ninth Cavalry, Fort Davis, Texas
Courtesy National Park Service

ON THE NEXT PAGE:
Aerial view of crumbling remains of once-thriving Fort Davis
Courtesy U.S. Signal Corps, National Archives

Lieutenant
Powhatan Clark
Courtesy of Fort Davis
National Historic Site,
Fort Davis, Texas

Boomer Leaders, circa 1884
Courtesy Western History Collections, University of Oklahoma Libraries

David L. Payne and his Boomers being escorted back to Kansas by
black soldiers of the Ninth and Tenth U.S. Cavalry, 1883
Courtesy Western History Collections, University of Oklahoma Libraries

Indian agents at the Pine Ridge, Rosebud, Cheyenne River, and Standing Rock reservations at first downplayed the importance of the Ghost Dance. By summer 1890, however, thousands of Indians were dancing themselves into an almost frenzied state. In August, Hugh Gallagher, an able and well-liked agent at Pine Ridge, attempted unsuccessfully to break up a dance at White Clay Creek. At Standing Rock James McLaughlin blamed Hunkpapa leader Sitting Bull for the troubles and wanted him arrested. According to the agent, the old chief was the "high priest and leading apostle of this latest Indian absurdity."[64] Agents Palmer and Reynolds at the Cheyenne River and Rosebud reservations reported that many of their Indians were armed and defiant.

The Ghost Dance craze and accompanying unrest were also disturbing to the military. In early November Brigadier General Thomas H. Ruger, commanding the Department of Dakota, investigated conditions on the reservation, which he found to be unsatisfactory but not explosive. General Miles, commanding the Division of the Missouri, was sufficiently alarmed to send military observers to the agencies.[65]

The craze might well have passed without major difficulty, but two events apparently triggered bloodshed. First, when Agent Gallagher fell victim to Indian Bureau politics, the totally inexperienced Dr. Daniel. F. Royer replaced him. The sight of milling, well-armed ghost dancers soon unnerved Royer, and on November 15 he telegraphed T. J. Morgan, commissioner of Indian affairs, informing him that "Indians are dancing in the snow and are wild and crazy." In the same message he frantically called for immediate protection of the agency and its personnel. "The leaders should be arrested and confined in some military post until the matter is quieted, and this should be done at once."[66]

Three days after Royer's call for troops, General Miles ordered Brigadier General John R. Brooke, commanding the Department of the Platte, to hasten a strong force to Pine Ridge and to station most of his remaining command along the rail and telegraph lines south and west of the reservations. At dawn on November 20, Brooke reached Pine Ridge with Companies F, I, and K of the Ninth, brought up from Fort Robinson; five companies of infantry; a Hotchkiss cannon; and a Gatling gun. On the same day, Lieutenant Colonel A. T. Smith, Eighth Infantry, reached the Rosebud

64 *Annual Report of the Commissioner of Indian Affairs for the Year 1891*, 125.
65 Utley, *Last Days of the Sioux Nation*, 119.
66 *Annual Report of the Commissioner of Indian Affairs for the Year 1891*, 128; Hyde, *Sioux Chronicle*, 254.

agency with three companies of his regiment, Companies A and G of the Ninth, and a Hotchkiss gun.[67]

Miles, wishing to avoid bloodshed, concentrated half the entire U.S. Army on or near the reservations. He sent Major Henry with D Company of the Ninth and two companies of infantry to Pine Ridge on November 25. On their heels came Colonel James W. Forsyth and eight companies of the Seventh Cavalry. Units of the First, Second, Fifth, Sixth, and Eighth Cavalry threw a formidable screen around the reservations. Such a force seemed sufficient to overawe even the most belligerent Lakotas.[68]

The appearance of so many troops frightened the Indians. Fearing a massacre was imminent, they fled the agencies and headed toward a stronghold in the Badlands some forty miles northwest of the Pine Ridge agency and prepared to fight. Miles launched a campaign of pressure and persuasion to induce the runaways to return and assemble in the vicinity of Pine Ridge. He met with some success, but the presence of troops set the stage for tragedy.

Agent McLaughlin, concluding that Sitting Bull was largely responsible for Lakota persistence in the Ghost Dance, decided to arrest him at Standing Rock when he arrived for annuities. With the military brought into the situation, however, he could act only with their consent and involvement. Given the widespread and intense fear among the Lakotas, McLaughin worried that the military's presence at the time the noted chief was arrested might ignite widespread panic that would end in violence. In the end he sent forty Indian police, supported by two companies of the Eight Cavalry, to make the arrest.[69]

The police arrived at Sitting Bull's lodge on Grand River at dawn on December 15. They took the chief into custody without difficulty and were preparing to take him away when they were attacked by more than one hundred of his followers. A bloody fight ensued in which Sitting Bull was killed. Only howitzer fire from the supporting troops rescued the Indian police.[70] Sitting Bull's death was a strong push toward a serious clash, for it compromised Miles's efforts to persuade the Indians that they had nothing to fear and strengthened the hands of the extremists among them.

---

67 *Annual Report of the Secretary of War for the Year 1891*, 179.
68 Ibid., 147–48.
69 Utley, *Last Days of the Sioux Nation*, 146–58; Utley, *Lance and the Shield*, 291–99.
70 Hyde, *Sioux Chronicle*, 286–89. Sitting Bull was killed by Sergeant Bullhead, who was himself also killed. In all, six police and eight of Sitting Bull's warriors died. *Annual Report of the Commissioner of Indian Affairs for the Year 1891*, 129.

Meanwhile, Miles instructed his commanders to push the Indians slowly toward Pine Ridge, avoiding contact but staying close enough to keep them on the move. These tactics were proving successful, but the whereabouts of Big Foot's band, known to contain a number of Sitting Bull's followers, was uncertain and a source of concern. At length Miles ordered Brooke at Pine Ridge to find and apprehend these people. On December 24 Major Henry with D, F, I, and K of the Ninth set out to find them.

Henry searched toward the northwest for fifty miles without success and took station at Harney Springs to scout the Badlands. It was rough work at best in bitter-cold weather. Private Charles Creek recalled later, "You late [sic] out in the cold like a dog, [often] not in a tent because the Indians gonna sneak up on you. It was so cold the [tobacco] spit froze when it left your mouth."[71] Private Creek suffered unnecessarily. The missing Big Foot, his band torn by dissension between fervent traditionalists and those who favored accommodation, had wavered at first but then turned south toward Pine Ridge.

When Henry failed to find Big Foot, Brooke sent out Major S. M. Whitside with four companies of the Seventh Cavalry and a platoon of Battery E, First Artillery, with two Hotchkiss guns. Whiteside marched northeast and, on the night of December 27, went into camp on Wounded Knee Creek. The next morning he sent out scouts, and they soon located the incoming Big Foot. When told he must surrender, the chief offered no resistance, and his band was escorted to the creek and encamped. Whiteside sent word of the roundup to Brooke, and Colonel Forsyth with four more companies of the Seventh and two additional pieces of artillery soon joined him.

Forsyth had orders to disarm Big Foot's band, and on the morning of December 29 he so informed the chief. After some hesitation, the Indians turned over a few antiquated arms, but Forsyth was not satisfied and ordered a detachment of troopers to search the lodges. Rifles and revolvers were found in quantities, and as the hunt continued a medicine man harangued the warriors. Some of these began their death chant, and suddenly one of them pulled a rifle from under his blanket and opened fire.

In a matter of seconds the site at Wounded Knee became a slaughter-house. Many Indians and troopers died in desperate hand-to-hand combat, while point-blank gunfire killed others. The deadly Hotchkiss guns opened,

71 Rickey, "Negro Regulars," 10.

tore the Indian camp to shreds, and then sought out those who chose to flee. It was all over in a matter of minutes. One hundred and forty-six Indian men, women, and children were dead, and fifty more were wounded. Forsyth's loss was twenty-six men killed and thirty-nine wounded.[72]

The roar of the Hotchkiss guns was heard at Pine Ridge, where more than six thousand Lakota had gathered as a result of Miles's drive. Swift Indian horsemen rode to investigate and soon returned with the news of Big Foot's fate. In minutes the Indian camps were a bedlam. Before the day was over, four thousand of them had stampeded, and many were heading for the Badlands, where hostile ghost dancers were in hiding. Forsyth and the Seventh, returning from the bloodbath at Wounded Knee, encountered knots of angry warriors, who skirmished with them. It was an ugly situation, and Brooke hastened to send off a courier to Major Henry.

Henry received Brooke's message just as his troopers were turning in after a fifty-mile scout through the Badlands. The command saddled immediately and set out in extremely cold weather. As they neared the agency, Henry left his train, escorted by Captain Loud and I, and pushed on with all possible speed to Pine Ridge with D, F, and K. He arrived just at dawn after an astonishing march of one hundred miles in a single day. Hardly had the half-frozen and weary troopers started fires to warm themselves, when Corporal William O. Wilson of Company D, having braved a gauntlet of pursuing Indians, charged into their midst with news of a possible catastrophe. Indians had surprised Captain Loud's advance detachment, killing Private Charles Haywood of D Company and threatening the battalion's supply wagons. Although Major Henry's men had rested less than two hours, they saddled up to rescue the threatened wagons. The Indians were beaten off, and the train was brought safely into the agency.[73]

The following morning, December 30, watchers at Pine Ridge saw columns of smoke rising in the direction of Drexel Mission, four miles below the agency. Forsyth and eight companies of the Seventh moved out to investigate. The command reached the mission, where the Indians had fired a small building, but they drew away as the troopers approached. Forsyth followed and marched down a narrow valley with steep bluffs to

72 Hyde, *Sioux Chronicle*, 301–5; Utley, *Last Days of the Sioux Nation*, 227–28; *Annual Report of the Commissioner of Indian Affairs for the Year 1891*, 130; *Annual Report of the Secretary of War for the Year 1891*, 150–51.

73 Brady, *Indian Fights and Fighters*, 353; Hyde, *Sioux Chronicle*, 305–6; Hutcheson, "Ninth Regiment of Cavalry," 287; Utley, *Last Days of the Sioux Nation*, 235–36.

the east and west, but for some unaccountable reason he failed to throw out flankers. Suddenly he found himself penned down by a leaden rain from Sioux riflemen who commanded the bluffs. Efforts to break out were thrown back, and Forsyth faced disaster.

The sound of gunfire alerted Major Henry. Although his buffalo soldiers again had managed no more than two hours' sleep, they quickly saddled and forced their feeble mounts to a trot toward Forsyth's engagement. At 1:30 P.M. Henry reached the mouth of the valley, surveyed the terrain at a glance, and went into action. Captain Wright with I and K spurred jaded animals and charged the east slope, while D and F under Loud and Captain C. S. Stedman dismounted and swept up the bluffs to the west. The warriors were thrown back and driven off, to the great relief of embattled Seventh Cavalry men, who raced to embrace their rescuers.[74] The Ninth, however, would not have been as capable of rescuing them had it not been for Corporal Wilson's brave dash, and the buffalo soldier received warm acclamations.

On New Year's Day, 1891, Major Henry's adjutant publicized his achievement in Order No. 1, which characterized the ride as "one involving much risk" in the face of large numbers of pursuing Indians. His willingness to risk his life had set an example "worthy of emulation" and one that "reflect[ed] great credit not only upon Corpl. Wilson but also upon the 9th Cavalry." Wilson's highest praise, however, came when he received the Medal of Honor for conspicuous gallantry during the fight.[75]

After Drexel Mission, Miles returned to his campaign of steady pressure combined with assurances of safety, decent treatment, and a redress of Indian grievances. Within two weeks more than four thousand Lakota had returned to Pine Ridge and surrendered, and all danger of a war had passed. On January 21 Miles held a grand review, and when Henry and his buffalo soldiers passed, the general raised his gloved hand in salute.[76] It was a fitting climax to the black troops' generation of service in the American West.

74   Beyer and Keydel, *Deeds of Valor,* 2:326; Brady, *Indian Fights and Fighters,* 354; Utley, *Last Days of the Sioux Nation,* 240; *Annual Report of the Secretary of War for the Year 1891,* 153–54.

75   Beyer and Keydel, *Deeds of Valor,* 2:326; Brady, *Indian Fights and Fighters,* 354; Utley, *Last Days of the Sioux Nation,* 240; *Annual Report of the Secretary of War for the Year 1891,* 153–54; Schubert, *Black Valor,* 126.

76   Utley, *Last Days of the Sioux Nation,* 269; *Annual Report of the Secretary of War for the Year 1891,* 155.

Epilogue

By the late 1880s the buffalo soldiers had compiled a record that more than justified their integration into the military services, but this was not to be. On the horizon were developments during the last decade of the nineteenth century and the first of the twentieth that threatened to toss their story into the dustbin of history. Chief among these was "Jim Crow," or de jure, segregation that grew apace in every southern state between 1890 and 1910.

Although segregation had existed earlier, it had not been universal in the South. With the region in political turmoil as struggling farmers revolted against the political order, southern whites disfranchised blacks by tying voting to poll taxes, residency requirements, literacy tests, and the grandfather clause that allowed those whose grandfathers had voted in 1867 to retain the ballot, thereby excluding blacks from the ballot box. To make matters worse, as a new generation of African Americans, who had never known slavery, achieved some prosperity or failed to act with sufficient obsequiousness, one southern state after another adopted Jim Crow laws that subjected blacks to degrading segregation.[1]

By the 1890s northerners, now subscribing increasingly to pseudoscientific theories of Anglo-Saxon superiority, were involved with southerners in a national reconciliation movement to overcome the lingering divisions from the Civil War era. Thus, they looked the other way as African Americans lost their rights. U.S. Supreme Court decisions, harking back to the civil rights cases of 1883, which held that the Fourteenth Amendment applied only to states and not individuals, furthered the national retreat from justice for blacks.

In 1896 *Plessy* v. *Ferguson* upheld segregation as long as it was "separate but equal." Two years later in *Williams* v. *Mississippi,* the Supreme Court

---

1 Woodward, *Strange Career of Jim Crow,* 3–65; Rabinowitz, *Race Relations in the Urban South,* 333–39.

sanctioned black disfranchisement. Finally, if segregation and disfranchisement failed to cow blacks into submission, then lynching instilled terror, especially in remote rural areas where blacks had recently migrated, such as the Gulf Plains, which extend from Florida to Texas, and in the cotton uplands of Louisiana, Arkansas, and Mississippi.[2]

In this new context, the black man in a uniform and armed with a gun was not a welcomed figure. When D. W. Griffith transformed Thomas Dixon's virulently racist 1905 novel *The Clansman* into the 1915 motion picture *Birth of a Nation,* the black soldier, Gus, was presented as a would-be rapist who caused the suicide of an innocent young white woman. When the Ku Klux Klan avenged her death, its violence was presented as a means of restoring a society based on virtue and honor since the men in the film demonstrated their willingness to protect white women. Because northerners as well as southerners applauded this film, it was evident that the effort at bringing about a total reconciliation of North and South was bearing fruit at the expense of African Americans in the United States.[3]

The motion picture's huge box-office receipts told blacks again that even though their men had donned their country's uniform and had fought and died under its flag, they had not yet won their right to full citizenship. Moreover, they still faced intense prejudice and discrimination despite their contributions and sacrifices. The fate of three soldiers who had won the Medal of Honor typified the era's lack of respect for black men who had met the highest standards of military service.

George Jordan, a young sharecropper from Tennessee, had enlisted in the Ninth Cavalry on Christmas Day, 1866. According to the record, he was five-feet, four-inches tall and weighed 130 pounds. He retired after thirty years of service with an impeccable record that included the Medal of Honor. Jordan took up residence in Crawford, Nebraska, where many of his Ninth Cavalry comrades from Fort Robinson had also retired. As was true of many old soldiers who had performed rigorous duty in remote areas, he was not in good health. In October 1904, when he became seriously ill, his doctor twice petitioned the commanding officer at Fort Robinson to permit Jordan to enter the post hospital for treatment. Both petitions were denied. On October 24 Jordan died, and his doctor wrote on his death certificate that

2 Woodward, *Strange Career of Jim Crow,* 67–109; David W. Blight, *Race and Reunion: The Civil War in American Memory,* 347–54; Ayers, *Promise of the New South,* 156–59.

3 Blight, *Race and Reunion,* 394–97.

the cause was "from want of care." The honored trooper left behind property valued at eleven dollars. As historian Frank Schubert observes, "In the
end Jordan's distinguished career availed him little."[4]

Clinton Greaves, born in Virginia in 1850, had enlisted in the Ninth
Cavalry in 1872. His records indicate that he was five-feet, seven-inches tall
and weighed almost two hundred pounds, slightly taller and heavier than
most buffalo soldiers. He retired due to ill health in 1892 after twenty years
of service. Although he had received the Medal of Honor for his role in a
close-quarter fight with Apache Indians in the Florida Mountains of New
Mexico in 1877, he was buried in an unmarked grave in Columbus, Ohio,
following his death in 1906.

Greaves's widow, Bertha, listed her occupation as "housework" and
applied repeatedly for a pension. Eventually, the War Department's Adjutant General's Office ruled that no evidence existed that Corporal Greaves
had ever played a role in any Indian campaign and denied her request. This
occurred despite ample official records to the contrary. Not until 1998,
ninety-two years after Clinton Greaves's death, was an appropriate marker
placed at the head of the grave of this intrepid soldier.[5]

The personal history of William McBryar coincided with the major
events that buffalo soldiers were involved in after the Indian wars. Twenty-
six years old and five-feet, five-inches tall, he had completed three years of
college when he enlisted in the Tenth Cavalry in 1887. He rose quickly to
sergeant and first sergeant and became the first Tenth Cavalry soldier to win
the Medal of Honor, awarded in 1890 for his service at Salt River in Arizona
against fugitive Apaches. When his regiment was sent to the northern plains,
McBryar served at Fort Custer in Montana and in 1893 transferred to the
Twenty-fifth Infantry. There, in a decade of labor strife, he and other buffalo
soldiers protected the Northern Pacific Railroad during the railroad workers' walkout in 1894 in support of striking workers at the Pullman Coach
factory outside Chicago.

In 1898, when the United States entered the Spanish-American War,
McBryar was serving as his company's quartermaster sergeant. By June that
year the Twenty-fifth was in Cuba, and in July he commanded the second
platoon in the battle of El Caney. There and at San Juan Hill the same day,

4 Schubert, *Black Valor*, 87–89 (quotation on 89). See also Schubert, *On the Trail of
the Buffalo Soldier*, 249.
5 Schubert, *Black Valor*, 47–48; Schubert, *On the Trail of the Buffalo Soldier*, 171.

his regiment played a major role in the victory over Spain. McBryar won such high praise that both his company commander and his regimental commander, Colonel Andrew S. Daggett, encouraged him to seek a commission in the regular army.

When the War Department created volunteer units of black men from the South to serve as occupation forces in Cuba, McBryar was commissioned lieutenant in the Eighth Volunteer Infantry. For that service he and other blacks who held such commissions emerged as heroes to their people at a time when African Americans were enduring the humiliations of losing the vote and adjusting to Jim Crow.

After the Eighth was mustered out in March 1899, McBryar reenlisted in the Twenty-fifth, this time as a private. Once more he rose quickly to battalion sergeant major, and as such he left with the Twenty-fifth for the Philippines, which the United States had taken from Spain as an overseas possession. McBryar continued to petition for a regular commission while he also sought appointment in either the Forty-eighth or Forty-ninth all-black volunteer units, with strong recommendations from Andrew J. Burt, the colonel commanding the Twenty-fifth, and regimental chaplain Theophilus G. Steward. His mother campaigned by writing President William McKinley that the U.S. Army had only one black officer (Charles Young) "notwithstanding the deeds of daring performed by the colored troops in the Spanish war." By November 1899 McBryar was serving as second lieutenant in the Forty-ninth U.S. Volunteer Infantry and held that rank until the entire regiment was mustered out in 1901.

McBryar continuously sought his commission in the regular army but to no avail. By 1905 he was serving as a private in the Ninth Cavalry after three-and a-half discouraging years as a civilian. Although he was soon promoted to corporal, age and rheumatism had taken their toll. By 1906 he was again a civilian, married, and taking low paying and short-term jobs. Although he tried to reenlist in 1916 during the border troubles with Mexico and again a year later when the United States entered World War I, he was too old for soldiering. After his death in 1941 at age eighty, and only months before Pearl Harbor, he was buried in Arlington Cemetery, where he had once worked as a night watchman. McBryar's career, as Frank N. Schubert observes, "raised the same questions brought up by the way in which George Jordan died: What were the Medal of Honor and a life of service worth to a black hero?"[6]

6   Schubert, *Black Valor*, 101–15; Schubert, *On the Trail of the Buffalo Soldier*, 275–76.

Lack of recognition was extended not only to the buffalo soldiers but to their officers as well, including Colonels Edward Hatch and Benjamin Grierson. The latter was particularly neglected, given his outstanding services during the Civil War. An innovative and courageous commander, he had earned the lasting respect of both Ulysses Grant and William T. Sherman. In the West he had functioned largely as a builder and peacekeeper since he refused to kill Indians for the sake of personal advancement.

Consequently, he found himself often characterized as a timid, inept fumbler who was unfit to wear the uniform of his country. Nonetheless, he proved his strategic ability when he outmaneuvered and outfought the Mimbres Apache chief Victorio in West Texas in a brilliant campaign of counterguerrilla warfare.[7] After the battle of Rattlesnake Springs, however, one source insisted that Grierson had hidden away in the West Texas mountains to avoid Victorio and his band. Passed over repeatedly for promotion to brigadier general in the regular army, Grierson finally won that rank shortly before his mandatory retirement in 1890.

Afterward, his record was all but lost to public view. On August 31, 1911, he died as a result of stroke. Leading the funeral procession was Guy Washington, a black man. As time passed, Grierson was largely ignored even in his hometown of Jacksonville, Illinois.[8]

Throughout much of the twentieth century, the story of the buffalo soldiers was little more than a distant memory. Almost half a century passed before they received any kind of recognition. In 1948 President Harry S. Truman, impatient over congressional failure to implement the recommendations to end "segregation, based on race, color, creed, or national origin" that his Civil Rights Committee had advanced in *To Secure These Rights*, took action on his own. On July 26, 1948, he issued an executive order mandating that all branches of the military were to offer "equality of treatment and opportunity for all persons in the armed services without regard to race, color, religion or national origin." By the time the United States entered the Korean War in June 1950, some of its military units had been quietly integrated.[9]

7 Leckie and Leckie, *Unlikely Warriors,* 256–68. Retired general J. J. Byrne, in a letter to a Texas congressman, accused Grierson of hiding from Victorio. See Alex E. Sweet and J. Armoy Knox, *On a Mexican Mustang through Texas: From the Gulf to the Rio Grande* (St. Louis: T. N. James, 1884), 525.

8 Ibid., 267–308. The sole exception to this neglect was D. Alexander Brown's excellent study, *Grierson's Raid,* which concerned Grierson's Civil War career and the national publicity he received as a result of his best-known raid through Mississippi in 1863.

9 Woodward, *Strange Career of Jim Crow,* 135–37.

These developments and a growing consciousness that the nation's treatment of blacks was leading to a loss of credibility with developing nations in Asia and Africa during the Cold War led to a growing scholarly interest in the history of race relations in the United States.[10] Although Theophilis Steward, the intellectual black chaplain for the Twenty-fifth Infantry, had published *The Colored Regulars in the United States Army* in 1904 as an account of African American contributions during the Spanish-American War, his work had received little attention.

The pioneering historian who ignited scholarly interest in black contributions in the military was Professor Kenneth Porter, the Harvard-trained professor who taught at many institutions but most notably at the University of Oregon. His work on military scouts who were the offspring of runaway slaves and Seminole Indians and their service in U.S. military campaigns appeared as "The Seminole Negro Indian Scouts, 1870–1881," in a 1952 issue of *The Southwestern Historical Quarterly*.[11] Soon after, Dudley T. Cornish's *The Sable Arm: Negro Troops in the Union Army, 1861–1865* brought to light the stunning contributions and sacrifices black soldiers had made to the Union victory in 1865.[12]

Further encouragement for those working in the emerging field of African American history came with the passage of the Civil Rights Bill in 1964 and the Voting Rights Act of 1965. These two major accomplishments of the civil rights movement were realized when President Lyndon B. Johnson harnessed the national grief over the assassination of President John F. Kennedy in 1963 and directed it toward ending Jim Crow and disfranchisement where they still existed in southern states.[13] This legislation assured African Americans that, although racism was not dead, they were now equal citizens under the law, a century after the Union victory in the Civil War.

It was in this context that the University of Oklahoma Press published *The Buffalo Soldiers: A Narrative of the Negro Cavalry in the West*. The book had been long in gestation, for the seed had been planted in William Leckie's favorable experience with black soldiers during World War II. As noted in the preface to the first edition, the military in World War II had discriminated against African American soldiers, but the objective of those men in

10   Ibid., 131–34
11   This work appeared in vol. 55, pp. 358–77.
12   This work first appeared in 1956 and was reissued by W. W. Norton in 1966.
13   Woodward, *Strange Career of Jim Crow*, 181–88.

serving their country had been the same as that of the buffalo soldiers earlier. They wanted to be treated fairly as soldiers and as men, and they had hoped that their service to their country would bring them acknowledgment of their full rights as citizens at long last.

Since the appearance of *The Buffalo Soldiers* in 1967, other scholars have examined the record of black soldiers in the post–Civil War western army. In 1971 Arlen L. Fowler published *The Black Infantry in the West, 1869–1891,* thereby recovering the history of the Twenty-fourth and Twenty-fifth Infantry, regiments whose service had been largely ignored.[14] Fowler did more than rescue these hardworking units from near oblivion. He also provided excellent insights into the educational system that the U.S. Army established for soldiers who were illiterate, which was the state of most black soldiers born into slavery. These educational reforms affected the entire army, for as noted earlier, by 1889 the U.S. military required schooling for all enlisted men who lacked an elementary-school education.

Furthermore, Fowler described the experience of Allen Allensworth, a former slave, Baptist minister, and a college-trained educator who had taught for the Freedmen's Bureau when he began his army career in service to the men of the Twenty-fourth Infantry at Fort Supply, Indian Territory. Fervently believing that education was the key to social advancement for his race, he later developed an effective literacy program complete with curriculum and lesson plans for his men at Fort Bayard, New Mexico. It, in turn, became a model for the military as a whole. Allensworth's military career was highly successful, for in 1904 he was one of four chaplains to win promotion to major. In 1906 he retired from the army with the rank of lieutenant colonel.[15]

Several studies appearing in the 1990s looked at the buffalo soldiers from the perspective of their effect on western regions. In 1991 Monroe Lee Billington's *New Mexico's Buffalo Soldiers, 1866–1900* focused on the contribution that black infantrymen and cavalrymen made to the settlement and development of New Mexico Territory in the post–Civil War era. In addition to manning, at various times, eleven out of sixteen of New Mexico's forts, they advanced the territory's economic development by building roads and telegraph lines and providing escorts for stages and security forces for water

14 The University of Oklahoma Press reprinted this work in 1996.
15 Fowler, *Black Infantry in the West,* 104–7; Schubert, *On the Trail of the Buffalo Soldier,* 6–8.

holes, herds, mines, and railroad construction crews. They also provided protection to newcomers, workers, and travelers in a region plagued by "robbers, horse thieves, and cattle rustlers," in addition to hostile Indians.

Finally, although western novels and films seldom note their presence, buffalo soldiers played peacekeeping roles in uprisings such as the Lincoln County War. Billington reminds his readers that, although the duties of the buffalo soldiers were similar to those of their white counterparts, their work was harder. They had to endure a "double dose" of prejudice "both because they were soldiers and because of their skin color."[16]

Billington's work was followed two years later by Frank N. Schubert's *Buffalo Soldiers, Braves, and the Brass: The Story of Fort Robinson, Nebraska.* Schubert's labor of love, the culmination of decades of research, examines the socioeconomic effect of the post on the surrounding region of the Pine Ridge country. The influence was profound since the fort served as the major catalyst for business in the area, and the soldiers' activities, including their visits to gambling parlors and houses of prostitution, provided the town with sources of taxable income.

Within the post, however, the military caste system meant that socially, officers and their families lived in one world, while the enlisted men and their families occupied another. African American chaplains, who held the rank of captain, existed in an intensely lonely no-man's world. Officers shunned them, and socializing with enlisted men violated military rules. In the court-martial of Reverend Henry Plummer, an incident in which he socialized with enlisted men played a role in his discharge from the army, although the charges of drunkenness against him were not proved and were probably leveled as a vendetta.

The more important factors in his dismissal were his zealous temperance crusade and his advocacy of a missionary venture in Africa for black soldiers. His travail proved that black enlisted men had an advantage that he lacked. Within their barracks and through their contacts with other African Americans in Crawford, they created their own world. Increasingly, it provided them with expanded opportunities for recreation, mutual support, and involvement in issues regarding the protection and advancement of their race.

Schubert also notes that military experience played a vital role in dispersing African Americans throughout the western United States. Spouses and

16 Billington, *New Mexico's Buffalo Soldiers,* xvii, xii, xvi.

relatives of soldiers who could find no housing at Fort Robinson, and later retired buffalo soldiers, made up most of the residents of Crawford's black community. It should be noted, however, that sometimes families of buffalo soldiers were living in town simply because a post commander had evaluated a soldier's wife, according to his own prejudice or caprice, as not respectable enough to occupy the hovels or stablelike quarters available to enlisted men's dependents at the post.[17]

In 1995 Schubert's *On the Trail of the Buffalo Soldier: Biographies of African Americans in the U.S. Army, 1866–1917* appeared in print. A compendium of biographical facts and sources rather than a standard historical narrative, it provides a gold mine of information on the lives of buffalo soldiers and remains a work of inestimable value to researchers in the field. Two years later Schubert published *Black Valor: Buffalo Soldiers and the Medal of Honor, 1870–1898*, a collective biography of men in the Ninth and Tenth Cavalry and Twenty-fourth and Twenty-fifth Infantry who distinguished themselves by receiving this high award during the Indian wars.

Charles L. Kenner also tackled the issue of relations between men and officers as his main subject in *Buffalo Soldiers and Officers of the Ninth Cavalry, 1867–1898*, which appeared in 1999. He found that both enlisted men and their officers sought "honor." For blacks this "meant respect and recognition of their entitlement to the privileges of citizenship; for the officers," he adds, "the term implied recognition from their peers and the approval of their superiors." To achieve their honor, blacks had to constantly battle the stereotypes that characterized them as "ignorant and irresponsible."[18] At the same time, their white commanders found that the prejudice directed toward the black soldiers spilled over onto the regiment and impeded their efforts to win the recognition and advancement they eagerly sought in an army in which promotion was notoriously slow and achieved only within one's regiment. Not surprisingly, some officers of the Ninth vented their frustrations by treating the men they commanded in insulting and, at times, sadistic ways.

Outstanding officers, such as Major Guy Henry, mitigated that situation somewhat by the late 1880s. Unfortunately, race relations in the United States were now entering the nadir for black Americans, and as an institution that reflected its larger society, the U.S. Army failed to give black soldiers

17   Schubert, *Buffalo Soldiers, Braves, and the Brass*, v–vi, 57–82, 126–37, 161–85.
18   Kenner, *Buffalo Soldiers and Officers of the Ninth Cavalry*, 3.

their due. In this context, an older work on African Americans in the military is still valuable. Marvin E. Fletcher's *The Black Soldier and Officer in the United States Army, 1891–1917*, published in 1974, not only describes the black military experience in the Spanish-American War, the Philippine Insurrection, and during the border troubles with Mexico in 1916, but it also contains excellent background on the deterioration of race relations in the United States in general and the institutionalization of a more vicious racism through segregation and disfranchisement by the early twentieth century.

Garna L. Christian chronicles the effect of this new, more virulent racism on the residents of border towns in Texas in *Black Soldiers in Jim Crow Texas, 1899–1917*. Although the citizens of these communities were largely Hispanic, they had absorbed the Anglo society's prejudices against blacks even while suffering from bias and discrimination themselves. The conflicts arose when black soldiers returned to Texas in 1899 after compiling an outstanding record in Cuba.

Armed confrontations broke out in October between Tenth Cavalry troops stationed at Fort McIntosh and city constables from the town of Laredo. Escalating tensions, arising in part from real or alleged attentions that Ninth Cavalry soldiers stationed at Fort Ringgold had paid to local women in Rio Grande City, led to even worse violence—the knifing of three troopers and the shooting of two others on October 17, 1899.

In 1900, on the surface, interracial trouble seemed unlikely in El Paso. The town's small African American population held relatively high status, and the population as a whole still harbored fond memories of the Ninth Cavalry's role in the Salt War of 1877. Nonetheless, racial conflict, which reared its ugly head between soldiers of the Twenty-fifth Infantry and townspeople, claimed the lives of a policeman and a corporal. In the context of these unfortunate occurrences, the series of events known as the Brownsville Raid was the culmination of deteriorating race relations and rising ethnic tensions on the Texas border.[19]

When soldiers of Companies B, C, and D of the Twenty-fifth Infantry arrived in the southernmost Texas town from duty in the Philippines and Fort Niobrara in Nebraska in July 1906, they immediately encountered intense hostility from its citizens. It became even more virulent after a white woman was allegedly attacked by a black serviceman. The soldiers were

19   Christian, *Black Soldiers in Jim Crow Texas.*

confined to their post, Fort Brown, by an eight o'clock curfew on August 13, when shooting broke out in town, claiming one life and leaving a police lieutenant injured.

Town residents told of seeing soldiers shooting in the street despite the curfew, the darkness of that night, and their distance from the actual scene of events. They also presented spent cartridges to the post's commanding officer, which they claimed they had retrieved from the streets. When the soldiers denied any involvement, stating that they had been in their barracks listening to the gunfire and believing themselves under siege, they were portrayed as uncooperative and involved in a conspiracy to cover up their actions.

Despite a grand jury's failure to return indictments against the soldiers, Inspector General Ernest A. Garlington, a South Carolinian who was contemptuous of blacks, argued for their dismissal from the service. On November 5 President Theodore Roosevelt summarily ordered all 167 Twenty-fifth Infantry soldiers at Brownsville discharged "without honor."[20] Later, however, Major Charles Penrose, the commanding officer at Brownsville, and the three officers commanding Companies, B, C, and D became convinced that the soldiers had not fired their guns that night and testified to that effect. To muddy the waters further, 14 men were allowed to petition for reenlistment, but the discharge of the other 153 soldiers stood.

John B. Weaver describes these incidents in his 1970 book, *The Brownsville Raid*.[21] Later he gave closer attention to the investigations that Senator Joseph B. Foraker of Ohio conducted on the soldiers' behalf in *The Senator and the Sharecropper's Son: The Exoneration of the Brownsville Soldiers*. In the twentieth century, ongoing historical investigations and Weaver's work on the raid convinced Augustus Hawkins, an African American member of Congress from California with a strong social conscience, that the soldiers had suffered a terrible injustice. In 1972 his persuasiveness led Acting Attorney General Richard Kleindienst to recommend that the army award the Twenty-fifth soldiers who were unjustly dismissed honorable discharges.

Dorsie Willis, the only survivor of this sad event and the son of a sharecropper, was at age eighty-eight still shining shoes in a Minneapolis barbershop when he received a settlement of $25,000. Asked if he were bitter, he answered "no," but added: "They can't pay me for the sacrifice I've made,

20 Ibid., 177.
21 For another work that discusses the effects of this event on national race relations, see Lane, *Brownsville Affair*.

Buffalo soldier statue by Eddie Dixon, at Fort Leavenworth, Kansas
Courtesy of Dennis Behling

ON THE PREVIOUS PAGES:
Ninth Cavalry Honor Guard at the funeral of Colonel Edward
Hatch, Fort Robinson, Nebraska, April 1889. Medal of Honor
winner Thomas Shaw is standing second from left. With Shaw,
right to left, are Sergeants James Wilson, David Badie, and Nathan
Fletcher. Seated right to left are Chief Trumpeter Stephen Taylor,
Sergeants Edward McKenzie, Robert Burley, and Zekiel Sykes.
Courtesy of United States Military Academy Library

"The Sentinal," by Renaldo "Sonny" Rivera, at Fort Selden, New Mexico
Photograph by Mark Erickson

the sacrifice that my family had to undergo. You can't pay for a lifetime. Some people feel the world owes them a living. I never thought that, but I did figure the world owed me an opportunity to earn a living. They took that away from me. That dishonorable discharge kept me from improving my life. Only God knows what it done to the others."[22]

William A. Dobak and Thomas D. Phillips in *The Black Regulars, 1866–1898*, published in 2001, eschew the term "buffalo soldiers." They see no evidence that the black soldiers saw that sobriquet as an honorific term and point to instances that suggest that some of them, at least, found the term insulting.[23] It is our hope that further research may illuminate this question in the future. Dobak and Phillips also disclose on the basis of their painstaking examination of the records that black regiments were not discriminated against in terms of their allocation or horses and weapons and equipment. Had the army done so, they persuasively argue, a large portion of its military would have been seriously handicapped in its ability to perform its functions. There were problems, but they point out that all regiments suffered from poor mounts and inadequate weapons at various times. Thus, the problems that Grierson and Hatch identified as arising from discrimination were those that occasionally plagued all commanders.

Dobak and Phillips also note that civilian populations were at times grateful to the buffalo soldiers for the services they supplied their communities. There is no disagreement here, for the first edition of this work also noted that fact. It also indicated, however, that such praise probably surprised black men who experienced intense prejudice in nineteenth-century America. And, as Garna Christian's work on black soldiers in Texas tells us, they experienced greater injustice and even violence and wrath rather than appreciation in many communities in the early decades of the twentieth century. The army's response was, as Christian tells us, that it "expected its charges to comply with all civilian laws and norms, just or not."[24] Nonetheless, the points that Dobak and Philips make are well taken, and their questioning of stereotypes about military policies regarding race represents a major contribution to historical studies of the black experience in the post–Civil War western army.

22 See Weaver, *Senator and the Sharecropper's Son*, xii–xvi, 212–13.
23 Dobak and Phillips, *Black Regulars*, xvii.
24 Christian, *Black Soldiers in Jim Crow Texas*, 176.

The attention that black military history has received in recent decades has given African Americans a stronger sense of the historical contributions their forbearers made to their country and a sense of well-earned pride in their ancestors' ability to endure and maintain their faith in their country. That, in turn, has led to the organization of buffalo soldier units in cities throughout the United States.

Many black Americans, and whites as well, have begun researching the buffalo soldiers' dress, weapons, and equipment, and they are compiling additional information and historical data. A national organization, the Ninth and Tenth Horse Cavalry Association, which dates its origin as 1866, has become the most prominent group in these endeavors. At its July 2001 national meeting in Atlanta, it claimed a membership of more than one thousand. As it does annually, it accepted new chapters from all parts of the United States, and thus the association is constantly growing.

The growing national interest has also spawned a movement to build monuments at western sites where buffalo soldiers had been stationed. By the turn of the twenty-first century, statues had been placed at Forts Bayard and Selden in New Mexico, Fort Huachuca in Arizona, Fort Bliss in El Paso, and Fort Leavenworth, Kansas. The last is the most impressive.

On July 25, 1992, the dedication ceremony for the monument was held before an audience estimated at between 18,000 and 20,000. The keynote speaker was then Chairman of the Joint Chiefs of Staff General Colin Powell, who described himself as a descendant of the buffalo soldiers. He also served as a catalyst for the statue's erection. While stationed at Leavenworth earlier, he had discovered that, although the Tenth Cavalry had been organized at that post, there was nothing there to commemorate that event.

The oversight was now corrected with the erection of a statue of a superbly mounted and armed buffalo soldier beside a spectacular artificial waterfall. The work of Lubbock, Texas, sculptor Eddie Dixon, the statue and its setting is an inspiring depiction of the enduring courage of the black soldier who served his country on remote western posts.

In his address General Powell spoke of Colonel Benjamin Grierson as commander of the Tenth Cavalry. His remarks ignited new interest in the almost-forgotten soldier. By 1996 Grierson was at last rescued from near oblivion. Citizens of Jacksonville, Illinois, began hosting the first of what is now an annual General Grierson Days celebration. This event attracts Civil

War reenactors, historians, and history buffs. It also includes a symposium at which the Grierson Society of Jacksonville presents the General Benjamin H. Grierson Humanitarian and Outstanding Achievement Award each year.

In contrast to the movement to erect monuments, motion picture producers have paid scant attention to the record of the Ninth and Tenth Cavalry, and only two efforts are worthy of mention. In 1960 Woodrow Strode starred in *Sergeant Rutledge.* His portrayal of a buffalo soldier falsely accused of the rape and murder of a white woman as well as the murder of her father, an officer, was a stirring and thought-provoking work. Directed by John Ford, it was a courageous film for Hollywood to produce in the context of the early 1960s, when the civil rights movement was controversial and dangerous for its participants.[25]

The other film, *The Buffalo Soldiers,* which featured Danny Glover, was unfortunately sentimental and ahistorical. Glover depicts a sergeant who leads a company of buffalo soldiers at Rattlesnake Springs and then surprises and captures the Apache leader Victorio and his Warm Springs band. After negotiations over coffee, the Apaches are permitted to leave. The main message of the production—which is false—is that black soldiers and American Indians sympathized with one another as people of color in white America during the Indian wars.[26]

From the perspective of today's world and the knowledge of the wrongs that white society has perpetrated against both African Americans and American Indians, there is admittedly a haunting irony to the fact that former slaves found themselves fighting against people who were in the process of being dispossessed of their land and whose culture was misunderstood and under attack. Nonetheless, that was not the view that black men who joined the U.S. Army had of their struggle.

Although individual black soldiers might have sympathized with Indians, just as individual white soldiers sometimes did, none of them would ever have captured an Apache chief, conversed with him, and then let him go. Moreover, many black soldiers saw the Indian with the same prejudices as their white counterparts. Native peoples, as the Utes had demonstrated tauntingly in their fight with the buffalo soldiers at the Milk River in September 1879, could return the compliment. Although every citizen today should abhor such prejudice and instead acknowledge the common human-

25 Willis Goldbeck produced this film.
26 This Turner Film production was made for television in 1997.

ity of all people, that attitude, unfortunately, is not yet universal. During the Indian wars it was often notably absent on all sides.

Another manifestation of expanding interest is in the appearance of artists portraying in paintings actual episodes from the buffalo soldier campaigns. Among these are Nick Eggenhofer's *Tenth Cavalry at the Battle of Rattlesnake Springs,* Bob Snead's *The Errand of Corporal Ross* and *Our Father Who Art in Heaven* (which depicts the burial of Corporal James Betters of the Ninth Cavalry's Company C after he was accidentally shot in New Mexico), and Clyde Heron's *Attack on the Eagle Springs Run.* Another important artwork is Mort Kunstler's depiction of four Tenth Cavalry soldiers, which appeared on the buffalo soldier stamp that the U.S. Postal Service issued in 1992 at the time of the Fort Leavenworth statue dedication. Finally, there is not a meeting of buffalo soldier enthusiasts that lacks a plentiful supply of lapel emblems, T-shirts, coffee mugs, photographs, and other such items. These are especially popular with the growing numbers who today are involved in the proliferating buffalo soldier reenactment groups.

A good beginning has been made, one that new scholars in western history and American military history will undoubtedly build on. In the future it is hoped that all Americans of whatever color will discover more about the men who served as buffalo soldiers. One area that descendents of these men may be able to provide information on concerns the question of how the buffalo soldiering experience affected black families and their communities.

In the end, the story of the buffalo soldiers is the story of individual men who sought to serve their country. If one wishes to identify a black man whose patriotism never flagged and whose service reached a high level of achievement, one would need to look no further than to Sergeant Augustus Walley. A native of Maryland, he enlisted in the Tenth Cavalry in 1877 and was assigned to Company E. In 1881 he was awarded the Medal of Honor for heroism against Nana's Apache band in the Cuchillo Negro Mountains, New Mexico. In 1898 he was commended for "great gallantry" during U.S. operations in Cuba. He retired in 1907, but when the United States entered World War I, the old warrior volunteered for service but was turned down because of his age, then being over sixty. In 1995, almost fifty-seven years after his death in 1938, a Medal of Honor marker was placed at Walley's grave in his hometown of Reisterstown, Maryland. Recognition and appreciation came to him at last.

At the same time, individual stories such as that of Augustus Walley are important because they fit into a larger narrative—the story of America. Walley's story and those of the buffalo soldiers chronicled above show us that blacks participated in virtually all American events. Among these was the expansion of the United States as it solidified its power and authority over a vast continent. Thus, the story of the buffalo soldiers is not simply a chronicle of black history. It is instead a chronicle of American history and a vital part of our common national heritage.

Bibliography

MANUSCRIPT MATERIALS

National Archives, Washington, D.C.
RECORDS OF THE OFFICE OF INDIAN AFFAIRS
   Letters Received by the Office of Indian Affairs, Kiowa Agency, 1864–80.

RECORDS OF THE WAR DEPARTMENT, ADJUTANT GENERAL'S OFFICE,
RECORD GROUP 94
   Annual Report of the Department of Texas for 1873.
   Correspondence, Adjutant General, Document File, 1876.
   "The History of the Fifth United States Cavalry from March 3, 1855, to December
       31, 1905," File 1102491.
   Letters Received, 1875–81.
   Letters Received, Affairs on the Rio Grande and Texas Frontier, 1875–81,
       Consolidated File 1653.
   Letters Received, File 554-1874.
   Letters Received, File 1305-1871.
   Letters Received, File 1405-1878.
   Letters Received, File 2815-1874.
   Letters Received, File 3144-1874.
   Letters Received, File 3300-1874.
   Letters Received, File 3490-1874.
   Letters Received, File 4447-1873.
   Letters Received, File 5993-PRD-1890.
   Letters Received, Selected Documents Relating to the Activities of the Ninth and
       Tenth Cavalry in the Campaign against Victorio, 1879–80, File 6058-1879.
   Medical History of Posts.
   Organizational Returns, Tenth Cavalry, 1866–86.
   Organizational Returns, Ninth Cavalry, 1866–93.
   Post Returns.
       Camp Supply.
       Fort Concho.
       Fort Davis.
       Fort Dodge.

Fort Grant.

Fort Griffin.

Fort Harker.

Fort Hays.

Fort Larned.

Fort McKavett.

Fort Richardson.

Fort Sill.

Fort Stockton.

Fort Thomas.

Fort Wallace.

Selected Documents from Letters Received, 1872–76.

Selected Letters Received, 1870–74.

Selected Letters Received, 1875–80.

Selected Letters Received, Department of Texas.

Selected Letters Received Relating to the Ninth and Tenth Regiments, U.S. Cavalry.

Selected Letters Received Relating to Texas, 1875–76.

"Tabular Statement of Murders, Outrages, Robberies, and Depredations Committed by Indians in the Department of Missouri and Northern Texas in
1868 and '69 (exclusive of military engagements) and officially reported to
Headquarters, Department of the Missouri."

RECORDS OF U.S. ARMY COMMANDS, RECORD GROUP 98

Bigelow, Major John, Jr. "Historical Sketch, Tenth U.S. Cavalry, 1866–92."

Letters Received, District of New Mexico, 1876–81.

Letters Sent, Department of the Missouri, 1876–81.

Letters Sent, District of New Mexico, 1876–81.

Letters Sent, Department of Texas, 1873–74.

Letters Sent, Tenth U.S. Cavalry, 1866–83.

Military Division of the Missouri, Special File 6181–1875.

Military Division of the Missouri, Special File, Victorio Papers, 1880.

Registers of Enlistments in the U.S. Army, 1798–1914. Microcopy 233.

Selected Letters Received Relating to the Tenth U.S. Cavalry, 1873–76.

Illinois State Historical Society, Springfield

Grierson, Brigadier General Benjamin H. "The Lights and Shadows of Life,
Including Experiences and Remembrances of the War of the Rebellion."

Papers of Benjamin H. Grierson.

Oklahoma State Historical Society, Oklahoma City

INDIAN ARCHIVES DIVISION

Cheyenne-Arapaho Files

Agents and Agency.

Battles.

    Depredations.
    Military Relations.
    Murders.
    Prisoners and Warfare.
  Kiowa Files
    Agents and Agency.
    Depredations.
    Military Relations.
    Trial of Satanta and Big Tree.

Texas Technological University, Lubbock

SOUTHWEST COLLECTION

Benjamin H. Grierson Papers, 1827–1941.

Grierson, Benjamin. Letters and Documents. Microcopy of MS 343A from the Edward Ayer Collection, Newberry Library, Chicago, Illinois.

The University of Oklahoma, Norman

THE PHILLIPS COLLECTION

Forsyth, George A., to Brevet Brigadier General C. M. McKeever, Assistant Adjutant General, Department of the Missouri. "Report of the Organization and Operations of a Body of Scouts Enrolled and Equipped at Forts Harker and Hays, Kansas, August 24, 1868," March 31, 1869.

"Extracts from Inspector General R. B. Marcy's Journal of an Inspection Tour while Accompanying the General in Chief during the Months of April, May, and June, 1871."

Sherman-Sheridan Papers. Typescript of Sherman-Sheridan Correspondence, 2 vols., Philip H. Sheridan Papers, Library of Congress, Washington, D.C.

GOVERNMENT PUBLICATIONS

Annual Report of the Commissioner of Indian Affairs, 1866–91.

Annual Report of the Secretary of War, 1866–91.

Day, James M., and Dorman Winfrey, eds. *Texas Indian Papers, 1860–1916.* 4 vols. Austin: Texas State Library, 1961.

Heitman, Francis B. *Historical Register and Dictionary of the United States Army.* 2 vols. Washington, D.C.: Government Printing Office, 1903.

Hodge, Frederick W. *Handbook of American Indians North of Mexico.* Bulletin 30, Bureau of American Ethnology. Washington, D.C.: Government Printing Office, 1912.

Kappler, Charles J. *Indian Affairs: Laws and Treaties.* Vol. II. Washington, D.C.: Government Printing Office, 1903.

Mooney, James. *Calendar History of the Kiowa Indians.* Seventeenth Annual Report of the Bureau of American Ethnology, 1895–1896. Washington, D.C.: Government Printing Office, 1898.

Mooney, James. "The Ghost-dance Religion." *Fourteenth Annual Report of the Bureau of American Ethnology, 1892–1893.* Washington, D.C.: Government Printing Office, 1896.

U.S. Army, Military Division of the Missouri. *Record of Engagements with Hostile Indians within the Military Division of the Missouri from 1868–1882.* Washington, D.C.: Government Printing Office, 1882.

U.S. Congress, House. H. Exec. Doc. 97, 40th Cong., 2d sess.

———. H. Misc. Doc. 139, 41st Cong., 2d sess.

———. H. Exec. Doc. 13, 42d Cong., 3d sess.

———. H. Exec. Doc. 1, 44th Cong., 2d sess.

———. H.R. 96, April 4, 1876, 44th Cong., 2d sess.

———. H. Exec. Doc. 1, pt. 2, 45th Cong., 2d sess.

———. H. Exec. Doc. 1, pt. 2, 45th Cong. 3d sess.

———. H. Exec. Doc. 10, 45th Cong., 1st sess.

———. H. Exec. Doc. 13, 45th Cong., 1st sess.

———. H. Exec. Doc. 18, 45th Cong., 1st sess.

———. H. Exec. Doc. 14, 45th Cong., 1st sess.

———. H. Exec. Doc. 64, 45th Cong., 2d sess.

U.S. Congress, Senate. S. Exec. Doc. 13, 40th Cong., 1st sess.

———. S. Exec. Doc. 7, 40th Cong., 3d sess.

———. S. Exec. Doc. 13, 40th Cong., 3d sess.

———. S. Exec. Doc. 18, 40th Cong., 3d sess.

———. S. Exec. Doc. 36, 40th Cong., 3d sess.

———. S. Exec. Doc. 40, 40th Cong., 3d sess.

———. S. Exec. Doc. 59, 41st Cong., 2d sess.

———. S. Exec. Doc. 16, 45th Cong., 2d sess.

United States Statues at Large. Vol. 15.

The War of the Rebellion: A Compilation of the Official Records of the Union and Confederate Armies. Washington, D.C.: Government Printing Office, 1891–98.

U.S. War Department. *Regulations of the Army of the United States and General Orders in Force on the 17th of February, 1881.* Washington, D.C.: Government Printing Office, 1881.

ARTICLES

Blount, Bertha. "The Apache in the Southwest, 1846–1886." *Southwestern Historical Quarterly* 23 (July 1919).

Burkey, Elmer R. "The Thornburgh Battle with the Utes on Milk Creek." *The Colorado Magazine* 13 (Denver 1936).

Cahill, Luke. "An Indian Campaign and Buffalo Hunting with 'Buffalo Bill.'" *The Colorado Magazine* 4 (August 1927).

Campbell, C. E. "Down among the Red Men." *Collections of the Kansas State Historical Society* 17 (Topeka 1929).

Carroll, H. Bailey. "Nolan's 'Lost Nigger' Expedition of 1877." *Southwestern Historical Quarterly* 14 (July 1940).

Clum, John P. "Geronimo." *New Mexico Historical Review* 2 (January 1928); 3 (April 1928).

Crimmins, Colonel M. L. "Captain Nolan's Lost Troop on the Staked Plains." *West Texas Historical Association Yearbook* 10 (October 1934).

———. "Colonel Buells's Expedition into Mexico." *New Mexico Historical Review* 10 (October 1934).

———. "Shafter's Explorations in West Texas." *West Texas Historical Association Yearbook* 9 (October 1933).

———. "Fort McKavett, Texas." *Southwestern Historical Quarterly* 38 (July 1934).

Davis, Theodore R. "A Summer on the Plains." *Harper's Monthly Magazine* 36 (February 1868).

Doran, Thomas F. "Kansas Sixty Years Ago." *Collections of the Kansas State Historical Society* 15 (Topeka 1923).

Dorst, Captain Joseph. "Ranald Slidell Mackenzie." *Cavalry Journal* 10 (December 1897).

Forsyth, George A. "A Frontier Fight." *Harper's Monthly Magazine* 91 (June 1895).

Garfield, Marvin. "Defense of the Kansas Frontier, 1864–1865." *The Kansas Historical Quarterly* 1 (February 1932).

Godfrey, Brigadier General E. S. "Some Reminiscences, Including an Account of General Sully's Expedition against the Southern Plains Indians, 1868." *Cavalry Journal* 36 (July 1927).

———. "Some Reminiscences, Including the Washita Battle, November 29, 1868." *Cavalry Journal* 37 (October 1928).

Haley, J. Evetts. "The Comanchero Trade." *Southwestern Historical Quarterly* 38 (January 1935).

Hazen, General William B. "Some Corrections of *Life on the Plains.*" *Chronicles of Oklahoma* 3 (December 1925).

Hinton, Harwood P., Jr. "John Simpson Chisum, 1877–1884." *New Mexico Historical Review* 31 (July 1956).

Hutcheson, Lieutenant Grote. "The Ninth Regiment of Cavalry." In *The Army of the United States: Historical Sketches of Staff and Line with Portraits of Generals-in-Chief,* edited by Theodore F. Rodenbough and William J. Haskin. New York: Maynard, Merrill, 1896.

Jenness, George B. "The Battle on Beaver Creek." *Transactions of the Kansas State Historical Society* 9 (1906).

Lamar, Howard R., and Sam Truett. "The Greater Southwest and California from the Beginning of European Settlement to the 1880s." In *The Cambridge History of the Native Peoples of the Americas.* Edited by Bruce G. Trigger and Wilcomb E. Washburn, vol. 1, pt. 2. New York: Cambridge University Press, 1996.

Merritt, Wesley. "Three Indian Campaigns." *Harper's New Monthly Magazine* 58 (April 1890).

Miles, Susan. "Fort Concho in 1877." *West Texas Historical Association Yearbook* 35 (October 1959).

Millbrook, Minnie Dubbs. "The West Breaks in General Custer." *Kansas Historical Quarterly* 36 (summer 1970).

Nunn, Curtis W. "Eighty-six Hours without Water on the Texas Plains." *Southwestern Historical Quarterly* 43 (January 1940).

Ogle, Ralph. "Federal Control of the Western Apaches." *New Mexico Historical Review* 14 (October 1939).

Opler, Morris E., and Catherine H. "Mescalero Apache History in the Southwest." *New Mexico Historical Review* 25 (January 1950).

Porter, Kenneth W. "The Seminole-Negro Indian Scouts, 1870–1881." *Southwestern Historical Quarterly* 15 (January 1952).

———. "Negroes and Indians on the Texas Frontier." *Southwestern Historical Quarterly* 53 (October 1949).

Pratt, Richard H. "Some Indian Experiences." *Cavalry Journal* 16 (December 1906).

"Publishing a Newspaper in a 'Boomer' Camp." *Chronicles of Oklahoma* 5 (December 1927).

Reddick, L. D. "The Negro Policy of the United States Army, 1775–1945." *The Journal of Negro History* 34 (January 1949).

Rister, Carl C. "Fort Griffin." *West Texas Historical Association Yearbook* 1 (June 1925).

———. "Colonel A. W. Evans' Christmas Day Indian Fight (1868)." *Chronicles of Oklahoma* 16 (September 1938).

Savage, W. Sherman. "The Role of Negro Soldiers in Protecting the Indian Frontier from Intruders." *The Journal of Negro History* 36 (January 1951).

Sibbald, John B. "Camp Followers All," *American West* 3 (spring 1966).

Smith, Sherry L. "Lost Soldiers: Re-searching the Army in the American West." *The Western Historical Quarterly* 29 (summer 1998).

Stewart, Miller J. "Army Laundresses: Ladies of the 'Soap Suds Row.'" *Nebraska History* 61 (winter 1980).

Sutton, Mary. "Glimpses of Fort Concho through Military Telegraph." *West Texas Historical Association Yearbook* 32 (October 1956).

Temple, Frank M. "Colonel B. H. Grierson's Victorio Campaign." *West Texas Historical Association Yearbook* 35 (October 1959).

———. "Federal Military Defense of the Trans-Pecos Region, 1850–1889." *West Texas Historical Association Yearbook* 30 (October 1954).

Thompson, Major W. A. "Scouting with Mackenzie." *Cavalry Journal* 10 (December 1897).

"Tribute to Captain Payne." *Chronicles of Oklahoma* 8 (March 1930).

Wallace, Edward S. "General John Lapham Bullis, Thunderbolt of Texas Frontier." *Southwestern Historical Quarterly* 55 (July 1951).

NEWSPAPERS AND MAGAZINES

Army and Navy Journal
Austin Daily Journal
Austin Daily State Journal
Dallas Daily Herald
Dodge City Times
Fort Griffin (Tex.) Echo
Flake's (Galveston, Tex.) Daily Bulletin
Galveston Daily News
Galveston News
Harper's Weekly Magazine
Mesilla (N.Mex.) Independent
San Antonio Daily Express
San Antonio Daily Herald
San Saba News
San Angelo Standard
New York Tribune
Winners of the West

BOOKS

Ayers, Edward L. *The Promise of the New South: Life after Reconstruction.* New York: Oxford University Press, 1992.

Armes, Colonel George A. *Ups and Down of an Army Officer.* Washington, D.C.: n. p., 1900.

Athearn, Robert C. *William Tecumseh Sherman and the Settlement of the West.* Norman: University of Oklahoma Press, 1956.

Ball, Eve. *In the Days of Victorio: Recollections of a Warm Springs Apache.* Norman: University of Oklahoma Press, 1970.

Barnett, Louise. *Ungentlemanly Acts: The Army's Notorious Incest Trial.* New York: Hill and Wang, 2000

Battey, Thomas C. *The Life and Adventures of a Quaker among the Indians.* Norman: University of Oklahoma Press, 1967.

Battles and Leaders of the Civil War. 4 vols. New York: Thomas Yodelef, 1956.

Berthrong, Donald J. *The Southern Cheyennes.* Norman: University of Oklahoma Press, 1963.

Beyer, Walter F., and Oscar F. Keydel, eds. *Deeds of Valor.* Detroit: Perrien-Keydel, 1903.

Billington, Monroe Lee. *New Mexico's Buffalo Soldiers, 1866–1900.* Niwor: University of Colorado Press, 1991.

Bourke, John G. *An Apache Campaign in the Sierra Madre.* New York: Charles Scribner's Sons, 1886.

——. *On the Border with Crook*. Chicago: Rio Grande, 1962.

Brady, Cyrus T. *Indian Fights and Fighters*. New York: McClure, Phillips, 1904.

Brown, D. Alexander. *Grierson's Raid*. Urbana: University of Illinois Press, 1954.

The Cambridge History of the Native Peoples of the Americas. North America, Volume I. eds. Bruce G. Trigger and Wilcomb E. Washburn. New York: Cambridge University Press, 1996.

Carlson, Paul H. *"Pecos Bill": A Military Biography of William R. Shafter*. College Station: Texas A&M University Press, 1989.

Carter, Robert G. *On the Border with Mackenzie*. Washington, D.C.: Eynon, 1935.

Carriker, Robert C. *Fort Supply, Indian Territory: Frontier Outpost on the Plains*. Norman: University of Oklahoma Press, 1970.

Casey, Robert J. *The Texas Border and Some Borderliners*. New York: Bobbs-Merrill, 1950.

Cashin, Herschel V., et al. *Under Fire with the Tenth Cavalry*. Chicago: American Publishing House, n.d.

Catton, Bruce. *A Stillness at Appomattox*. Garden City, N.Y.: Doubleday, 1954.

——. *This Hallowed Ground: The Story of the Union Side of the Civil War*. Garden City, N.Y.: Doubleday, 1956.

Cherny, Robert W. *Populism, Progressivism, and the Transformation of Nebraska Politics, 1885–1915*. Lincoln: University of Nebraska Press, 1981.

Christian, Garna L. *Black Soldiers in Jim Crow Texas, 1899–1917*. Centennial Series of the Association of Former Students, Texas A&M University, No. 57. College Station: Texas A&M University Press, 1995

Clum, Woodworth. *Apache Agent*. Boston: Houghton Mifflin, 1936.

Coffman, Edward M. *The Old Army: A Portrait of the American Army in Peacetime, in 1784–1898*. New York: Oxford University Press, 1986.

Cook, John R. *The Border and the Buffalo*. Topeka, Kans.: Crane, 1907.

Cornish, Dudley T. *The Sable Arm*. New York: Longman's, 1956.

Crawford, Samuel J. *Kansas in the Sixties*. Chicago: A. C. McClurg, 1911.

Cullum, George W. *Biographical Register of Officers and Graduates of the United States Military Academy at West Point, New York, 1802–1867*. New York: D. Van Nostrand, 1868.

Custer, Elizabeth. *Tenting on the Plains; or, General Custer in Kansas and Texas*. New York: Charles L. Webster, 1887.

Dale, Edward Everett. *The Indians of the Southwest: A Century of Development under the United States*. Norman: University of Oklahoma Press, 1971.

Davis Britton. *The Truth about Geronimo*. New Haven, Conn.: Yale University Press, 1929.

Debo, Angie. *Geronimo: The Man, His Time, His Place*. Norman: University of Oklahoma Press, 1976.

Dixon, David. *Hero of Beecher Island: The Life and Military Career of George A. Forsyth*. Lincoln: University of Nebraska Press, 1994.

Dobak, William A., and Thomas D. Phillips. *The Black Regulars, 1866–1898.* Norman: University of Oklahoma Press, 2001.

Dunn, J. P., Jr. *Massacres of the Mountains.* New York: Archer House, 1886.

Dupuy, R. Ernest, and Trevor N. Dupuy. *Military Heritage of America.* New York: McGraw-Hill, 1956.

Eastman, Elaine G. *Pratt, the Red Man's Moses.* Norman: University of Oklahoma Press, 1935.

Emmett, Chris. *Fort Union and the Winning of the Southwest.* Norman: University of Oklahoma Press, 1965.

Emmitt, Robert. *The Last War Trail: The Utes and the Settlement of Colorado.* Norman: University of Oklahoma Press, 1954.

Fletcher, Marvin E. *The Black Soldier and Officer in the United States Army, 1891–1917.* Columbia, Missouri: University of Missouri Press, 1974.

Flipper, Henry O. *Negro Frontiersman.* El Paso: Texas Western College Press, 1963.

Foner, Eric. *Reconstruction: America's Unfinished Revolution, 1863–1877.* The New American Nation Series. New York: Harper & Row, 1988.

Foner, Jack D. *The United States Soldier between Two Wars: Army Life and Reforms, 1865–1898.* New York: Humanities Press, 1970.

Fowler, Arlen. *The Black Infantry in the West., 1869–1898.* Contributions in Afro-American and African Studies, No. 6. Westpoint, Conn.: Greenwood and Negro University Press, 1971. Reprint, Norman: University of Oklahoma Press, 1996.

Frazer, Robert W. *Forts of the West.* Norman: University of Oklahoma Press, 1965.

Ganoe, William A. *The History of the United States Army.* New York: D. Appleton, 1924.

Gard, Wayne. *Frontier Justice.* Norman: University of Oklahoma Press, 1949.

Garrett, Pat F. *The Authentic Life of Billy the Kid.* Norman: University of Oklahoma Press, 1954.

Crook, George. *General George Crook: His Autobiography.* Edited by Martin F. Schmitt. Foreword by Joseph C. Porter. Norman: University of Oklahoma Press, 1986.

Gibson, A. M. *The Kickapoos: Lords of the Middle Border.* Norman: University of Oklahoma Press, 1963.

Glass, Major E. N. *History of the Tenth Cavalry.* Tucson: Acme Printing, 1921.

Grierson, Alice Kirk. *The Colonel's Lady on the Western Frontier: The Correspondence of Alice Kirk Grierson.* Edited by Shirley A. Leckie. Women in the West. Lincoln: University of Nebraska Press, 1989.

Grinnell, George B. *The Fighting Cheyennes.* Norman: University of Oklahoma Press, 1956.

Hagan, William T. *Quanah Parker, Comanche Chief.* Oklahoma Western Biographies. Norman: University of Oklahoma Press, 1993.

Haley, J. Evetts. *Fort Concho and the Texas Frontier.* San Angelo, Tex.: *San Angelo Standard-Times,* 1952.

Higginson, Thomas Wentworth. *Army Life in a Black Regiment.* East Lansing: Michigan State University Press, 1960.

Hoig, Stan. *The Peace Chiefs of the Cheyennes.* Foreword by Boyce D. Timmons. Norman: University of Oklahoma Press, 1980.

Humfreville, J. Lee. *Twenty Years among Our Hostile Indians.* New York: Hunter, 1889.

Hutton, Paul A. *Phil Sheridan and His Army.* Lincoln: University of Nebraska Press, 1985.

Hyde, George E. *A Sioux Chronicle.* Norman: University of Oklahoma Press, 1956.

Jones, Jacqueline. *Labor of Love, Labor of Sorrow: Black Women, Work, and the Family, from Slavery to the Present.* New York: Vintage, 1985.

Keim, De Benneville R. *Sheridan's Troopers on the Borders: A Winter Campaign on the Plains.* Philadelphia: D. McKay, 1885.

Keleher, William A. *Violence in Lincoln County.* Albuquerque: University of New Mexico Press, 1957.

Kenner, Charles L. *Buffalo Soldiers and Officers of the Ninth Cavalry, 1867–1898: Black and White Together.* Norman: University of Oklahoma Press, 1999.

King, James T. *War Eagle: A Life of General Eugene A. Carr.* Lincoln: University of Nebraska Press, 1963.

Knapp, Frank Averill, Jr. *The Life of Sebastian Lerdo de Tejada, 1823–1889.* Austin: University of Texas Press, 1951.

Koller, Larry. *The Fireside Book of Guns.* New York: Simon and Schuster, 1959.

Kraft, Louis. *Gatewood and Geronimo.* Albuquerque: University of New Mexico Press, 2000.

Lane, Ann J. *The Brownsville Affair: National Crisis and Black Reaction.* Port Washington, N.Y.: National University Publications: Kennikat Press, 1971.

Leckie, Shirley A. *Elizabeth Bacon Custer and the Making of a Myth.* Norman: University of Oklahoma Press, 1993; paperback ed. 1998.

Leckie, William H. *The Military Conquest of the Southern Plains.* Norman: University of Oklahoma Press, 1963.

Leckie, William H., and Shirley A. Leckie. *Unlikely Warriors: General Benjamin Grierson and His Family.* Norman: University of Oklahoma Press, 1984; Reprint. 1998.

Litton, Gaston. *History of Oklahoma.* 4 vols. New York: Lesis Historical Publishing, 1957.

Lockwood, Frank E. *The Apache Indians.* New York: Macmillan, 1938.

McCracken, Harold, ed. *Frederick Remington's Own West.* New York: Dial, 1960.

McPherson, James M. *Battle Cry of Freedom: The Civil War Era.* New York: Oxford University Press, 1988.

McReynolds, Edwin C. *Oklahoma: A History of the Sooner State.* Norman: University of Oklahoma Press, 1954.

Mayhall, Mildred. *The Kiowas.* Norman: University of Oklahoma Press, 1962.

Miles, General Nelson A. *Personal Recollections of General Nelson A. Miles.* Chicago: Werner, 1896.

Nolan, Frederick W. *The Life and Death of John Henry Tunstall.* Albuquerque: University of New Mexico Press, 1965.

Nye, Wilbur S. *Carbine and Lance: The Story of Old Fort Sill.* Norman: University of Oklahoma Press, 1943.

Parkes, Henry Bamford. *A History of Mexico.* Boston: Houghton Mifflin, 1928.

Pierce, Michael D. *The Most Promising Young Officer: A Life of Ranald Slidell Mackenzie.* Norman: University of Oklahoma Press, 1993.

Porter, Joseph C. *Paper Medicine Man: John Gregory Bourke and His American West.* Norman: University of Oklahoma Press, 1986

Pratt, Richard Henry. *Battlefield and Classroom: Four Decades with the American Indian, 1867–1904.* Edited by Robert M. Utley. New Haven: Yale University Press, 1964.

Price, George F. *Across the Continent with the Fifth Cavalry.* New York: D. Van Nostrand, 1883.

Quarles, Benjamin. *The Negro in the Civil War.* Boston: Little, Brown, 1953.

Rabinowitz, Howard N. *Race Relations in the Urban South, 1865–1900.* New York: Oxford University Press, 1978.

Randall, James G. *The Civil War and Reconstruction.* Boston: D. C. Heath, 1937.

Rathjen, Frederick W. *The Texas Panhandle Frontier.* Austin: University of Texas Press, 1973.

Richardson, Rupert N. *The Comanche Barrier to South Plains Settlement.* Glendale, Calif.: Arthur H. Clark, 1933.

Rickey, Don, Jr. *Forty Miles a Day on Beans and Hay.* Norman: University of Oklahoma Press, 1963.

Rister, Carl C. *Land Hunger: David L. Payne and the Oklahoma Boomers.* Norman: University of Oklahoma Press, 1963.

Robinson, Charles M., III. *The Court Martial of Lieutenant Henry Flipper.* El Paso: Texas Western Press, 1994.

———. *General Crook and the Western Frontier.* Norman: University of Oklahoma Press, 2001.

———. *Satanta: The Life and Death of a War Chief.* Foreword by William H. Leckie. Austin: State House Press, 1996.

Roe, Frances M. A. *Army Letters from an Officer's Wife, 1871–1888.* New York: Appleton, 1909. reprint with introduction by Sandra L. Myres. Lincoln: University of New Mexico Press, 1984.

Schubert, Frank N. *Black Valor: Buffalo Soldiers and the Medal of Honor, 1870–1898.* Wilmington, Del.: SR Books, 1997.

———. *Buffalo Soldiers, Braves, and the Brass: The Story of Fort Robinson, Nebraska.* Shippensburg, Penn.: White Mane, 1993.

———. *On the Trail of the Buffalo Soldier: Biographies of African Americans in the U.S. Army, 1866–1917.* Wilmington, Del.: SR Books, 1995.

Sheridan, Philip H. *Personal Memoirs.* 2 vols. New York: Charles L. Webster, 1888.

Sherman, General W. T. *Memoirs of General W. T. Sherman.* 2 vols. New York: Charles L. Webster, 1892.

Sonnichsen, C. L. *The Mescalero Apaches.* Norman: University of Oklahoma Press, 1958.

――――. *Tularosa: Last of the Frontier West.* New York: Devin-Adair, 1960.

Stallard, Patricia Y. *Glittering Misery: Dependents of the Indian-Fighting Army.* San Rafael, Calif., and Fort Collins, Colo.: Presidio Press and Old Army Press, 1978.

Steward, Theophilus G. *The Colored Regulars in the United States Army.* Philadelphia: A.M.E. Book Concern, 1904.

Tate, Michael L. *The Frontier Army in the Settlement of the West.* Norman: University of Oklahoma Press, 1999.

Tatum, Lawrie. *Our Red Brothers and the Peace Policy of President Ulysses S. Grant.* Philadelphia: J. C. Winston, 1879.

Thrapp, Dan L. *The Conquest of Apacheria.* Norman: University of Oklahoma Press, 1967.

――――. *Victorio and the Mimbres Apaches.* Norman: University of Oklahoma, 1974.

Twitchell, Ralph E. *The Leading Facts of New Mexican History.* 2 vols. Cedar Rapids, Iowa: Torch, 1912.

Utley, Robert M. *Billy the Kid: A Short and Violent Life.* Licoln: University of Nebraska Press, 1989.

――――. *Cavalier in Buckskin: George Armstrong Custer and the Western Military Frontier.* Rev. ed. Norman: University of Oklahoma Press, 2001.

――――. *Frontier Regulars: The United States Army and the Indian, 1866–1891.* New York: Macmillan, 1974.

――――. *High Noon in Lincoln: Violence on the Western Frontier.* Albuquerque: University of New Mexico Press, 1987.

――――. *The Indian Frontier of the American West, 1846–1890.* Albuquerque: University of New Mexico Press, 1985.

――――. *The Lance and the Shield: The Life and Times of Sitting Bull.* New York: Henry Holt, 1993.

――――. *The Last Days of the Sioux Nation.* New Haven: Yale University Press, 1963.

Weaver, John B. *The Brownsville Raid.* New York: W. W. Norton, 1970.

――――. *The Senator and the Sharecropper's Son: The Exoneration of the Brownsville Soldiers.* College Station: Texas A&M University, 1996.

Webb, Walter P. *The Texas Rangers: A Century of Frontier Defense.* Boston: Houghton Mifflin, 1935.

West, Elliot. *The Contested Plains: Indians, Goldseekers, and the Rush to Colorado.* Lawrence: University Press of Kansas, 1998.

――――. *The Way West: Essays on the Central Plains.* Albuquerque: University of New Mexico Press, 1995.

Wheeler, Homer W. *Buffalo Days.* New York: Bobbs-Merrill, 1925.

Whitman, S. E. *The Troopers.* New York: Hastings House, 1962.

Wilbarger, J. W. *Indian Depredations in Texas.* Austin: Hutchings Printing House, 1889.

Williams, George W. *A History of the Negro Troops in the War of the Rebellion, 1861–1865.* New York: Harper and Brothers, 1888.

Woloch, Nancy. *Women and the American Experience.* 3d ed. Boston: McGraw-Hill, 2000.

Woodward, C. Vann. *The Strange Career of Jim Crow.* 3d rev. ed. New York: Oxford University Press, 1974.

Wooster, Robert. *History of Fort Davis, Texas.* Southwest Cultural Resources Center. Professional Papers 24. Santa Fe: National Park Service, 1990.

———. *Nelson A. Miles and the Twilight of the Frontier Army.* Lincoln: University of Nebraska Press, 1993.

WPA Oklahoma Slave Narratives. Edited by T. Lindsay Baker and Julie P. Baker. Norman: University of Oklahoma Press, 1996.

Worcester, Donald E. *The Apaches: Eagles of the Southwest.* Norman: University of Oklahoma Press, 1979.

UNPUBLISHED MATERIALS

Dinges, Bruce. "The Making of a Cavalryman: Benjamin H. Grierson and the Civil War along the Mississippi, 1861–1865." Ph.D. dissertation, Rice University, 1978.

Kubela, Marguerite E. "History of Fort Concho, Texas." Master's thesis, University of Texas, 1936.

Lamm, Alan K. "Buffalo Soldier Chaplains: A Case Study of the Five Black United States Army Chaplains, 1884–1901." Ph.D. dissertation, University of South Carolina, 1995.

Rickey, Don, Jr., "The Negro Regulars: A Combat Record, 1866–1891." Paper delivered at the Western History Association meeting at Helena, Montana, October, 1965.

Index